HISTORY

OF THE

PROGRESS AND SUPPRESSION

OF THE

REFORMATION IN ITALY

IN THE SIXTEENTH CENTURY

INCLUDING

A SKETCH OF THE HISTORY OF THE

REFORMATION IN THE GRISONS.

By THOMAS McCRIE, D.D.

WIPF & STOCK · Eugene, Oregon

Wipf and Stock Publishers
199 W 8th Ave, Suite 3
Eugene, OR 97401

History of the Progress and Suppression
of the Reformation in Italy in the Sixteenth Century
Including a Sketch of the History of the Reformation in the Grisons
By McCrie, Thomas
Softcover ISBN-13: 978-1-7252-9918-4
Hardcover ISBN-13: 978-1-7252-9919-1
eBook ISBN-13: 978-1-7252-9920-7
Publication date 2/1/2021
Previously published by Presbyterian Board of Publication, 1842

This edition is a scanned facsimile of
the original edition published in 1842.

CONTENTS.

	Page
PREFACE,	5

CHAPTER I.

State of Religion in Italy before the era of the Reformation,   9

CHAPTER II.

Introduction of the Reformed opinions into Italy, and causes of their Progress,   46

CHAPTER III.

Progress of the Reformation in the different States and Cities of Italy,   76

CHAPTER IV.

Miscellaneous Facts respecting the state of the Reformed opinions in Italy,   141

CHAPTER V.

Suppression of the Reformation in Italy,   179

CHAPTER VI.

Page.

Foreign Italian Churches, with Illustrations of the Reformation in the Grisons, - - - - - 291

APPENDIX, - - - - - - 367

PREFACE.

A CONSIDERABLE number of years has elapsed since I was convinced that the reformed opinions had spread to a much greater extent in Italy than is commonly supposed. This conviction I took an opportunity of making public, and, at the same time, expressed a wish that some person who had leisure would pursue the inquiry, and fill up what I considered as a blank in the History of the Reformation. Hearing of none who was willing to accept the invitation, I lately resolved to arrange the materials relating to the subject which had occurred to me in the course of my reading, with the addition of such facts as could be discovered by a more careful search into the most probable sources of information.

To some of the quarters from which the most interesting information might be expected, I entertained no hope of finding access; nor shall I inquire at present why the late revolutions which have led to the disclosure of the mysteries of the Spanish, should have sealed up those of the Roman Inquisition.

Unfortunately, none of the Italian Protestants in the sixteenth century thought of recording the facts connected with the religious movement which issued in their expulsion from their native country; a task which was not altogether neglected by those who were driven from Spain for their attachment to the same cause. On the other hand, writers of the Roman Catholic persuasion appear to have agreed, from an early period, to pass over a subject at once dangerous to themselves and ungrateful to their countrymen; or, if they did touch it, to represent any agitation which took place as exceedingly slight and transient, and as produced by a few individuals of no note or consideration, who had suffered themselves to be led astray by fondness for novelty. Facts which contradicted this representation were indeed to be found in writings composed during the struggle, but these were afterwards carefully suppressed; and the *Index Expurgatorius* of Rome was itself reformed, with the view of preventing it from being known that certain names had once been branded with the stigma of heresy. In these circumstances, the modern historian, if he does not choose to rest in general statements must have recourse to the tedious process of examining the epistolary correspondence of those who lived in that age, the memoirs of private individuals, and dedications and prefaces to books on various subjects; while, at the same time, he must carefully ascertain that the editions which he consults are original, or at least unmutilated.

The labour attending this task has been in no small degree lightened by the numerous and valuable collections relating to literary and ecclesiastical history which John George Schelhorn, the learned superintendent and librarian of Memmingen, published in Latin and in his native tongue, during the first half of the eighteenth century. Some of his statements respecting the progress which the Reformation had made in Italy brought forward Cardinal Quirini, the honorary and learned keeper of the Vatican Library; and, as usual in such cases, truth was elicited from the controversy which ensued. In 1765, the *Specimen Italiæ Reformatæ* of Daniel Gerdes, well known by his general History of the Reformation, made its appearance, in which that indefatigable writer collected all the facts which he had met with connected with that subject. This work is scarcely known in Britain, and has not, so far as I have observed, been mentioned by any of our writers. Though labouring under the defects of a posthumous publication, it is of great utility, and has induced later Italian writers to bring forward facts which they might otherwise, like their predecessors, have passed unnoticed. Had I seen this work earlier, it might have saved me much trouble; but I do not regret the circumstance of its having come so late into my hands, as I was led, in the absence of such a help, to make researches which I would have been tempted to decline, but which have enabled me to supply in part its defects, and to correct some of the mistakes into which its author had inadvertently fallen.

The *Historia Reformationis Ræticarum Ecclesiarum,* by Rosius de Porta, has furnished me with a number of important facts respecting the Italian refugees. To throw light on the settlements which they formed in the Grisons, I have given a sketch of the history of the Reformation in that country, which I trust will not be unacceptable to the reader.

It has not been in my power to procure several Italian works, which, I have reason to think, would have helped to illustrate parts of my subject. Some of the most curious and valuable of those quoted in the following pages I had the opportunity of examining in Holland, and particularly in the library of the venerable Mons. Chevalier, one of the pastors of the French church in Amsterdam, whose uncommon politeness I have to acknowledge, in not only allowing me the freest use of his books, but also in transmitting to me a number of extracts which I had not time to make during my short stay in that city.

Amidst such a multiplicity of facts, as to many of which I had not the advantage arising from a comparison of different authorities, I do not flatter myself that, with all my care, I have kept free from mistakes; and shall feel obliged to any one who shall put it in my power to correct the errors which I may have committed.

It was my intention, even after the work went to the press, to include in this volume an account of the progress and suppression of the Reformation in Spain. This I have found impracticable, and accordingly have reserved that part of my undertaking for a separate publication. I regret this delay the less, that it will enable me to avail myself of an extensive collection of Spanish books which has been lately purchased by the Faculty of Advocates.

EDINBURGH, 4*th May*, 1827.

ADVERTISEMENT

TO

THE SECOND EDITION.

THE interest, perhaps partial, which I feel in the subject of the following work, has led me to take more pains in preparing this edition for the press than many readers may think to have been necessary. In the introductory chapter, a fuller account has been given of the state of religion in Italy before the Reformation. From books to which I have had access since the first edition was submitted to the public, I have been enabled to bring forward several new and not unimportant facts as to the progress of the Reformed doctrine and the treatment of its friends, especially within the states of Tuscany and Modena. And a number of interesting papers will be found added to the Appendix.

EDINBURGH, 20th *June*, 1833.

HISTORY

OF THE

REFORMATION IN ITALY.

CHAPTER I.

STATE OF RELIGION IN ITALY BEFORE THE ERA OF THE REFORMATION.

It is an undoubted fact, though it may appear improbable to those who are imperfectly acquainted with ecclesiastical history, that the supremacy claimed by the bishops of Rome was resisted in Italy after it had been submitted to by the most remote churches of the west. The diocese of Italy, of which Milan was the capital, remained long independent of Rome, and practised a different ritual, according to what was called the Ambrosian Liturgy. It was not till the eleventh century that the popes succeeded in establishing their authority at Milan, and prevailed on the bishops of that see to procure the archi-episcopal pall from Rome. When this was first proposed, it excited great indignation on the part of the people, as well as of the clergy, who maintained that the Ambrosian church had been always independent; that the Roman pontiff had no right to judge in its affairs; and that, without incurring disgrace, they could not subject to a foreign yoke that see which had preserved its freedom during so many ages.*

* Petri Damiani Opusc. p. 5. The archbishop of Milan having consulted Roboald, bishop of Alva, the latter replied, that " he would sooner have his nose slit," than advise him to comply with the de-

During the pontificate of Nicolas II. the papal claims were strenuously resisted by Guido, archbishop of Milan.† And, in the year 1074, when Gregory VII., the noted Hildebrand, issued his decree against the marriage of the clergy, the Milanese ecclesiastics rejected it, branded the pope and his adherents as heretics, and were prevented from making a formal separation from the Church of Rome only by the arms of Estembald.‡

As the supremacy of the bishop of Rome met with strenuous opposition, so were there individuals in the darkest age who resisted the progress of those superstitions which proved the firmest support of the pontifical power. Among these was Claude, bishop of Turin, who, in the ninth century, distinguished himself not only by his judicious commentaries on the Scriptures, but also by his vigorous opposition to the worship of images and pilgrimages to Rome; on which account, he, with his followers in Italy, have been branded as Arians by popish historians, who are ever ready, upon the slightest pretexts, to impute odious opinions to those who may dissent from the dominant church.§

Scarcely had the bishops of Rome secured the obedience of the Italian clergy, and silenced the opposition which arose from Turin, when their attention was called to other opponents. Among these were the Arnoldists, who take their name from Arnold of Brescia, a disciple of Abelard, and a man of great learning and spirit, who maintained publicly that the possessions and rents of the popes, bishops, and monasteries, should be transferred to the supreme rulers of each state, and that nothing should be left to the

---

mand of pope Honorius—" quod prius sustineret nasum suum scindi usque ad oculos, quam daret sibi consilium ut susciperet Romæ stolam," &c. (Ughelli Italia Sacra, tom. iv. p. 189.)

† Landulphi Sen. Hist. Mediolan. l. ii. c. 35. Arnulphi, Hist. Mediolan. l. iii. c. 12. Muratori, Script. Rer. Ital. tom. iv.

‡ Arnulphi, l. iv. c. 6, 9, 10.

§ Jo. Alb. Fabricii Bibl Med. et Infim. Ætatis, tom. i. p. 388. Simon, Hist. Crit. du N. Testament, chap. xxv. Weismanni Memorab. Hist. Eccles. tom. i. p. 761.

ministers of religion but a spiritual authority, and a subsistence drawn from the tithes and the voluntary contributions of the people. He was condemned by the council of the Lateran in 1139, and obliged to retire to Zurich; but returning, on the death of Innocent II., and finding Rome in a state of great agitation, from the contest between the pope and the emperor, he persuaded the inhabitants to throw off the degrading yoke of a priest, and secure their independence by reviving the ancient authority of the senate. The circumstances of the time, and the degenerate spirit of the Romans, equally forbade the success of such an attempt. Arnold was obliged to fly, and being taken, was crucified, and his body reduced to ashes; but he left behind him a great number of disciples, who inherited the zeal and intrepidity of their master, and were always ready, on a favourable opportunity, to take part in any design which had for its object the reformation of the church.*

In the twelfth century, those Christians known in history, under the several names of Vaudois, Waldenses, and Albigenses, as the hereditary witnesses for the truth against the corruptions of Rome, penetrated through the Alps into Italy. As early as the year 1180, they had established themselves in Lombardy and Puglia, where they received frequent visits from their brethren in other countries;† and, at the beginning of the thirteenth century, they were to be found in the capital of Christendom. In the year 1231, pope Gregory IX. published a furious bull against them, ordaining that they should be sought out and delivered to the secular arm to be punished, and that such as harboured them should be declared infamous, along with their children to the second generation. The senator or chief magistrate of Rome set on foot an inquisition agreeably to the municipal laws of the city, in consequence of this bull, which was also sent by the pope to the archbishop of Milan,

* Allix's Churches of Piedmont, p. 169—174. Mosheim's Eccl. Hist. cent. xii. ch. v. sect 10.
† Leger, Hist. des Eglises Evangeliques, part i. p. 202.

with injunctions to see it executed in his diocese, and those of his suffragans, where heresy had already made an alarming progress. Some curious facts, relating to the state of the Waldensian churches to the south of the Alps, are furnished by a letter from Ivo of Narbonne to Gerard, archbishop of Bordeaux. Having been summoned by the inquisitor of heretical pravity, unjustly, according to his own account, Ivo fled into Italy. At Como he became acquainted with certain persons belonging to the sect of the Paterins, (as the Waldenses were called in Italy,) and pretending that he was banished for holding their opinions, was kindly received by them, and admitted into their confidence. After he had given them his oath of fidelity, and promised to exert himself in propagating the true faith in the places which he visited, they told him, that they had churches in almost all the towns of Lombardy, and in some parts of Tuscany, which sent apt young men to Paris to be instructed in the scholastic logic and theology, with the view of their being qualified for entering the lists with the advocates of the church of Rome; and that their merchants, in frequenting fairs and markets, made it their business to instil their tenets into the minds of the rich laymen with whom they traded, and the landlords in whose houses they lodged. On leaving Como, he was furnished with letters of recommendation to professors of the same faith in Milan; and, in this manner, he passed through all the towns situate on the Po, through Cremona and the Venetian States, being liberally entertained by the Paterins, who received him as a brother, on producing his letters, and giving the signs which were known by all that belonged to the sect.*

That their opinions had also spread in Naples and Sicily, appears from a letter to the pope by the emperor Frederick II, who condemned such as were

* This letter, which has attracted less notice from its being entitled *De Tartaris*, is inserted at length in Mat. Paris, Hist Maj. (under the year 1243,) p 538, 539, edit. Wats, Lond. 1684. It is to be remembered, however, that Ivo, according to his own profession, joined the Paterins from motives of conveniency.

convicted of heresy to the fire, but allowed the bishops to show mercy where they thought it proper, "provided the tongues of those who should be pardoned were cut out, so that they might not again blaspheme."* In Genoa, and some of the neighbouring cities, they had houses in which they assembled for worship, with their *barbs*, or religious teachers.† Notwithstanding the persecutions to which they were exposed, the Waldenses maintained themselves in Italy, kept up a regular correspondence with their brethren in other countries, and, in the fourteenth century, had academies in Lombardy, which were frequented by young men, and supported by contributions, from churches of the same faith in Bohemia and Poland.‡

In the year 1370, the Vaudois who resided in the valleys of Pragela, finding themselves straitened in their territories, sent some of their number into Italy to look out for a convenient settlement. The deputies bargained with the proprietors of the soil for liberty to plant a colony in an uncultivated and thinly peopled district of Calabria. Within a short time the place assumed a new appearance; villages rose in every direction; the hills resounded with the bleating of flocks, and the valleys were covered with corn and vines. The prosperity of the new settlers excited the envy of the neighbouring villagers, who were irritated at the distance which they preserved, and at their refusal to join with them in their revels and dissipation. They regularly paid their tithes, according to the stipulation entered into by their deputies; but the priests, perceiving that they practised none of the ceremonies usual at the interring of the dead, that

* Rainaldi Annal. ad ann. 1231, n. xiv. 18—20. Compare the first document in the appendix to Allix's Remarks on the History of the Ancient Churches of Piedmont, p 297, 298.

† Weismanni Memor. Hist. tom. 1. p. 1096. Mons Court de Gebelin, in his *Dictionnaire Etymologique*, says, that the Vaudois were called *Barbets*, "parce que leur pasteurs s'appelloient *Barbe*, du mot Venetien *Barba*, un ancien, un chef a Barbe"

‡ Wolfii Memor. Lect tom. 1. 312. Beze. Hist. Eccl des Eglises Ref. de France, tom. 1. p 35, 36 Perrin, Hist. des Vaudois, part 1. p. 240—242. Leger, part 11. p. 336.

they had no images in their chapels, did not go in pilgrimage to consecrated places, and had their children educated by foreign teachers, whom they held in great honour, began to raise the cry of heresy against the simple and inoffensive strangers. But the proprietors, gratified to see their grounds so highly improved, and to receive large rents for what had formerly yielded them nothing, interposed in behalf of their tenants; and the priests, finding the value of their tithes yearly to increase, resolved prudently to keep silence.* The colony received accessions by the arrival from time to time, of those who fled from the persecutions raised against them in Piedmont and France;† it continued to flourish when the Reformation dawned on Italy; and, after subsisting for nearly two centuries, was basely and barbarously exterminated.‡

It is a curious circumstance, that the first gleam of light, at the revival of letters, shone on that remote spot of Italy where the Vaudois had found an asylum. Petrarch first acquired the knowledge of the Greek tongue from Barlaam, a monk of Calabria; and Boccaccio was taught it by Leontius Pilatus, who was a hearer of Barlaam, if not also a native of the same place, and for whom his grateful pupil procured an appointment among the professors of Florence.§ The example and the instructions of two individuals, how eminent soever for genius and popularity, could not impart a permanent impulse to the minds of their countrymen, or overcome the obstacles which opposed the cultivation of ancient letters. But the taste which they had been the means of creating was revived, in the beginning of the fifteenth century, by those learned Greeks whom the feeble successors of Constantine

* Perrin, i. 196—198. Leger, part ii. p. 333.

† About the year 1500, many left the valley of Fresiniere to take up their residence in the city Volturata, not far from the settlements of their brethren.—At Florence, the barbs possessed a house, with the requisite funds to defray their expenses. (Gilles, Hist. Eccles. des Eglises Ref. ou Vaudoises, p. 20.)

‡ Perrin, i. 199. Leger, p. ii. chap. i. p. 7. Morland, Hist. of the Evang. Churches of Piedmont, p. 194.

§ Sismondi, Histoire des Republiques Italiennes, tom. vi. p. 160—162, 168—170. Hodius de Græcis Illustribus, p. 2—5.

sent to the papal court to implore succours against the overwhelming power of the Turks, and who were induced to teach their native language in different parts of Italy. The fall of the eastern empire, and the taking of Constantinople in 1453, brought them in greater numbers to that country, while it added immensely to the stock of manuscripts which individuals had for some time before been in the habit of procuring from the east.* And the art of printing, which was invented about the same period, from its novelty, and its tendency to multiply the number of copies of a book indefinitely, and to afford them at a cheap rate, gave an incalculable acceleration to the human mind in its pursuit of knowledge.

Ancient literature was now cultivated with the greatest enthusiasm; it spread with amazing rapidity through Italy, and, surmounting the Alps, reached, within a short period, the northern extremities of Europe. The human mind was roused from the slumber by which it had been oppressed for ages; its faculties were sharpened by the study of languages; the stores of ancient knowledge were laid open; the barbarism of the schools was exploded; and opinions and practices which had long been held sacred, and which a little before it would have been deemed impious to suspect, were now openly called in question, opposed, and repudiated. The rise of the papal monarchy, and the corruption of Christianity, may be

* Ginguené is of opinion, that too much influence has been ascribed to the fall of the eastern empire in producing the revival of letters, and remarks that Florence would have become the new Athens, though the ancient one, with all its islands, and the city of Constantine, had not fallen under the stroke of an ignorant and barbarous conqueror. (Histoire Littéraire d'Italie, tom. iii. p. 18.) The remark of this elegant writer is not unnatural in one who, by minute investigations, had become acquainted with all the concurring causes of a great revolution. But he has himself owned that Boccaccio's knowledge of Greek was extremely limited, and that the study of ancient literature languished after his death; it is undeniable that it was afterwards revived by the arrival of natives of Greece; and what was the fall of Constantinople but the completion of those calamities which at first induced these learned men to visit Italy, to which their successors now transferred their fixed residence and the wreck of their literary treasures?

traced in a great measure to the ignorance and barbarism which fell on western Europe, and increased during the middle ages. The revival of letters, by banishing the darkness, broke the spell on which the empire of superstition rested, and opened the eyes of mankind on the chains with which their credulity had suffered their spiritual rulers to load them.

A taste for letters does not, indeed, imply a taste for religion, nor did the revival of the former necessarily infer the reformation of the latter. Some of the worst of men, such as pope Alexander VI. and his sons, encouraged literature and the arts; and in the panegyrics which the learned men of that age lavished on their patronesses, we find courtezans of Rome joined with ladies illustrious for their birth and virtue.* The minds of many of the restorers of literature in the fifteenth century were completely absorbed by their favourite studies. Their views did not extend beyond the discovery of an old manuscript, or printing and commenting on a classical author. Some of them carried their admiration of the literary monuments of pagan Greece so far as to imbibe the religious sentiments which they inculcated; and, in the excess of their enthusiasm, they did not scruple to give a species of adoration to the authors of such "divine works."† Others showed, by their conduct, that they were as great slaves to worldly passions as the most illiterate, and ready to support any establishment, however corrupt, which promised to gratify their avarice, their ambition, or their love of pleasure. Lorenzo de Medici, the munificent patron of letters, and himself an elegant scholar, testified the most extravagant joy at his son's being elected a cardinal at seven years of age,‡ and gave the destined pontiff

* Roscoe's Life of Leo X. vol. i. p. 335, 336, vol. ii 220.
† Marsil. Ficini Pref. in Plotinum, et Epist. lib viii. p 144. Sismondi, Hist. des Rep. Ital tom. viii. p. 238, 239. Roscoe's Life of Lorenzo de Medici, vol. i. p 162, 163, 169. Ginguené, Hist. Litt. d'Italie, tom. iii. p. 362.
‡ Roscoe's Life of Leo X. vol i p. 19. Another learned man did not scruple to write, on the occasion of this advancement, in the following strain:—" Semen autem Joannis ejusdem, *in quo benedicentur*

an education better fitted for a secular potentate than for the head of the church; a circumstance, however, which probably contributed more to bring about the Reformation than all the patronage he lavished on literature and the arts. Bembo and Sadoleti were apostolical secretaries, and, in their official character, composed and subscribed the most tyrannical edicts of the court of Rome. The former, of whom it has been said, that he "opened a new Augustan age, emulated Cicero and Virgil with equal success, and recalled in his writings the elegance and purity of Petrarca and of Boccaccio," has his name affixed to the infamous bull vindicating the sale of indulgences; and the latter disgraced his elegant pen, by drawing and signing the decree which condemned Luther as a heretic, ordaining that, if he continued obstinate, he should be seized and sent to Rome, and authorizing the sentence of excommunication and interdict to be pronounced against all powers, civil or ecclesiastical, (the emperor excepted,) secular or regular, dukes, marquises, universities, and communities, by whom he might be received or harboured.* Thus did these two polite scholars divide between them the odium of measures which had it for their object to crush the most glorious attempt ever made to burst the chains of despotism; and in compensation for the stigma inflicted upon literature by the conduct of its representatives, we must be contented with being told, that they "first demonstrated that the purity of the Latin idiom was not incompatible with the forms of business, and the transactions of public affairs." There are, I doubt not, persons who will be gratified with the information which I have it in my power to afford them, that, before the Reformation, there were sums issued from the exchequer of the Vatican, as salaries to learned men, whose task it was to reform the *bul-*

omnes gentes, est Joannes Laurentiæ genitus, cui adhuc adolescentulo divina providentia mirabiliter Cardineam contulit dignitatem, futuri pontificis auspicium." (Ficini Epist. lib. ix. p. 159. Venet. 1495.)

* Roscoe's Leo X. vol. iii. App. no. cli. and clix.

larium, by picking out all the solecisms which had crept into it, and substituting purer and more classical words in their room.* Who knows to what advantages this goodly work of expurgation would have led? What elegant reading might not the papal bulls have furnished to our modern literati, if the barbarous reformers had not interfered, and, by their ill-timed clamour, turned the public attention from words to things—from blunders in grammar to perversions of law and gospel!

But the subject is too serious for ridicule. In fact, the passion for the sciences and fine arts, which was at that time so general in Italy, had a direct tendency to infidelity and heathenish atheism, and, had not the Reformation taken place, it is difficult to say how far the infection would have spread. The fine spirits of that age made the mysteries of religion the butt of their wit, and treated the sacred Scriptures as a godly song or mythological fable; so that the reformation of the Christian faith in the sixteenth century resembled the first introduction of Christianity, which had to contend with intellectual luxury, refined sensuality, and the corroding poison of the Epicurean philosophy. Had the Romish church felt any real concern for the interests of religion and the welfare of the people, she would have taken part with those who united a love of the arts and sciences with a desire to restore the true faith, and to imbue the minds of men with the ancient spirit of Christian piety. But she threw all the weight of her authority into the opposite scale. A love of refined heathenism was the ruling passion of Leo X., and influenced all his other passions. This was also the character of the learned men who frequented his court, or shared his patronage and liberality. The poems of Pontano, Sanazzaro, and others, were constructed on the principles of the ancient mythology; and Marullus published a collection of such

* " Ante paucos annos, Rhomæ, ex ærario pontificis, eruditis aliquot salarium dari solitum est, qui, e pontificum literis, solœcismos tollerent" (Erasmi Roterd. Apologia, refellens suspiciones D. Jacobi Latomi, p. 16. Lovanii, 1519.)

pieces, in which the praises of the gods of Greece and Rome are celebrated with great splendour and devotion. Even the clergy followed the example; and, in several instances, their writings were more spotted with ribaldry and profane wit than those of laymen. They were ashamed of the Bible on account of its barbarisms, and would not read it lest it should spoil their fine Latin style; but they made no scruple of seasoning their discourses and writings with quotations from heathen antiquity. They found in pagan theology antitypes of the sacred persons mentioned in Scripture, not excepting the Holy Trinity. God, the Father, was Jupiter Optimus Maximus; the Son, Apollo or Esculapius; and the Virgin Mary, Diana. Erasmus, in one of his letters, has given an account of a sermon which he heard preached, before Pope Julius II. and his cardinals, on the sufferings and death of Jesus. The preacher began with the praises of the Pope, whom he represented as a second Jupiter, holding in his almighty hand the thunderbolt, and ruling the affairs of the world by his nod. When he came to the sufferings of Christ, he reminded his hearers of Decius and Curtius, who leapt into the gulf for the salvation of their country. He mentioned, with high eulogium, Cecrops and Menacius, Iphigenia and others, who nobly preferred their country to their lives. When he wished to move his hearers to compassion by the tragical fate of Jesus, he described the gratitude which the heathen testified for their heroes and benefactors, by deifying them and raising monuments to their memory, while the Jews treated the deliverer of mankind with ignominy, and crucified him. The death of Christ was then compared with that of other celebrated men, who died innocently, suffering for the common welfare;—a Socrates and a Phocion, who, though they had committed no crime, drank the poisoned cup; an Epaminondas, who, after performing many renowned deeds, was obliged to defend himself against a public charge of high-treason; a Scipio, whose numerous services were rewarded with banishment; and an Aristides, who was expelled from his native country, because he was surnamed the Just.*

But though many of the revivers of literature intended anything rather than a reformation of religion, they, nevertheless, contributed greatly to forward this desirable object. It was impossible to check the progress of the light which had sprung up, or to prevent the new spirit of inquiry from taking a direction towards religion and the church. Among other books which had long remained unknown or neglected, copies of the sacred writings, in the original languages, with the works of the Christian fathers, were now eagerly sought out, printed, and circulated, both in the original and in translations; nor could persons of ordinary discernment and candour peruse these, without perceiving that the church had declined far from the Christian standard, and the model of primitive purity, in faith, worship, and morals. This truth forced itself on the minds even of those who were interested in the support of the existing corruptions. They felt that they stood on unsafe ground, and trembled to think that the secret of their power had been discovered, and was in danger of becoming every day better and more extensively known. This paralysed the exertions which they made in their own defence, and was a principal cause of that dilatory, vacillating, and contradictory procedure which characterized the policy of the court of Rome, in its first attempts to check the progress of the reformed opinions.

The poets of the middle ages, known by the name of Troubadours, had joined with the Vaudois, in condemning the reigning vices of the priests; and several of the superstitious notions and practices, by which the clergy increased their power and wealth, were assailed in those lively satires which were written in the ancient language of Provence, but read by the inhabitants of Italy and Spain. It is a circumstance

---

* Erasmi Epist. l. xx. ep. 14. Ciceronianus, p. 39—43 Roscoe's Life and Pontificate of Leo X. vol iii. p. 143—147. Marheinecke, speaking of this work of Mr. Roscoe, says, "As was the hero, so is his historian." (Geschichte der Teutchen Reformation, th. 1 p. 24.)

deserving of notice, and reflecting honour on a sect which has been so unmercifully traduced by its adversaries, that the *Nobla Leyçon,* and other religious poems of the Vaudois, which are among the earliest and rarest monuments of *Provençal* poetry, contain few of those satirical reflections on the clergy, which abound in the writings of their contemporaries who remained in the Romish Church. "Indulgences," says one of the troubadours, "pardons, God and the devil—all, the priests make use of. To some men they allot paradise by their pardons; others they send to hell by their excommunications. There are no crimes for which pardon cannot be obtained from the monks: for money they grant to renegades and usurers that sepulture which they deny to the poor who have nothing to pay. To live at ease, to enjoy good fish, fine wheat-bread, and exquisite wines, is their great object during the whole year. God grant me to be a monk, if salvation is to be purchased at this price!" "Rome!" says another, "thou hast established thy see in the bottom of the abyss, and of perdition. How much innocent blood hast thou spilt! Falsehood, disgrace, and infamy, reign in thy heart. With the exterior of a lamb, thou art within a ravening wolf and a crowned serpent. Go, then, Sirvente, and tell the false clergy, that he who gave them dominion over us is dead." "If God," says a third, "save those whose sole merit lies in loving good cheer, and paying their court to women—if the black monks, the white monks, the templars, the hospitallers, gain heaven, then St. Peter and St. Andrew were great fools to submit to such torments for the sake of a paradise which cost others so little."[*]

> [*] Si monge niers vol dieus que sian sal,
> Per pro manjar ni per femnas tenir,
> Ni monge blanc, per boulas a mentir,
> Ni per erguelh Temple ni Espital,
> Ni canonge per prestar a renieu,
> Bene tene per fol sanh Peir', sanh Andrieu,
> Que sofriro per Dieu aital turmen,
> S'aquest s'en van aissi a salvamen.

(Raymond de Castelnau; Renouard, Choix des Poesies Orig. des Troubadours, tom. iv. p. 383.)

From the earliest dawn of letters in Italy, the corruptions of the Roman Church had been discovered by persons who entertained no thought of renouncing her communion. These were exposed by the poets, under the protection of that license which they have enjoyed in every age, and among almost every people. The *Divina Comedia* of Dante is founded on some of the leading tenets of the Roman Catholic Church, in which he was a sincere believer; but there is much less in it favourable to popery than this circumstance would have led us to expect, while it abounds with complaints of the corruption of Christianity. Dante appears to have had no faith in the infallibility of either popes or general councils. While he freely bestows the keys on St. Peter, and speaks honourably of his early successors, he expresses himself doubtfully of Rome's claim to be the mistress of Christendom.* He gives but slender comfort to those who go into purgatory, by his advice, "Think on what succeeds," and by telling them, that no prayer on earth can avail them but what "riseth up from heart which lives in grace."† Priestly absolution he reduces to a conditional declaration of pardon, by teaching, that "no power can the impenitent absolve."‡ In paradise he makes a confession of his faith, at the desire of St. Peter; it is what every sound Protestant could subscribe; and when asked by the apostle as to the source from which he derived his faith, he answers,

> From that truth
> It cometh to me rather, which is shed
> Thro' Moses, the rapt prophets, and the Psalms,
> The Gospel; and what ye yourselves did write,
> When ye were gifted of the Holy Ghost.

When asked how he knew these to be the word of God, he does not reply by appealing to the authority of the Church or tradition, but says, "The works that followed, evidence their truth;" and when still further questioned, by St. Peter, how he knew that, his reply

* Infc. c. ii. † Purg. c. iv. x. ‡ Inf. c. xxvii.

is at once just and strikingly illustrative of his sentiments.

> "That all the world," said I, "should have been turn'd
> To Christian, and no miracle been wrought,
> Would, in itself, be such a miracle,
> The rest were not a hundredth part so great.
> E'en thou wentest forth, in poverty and hunger,
> To set the goodly plant, that, from thy vine
> It once was, now is grown unsightly bramble."*

It is impossible to pronounce a clearer and more decisive judgment on one of the leading and most important points of controversy between the Popish and Protestant Churches, than Dante has given in this part of his poem. The poet repeatedly inculcates a simple adherence to Scripture, in opposition to the human inventions and fables with which it was mixed up in his time.

> E'en they whose office is
> To preach the gospel, let the gospel sleep,
> And pass their own inventions off instead.

And having given some specimens of this, he adds,

> The sheep, meanwhile, poor witless ones, return
> From pasture, fed with wind; and what avails
> For their excuse, they do not see their harm?

Dante has exhibited, in his pictorial style, the indecent buffoonery which disgraced the pulpit in that age; and he treats the credulity of the people with almost as much severity as the impudence and imposture of the priests and friars.

> The preacher now provides himself with store
> Of jests and gibes; and, so there be no lack
> Of laughter, while he vents them, his big cowl
> Distends, and he has won the meed he sought.
> Could but the vulgar catch a glimpse the while,
> Of that dark bird which nestles in his hood,
> They scarce would wait to hear the blessing said,
> Which now the dotards hold in such esteem.†

He celebrates the virtues of St. Francis and St. Dominic, but pronounces a severe censure on the degene-

* Parad. c. xxiv, Carey's Translation.   † Parad. c. xxix.

racy of their respective orders.* He is warm in his praises of the Virgin, but puts them into the mouth of St. Bernard, the great opponent of those who ascribed to her the honours due to the Saviour.† His *Hell*, as well as his *Purgatory*, are peopled with clergy, from popes down to begging friars. The court of Rome is repeatedly compared by him to the idolatrous Babylon of the Apocalypse.

> Of shepherds like to you, th' Evangelist
> Was ware, when her, who sits upon the waves,
> With kings in filthy whoredom he beheld;
> She who with seven heads tower'd at her birth,
> And from ten horns her proof of glory drew,
> Long as her spouse in virtue took delight.
> Of gold and silver ye have made your god,
> Diff'ring wherein from the idolater,
> But that he worships one, a hundred ye.
> Ah! Constantine, to how much ill gave birth,
> Not thy conversion, but that plenteous dower
> Which the first wealthy father gained from thee?‡

In describing the avarice and luxurious living of the clergy,§ he seems sometimes at a loss whether to employ the language of ridicule or of indignation, and, therefore, combines them; as in the following passage, put into the mouth of a cardinal, who, by a rare fate, had escaped both hell and purgatory.

> I was constrain'd to wear the hat, that still
> From bad to worse was shifted.—Cephas came,
> He came who was the Holy Spirit's vessel,
> Barefoot and lean; eating their bread, as chanc'd,
> At the first table. Modern shepherds need
> Those who on either hand may prop and lead them,
> So burly are they grown; and from behind
> Others to hoist them. Down the palfrey's sides
> Spread their broad mantles, so as both the beasts
> Are cover'd with one skin. Oh! patience, thou
> That look'st on this, and dost endure so long!‖

---

* Parad. c. xi. xii.   † Ibid. c. xxxiii.
‡ Inf c xix. conf. Purg. c. xxxii.
§ In a similar strain did Ariosto afterwards write on this subject, and, speaking of avarice, he says,

> Worse did she in the court of Rome, for there
> She had slain popes and cardinals.
>   *Orl. Fur.* c. xxvi. st. 32.

‖ Para . c. xxi.

With such a deep impression of the corruptions of the popedom on his spirit, we need not be surprised to find the poet writing in a strain which may be interpreted as prophetic of its speedy downfall, and of the Reformation.

> Yet it may chance, ere long, the Vatican,
> And other most selected parts of Rome,
> That were the grave of Peter's soldiery,
> Shall be delivered from th' adult'rous bond.*

Nor were these the mere effusions of poetical exaggeration. In his treatise on monarchy, he inveighs against the abuses of the church with as great freedom as in his poem; and, not contented with depriving the popes of their temporal authority, he attacks tradition, the main pillar on which they have always rested their claim to spiritual authority.†

Petrarch followed in the steps of Dante, and he is still more severe against the papal court in his prose compositions than in his poetical. In proof of this, we need not refer to a letter, ascribed to him, which was dropt in the consistory at Rome, and read in the presence of Clement VI. and his whole court. It was inscribed, "Leviathan, prince of darkness, to pope Clement, his vicar, and the cardinals, his counsellors and good friends;" contained an enumeration of the crimes committed by the prelates of the court, for which he expressed his thanks, exhorting them to continue in the same course, by which they would merit, more and more, his favour; and concluded with these words—" Given at the centre of hell, in the presence of a crowd of demons." In his confidential letters, Petrarch seems at a loss for words to express his detestation of the sins of the papal court. "I am

---

* Parad. c. ix.
† Speaking of the decretalists, or masters of canon law, he says, "I have heard one of them saying, and impudently maintaining, that traditions are the foundation of the faith of the church." (*De Monarchia*, lib iii.) The *Monarchia* of Dante has a place in the *Index Prohibitorius* of Rome for 1559; and it is not improbable that his *Heaven* and *Hell* would have shared the same fate, had not *Purgatory* come between, and saved them.

at present," says he to a friend, "in the western Babylon, than which the sun never beheld any thing more hideous, and beside the fierce Rhone, where the successors of the poor fishermen now live as kings. Here the credulous crowd of Christians are caught in the name of Jesus, but by the arts of Belial; and being stripped of their scales, are fried to fill the belly of gluttons. Go to India, or wherever you choose, but avoid Babylon, if you do not wish to go down alive to hell. Whatever you have heard or read of as to perfidy and fraud, pride, incontinence and unbridled lust, impiety and wickedness of every kind, you will find here collected and heaped together. Rejoice, and glory in this, O Babylon, situated on the Rhone, that thou art the enemy of the good, the friend of the bad, the asylum of wild beasts, the whore that hast committed fornication with the kings of the earth! Thou art she whom the inspired evangelist saw in the spirit; yes, thee, and none but thee, he saw, 'sitting upon many waters.' See thy dress—'A woman clothed in purple and scarlet.' Dost thou know thyself, Babylon? Certainly what follows agrees to thee and none else—'Mother of fornications and abominations of the earth.' But hear the rest—'I saw,' says the evangelist, 'a woman drunk with the blood of the saints, and the blood of the martyrs of Jesus.' Point out another to whom this is applicable but thee."*
In this strain does Petrarch go on to comment on the description of the apocalyptic Babylon, and to inveigh against the monstrous vices, heresies, and false miracles of the papal court.† Several of his Latin eclogues

* Epistolæ sine titulo, ep. 4, 12, 15, 16. Abbé Sade complains that the Protestants "have, in their declamations against the church of Rome, abused certain secret letters which Petrarch wrote to his friends, in which he opens his heart with a little too much freedom." (Memoires de Petrarche, tom. iv p 3, 4.) The only way in which they have abused them, is by quoting them, which the Abbé has prudently avoided amidst his copious extracts; and, when he calls the letters "secret," he seems to have forgotten that Petrarch himself had carefully collected them into a volume by themselves, intended for public use, as appears from his preface, and his having suppressed the names of the persons to whom they were written.

† It is true that Petrarch refers to the residence of that court at

are concealed satires on the popes and their clergy.
In his sonnets the satire is avowed, and the holy see
is characterized as " impious Babylon—avaricious
Babylon—the school of error—the temple of heresy—
the forge of fraud—the hell of the living.* The following may be given as a specimen.†

>The fire of wrathful heaven alight,
>And all thy harlot tresses smite,
>   Base city! thou, from humble fare,
>Thy acorns and thy water, rose
>To greatness, rich with others' woes,
>   Rejoicing in the ruin thou didst bear.
>
>Foul nest of treason! Is there aught
>Wherewith the spacious world is fraught
>   Of bad or vile—'tis hatch'd in thee,
>Who revellest in thy costly meats,
>Thy precious wines, and curious seats,
>   And all the pride of luxury.
>
>The while within thy secret halls,
>Old men in seemly festivals
>   With buxom girls in dance are going;
>And in the midst old Beelzebub
>Eyes, through his glass, the motley club,
>   The fire with sturdy bellows blowing.
>
>In former days thou wast not laid
>On down, nor under cooling shade;
>   Thou naked to the winds wast given,
>And through the sharp and thorny road
>Thy feet without the sandals trod;
>   But now thy life is such, it smells to Heaven.

The alternate style of broad humour and keen wit
with which Boccaccio exposed the superstition and
knavery of churchmen was at once more fatal to
them, and more suited to the spirit of the age in which

Avignon in France, (where it continued during his lifetime;) and he sometimes deplores its transference from Rome, under the name of a captivity. But the chief part of his description is borrowed from that of Dante, which preceded that event; and he himself traces the deplorable change on the face of the church to a much higher period.

* Petrarchi Opera, tom. iii. p 149

† Fiamma del ciel su le tue treccie piova,
    Malvagia, &c.
        (Le Rime del Petrarcha, edit. Lod. Castelvetro,
        tom. i. p. 325.

he lived, than the lofty and severe invective of his master. Poggio Bracciolini, the author of an eloquent and pathetic description of the martyrdom of Jerome of Prague, of which he was an eye-witness, employed his wit in exposing the vices of the clergy, and the ignorance and absurdities of the preachers of that time, in his dialogues on avarice, luxury, and hypocrisy. That such freedoms should have been permitted in a pontifical secretary, must excite surprise; and tolerant and friendly to learned men as Nicholas V. was, it is probable that Poggio would have suffered for his temerity, had he not secured the protection of his master, by writing an invective against his rival, the anti-pope Amedæus.* It would be endless, however, to give examples from him or the other ancient poets and novelists of Italy, whose satires against the clergy, and especially their lampoons on the monks and friars, were afterwards imitated or translated by writers in the different countries of Europe. The practice was continued by Ariosto and Berni down to the very time of the Reformation. After that period, when no poet who wished his works to be circulated would venture on such freedoms, the task was taken up by the writers of pasquinades and other anonymous satires, who often employed the images and language of their illustrious predecessors.†

* Ginguene, vol vii. p. 308, 313, 319. Shepherd's Life of Poggio Bracciolini, p. 88, 428.
† The following verses, on the death of Alexander VIII., are transcribed from an Italian MS in the Advocate's Library, entitled, "Raccolta delle migliori Satire venute alla luce in occasione di diversi Conclavi da quello di Alessandro VIII "

> *Sacro Nume del Ciel, non diro mai,*
> *Che tu facesti far papa Alessandro,*
> *Che al Tebro cagione piu danno assai,*
> *Di quel che fece il fuoco alla Scamandro.*
>
> *Sempre voleva dir qualche saldonia,*
> *Parlando ancor di cosa alta e divina;*
> *E avea quasi ridotta in Babilonia,*
> *Questa di Dio Jerusalem Latina.*
>
> *Che piu ? Si vedde al suo ponteficato,*
> *Liberta di concienza, e di costumi,*

The corruptions of the Church of Rome were attacked by others in a graver style. In the beginning of the fifteenth century, Laurentius Valla, "who rescued literature from the grave, and restored to Italy the splendour of her ancient eloquence,"* wrote against the pretended donation of Constantine, and various papal abuses. This learned Italian had advanced far before his age in every species of knowledge; as a grammarian, a critic, a philosopher, and a divine, he was equally distinguished. His scholia on the New Testament, in which he proposes numerous corrections on the Vulgate, display an intimate acquaintance with the Greek language; and in his dialogue on free-will, he defends, with much acuteness, the doctrine on that subject, and on predestination, afterwards espoused by Luther and Calvin.† The freedom of his sentiments roused the resentment of the patrons of ignorance and fraud; and Valla was condemned to the flames, a punishment from which he was saved by the protection of Alphonsus V. of Arragon.‡ The writings of Baptista, the modern poet of Mantua, who flourished in the end of the fifteenth century, abound with censures of the corrupt manners

> *E il solo non peccar, era peccato,*
> *Per far contro le stelle, e scorno a Numi.*

> Spirit of heaven, it never shall be said,
> That thou for Pope this Alexander made,
> Who caused the Tiber more to mourn his name,
> Than that Scamander once the Grecian flame.

> His wish was still to have his sprightly quips,
> E'en then when truths divine forsook his lips;
> But this Jerusalem, God's chosen throne,
> He had well nigh reduced to Babylon.

> Truly, when he was pontiff, man was free,
> Conscience and conduct both had liberty,
> When one might scoff the stars, and stand secure
> In every crime, but one—the being pure.

* Erasmi Epist. lib. vii. ep. 3.
† Laurentii Vallæ Opera, Basileæ, 1540, fol.
‡ Cave, Hist. Liter. App. 121, 122. Wolfius, Lect. Mem. ii. 7. Ginguené, Hist. Litter. d'Italie, tom. vii. p. 349.

of the court of Rome, which deserve the more credit, as they proceeded from a friar, whose verses are distinguished for their moral purity still more than for their classical elegance.*

It has been common to place Savonarola among the witnesses of the truth before the Reformation; and some have called him the Luther of Italy.† By others, he is described as a delirious fanatic and turbulent demagogue, who, by pretending to the gift of prophecy, and immediate intercourse with heaven, sought to excite the populace against their rulers, civil and ecclesiastical, and to gratify his own ambition by humbling his superiors. In this last light he has been represented, not only by the interested advocates of the church of Rome, but also by the warm admirers of the house of Medici.‡ Those who impartially consider the character of the Florentine reformer, will not be disposed to adopt either the one or the other of these representations. It cannot be denied that the fervour of his zeal betrayed him into extravagance, and that, in prosecuting his plans of reform, he yielded to the illusions of an overheated imagination, and persuaded himself that he was possessed of supernatural gifts; but instances of this kind were not uncommon among those who, like him, had been brought up in a cloister. On the other hand, the best and most enlightened men of that age bear unequivocal testimony to his integrity, sanctity, and patriotism.§ It

---

*   Venalia nobis
Templa, sacerdotes, altaria, sacra, coronæ,
Ignes, thura, preces, cœlum est venale, Deusque.
Ite lares Italos, et fundamenta malorum,
Romuleas arces et pontificalia tecta,
Colluviem scelerum, &c.
          (Baptista Mantuanus, lib. III De Calam. Temp.)

† M. Flacii Illyrici Testes Veritatis, p 890. Wolfii Lect. Memor. tom. I. p 800. Bezæ Icones, sig Biiij.

‡ Roscoe's Life of Lorenzo de Medici, vol. ii. p 158, 269, and Life of Leo X. vol I. p. 278.

§ Marsilii Ficini Epist lib. xII. f. 197. Joan. Fr. Pici Mirandulæ Opera, tom II. p 40. Guicciardini, Istor lib III. Petri Martyris Anglerii Opus Epistol. ep. 191.—John Francis Budæus, in his youth, published a dissertation unfavourable to Savonarola, of which he afterwards candidly wrote a refutation. Both treatises are included in his *Parerga Historica-Theologica*

has been supposed, but without satisfactory proof, that he held the doctrines concerning justification, the communion under both kinds, indulgences, and tradition, which were afterwards called Protestant. The reform which he sought had, for its object, a change on the manners, not the faith, of the Christian world. He believed that the discipline of the church was corrupted, and that those who had the charge of souls, from the highest to the lowest, were become unfaithful. To this persuasion he joined an ardent passion for political liberty, which qualified him for being the organ of those of his countrymen, who felt as Christians for the dishonours done to religion, and as citizens for the encroachments made on their political rights. The appearance of such a person, at a time when the papal throne was filled by a man of the most profligate character, and the Italian republics were on the eve of being stripped of the last remains of their freedom, claims the attention of the inquirer into the causes of the Reformation.

Jeronimo Savonarola was descended from an illustrious family, originally belonging to Padua, and was born at Ferrara in the year 1452. He distinguished himself early in his studies, which were chiefly directed to theology; and, in the twenty-third year of his age, entered the Dominican convent at Bologna. His ardent piety, and his talents, recommended him to the superiors of his order, from whom he received an appointment to read lectures on philosophy. The admiration which he gained in the academical chair was forfeited when he ascended the pulpit; his voice was at once feeble and harsh, and his address ungraceful. But he exerted himself, in conquering these natural defects, with all the enthusiastic perseverance of the Athenian orator; and those who heard him, in 1488, modulating a deep-toned voice, accompanied with all the graces of action, could not believe he was the same person to whom they had listened with impatience six years before. The piety of Savonarola took alarm at the success of his own eloquence; he redoubled his monastic austerities; and it has been supposed, not without probability, that this metamorphose first suggested to him the idea of his divine mission. In 1484 he began to preach on the book of the Revelation at Brescia, and, inveighing against the vices of its inhabitants, told them that their walls should one day be deluged with blood; a threatening which was thought to be accomplished two years after his death, when the city was sacked by the French. In 1489 he fixed his abode at Florence, in the convent of St. Marc. Lorenzo de Medici, aware of the influence he exerted over the public mind, strove to attach him to his interest; but Savonarola resisted all his advances, and would not so much as visit the man whom he regarded as the usurper of the liberties of his country. Lorenzo, on his death-bed, sent for the monk, who asked him if he had an entire confidence in the mercy of God; if he was willing to make restitution of all goods which he had procured unlawfully; and if he was prepared to restore the Florentine republic to its former liberty. To the two first questions the dying man replied in the affirmative, but was silent at the last request; upon which Savonarola left him, without administering absolution.* During the government of Pietro, the haughty and luxurious successor of Lorenzo, the influence of Savonarola increased, and his enthusiasm kept pace with his popularity. He spake to the people, in the name of heaven, of the calamities which were approaching, and summoned them to speedy repentance; he painted, with all the force of a brilliant and fervid imagination, the luxury and immorality which prevailed among all classes of the citizens, the disorders of the church and the corruption of its prelates, the disorders of the state and the tyranny of its rulers. The effect of his denunciations was greatly heightened by the rumours of the invasion of Italy by Charles VIII. of France, whom Savonarola did not scruple to announce as the monarch whom Providence had raised up to punish

* Roscoe disputes the accuracy of this statement, (vol. ii p. 238;) but it has been adopted by the more impartial Sismondi, who had access to all the authorities. (Hist. des Repub. Ital. tom. xii. p. 69.)

the vices of his native country, to introduce a salutary reform into the church, and to break the fetters of political bondage. The preacher had the satisfaction of, at least, witnessing the success of his exhortations on the inhabitants of Florence; luxury was repressed, the women gave an example of modesty in their dress, and a change of manners became visible over the whole city. On the expulsion of the Medici, Savonarola lent all the weight of his authority to those who established a popular government in Florence, and his advice had the greatest influence on the counsels of the new republic; but he continued still to keep in view his main object, of preserving a rigorous morality in the state.

Without possessing the prophetic powers claimed by Savonarola, it was easy to foresee what his fate would be. He was equally hated by the secret adherents of the house of Medici, and the dissolute portion of the citizens, which submitted with impatience to the freedom of his reproofs and the severity of the laws which he had procured. To accomplish his ruin, they had recourse to Rome. Savonarola had preached, that it behoved the reform, which was indispensably necessary, to begin with the head of the church; and, in his invectives, he had not spared the reigning pontiff, Alexander VI. The crimes which, in 1497, disgraced the family of the pope, and scandalized all Italy, were publicly denounced by the Florentine monk; and thus, personal resentment was added to the fears which Alexander entertained, lest the reforms introduced into Florence should be pleaded as an example against the court of Rome. He accused Savonarola as a heretic, interdicted him from preaching, and finally launched the sentence of excommunication against him. At the request of the senate, the preacher desisted, for some time, from the exercise of his office, and sought to pacify the irritated pontiff; but, resuming courage, and acting on the principle which afterwards induced Luther to burn the bull of excommunication by Leo X., he appeared in public, declared that an unjust sentence of the pope was invalid, that relaxation from it was not to be sought, that the inspiration of the Almighty obliged him to renounce obedience to a corrupt tribunal; and, having celebrated mass, and communicated along with his brethren and a great number of secular persons, he conducted a solemn procession round the convent, after which he preached in the cathedral church to greater crowds than ever. Defeated in this attempt, the pope stirred up the Augustinian and Franciscan monks against the object of his hatred. Fransesco de Pouille, a preacher of the Minor Observantines, who was sent from Rome, publicly denounced him as a heresiarch who had seduced the republic, and called upon the senate to silence him instantly, under the pain of having their territory laid under an interdict, and the property of their merchants confiscated in foreign countries. Deprived of the assistance of France, and alarmed at the consequences of an open breach with the pope, the Florentines yielded, and Savonarola was ordered to desist from preaching.

Pursuing his advantage, Pouille next declared, from the pulpit, that he understood that Savonarola spoke of confirming his false doctrines by a miracle. He therefore offered to submit to the trial with his adversary, by walking through the flames. Savonarola, suspecting a snare on the part of his enemies, declined the fiery contest; but Bonvicini, one of his disciples, zealous for his master's honour, accepted the challenge. The whole city took a deep interest in this strange affair, and the chief officers of the republic were engaged in making preparations for it. The pope wrote to the Franciscans of Florence, praising their zeal for the honour of the holy see, and declaring that the memory of the glorious exploit would be imperishable. On the 7th of April, 1498, the combustibles being prepared, the champions, accompanied by their friends, appeared on the spot, surrounded by an immense crowd of eager spectators, consisting of the inhabitants of the city and adjoining territories. Pouille had previously excused himself, on the pretext that he would enter the fire with none but the heresiarch himself; and another Franciscan, named Rondinelli, appeared as his substitute. After the religious ceremonies had been performed, and the people waited in breathless anxiety to see the champions enter the flames, which were already kindled, the Franciscans began to raise difficulties. First, they urged that the Dominican might be an enchanter, and therefore insisted that he should be stripped of his raiment, and clothed with a suit of their choosing. This having been complied with, they next objected to their opponent bearing the host along with him, alleging that it was an impious act to expose the body of Christ to the risk of being consumed by the flames. But on this point Savonarola was inflexible, and urged that it was unreasonable to deprive his friend of that which was the comfort of all Christians in their trials, and the pledge of their safety. The dispute on this point continued to a late hour; and, while it was yet undecided, a violent and unexpected shower of rain extinguished the fire, upon which the senate dismissed the assembly, to the satisfaction, it may be presumed, of both parties. It was not, however, to the satisfaction of the multitude, whose curiosity, wrought up to the highest pitch, was now converted into ridicule and indignation. They were ignorant of the real ground of the dispute between the monks which had prevented the spectacle; but they heard that Savonarola had refused to comply with some condition required by the opposite party, and he was insulted as he passed through the crowd. On reaching his convent, he addressed the people, and gave an explanation of the affair; but an unfavourable impression had already been made on their minds. Next day he preached with great unction; and, at the close of his sermon, as if foreseeing what would befall him, took farewell of his audience, and declared himself ready to offer his life in sacrifice to God. In fact, his enemies availed themselves of the temporary dissatisfaction, to irritate the public mind against him, by representing him as a false prophet, who, at the moment of danger, drew back from the proof of his mission which he had affected to court. Having collected in the cathedral church that same night, they raised the cry, during the time of divine service—"To arms! To St. Marc!" Instantly an infuriated mob rushed, with hatchets and lighted torches, to the convent, forced open its gates, and seizing Savonarola and two other monks, conducted them to prison amidst insults and threatenings. Without allowing the ferment to cool, the conspirators conducted the mob through the city, killed many of the popular party, and forced others to abdicate their places, which were immediately filled with persons belonging to the libertine faction. The carnival which was proclaimed in the city, and the renewal of the sports which had been suppressed for several years, conveyed to Savonarola the intelligence that the government had passed into different hands, and that his favourite reform was overthrown.

One of the first things done by the insurgents was to dispatch a courier to the Pope, to inform him of the imprisonment of Savonarola. Alexander urged that he should be sent to Rome; and, with the view of obtaining his request, granted indulgences to the Florentines, with power to reconcile to the church all those who had incurred excommunication, by attending the sermons of the heretical monk. The senate insisted, however, that he should be tried in Florence, and requested the pope to depute two ecclesiastical judges to conduct the process. On their arrival, the process commenced with the torture; and Savonarola, whose constitution, originally feeble, had been further weakened by austerities and labours, being unable to endure the rack, confessed that his prophecies were only simple conjectures; but when his deposition was afterwards read to him, he declared that it was extorted by bodily agony, and maintained anew the truth of his revelations, and of the doctrines he had preached. A second attempt was made with exactly the same results.* Being condemned to the flames, along with

* Roscoe has given an incorrect account of the trial; and, indeed, his whole account of Savonarola is marked with partiality. (Life of Lorenzo de Medici, vol. II. p. 269—272.)

his two companions, Savonarola spent the interval in composing a commentary on the fifty-first psalm, which, in lecturing through the psalter, he had passed by, saying, he would reserve it for the time of his own calamity. On the 23d of May 1498, a pile of faggots was erected on the spot where the voluntary trial by fire was to have taken place; and the three monks, after being degraded, were bound to the stake. When the presiding bishop declared them separated from the church, Savonarola exclaimed, "From the militant;" intimating that he was about to enter into the triumphant church. This was all that he spoke. The fire was applied to the pile by one of his enemies, who took upon him the office of the executioner. Strict orders were given by the magistrates to collect the ashes of the three monks, and to throw them into the Arno; but some relics were preserved by the soldiers who guarded the place, and are still shown at Florence for the adoration of the devout.*

From the time of the council of Constance, or rather from that of Pisa, held in the year 1409, a reformation of the church, both in its head and members, had been loudly demanded. This demand was repeated, at the beginning of the sixteenth century, in the council which the pope was compelled to convocate; as appears from the decrees which that assembly passed during its sitting at Pisa, and from the orations delivered in it after its translation to the Lateran, where it sat under the eye of the supreme pontiff. Among these, the most noted were the speeches of Egidio of Viterbo, general of the order of Augustinians, and Gianfransesco Pico, the learned and pious count of Mirandula; both of whom denounced, with singular freedom and boldness, the abuses which threatened the ruin of the church and the utter extinction of religion.†

* Jacopo Nardi, Hist. Fior. lib. ii. Guicciardini, lib. iii. Della Storia e delle gesta del Padre Girolamo Savonarola, Livorno, 1782 Sismondi, Hist. des Rep. Ital. tom xii. p. 73, 237, 261, 450, 474. Specimens of Savonarola's eloquence may be seen in Tiraboschi, Stor. della Letter. Ital tom. vi p. 1160.
† The speech of Egidio is published by Gerdesius, Hist. Reform.

Secure in the plenitude of their authority, and lulled asleep amidst wealth and luxury, the popes had overlooked the influence of satirical effusions from the press, and become habituated to censures, which, though sometimes uttered with offensive boldness, seldom reached beyond the walls within which the fathers, assembled in general council, were permitted at intervals to give vent to their zeal. But at length these complaints began to find their way into the pulpit, and to reach the ears of the people. This was a mode of attack which could not be safely tolerated; and, accordingly, in 1516, a papal bull was issued, which, after reprimanding certain irregularities, forbade preachers to treat in their sermons of the coming of Antichrist.* But it was too late. In the course of the following year, a cry was raised in the heart of Germany, and the ominous sounds, Antichrist and Babylon, reverberating from every corner of Europe, struck the Vatican, and awoke its astounded inmates from the security in which they had slumbered for ages.

It would be unsuitable to enter here into a minute detail of the ecclesiastical grievances which were the subject of such general complaint and remonstrance. Suffice it to say, that all of them existed, and some of them in an aggravated form, in Italy, if we except such as were felt by other countries on account of their distance from Rome. The vices of the clergy, their neglect of religious instruction, the consequent ignorance of the people, the sale of ecclesiastical offices, and the prostitution of sacred things to worldly purposes, had grown to the greatest height among the Italians. The court of Rome had become more corrupt than any of the secular courts of Europe, by the confession of popish writers, and of persons who, from their official situations, were admitted into all its secrets. The unprincipled and faithless character of

tom. i. app. no. v; and that of Pico, by Roscoe, in his Life of Leo X. vol iii app. no. cxlvi. See also Wolfii Lect. Memor tom. i. p 30—35.

* Loescher, Vollstandige Reformationsacta, tom. i. p. 104.

its policy had become proverbial. It was a system of intrigue, cabal, and bribery; and its ministers, while they cordially agreed in duping the world, made no scruple of deceiving and supplanting one another, whenever their personal interests happened to interfere. The individuals who filled the papal chair for some time before the Reformation openly indulged in vices, over which the increasing knowledge of the age should have taught them, in point of prudence, to throw a veil.* During the pontificate of Sixtus IV. we are presented with the horrid spectacle of a supreme pontiff, a cardinal, and an archbishop, associating themselves with a band of ruffians to murder two men who were an honour to their age and country, and agreeing to perpetrate this crime during a season of hospitality, within the sanctuary of a Christian church., and at the signal of the elevation of the host. Alexander VI. was so notorious for his profligate manners and insatiable rapacity, that Sanazzaro has compared him to the greatest monsters of antiquity—to Nero, Caligula, and Heliogabalus. Julius II. was more solicitous to signalize himself as a soldier than a bishop, and by his ambition and turbulence kept Italy in a state of continual ferment and warfare. Leo X., though distinguished for his elegant accomplishments, and his patronage of literature and the arts, disgraced the ecclesiastical seat by his luxury and voluptuousness, and scandalized all Christendom by the profane methods of raising money to which he had recourse for the purpose of gratifying his love of pleasure and his passion for magnificent extravagance.

To this rapid sketch I shall add the description of the papal court, drawn by the pen of an Italian who lived in the age of the Reformation, in whose writings we sometimes find the copiousness of Livy combined with the deep-toned indignation against tyranny which

* Julius; Dialogus, in quo impietas Julii II. Papæ depingitur, lectu utilis ad judicandum de moribus, vita et studiis Pontificum Romanorum. Addita sunt Hutteni Epigrammata ejusdem argumenti, 1567. Erasmus was the author of this dialogue, which was originally published soon after the accession of Leo X. to the pontificate.

thrills through our veins in perusing the pages of Tacitus. The reader need not be told that the following passage was struck out by the censors of the press, before the work was allowed to be published in Italy: "Having raised themselves to earthly power on this basis, and by these methods, the popes gradually lost sight of the salvation of souls and divine precepts; and, bending their thoughts to worldly grandeur, and making use of their spiritual authority solely as an instrument and tool to advance their temporal, they began to lay aside the appearance of bishops, and assumed the state of secular princes. Their concern was no longer to maintain sanctity of life, to promote religion, or to show charity to mankind; but to accumulate treasures, to raise armies, to wage wars against Christians. The sacred mysteries were celebrated with thoughts and hands stained with blood; and, with the view of drawing money from every quarter, new edicts were issued, new arts invented, new stratagems laid, spiritual censures were fulminated, and all things, sacred and profane, sold without distinction and without shame. The immense riches amassed in this way, and scattered among the courtiers, were followed by pomp, luxury, licentiousness, and the vilest and most abominable lusts. No care was taken to maintain the dignity of the Pontificate; no thought bestowed on the character of those who should succeed to it: the reigning pope sought only how he might raise his sons, nephews, and other relations, to immoderate wealth, and even to principalities and kingdoms; and, instead of conferring ecclesiastical dignities and emoluments on the virtuous and deserving, he either sold them to the best bidder, or lavished them on those who promised to be most subservient to his ambition, avarice, and voluptuousness. Though these things had eradicated from the minds of men all that reverence which was once felt for the popes, yet their authority was still sustained to a certain degree by the imposing and potent influence of the name of religion, together with the means which they possessed of gratifying princes and their courtiers, by bestowing on them dignities and other ecclesiastical favours. Presuming on the respect which men entertained for their office—aware that any prince who took up arms against them incurred general odium, and exposed himself to the attack of other powers, and knowing that, if victorious, they could make their own terms, and, if vanquished, they would escape on easy conditions—the pontiffs abandoned themselves to their ruling passion of aggrandizing their friends, and proved, for a long time, the instruments of exciting wars, and spreading conflagrations over the whole of Italy."*

On the other hand, the obstacles to ecclesiastical reform, and the reception of divine truth, were numerous and formidable in Italy. The Italians could not, indeed, be said to feel at this period a superstitious devotion to the see of Rome. This did not originally form a discriminating feature of their national character; it was superinduced, and the formation of it can be distinctly traced to causes which produced their full effect subsequently to the era of the Reformation. The republics of Italy, in the middle ages, gave many proofs of religious independence, and singly braved the menaces and excommunications of the Vatican, at a time when all Europe trembled at the sound of its thunder. That quick-sighted and ingenious people had, at an early period, penetrated the mystery by which the emptiness of the papal claims was veiled, while the opportunity which they enjoyed of narrowly inspecting the lives of the Popes, and the real motives by which they were actuated in the most imposing of their undertakings, had dissipated from their minds those sentiments of veneration and awe for the holy see which continued to be felt by such as viewed it from a distance. The consequence of this, under the corrupt form in which Christianity every where presented itself, was the production of a spirit of indifference about religion, which, on the revival of learning, settled into scepticism, masked by an exter-

* Guicciardini Paralipomena, ex autographo Florentino recensita, p. 46—48. Amstel. 1663.

nal respect to the established forms of the Church. In this state did matters remain until the middle of the sixteenth century, when, from causes to be explained hereafter, bigotry and superstition took the place of irreligion and infidelity, and the Popes recovered that empire over the minds and consciences of their countrymen which they had almost entirely lost. If, before this period, there were few heretics in Italy, or if those who swerved from the received faith were less eagerly inquired after, and less severely punished there than in other countries, it was because the people did not give themselves the trouble to think on the subject. Generally speaking, devotion, even according to the principles authorized by the Roman Church, was extinct among the Italians. They were not attached to the Church either by a lively faith or an ardent enthusiasm, by the convictions of the understanding or the sentiments of the heart. The religion of the statesmen resolved itself into their secular interest; the learned felt more respect for Aristotle or Plato, than for the sacred Scriptures or the writings of the Christian fathers; and the people, always under the influence of their senses and imagination, were attracted to the services of the Church by the magnificence of its temples, and by the splendour and gaiety of its religious festivals.*

On a superficial view of the matter, we may be apt to think that a people, who felt in the manner which has been described, might have been detached, without much difficulty, from their obedience to the Church of Rome. But a little reflection will be sufficient to satisfy us, that such expectations are unreasonable. None are more impervious to conviction, or less disposed to make sacrifices to truth, than those who have sunk into indifference about religion under the practice of its forms. The spiritual and humbling doctrines of the gospel, as brought forward, simply and without disguise, by the first reformers, are offensive to the pride of the human mind; and experience has shown, that men, whose minds were emancipated

* Sismondi, Hist. des Rep. Ital. tom. viii. p. 237-240.

from vulgar prejudices, but whose hearts were dead to religious feeling, have yielded as ready a support to established systems of error, and proved as bitter enemies and persecutors of the truth, as the most superstitious and bigoted. But this is not all. The want of religious principle was, on the present occasion, supplied by national vanity and a regard to national interest; two principles which had operated, for more than a century before the Reformation, in strengthening the attachment of the Italians to the Roman see. By the removal of the Papal court to Avignon, the wealth and importance of the city of Rome had been greatly diminished. After the return of the Popes to their ancient seat, and the revival of the pontificate from the deadly wound inflicted on it by the schism of the anti-popes, the Romans congratulated themselves on the recovery of their former distinction. In this feeling, their countrymen in general participated; and the passion for political liberty, by which they had been animated, having subsided, they seemed to think that the loss of the ancient glory of Italy as the mistress of the world was compensated by the flattering station to which she was now raised as the head of Christendom. Accordingly, when the councils of Pisa, Constance, and Basle, attacked the corruptions of the Roman court, and sought to abridge its extensive authority, the Italians came forward in its defence. They felt themselves dishonoured, as a nation, by the invectives which were pronounced against the "Italian vices" of the pontiffs; and they saw that the reforms, which were so eagerly pressed, would cut off or drain those pecuniary resources by which they hoped to be enriched. The Popes were careful to foster this spirit. By a system of artful policy, they had taken effectual care that the power, which they had gradually acquired over the nations of the west, should not be empty or unproductive; and the wealth of Europe continued to flow in various channels to Rome, from which it was distributed through Italy. Under the name of annats, the pope received the first year's produce of all ecclesiastical livings after every vacancy. He drew large sums of money for the confirmation of bishops, and for the gift of archi-episcopal palls. His demands on the clergy for benevolences were frequent, besides the extraordinary levy of the tenths of benefices, on pretence of expeditions against the Turks, which were seldom or never undertaken.* Add to these, the sums exacted for dispensations, absolutions, and indulgences, with the constant and incalculable revenue arising from law-suits, brought from every country by appeal to Rome, carried on there at great expense, and protracted to an indefinite length of time. The pope had also an extensive right of patronage in every country which owned his authority: he presented to all benefices which came under the name of *reserved*, and to those vacant by translation, or which had been possessed by persons who died at Rome, or within forty miles of it, on their journey to or from that city.† These, if not sold to the highest bidder, were generally conferred on Italians, upon whom the pope could rely with more implicit confidence than on foreigners, for extending his authority, and supporting him in those contests in which his ambition involved him with the secular powers. In consequence of the influence which the court of Rome had come to exert in the political affairs of Europe during the fifteenth century, almost every sovereign strove to procure for his near relations, or for some of his subjects, seats in the sacred college; and these were usually purchased by the gift of the richest benefices within his kingdom to those who, from their situation or connections, had it most in their power to serve

---

* The chief of the new Pharisees meantime
Waging his warfare near the Lateran,
Not with Saracens or Jews; his foes
All Christians were.
Dante, Inf. c. xxvii.

† Rymer's Fœdera, vol x. and xi. Appellatio Univers. Paris.; apud Richer. Hist. Concil. Gen lib. iv. p. 2 cap iv. § 15. Georgii Gravamina, p. 363, 522. Kappe, Nachlese Ref Urkunden, P. ii. p. 399, 435; P. iii. p. 246—350. Robertson's Charles V. vol. ii. p. 148—150, 273. Llorente, Hist. de l'Inquisition d'Espagne, vol. i. p. 239—256.

his interests in the conclave. There was not an Italian state or town which did not, on these accounts, depend on the papal court; nor a great family which had not some of its relations in offices connected with it. The greater part of the learned either held ecclesiastical benefices, or enjoyed pensions which they drew from them. Italy was a land of priests. The regular clergy, the sworn clients of the popedom, formidable by their numbers, and by the privileges which they enjoyed, were always prepared to take part with the court of Rome, which, in its turn, supported them against every attempt of the government under which they lived to resist their encroachments, or to correct their most flagrant vices.* Though the states of the church, properly so called, even after they had been enlarged by the warlike Julius, were confined within narrow bounds, yet the pontiffs had taken care to preserve their paramount power over those districts or cities which withdrew from their government, by transferring it to particular families, under the title of vicars of the church. Indeed, there were few places in Italy to which they had not, at one time or an-

* In 1562, the city of Florence alone contained four thousand three hundred and forty-one monks, divided into forty-five monasteries. Cosmo, duke of Tuscany, in 1545, ordered the Dominican Observantines, who had disturbed his government, to quit the monastery of St. Marco, which he gave to the Augustinians. The expelled monks complained to the pope, who ordered the Augustinians, under the highest pains, to retire instantly from the convent, endeavoured to stir up all Christian princes against the duke, as an innovator in religion; and issued a brief, threatening him with excommunication, if he did not, within three days, remit the whole cause to be judged at Rome. In consequence of this, the Dominicans returned to their convent in triumph. Cosmo was equally unsuccessful in his attempts to abridge the privilege of the monks to exemption from secular jurisdiction, which was deluging the country with crimes of every description; and he was obliged to supplicate his holiness to send a legate, " il quale avesse autorità di castigare li Frati nei delitti di eresia, monasteri, bestemia, &c.; perchè i Frati non gli castigano ancora di assassinio e omicidio, e che non gli castighino in abbiamo provato infinite volte. Ancora avesse autorità di castigare li Preti che dai loro Vescovo non fossero puniti secondo i canoni, perchè ogni giorno vediamo grandissime stravaganze, e voremmo castigando noi li Laici che ancor li Frati e li Preti con l'impunità non dessero simili esempio." (Galuzzi, Istoria del Granducato di Toscana, tom. i. 66—68, 73, 139, 365.)

other, advanced a claim, founded on real or pretended grants;* and provided any prince testified a disposition to withdraw his allegiance from the see of Rome, or to resist its authority, it was easy for the pope to revive his dormant claim, and having launched the sentence of excommunication, to add the forfeited possessions to the patrimony of the church, or to bestow them on some neighbouring rival of the rebellious heretic.†

When these things are taken into consideration, it will be matter of surprise, that the reformed doctrine made so much progress in Italy as we shall find it to have made; and we can easily account for the mistake into which some writers, guided by theory rather than fact, have fallen, when they assert that it had few converts in that country.‡

CHAPTER II.

INTRODUCTION OF THE REFORMED OPINIONS INTO ITALY, AND CAUSES OF THEIR PROGRESS.

A CONTROVERSY, which had been carried on for several years with great warmth in Germany, and which was at last brought before the papal court for deci-

* Franc Guicciardini Paralipomena: Discorso levato del tutto via dell'historia nel quarto libro, p. 35—42, 44

† So late as the year 1555, the Pope, Paul IV., not only excommunicated Marc-antonio Colonna, and deprived him of the dukedom of Paliano, but ordered a legal process to be commenced, in the apostolical chamber, against Philip II, king of Naples, as a schismatic and favourer of heresy, inferring, if proved, that he should be deprived of the crown of the two Sicilies, as a fief of the holy see, and sentence would have been pronounced against him, had not the duke of Alva advanced with his troops from Naples to Rome. (Llorente, ii. 172—181.)

‡ "Peu de personnes prirent le parti de Luther en Italie. Ce peuple ingenieux occupé d'intrigues et de plaisirs n'eut aucun part à ces troubles." (Voltaire, Essai sur les Mœurs, chap cxxviii.) Voltaire is not the only author who has committed this error.

sion, deserves notice here, as having contributed, in no small degree, to direct the attention of the Italians, at an early period, to the reformed opinions. A suspicious convert from Judaism, either from hostility to learning, or with the view of extorting money from his countrymen, leagued with an inquisitor of Cologne, and obtained from the imperial chamber a decree, ordaining all Jewish books, with the exception of the Bible, to be committed to the flames, as filled with blasphemies against Christ. John Reuchlin, or Capnio, a learned man of Suabia, and the restorer of Hebrew literature among Christians,* exerted himself, both privately and from the press, to prevent the execution of this barbarous decree. His successful opposition exposed him to the resentment of the clergy, and sentence was pronounced against him, first by the divines of Cologne, and afterwards by the Sorbonne at Paris. Reuchlin appealed to Rome, and the friends of learning determined to make his cause a common one. Erasmus and other distinguished individuals wrote warmly in his favour to their friends at Rome, several of whom belonged to the sacred college; and the monks exerted themselves with equal zeal to defeat a party which they had long hated, and from which they had much to dread. No cause of the kind had, for a long time, excited such general interest. On the one side were ranked the monks, the most devoted clients of the papal throne; on the other, the men who had attracted the admiration of Europe by their talents and writings. The court of Rome was afraid of offending either side, and by means of those arts which it knew so well how to employ in delicate cases, protracted the affair from time to time. During this interval, the monks and

* It ought to be mentioned to the honour of the Netherlands, that Reuchlin received his first knowledge of Hebrew from John Wessel, a native of Groningen. (Maius, Vita J. Reuchlini Phorcensis, p. 154.) To this singular man, Luther gives the title of *God taught;* and, in an epistle prefixed to his works, he says, " If I had read them before, my enemies might have said, that Luther had borrowed every thing from Wessel, so much do our writings breathe the same spirit." (Luther's Saemmtliche Schriften, tom. xiv. p. 219—223.) Wessel died in 1489.

their supporters were subjected to the lash of the most cutting satires,* and the ultimate sentence, enjoining silence on both parties, was scarcely ratified, when the controversy between Luther and the preachers of indulgences arose, and was brought before the same tribunal for decision †

The noise excited by the late process had fixed the attention of the Italians on Germany; the facts which it brought to light abated the contempt with which they had hitherto regarded the inhabitants of that country; Luther had taken part with Reuchlin ‡ and some of the keenest and most intrepid defenders of the latter, such as Ulrich Hutten, declared, at an early period, in favour of the religious opinions of the former.

It was not to be expected, after all, that a dispute managed by a friar, in an obscure part of Germany, against the sale of indulgences, a traffic which had long been carried on under the auspices and for the profit of the see of Rome, would attract much attention in Italy. But the boldness of his own mind, and the provoking impudence of his antagonists, having led Luther to persevere in his opposition, and gradually to extend his censure to other abuses, his name and opinions soon became the topic of general conversation beyond the limits of his native country.

---

* Of these, the most celebrated was the work entitled, Epistolæ Obscurorum Virorum, the joint production of several learned men.

† Maii Vita Reuchlini, *passim*. Schlegel, Vita Georgii Spalatini, p. 24, 25 Bulæi Hist. Univ. Paris. tom. vi. p. 47—57. Beside the works mentioned by Maius, Pfefferkorn published, "Speculum adhortationis Judaicæ ad Christum," and "Libellus de Judaica confessione, sive sabbato afflictionis." Both were printed at Cologne in 1508, and evince a bitter hostility to his countrymen.

‡ Luther's Saemmtliche Schriften, tom. xxi. p. 518—521. A letter from him to Reuchlin is to be found in Illustrium Virorum Epistolæ ad Joannem Reuchlin. Liber Secundus, sig. C 3. Hagenoæ, 1519. The interest which he took in the affairs of that scholar, appears from the incidental reference which he made to him, in the midst of his own trials:—" Minacibus illis meis amicis nihil habeo quod respondeam, nisi illud Reuchlinianum, Qui pauper est, nihil timet, nihil potest perdere. Res nec habeo, nec cupio." (Epistola ad J. Staupicium, die S. Trinitatis, 1518. Opera Omn. tom. i. f. 74. Jenæ, 1564.)

Within two years from the time of his first appearance against indulgences, his writings had found their way into Italy, where they met with a favourable reception from the learned. It must have been highly gratifying to the reformer, to receive the following information, in a letter addressed to him by John Froben, a celebrated printer at Basle:—" Blasius Salmonius, a bookseller at Leipsic, presented me, at the last Frankfort fair, with certain treatises composed by you, which being approved by learned men, I immediately put to press, and sent six hundred copies to France and Spain. My friends assure me, that they are sold at Paris, and read and approved of even by the Sorbonnists. Several learned men there have said, that they have long wished to see divine things treated with such becoming freedom. Calvus, a bookseller of Pavia,* himself a scholar and addicted to the muses, has carried a great part of the impression into Italy. He promises to send epigrams written in your praise by the most enlightened men in that country;† such favour have you gained to yourself and the cause of Christ, by your constancy, courage, and dexterity."‡ A letter has also been preserved, written about this time by an individual in Rome, in which the spirit and writings of Luther are applauded.§

* The person referred to in the text is Francesco Calvi, often mentioned in the letters of Erasmus, and highly praised by Andrea Alciati, the civilian, and other learned men. (Tiraboschi, vii. 365.) Speaking of the difficulty of disposing of books in Italy, Cælio Calcagnini says, in a letter dated from Ferrara, 17 kal. Febr 1525, "Unus fuit Calvus, ejus Calvi frater qui rem impressoriam curat Romæ, qui non pecuniam sed librorum permutationem obtulit." (Calcagnini Opera, p. 115.)

† Schelhorn (Amœnit. Hist. Eccles. et Liter. tom. ii. p. 624.) has published a copy of verses in praise of Luther, composed at Milan, in 1521, which conclude thus.—

    Macte igitur virtute, pater celebrande Luthere,
      Communis cujus pendet ab ore salus:
    Gratia cui ablatis debetur maxima monstris,
      Alcidæ potuit quæ metuisse manus.

‡ Miscellanea Groningana, tom. iii. p. 61—63. Froben's letter is dated, " Basileæ d. 14. Februar. 1519." A letter to the same purpose by Wolfgangus Fabricius Capito, dated " 12 kal. Martii, 1519," is inserted in Sculteti Annal. Reform. p. 44.

§ Riederer, Nachrichten fur Kirchengelehrten und Buchergeschichte, tom. i. p. 179.

Burchard Schenk, a German nobleman who had embraced a monastic life and resided at Venice, writes, on the 19th of September 1520, to Spalatin, the chaplain of the Elector of Saxony:—" According to your request, I have read the books of Martin Luther, and I can assure you that he has been much esteemed in this place for some time past. But the common saying is, 'Let him beware of the pope!' Upwards of two months ago, ten copies of his books were brought here, and instantly purchased, before I had even heard of their arrival; but, in the beginning of this month, a mandate from the pope and the patriarch of Venice arrived, prohibiting them; and a strict search having been instituted among the booksellers, one imperfect copy was found and seized. I had endeavoured to obtain that copy, but the bookseller durst not dispose of it."* In a letter written during the following year, the same person states, that the senate of Venice had at last reluctantly consented to the publication of the papal bull against Luther, but had taken care that it should not be read until the people had left the church.† Two circumstances of a curious kind appear from this correspondence. The one is, that Schenk had received a commission from the Elector of Saxony to purchase relics for the collegiate church of Wittemberg; but the commission was now revoked, and the relics sent back to Italy, to be sold at what price they would bring; "for," writes Spalatin, "here even the common people despise them, and think it sufficient (as it certainly is) if they be taught from Scripture to have faith and confidence in God, and love to their neighbour."‡ The other fact is, that the person employed by Schenk to collect relics for the elector was Vergerio, afterwards bishop of Capo d'Istria, and legate from the pope to the German princes, but who ultimately renounced popery, and became eminently instrumental in spreading the reformed doctrine in Italy and elsewhere. The character given of him, at this early

* Seckendorf. Hist. Lutheranismi, tom. p. 115.   † Ibid. p. 116.
‡ Schlegel, Vita Spalatini, p. 59.

period of his life, is worthy of notice, as the popish writers, after his defection, endeavoured, in every possible way, to discredit his authority and tarnish his reputation. Schenk describes him as " a most excellent young man, who had distinguished himself among the students of law at Padua, and was desirous of finishing his studies at Wittemberg, under the auspices and patronage of the elector Frederick."*

In spite of the terror of pontifical bulls, and the activity of those who watched over their execution, the writings of Luther and Melancthon, Zuingle and Bucer, continued to be circulated and read with avidity and delight in various parts of Italy. Some of them were translated into the Italian language,† and, to elude the vigilance of the inquisitors, were published under disguised and fictitious names, by which means they made their way into Rome and even into the palace of the Vatican; so that bishops and cardinals unwittingly read and praised works, which, on discovering their real authors, they were obliged to pronounce dangerous and heretical. The elder Scaliger relates an incident of this kind, which happened when he was at Rome. " Cardinal Seraphin," says he, " who was at that time counsellor of the papal Rota, came to me one day, and said, 'We have had a most laughable business before us to-day. The Common Places of Philip Melancthon were printed at Venice with this title, *par Messer Ippofilo da Terra Negra*.‡ Being sent to Rome, they were freely bought for the space of a whole year, and read with great applause, so that the copies being exhausted, an order was sent to Venice for a fresh supply; but, in the mean time, a Franciscan friar, who possessed a copy of the origi-

---

* Seckend tom. i. p 223.

† Luther's Shorter Catechism, and his Exposition of the Lord's Prayer, the Creed, the Decalogue, &c. were printed in Italian. (Ukert, Luther's Leben, tom. ii. p. 305)

‡ *Schwartzerd*, which was his proper name, signifies in German, as *Melancthon* does in Greek, and *Terra Negra* in Italian, *black earth*. The Italian translator of the Common Places is erroneously supposed by Fontanini to have been the celebrated critic, Ludovico Castelvetro. (Della Eloquenza Italiana, p. 490–509.)

nal edition, discovered the trick, and denounced the book as a Lutheran production from the pen of Melancthon. It was proposed to punish the poor printer, who probably could not read one word of the original; but, at last, it was agreed to burn the copies and suppress the whole affair.' "* A similar anecdote is told of Luther's preface to the Epistle to the Romans, and his treatise on justification, which were eagerly read for some time, as the productions of Cardinal Fregoso.† The works of Zuingle were circulated under the name of Coricius Cogelius;‡ and several editions of Martin Bucer's commentary on the Psalms were sold in Italy and France as the work of Aretius Felinus. In this last instance, the learned stratagem was used with the consent of the author. "I am employed," says Bucer, in a letter to Zuingle, "in an exposition of the Psalms, which, at the urgent request of our brethren in France and Lower Germany, I propose to publish under a foreign name, that the work may be bought by their booksellers; for it is a capital crime to import into these countries books which bear our names. I therefore pretend that I am a Frenchman, and, if I do not change my mind, shall send forth the book as the production of *Aretius Felinus*, which, indeed, is my name and surname, the former in Greek, and the latter in Latin."§

* Scaligerana Secunda, art *Rota* See also Brucker, Miscel. Hist. &c. part. ii. p 323, 333. Greater mistakes than this have been committed in Italy since that period. "My hostess, the good mother Coleti," says Chardon de la Rochette, "says her prayers every day before a beautiful miniature, which represents Luther on the one side and Melancthon on the other. She believes them to be portraits of St. Peter and St. Paul." (Litterarische Analekten von F. A. Wolf, vol i. p. 405)
† Vergerii Adnot. in Catal Hæret. Romæ, 1559.
‡ Gerdesii Ital Ref. p. 12–14
§ Le Long, edit. Masch, vol iii. part. ii. p. 520. Colomesii Notæ in Scaliger. Secund p. 538. Fontanini, Della Eloquenza Ital. p. 490. The work was printed first at Strasburg in 1529, under this title " Psalmorum Libri quinque ad Ebraicam veritatem versi, et familiari explanatione elucidati. Per Aretium Felinum Theologum." The dedication to the Dauphin of France is dated " Lugduni iii. Idus Julias Anno M.D.XXIX." Bucer also assumed the names of *Treu von Friedesleben*, and *Waremund Luithold*.

It is one thing to discover the errors and abuses of the Church of Rome, and it is another, and a very different thing to have the mind opened to perceive the spiritual beauty and to feel the regenerating influence of divine truth. Many who could easily discern the former, remained complete strangers to the latter, as preached by Luther and his associates; and it is not to be expected that these would make sacrifices, and still less that they would count all things loss, for the excellent knowledge of Christ. Persons of this character abounded at this period in Italy. But the following extracts show that many of the Italians "received the love of the truth;" and they paint in strong colours the ardent thirst for knowledge which the perusal of the first writings of the reformers had excited in their breasts. "It is now fourteen years," writes Egidio di Porta, an Augustinian monk on the Lake of Como, to Zuingle, "since I, under the impulse of a certain pious feeling, but not according to knowledge, withdrew from my parents and assumed the black cowl. If I did not become learned and devout, I at least appeared to be so, and for seven years discharged the office of a preacher of God's word, alas! in deep ignorance. I savoured not the things of Christ; I ascribed nothing to faith, all to works. But God would not permit his servant to perish for ever. He brought me to the dust. I was made to cry out, Lord, what wilt thou have me to do? At length my heart heard the delightful voice, Go to Ulric Zuingle, and he will tell thee what thou shouldst do. O ravishing sound! my soul found ineffable peace in that sound. Do not think that I mock you; for you, nay not you, but God, by your means, rescued me from the snare of the fowler. But why do I say *me?* for I trust you have saved others along with me."* In these enthusiastic strains does Porta communicate the intelligence, that he had been enlightened by the writings of the Swiss reformer which Providence had thrown in his way, and that he had

* Epistola Ægidii a Porta, Comensis, Dec. 9, 1525: Hottinger, Hist. Eccl. Sec. xvi. tom. ii. p. 611.

imparted the knowledge of the truth to some of his brethren of the same convent. In another letter, he adjures Zuingle to write him a letter which might be useful for opening the eyes of others belonging to his religious order. "But let it be cautiously written," continues he, "for they are full of pride and self-conceit. Place some passages of Scripture before them, by which they may perceive how much God is pleased to have his word preached purely and without mixture, and how highly he is offended with those who adulterate it and bring forward their own opinions as divine."* The same spirit breathes in a letter addressed by Baltasare Fontana, a Carmelite monk of Locarno, to the evangelical churches of Switzerland. "Hail! faithful in Christ. Think, O think of Lazarus in the gospels, and of the lowly woman of Canaan, who was willing to be satisfied with the crumbs which fell from the table of the Lord. As David came to the priest in a servile dress and unarmed, so do I fly to you for the show-bread and the armour laid up in the sanctuary. Parched with thirst, I seek the fountains of living water; sitting like the blind man by the wayside, I cry to him that gives sight. With tears and sighs we, who sit here in darkness, humbly intreat you who are acquainted with the titles and authors of the books of knowledge, (for to you it is given to know the mysteries of the kingdom of God,) to send us the writings of such elect teachers as you possess, and particularly the works of the divine Zuingle, the far-famed Luther, the acute Melancthon, the accurate Ecolampade. The prices shall be paid to you through his excellency, Werdmyller. Do your endeavour that a city of Lombardy, enslaved by Babylon and a stranger to the gospel of Christ, may be set free."†

The attention which had been paid to sacred literature in Italy contributed, in no small degree, to the

* Epist. Dec. 9, 1525. Hottinger, Hist. Eccl. Sec. xvi. tom. ii. p. 16.

† Apud Comum, 15to Decembris 1526." Another letter from the same individual, dated, "Ex Locarno Kal. Mart. anno 1531," is published by Hottinger, Hist. tom. vi. part. ii. p. 618, 620, 271. Tempe Helvetica, tom. iv. p. 141.

spread of the reformed opinions. In this, as well as in every other literary pursuit, the Italians took the lead, though they were afterwards outstripped by the Germans. From the year 1477, when the psalter appeared in Hebrew, different parts of the Old Testament, in the original, continued to issue from the press; until at last, in the year 1488, a complete Hebrew Bible was printed at Soncino, a city of the Cremonese, by a family of Jews, who, under the adopted name of Soncinati, established printing-presses in various parts of Europe, including Constantinople. This department of typography was almost entirely engrossed by the Jews, until the year 1518, when an edition of the Hebrew Scriptures, accompanied with various readings and Rabbinical commentaries, proceeded from the splendid press which Daniel Bomberg had recently erected at Venice.*

A minute investigation of ancient documents shows that the knowledge of Hebrew was not quite extinct among Christians in Italy anterior to the revival of letters. An individual now and then had the curiosity to acquire some insight into it from a Jew, or had the courage to grapple, in his own strength, with the difficulties of a language whose very characters wore a formidable aspect to European eyes; and persons who, like Fra Ricoldo of Florence, and Ciriaco of Ancona, travelled into Turkey, Syria, and adjacent countries, picked up some acquaintance with other languages of the east. In the literary history of Italy, during the early part of the fifteenth century, several persons are spoken of as Hebrew and Arabic scholars; the most distinguished of whom was Giannozzo Manetti, a Florentine, who drew up a triglot psalter, containing a Latin translation made by himself from the original.† But the study of Hebrew in Italy, properly speaking, was coeval with the printing of the

* De Rossi, De Heb. Typog. Origin. Wilhelm Fried. Hetzels Geschichte der Hebraischen Sprache und Litteratur, p. 143—176. Le Long, Bibl. Sac. edit. Masch, vol. 1. par. 1. Baueri Crit. Sac. p. 230, 232.

† Tiraboschi, Storia della Letteratura Italiana, tom. vi. p. 792, 679.

Hebrew Scriptures; and it was facilitated by the severe measures taken by Ferdinand and Isabella, at the instigation of the inquisitors, against the Jews, which induced many of that people to emigrate from Spain to Italy, where, from lucrative motives, they were favourably received by the popes.*

One of the earliest students of the oriental tongues in Italy was Giovanni Pico, a young man of rank, and the prodigy of his age for learning. He was the son of Gianfrancesco Pico, prince of Mirandula and Concordia. From early youth he possessed so quick an apprehension, and so retentive a memory, as to forget nothing which he heard or read. After studying in the most celebrated universities of his native country and France, he came to Rome, with the reputation of knowing twenty-two languages; and, in the twenty-fourth year of his age, published nine hundred propositions relating to dialectics, morals, physics, mathematics, metaphysics, theology, and natural magic, as treated by the Chaldean, Arabian, Greek, and Latin philosophers, and by the Christian fathers and schoolmen, declaring that he was ready to dispute with any person upon every one of them.† The challenge was not accepted; and it exposed Pico to a more serious charge than that of vanity. He was accused to Innocent VIII. as a heretic; and thirteen propositions, selected from his work, having been submitted to certain divines, the pope condemned them as suspicious and dangerous, but exempted the author from punishment, because he had protested, on oath, his willingness to submit in all things to the judgment of the church. In the meantime, he published a large apology for the offensive articles, in which he

* Basnage, Histoire des Juifs, liv. vii. chap. xxix. sect. iv.—vii. Sadoleti Epist. lib. xii. p. 5, 6. Llorente, Hist. de l'Inquisition d'Espagne, tom. i. p. 161—170.

† A MS. copy of the propositions, preserved in the library of Vienna, has, at the end, the following notification in Latin.—" The dispute on these conclusions will not take place until after Epiphany. In the meantime, they will be published in all the academies of Italy; and if any philosopher or divine choose to come from the remotest parts of Italy to dispute, his expenses shall be borne." (Lambacher, Biblioth. Civit. Vindobon. p. 286.)

showed much ingenuity in reconciling them to the
catholic doctrine. This produced a fresh summons,
from the effects of which he was saved by the demise
of Innocent; and, after remaining for some time at
Florence, he obtained, through the good offices of his
friends, a brief of absolution and security from the
new pope, Alexander VI.* At Florence he contracted an intimate friendship with Lorenzo de Medici, and other men of genius, by whom he was
courted for his erudition and taste. But his mind
underwent a great change about this time; and, having relinquished the pursuit of secular learning, and
committed to the flames a collection of his Italian and
Latin poems, which had been revised and approved
of by Politiano, he devoted himself to sacred studies
and the practice of piety. In the midst of these exercises, he was seized with a fever in 1494, and prema-
turely cut off in the thirty-second year of his age.†
Pico had begun the study of the oriental languages
before he became decidedly pious. He was instructed
in Hebrew by a Jew, called Jochana.‡ His teacher
in Chaldee was one Mithridates, of whom he gives
the following singular account, in a letter to a friend:
" As to your request for the Chaldee alphabet, you
cannot obtain it from Mithridates, nor from me, who
am always ready to grant you every thing. For this
man would not agree to teach me the Chaldee tongue
until I had taken an oath, in express words, that I

* The papal brief is prefixed to the edition of his works printed at Basle in 1572. Among the condemned propositions are the two following.—That Christ did not descend into hell truly, or in respect of real presence; and that neither the cross of Christ, nor any other image, is to be adored with the worship called *latria*, as taught by Thomas Aquinas. There are other propositions in the work which, it might have been supposed, would have given equal offence, such as, that the will of God is the sole reason why he reprobates some, and elects others; that the true body of Christ is in heaven locally, and on the altar sacramentally, and that the same body cannot be made, by the power of God, to exist in different places at the same time. (Opera J. Pici, p. 62—65.)

† Biblioteca Modonese, dal Girol. Tiraboschi, tom. iv. p. 95—103. Roscoe's Lorenzo de'Medici, vol. ii. p. 91—95

‡ Opera J. Franc. Pici, p. 1371.

would impart it to nobody. Of this you may be assured by the testimony of our friend Geronimo Benivieni, who, happening to be present one day when I was about to receive a lesson, Mithridates, in a rage, drove him out of the room. But, not to disappoint you altogether, instead of the Chaldee, you will receive with this packet the Arabic characters, which I copied with my own hand."* Judging from the writings of Pico, his knowledge of Hebrew was not inconsiderable;† of the enthusiasm with which he studied it and the cognate languages of the east, we have the most satisfactory evidence in his confidential letters. Writing to his nephew, he says—" The reason why you have not had an answer to your letter is, that I have met with certain Hebrew books, which have occupied me for a whole week, night and day, so that I am nearly blind. They were brought me twenty days ago by a Jew from Sicily, and, as I am afraid that they may be recalled, you must not expect to hear a word from me till I have thoroughly examined their contents. When that is done, I shall overwhelm you with letters."‡ In a letter to Marsilio Ficino, he writes—" You could not have demanded back your Latin Mahomet at a more convenient time, as I expect shortly to be able to read him in his native tongue. Having laboured a whole month in studying the Hebrew language, I am about to apply myself to Arabic, and am not afraid but that I shall make as much proficiency in it, as I have done in Hebrew, in which I can now write a letter correctly, though not with elegance. You see what resolution, accompanied with labour and diligence, can do, even when the bodily strength is small. Certain books, in both languages, which have come into my hands, not by chance, but by the direction of a kind providence favouring my studies, have encouraged and compelled me to lay aside everything for the

* Opera J. Pici, p. 385.
† See his *Heptaplus*, or treatise on the Mosaic account of the creation, in the collection of his works.
‡ Opera. p. 360.

sake of acquiring the knowledge of Arabic and Chaldee. Having obtained these, (shall I call them books or treasures?) I was inflamed with the desire of being able to read them without an interpreter—a task at which I am now toiling with all my might. Do not think, however, that I forget your favourite Plotinus."* We need not wonder that the enthusiasm of this scholar made him the dupe of designing and covetous men. Perceiving his strong desire to demonstrate the truth of the Christian religion, and its mysteries, from the recondite sources of Pythagorean and Jewish philosophy, certain impostors interpolated some Cabalistic books, of which they sold him seventy volumes at a great price, with a solemn assurance that they were written under the direction of Ezra, and contained that interpretation of the law which the Jews had hitherto religiously concealed from Christians.† The same thing happened to his contemporary and countryman, Annius, or Nanni, of Viterbo, who was induced to publish a number of fabulous works, as the authentic productions of Berosus, Manetho, Fabius Pictor, and other ancient writers;‡ and similar impositions have been practised upon literary men in later and more enlightened times. Gianfrancesco Pico inherited his uncle's taste for Hebrew literature;§ and other scholars arose, who cultivated it, not indeed with equal zeal, but certainly with more success.

Germany had the honour of giving to the world the first elementary work on Hebrew which was written by a Christian, or in the Latin language, in the grammar and lexicon of John Reuchlin, printed at Pfortzheim in the year 1506; but, as early as 1490, the *Book of Roots*, or lexicon, of the celebrated Jewish grammarian, David Kimchi, was published in

* Opera J. Pici, p. 367, 368.
† Ib. p. 123. Reuchlin, De Arte Cabalistica, lib i. f. 13, b Bruckeri Hist. Philos. tom. ii p. 660, 919. Simon, Lettres Choisies, tom. ii. p. 188.
‡ Tiraboschi, Lett. Ital tom. vi. part ii p. 17.
§ Opera Joan. Francisci Pici, p. 1371. Colomesii Italia Orientalis, p. 46—51.

the original at Venice.* Francesco Stancari of Mantua, who afterwards embraced the Protestant religion, and excited great commotions in Poland, published a Hebrew grammar in 1525.† Felix of Prato, a converted Jew, who published a Latin translation of the Psalms in 1515, appears to have been the first Christian in Italy who taught Hebrew, being invited to Rome, for this purpose, in 1518, by Leo X.‡ About the same time, Agathias Guidacerio, a native of Catano, also taught it at Rome, from which he was called by Francis I. to be professor of the sacred tongue in the Trilingual college at Paris, in which Paolo Paradisi, or Canossa, his countryman, and, like him, the author of a work on Hebrew Grammar, afterwards held the same situation.§

As early as 1514, a collection of prayers was printed in the Arabic language and character at Fano, in the ecclesiastical states, at a press which had been founded by the warlike pontiff, Julius II.‖ Previous to this, an edition of the Koran, in the original language, had been begun, and a part of it at least printed at Venice, by Pagnino de Pagninis.¶ But the principal work in this language, so far as biblical literature is concerned, was produced by Agostino Justiniani, bishop of Nebio in Corsica, in a polyglot psalter, containing the Hebrew, Chaldaic, Arabic, Greek, and Latin; printed at Genoa in the year 1516, and intended as a specimen of a polyglot bible, which the author had been long engaged in preparing for the press.** This

* Hirts Orientalische und Exegetische Bibliothek, tom. i p. 35, 44. G. Laur Baueri Hermeneutica Sacra, p. 175.

† Tiraboschi, tom. vii. p. 1087. Stancari became professor of Hebrew, first in the university of Cracow, and afterwards in that of Konigsberg. (Harknochs Preussische Kirchenhistorie, p. 333) Hetzel speaks as if none of his grammatical works appeared before 1547. (Geschichte der Heb. Sprache, p 169)

‡ Tiraboschi, vii. 1083. Colomesii Ital. Orient. p 19. Le Long, edit Masch, vol i. part. i p 97; vol. ii part. ii. p. 534.

§ Præfat. in Lib. Michlol, per Agathiam Guidacerium; Parisiis in Collegio Italorum, 1540. Conf Colomesii Ital. Orient p. 60, 68—70.

‖ Schnurreri Bibliotheca Arabica, p 231—234.

¶ Ibid. p 402—404

** Dedic. Justiniani ad Leonem X. Conf. Le Long. edit. Masch, vol i. part i p 400.

work procured him an invitation from Francis I. to teach the oriental tongues at Paris.* Juan Leon, a native of Elvira in Spain, better known as a historian by the name of Leo Africanus, instructed many of the Italians in Arabic, and, among others, Egidio of Viterbo, a prelate still more distinguished for elegant taste and extensive learning than for rank, who zealously promoted oriental studies among his countrymen both by example and patronage. The master went to Tunis, and relapsed to Mahometanism; the scholar was advanced to the purple, and sent as ambassador to Constantinople.†

Certain deputies sent to Rome, from the Christians of Abyssinia, during the sitting of the Lateran council in 1512, were the means of introducing into Europe the knowledge of the Ethiopic, or, as they called it, Chaldean language, in which their countrymen continued to perform the religious service. In consequence of instructions received from them, John Potken, provost of St. George's at Cologne, was able, in 1513, to publish, at Rome, the Psalter and Song of Solomon in Ethiopic, with a short introduction to that language.‡ At a subsequent period, a learned abbot of that country, named Tesso-Sionis Malhesini, or, as he called himself in Europe, Peter Sionita, who resided at Rome under the patronage of cardinal Marcello Cervini, taught his native tongue to Pierpaolo Gualtieri and Mariano Vittorio, afterwards bishop of Rieti; and, with their assistance, and that of two of his own countrymen, he published the New Testament in Ethiopic, at Rome, in the year 1548. Four

* Tiraboschi, tom. vii. p. 1067. Colomesii Ital. Orient. p 31—36. Sixt. Senensis Bibl. Sacr p. 327. Justiniani himself says, " Mi fece suo consigliero e suo elemosinaro,—e mi mandò in Parigi, dove me detenni insino al quinto anno, & lessi & piantai in l'universita Parisiense le litere Hebree " (Castigatissimi Annali della Republica di Genova, lib iii. a. 1537.)

† Widmanstaedter's Dedication, to the Emperor Ferdinand, of his edition of the Syriac New Testament. Compare the testimonies to Egidio's merits, collected by Colomies. (Ital. Orient. p. 41—46.) Hetzel's Geschichte, p. 180.

‡ Le Long, edit. Masch, vol. i. par. ii p. 146, 147.

years after this, the first grammar of that language was given to the public by Vittorio.*

It may appear strange, that no part of the Syriac version of the Scriptures should as yet have come from the press. Bomberg intended to print the gospel according to Matthew in that language, from a copy of the four gospels which was in his possession, but delayed the work in expectation of obtaining additional manuscripts.† Teseo Ambrogio, of the noble family of the Conti d'Albonese, a doctor of laws and canon regular of St. John's of the Lateran, who had received instructions in Ethiopic from the Abyssinians who visited Rome in 1512, was initiated into the Syriac language by one of three individuals, Joseph Acurio, a priest, Moses, a deacon, and Elias, a subdeacon, whom Peter, patriarch of the Maronites, had sent as a deputation to Rome, soon after the advancement of Leo X. to the pontificate. From that time Ambrogio became passionately fond of these languages, and being appointed to teach them at Bologna, gave from the press a specimen of his qualifications for that task in his Introduction to the Chaldaic, Syriac, Armenian, and ten other languages, with the characters of about forty different alphabets.‡ Various untoward events prevented him from executing his favourite design of publishing the gospels in Syriac, which, at an accidental interview, he devolved on Albert Widmanstaedter, the learned chancellor of Eastern Austria. In the year 1552, Ignatius, patriarch of Antioch, sent Moses Mardineus, as his "orator" to the Roman pontiff, to obtain, among other things, the printing of an edition of the Syriac New Testament, for the use of

* Tiraboschi, tom. vii. p. 1073. Le Long, edit Masch, vol. 1 part ii p 152—154. Colomesii Ital. Orient p. 107, 108, art. Marianus Victorius Reatinus. Michaelis, Introd to the New Testament, by Marsh, vol. ii. part 1. p. 612.

† Postel, Linguarum Duodecim Alph. Introd. sig. Biiij Parisiis 1538. Conf Postelli Epist. prefix Vers. N. Test. Syriaci, Vien. Austr. 1555

‡ Introductio in Chaldaicam linguam, Syriacam, &c. Papiæ, 1539. Tiraboschi, vii. 1068—1072. Henr. a Porta, (Prof. Linguarum Oriental. apud. Acad. Ticin.) De Ling. Orient. Præstantia, p 189.

the churches under his inspection. The orator exerted his eloquence in vain at Rome, Venice, and other places of Italy; and, after wasting nearly three years, was about to return home in despair, when he was advised to apply to Widmanstaedter, by whose zealous exertions the work was published in 1555, at Vienna.* Thus was Italy deprived of the honour of giving to the world the New Testament in the best and most venerable of all the ancient versions.

The first edition of the Septuagint came from the Aldine press in 1518, under the direction of Andrew of Asolo. In 1516, Erasmus published at Basle his edition of the Greek text of the New Testament, accompanied with a Latin version formed by himself; to which his fame gave an extensive circulation in Italy. And in 1527, Sante Pagnini of Lucca published his Latin translation of the whole Bible, which had excited great expectations, from the reputation which the author enjoyed as a Hebrew scholar, and its being known that he had spent upwards of twenty-five years on the work.

The publication of the Scriptures in the original languages, and in various versions, was followed by illustrations of them, which were neither without merit nor utility. The work of Pietro Colonna, commonly called, from his native place, Galatinus, from which later writers on the Jewish controversy have drawn so many of their materials, was not the less useful, that it was afterwards found to be a compilation from the unpublished work of another author.† Besides his own paraphrases, Erasmus edited the notes of Laurentius Valla on the New Testament, which came recommended to the Italians as the work of one of their countrymen, who had distinguished himself as a reviver of letters, but whom Bellarmine afterwards

* Dedic. et Præfat. in N. Test. Syriac. Vien. Austr. 1555. Assemani Bibl. Orient. tom. 1 p. 535. Le Long, edit. Masch, vol 1. par. ii p. 71—79. Michaelis, Introd. by Marsh, vol. ii. part 1. p. 8, 535 —540.

† Galatinus, De Arcanis Catholicæ Veritatis, Ortonæ, 1518. See the account of the *Pugio Fidei* of Raymond Martini, given in the History of the Reformation in Spain, p. 66.

called, not without reason, the precursor of the Lutherans.* The scriptural simplicity which characterizes the commentaries of Cardinal Cajetan, and a few others, forms a striking contrast to the writings of the scholastic divines who preceded them. Cardinal Sadolet's commentary on the epistle to the Romans was the work of an orator, who wished to correct the barbarisms of the vulgate, and combat the tenets of St. Augustine † The works of Agostino Steuchi, or Steuco, of Gubbio, discover an extensive acquaintance with the three learned languages, mixed with cabalistical and Platonic ideas. I shall afterwards have occasion to speak of the commentaries of Folengo. Isidoro Clario, a Benedictine abbot of Monte Cassino, who was advanced to the bishoprick of Foligno, published the vulgate, corrected from the original Hebrew and Greek, and accompanied with preliminary dissertations and explanatory notes; but as the work did not appear till 1542, when the progress of heresy had alarmed his brethren, it, in consequence, underwent the process of expurgation, and the prolegomena were suppressed.‡ He gave great offence by saying in his preface, that he had corrected the version of the Old Testament by the Hebrew, and of the New by the Greek verity.§ The author had also availed himself of the notes of the Protestants, but tacitly; " for, in the time in which he wrote, to cite a Protestant author was an unpardonable crime," as Tiraboschi candidly owns. "Heresy," says another modern writer, " was a pest, the very touch of which created horror; the cordon of separation or precaution was drawn all around; Clario did not dread the contagion for himself, but he dreaded to appear to have braved it, and his prudence excuses his plagiarism."‖

By means of these studies, the minds of the learned

* Simon, Hist. Crit. des Commentateurs du N. Test. p. 484—487
† Ibid. p. 550—556 Sadolet was thrown into great distress, in consequence of the master of the sacred palace refusing to approve of his commentary. (Tiraboschi, tom. vii p. 313—315.)
‡ Riveti Opera, tom. ii. p. 916.
§ Tiraboschi, tom. vii. p. 348.   ‖ Ginguene, tom. vii. p. 36.

in Italy were turned to the Scriptures, and prepared for taking part in the religious controversy which arose. Individuals in the conclave, such as Egidio, Fregoso, and Aleander, were skilled in the sacred tongues, which were now studied in the palaces of bishops and in the cells of monks. All were not concerned to become acquainted with the treasures hid in those books, which they turned over by night and by day, and still less were they led by them to renounce a system to which, among other secular advantages, they owed their literary leisure; but neither, on the other hand, were men disposed, at that period, as they were at a subsequent one, to employ sacred criticism as an art to invent arguments for supporting existing abuses; and there were always individuals, from time to time, whose minds welcomed the truth, or were accessible to conviction. Accordingly, we shall find among the converts to the reformed doctrine, men eminent for their literary attainments, the rank which they held in the Church, and the character which they had obtained for piety in those orders to which the epithet religious had long been appropriated. The reformers appealed from the fallible and conflicting opinions of the doctors of the Church to the infallible dictates of revelation, and from the vulgate version of the Scriptures to the Hebrew and Greek originals; and in these appeals they were often supported by the translations recently made by persons of acknowledged orthodoxy, and published with the permission and warm recommendations of the head of the church. In surveying this portion of history, it is impossible not to admire the arrangements of Providence, when we perceive monks and bishops, cardinals and popes, active in forging and polishing those weapons which were soon to be turned against themselves, and which they afterwards would fain have blunted and laboured to decry as unlawful and empoisoned.

The works which have been described were confined to the learned; and, however useful they were, it is not probable that any impression would have been made on the public mind in Italy, unless the means of religious knowledge had been laid open to the people at large. As the church of Rome has strictly confined the religious service to an unknown tongue, we need not be astonished at the jealousy with which she has always viewed translations of the Scriptures into vulgar languages. There would be still less reason for astonishment at this, if we might believe the statement of a learned Italian, that, down to the sixteenth century, all the sermons preached in churches were in Latin, and that those in Italian were delivered without the consecrated walls, in the piazzas or some contiguous spot.* This statement, however, has been controverted. The truth appears to be, that, in the thirteenth century, the sermons were preached in Latin, and afterwards explained in Italian to the common people; and that instances of this practice occur in the history of the fifteenth century.† It was pleaded, that the dignity of the pulpit and the sacredness of the word of God suffered by using a different method; and with equal force might it be urged, that "the sacred Scriptures were vilified by being translated into the vulgar tongue."‡ But, in spite of this prejudice, translations of the Bible into Italian were attempted, as soon as the language had been purified by Dante, Petrarch, and others; and they came from the press within a few years after the invention of the art of printing.

Jacopo da Voragine, bishop of Genoa, and author of the Golden Legend, is said to have translated the Scriptures into the language of Italy as early as the

---

* Fontanini, Della Eloquenza Italiana, lib. iii. cap. ii. p. 250–254. It is certain that, so late as the middle of the sixteenth century, Isidoro Clario, bishop of Foligno, preached in Latin to a crowded assembly of men and women—" Frequens istem, quem cerno, virorum, *mulierumque*, conventus," says the preacher. (Orationes Extraord. Venet. 1567, tom. i. orat. xvi.)

† Apostolo Zeno, Note alla Biblioteca del Fontanini, tom ii. p. 424. Sig. Domenico Maria Manni, Prefaz. alle Prediche di Fra Giordano: Tiraboschi, tom. iv. p. 496—498.

‡ "*Avvilire* la sacra Scrittura il tradurla in lingua volgare," says Passavanti, in his *Specchio di vera Penitenza*, quoted by Fontanini, p. 674.

middle of the thirteenth century.* It is certain, that this task was undertaken by more than one individual in the subsequent age, but executed, as may be supposed, in a rude and barbarous manner.† An Italian version of the Scriptures, by Nicolo Malermi or Malerbi, a Camaldolese monk, was printed at Venice so early as the year 1471,‡ and is said to have gone through no fewer than nine editions in the fifteenth and twelve editions in the sixteenth century;§ a proof that the Italians were addicted to reading in their native tongue, if there did not exist among them at that time a general desire for the word of God. We find an additional proof of this in the Italian versions of parts of Scripture which appeared about the same period.|| Malermi's translation, like those on which

* Le Long doubts if there ever was such a version. (Bibl. Sac. tom. i. p. 352. edit. 3.) Fontanini denies its existence. (Della Eloq. Ital. p. 673.)

† Fragments of such translations were to be found in libraries during the fifteenth century. Malermi expressly mentions one of them, which contained, he says, "cose enormi, que non lice ser dicte, ne da esser leggiute." (D Abbate Giov Andres, Dell' Origine d'ogni Letteratura, tom. xix. p. 200.) Girolamo Squarzafico, a learned man, who wrote a preface to the edition of the Bible in 1477, says:—"Venerabilis Dominus Nicolaus de Malermi (aut de Malerbi) sacra Biblia ex Latino Italice reddidit, eos imitatus, qui vulgares antea versiones, si sunt hoc nomine, et non potius confusiones nuncupantur, confecerunt." (Lettera Critica dal Signor Abbate N. N. all' Erud. Padre Giov. degli Agostini, p 8. Roveredo, 1739.)

‡ Fontanini, p 673. De Bure, (Partie de la Theologie,) p. 89. It was printed, "Kal. Aug. 1471," by "Vind. de Spira," and contains a prefatory epistle by Nicolo di Malherbi. Another version of the Bible was printed in the month of October of the same year, without notice of the translator, printer, or place of printing. (Dibdin's Ædes Althorp. vol. ii. p. 44. Bibl. Spencer. vol. i. p. 63)

§ Foscarini, Della Letteratura Veneziana, vol. i. p. 339. Dr. Geddes says it went through thirteen editions in the space of less than half a century. (Prospectus of a New Translation, p. 103.) Andrew Rivet possessed a copy of the edition printed in 1477. (Opera, tom. ii p. 920.) Père Simon, who is not always so accurate as a severe critic on the works of others should be, speaks of Malermi's version as published for the first time in 1541. (Hist. Crit de V. Test. p. 371, 598 edit. 1680)

|| The two following are mentioned by Maffei —"Li quattro volumi de gli Evangeli volgarizzati da frate Guido, con le loro esposizioni fatte per Frate Simone da Cascia, Ven. 1486." "L'Apocalisse con le chiose de Nicolo da Lira; traslazione di Maestro Federico da

it was founded, was made from the vulgate, and written in a style unsuited to the sixteenth century. A version less barbarous in its diction and more faithful to the original had long been desired by the learned. This was at last executed by Antonio Brucioli, of whose history and qualifications as a biblical interpreter I shall afterwards have occasion to speak. His Italian version of the New Testament was printed at Venice in 1530,* and his version of the whole Bible came from the same press in 1532.† The latter was reprinted with greater accuracy in 1541;‡ and, in an advertisement prefixed to it, the translator seems to intimate that the whole work appeared in 1530;§ but as no copy of the Old Testament printed in that year has ever been heard of, it is probable that he referred only to the New Testament. So great was the success of this work, that other translations were produced within a few years; and the Roman Catholics reckoned it necessary to oppose versions of their own to those which came from Protestants, or which were thought favourable to their views. This was the origin of the Italian

---

Venezia, lavorata nel 1394, e stampata Ven. 1519." (Esame del Sig. Marchese Scipione Maffei, p. 19 Roveredo, 1739)

* It came from the press of his countryman, Luca Antonio Giunti A copy of this rare book is to be found in the royal library at Berlin.

† Le Long, Bibl Sac. par. II. p. 125, 126, edit Boerneri. Wolfii Notæ ad Colom Ital. Orient. p. 59. Gerdes, Ital Ref p. 190. Miscell Groningana, tom II p 658 Simon. Hist. Crit de V Test. l. II chap 22, and Disquis. Crit p 193 The most accurate account is given by Schelhorn, Ergoetzlichkeiten aus der Kirchenhistorie und Literatur, tom. I p. 401—419, 643—647

‡ The following is the title of this edition :—" La Biblia la quale in se contiene i sacro santi Libri del vecchio & nuovo Testamento, i quali ti apporto Christianissimo Lettore, nuovamente tradotti da la Hebraica & Greca verita in lingua Toscana per Antonio Brucioli Con le Concordantie di tutta essa scrittura santa Et con due tavole d'una delle quali montra i luoghi & ordine di quella, & l'altra dichiara tutta le materie che si trattono in essa, remittendo a suvi luoghi i Lettori. Cosa nuova, & utilissima à tutti i Christiani. In Venetia nel MDXLI." At the end is, "Impresso in Venetia nelle case di Francesco Brucioli & i Frategli nel mese di Agosto MDXLI" (Schelhorn, Ergotzlich. aus der Kirchenhist. und Literat. tom 1 p 410)

§ Brucioli complains of the incorrectness of this impression, and states that he will not acknowledge as his translations any that have not been executed by the printers of the edition in 1541

Bible by Sante Marmochini,* which, though professing to be translated from the Hebrew and Greek, is in reality a version of the vulgate, except when it slavishly copies Brucioli. Fra Zaccario, in his version of the New Testament,† followed Marmochini. Subsequently, the New Testament was translated by Massimo Teofilo,‡ and the whole Bible by Filippo Rusticio.§ Both of them profess it as their object to preserve the purity of the Italian language, which had been neglected by those who had gone before them; and, in their prefatory and subjoined discourses, they defend the reading of the Scriptures in the vulgar tongues, and write on this subject in every respect as Protestants.‖

The new opinions were also propagated in Italy by the intercourse which letters and travelling had established between it and the protestant parts of Europe. It had long been the custom for the German youth to finish their education, especially in law and medicine, at Padua, Bologna, and other Italian universities. The Italians began now, in their turn, to visit the schools of Switzerland and Germany, whose literary reputation was daily advancing; and many of them were attracted to Wittemberg by the fame of Melancthon, who was known to most of the learned in Italy, and with whom Bembo and Sadoleti did not scruple to maintain a friendly correspondence.¶ The effects of this intercourse were so visible, that it was repeatedly complained of by the more zealous defenders of the old religion; and a writer of that age gives it as his advice, "that a stop should be put to all commerce and intercourse, epistolary or otherwise, between the Germans and Italians, as the best means of preventing heresy from pervading the

* Printed at Venice in 1538.
† Printed in 1542.
‡ Printed at Lyons in 1551.
§ Printed at Geneva in 1562.
‖ Henr a Porta De Ling. Orient. p. 71. Abbate D Giov. Andres, D'Ogni Letteratura, tom. xix. p. 242. Schelhorn, Ergotz. tom. i. p. 418, 645, 646. Gerdes, Ital. Ref. p. 329, 340.
¶ Melancthon, Epist. coll. 368, 373, 712, 728, 733, 758, edit. Lond.

whole of Italy."* At a later period, the reformed opinions and books were imported by merchants belonging to Lyons, and other parts of France, who traded with the Italian states †

War, which brings so many evils in its train, and which proved such a scourge to Italy during the first half of the sixteenth century, was overruled by Providence for disseminating in that country the inestimable blessings of the gospel. The troops which Charles V. brought from Germany to assist him in his Italian expeditions, and the Swiss auxiliaries who followed the standard of his rival Francis I., contained many Protestants.‡ With the freedom of men who have swords in their hands, these foreigners conversed on the religious controversy with the inhabitants among whom they were quartered. They extolled the spiritual liberty which they enjoyed at home, derided the frightful idea of the reformers which the monks had impressed on the minds of the people, talked in the warmest strains of Luther and his associates as the restorers of Christianity, contrasted the purity of their lives and the slender income with which they were contented, with the wealth and licentiousness of their opponents, and expressed their astonishment that a people of such spirit as the Italians should continue to yield a base and implicit subjection to an indolent and corrupt priesthood, which sought to keep them in ignorance, that it might feed on the spoils of their credulity. The impression which these representations were calculated to make on the minds of the people, was strengthened by the angry manifestoes which the pope and the emperor published against each other. Clement charged the emperor with indifference to religion, and complained that he had enacted laws, in various parts of his dominions,

* Busdragi Epistola de Italia a Lutheranismo preservanda; in Scrin. Antiq. tom. i. p. 324. It has been supposed by some, that *Vergerio* concealed himself under the feigned name of *Gerardus Busdragus*, and that the whole letter is a piece of irony
† Galluzzi, Istoria del Granducato di Toscano, tom. i. p 142.
‡ Robertson's Charles V. vol. ii. p. 356 Gerdes Ital. Ref. p. 17.

which were highly injurious to the interests of the Church and derogatory to the honour of the holy see. Charles recriminated, by accusing the pope of kindling the flames of war in Europe, that he might evade, what was universally and loudly called for, the reformation of the church in its head and members: he wrote to the cardinals to summon a general council for this purpose; and threatened that, if this were not done, he would abolish the jurisdiction of the pope throughout Spain, and convince other nations, by his example, that ecclesiastical abuses might be corrected and the ancient discipline of the church restored without the intervention of papal authority.*

Nor did the emperor rest in threatenings. His general, the duke of Bourbon, having entered the papal territories, Rome was taken and sacked; and the pontiff, after enduring a siege in the castle of St. Angelo, was obliged to surrender to the imperial troops, and to remain for a considerable time as a captive in their hands. According to the accounts given by Roman Catholic historians, the Germans in the emperor's army behaved with great moderation towards the inhabitants of Rome after the first day's pillage, and contented themselves with testifying their detestation for idolatry; the Spaniards never relented in their rapacity and cruelty, torturing the prisoners to make them discover their treasures; while the Italians imitated the Spaniards in their cruelty, and the Germans in their impiety.† A scene which was exhibited during the siege of the castle, will convey an idea of the indignity shown to all which had been held sacred in the Roman see. A party of German soldiers, mounted on horses and mules, assembled one day in the streets of Rome. One of them, named Grunwald, distinguished by his majestic countenance and stature, being attired like the pope, and wearing

* Pro divo Carolo ejus nominis quinto, Apologetici libri duo, Mogunt. 1527. Sleidan, Comment. tom. i. p. 332—336, edit. Am Ende. De Thou, Hist. lib 1. sect. 11.

† Guicciardini, Il Sacco di Roma, and the authorities quoted by Sismondi, Hist. des Rep. Ital. tom. xv. p. 274—276.

a triple crown, was placed on a horse richly caparisoned. Others were arrayed like cardinals, some wearing mitres, and others clothed in scarlet or white, according to the rank of those whom they personated. In this form they marched, amidst the sounding of drums and fifes, and accompanied by a vast concourse of people, with all the pomp and ceremony usually observed in a pontifical procession. When they passed a house in which any of the cardinals was confined, the procession stopped, and Grunwald blessed the people by stretching out his fingers in the manner practised by the pope on such occasions. After some time he was taken from his horse, and borne on the shoulders of one of his companions on a pad or seat prepared for the purpose. Having reached the castle of St. Angelo, he drank from a large cup to the safe custody of Clement, in which he was pledged by his attendants. He then administered to his cardinals an oath, in which they engaged to yield due obedience and faithful allegiance to the emperor, as their lawful and only prince; and not to disturb the peace of the empire by intrigues, but, as became them, according to the precepts of Scripture and the example of Christ and his apostles, to be subject to the civil powers. After a speech, in which he rehearsed the civil, parricidal, and sacrilegious wars excited by the popes, and acknowledged that providence had raised up the emperor Charles V. to revenge these crimes and bridle the rage of wicked priests, the pretended pontiff solemnly promised to transfer all his authority and power to Martin Luther, that he might remove the corruptions which had infected the apostolical see, and completely refit the ship of St. Peter, that it might no longer be the sport of the winds and waves, through the unskilfulness and negligence of its governors, who, intrusted with the helm, had spent their days and nights in drinking and debauchery. Then raising his voice, he said, "All who agree to these things, and would see them carried into execution, let them signify this by lifting up their hands;" upon which the whole band of soldiers, raising their hands, exclaimed, "Long live pope Luther! Long live pope Luther!" All this was performed under the eye of Clement VII.*

In other circumstances, such proceedings would have been regarded in no other light than as the unbridled excesses of a licentious soldiery, and might have excited compassion for the captive pontiff; but at this time it was the general conviction, that the wars which had so long desolated Italy were chiefly to be ascribed to the ambition and resentment of the popes; the conduct of Clement, in provoking a powerful enemy whom he was incapable of resisting, appeared to be the effect of a judicial infatuation; the disasters which befel the papal see and the city of Rome were interpreted as marks of divine displeasure; and those who insulted over them were regarded as heralds employed to denounce the judgments of heaven against an incorrigible court, and a city which was desecrated and defiled by all manner of wickedness. These were not merely the sentiments of the vulgar, or of such as had already imbibed the reformed opinions; they were entertained by dignitaries of the Roman church, and uttered within the walls of the Vatican. We have a proof of this in a speech delivered by Staphylo, bishop of Sibari, at the first meeting of the apostolical Rota held after Rome was delivered from a foreign army. Having described the devastations committed on the city, the bishop proceeds in the following strain:—"But whence, I pray, have these things proceeded? and why have such calamities befallen us? Because all flesh have corrupted their ways: because we are citizens, not of the holy city of Rome, but of Babylon the wicked city. The word of the Lord spoken by Isaiah is accomplished in our times—'How is the faithful city become an harlot! It was full of judgment and holiness: righteousness formerly dwelt in it; now sacri-

* Narratio Direptionis Expugnatæ Urbis, ex Italico translata a Casparo Barthio: Fabricii Centifol Lutheran. tom. 1. p 96—98. The principal facts in this narrative are confirmed by the popish writers, Cochlæus, Spondanus, &c.

legious persons and murderers! Formerly it was inhabited by a holy nation, a peculiar people, but now by the people of Gomorrah, a depraved seed, wicked children, unfaithful priests, the companions of thieves!' Lest any should suppose," continued the bishop, " that this prophetic oracle was fulfilled long ago in the overthrow of the Babylonish Jerusalem by the Roman emperors Vespasian and Titus, seeing the words appear to refer to the time in which the prophet lived, I think it proper to observe, agreeably to ecclesiastical verity, that future things were set before the eyes of the prophet's mind as present. This is evident from the sacred writings throughout—' The daughter of Zion shall be forsaken and made desolate by the violence of the enemy.' This daughter of Zion, the apostle John, in the book of Revelation, explains as meaning not Jerusalem, but the city of Rome, as appears from looking into his description. For John, or rather the angel explaining to John the vision concerning the judgment of the whore, represents this city as meant by Babylon. ' The woman whom thou sawest is that great city which reigns (he refers to a spiritual reign) over the kings of the earth.' Again John says—' She sits on seven hills;' which applies properly to Rome, called, from ancient times, *the seven-hilled city.* She is also said to ' sit on many waters,' which signify people, nations, and various languages, of which, as we see, this city is composed more than any other city in the Christian world. He says also, ' She is full of names of blasphemy, the mother of uncleanness, fornications, and abominations of the earth.' This supersedes the necessity of any more specific proof that Rome is the city referred to; seeing these vices, though they prevail everywhere, have fixed their seat and empire with us."*

If such was the impression which this event made on the mind of a bishop, and such the language held within the hearing of the sovereign pontiff, what must

* Oratio habita ad Auditores Rotæ, de causis Excidii Urbis Romæ, anno 1527; inter Rerum German. Scriptores, a Schardio, tom. ii. p. 613, &c. Wolfii Lect. Memor. tom. ii. p. 300.

have been the feelings and the language of those who were less interested in the support of the ecclesiastical monarchy, and who were still greater sufferers from the ambition and tyranny of those who administered its affairs? The mysterious veil of sanctity, by which the minds of the vulgar had been long overawed, was now torn off, and, when revealed, the claims of the priesthood appeared to be as arrogant and unfounded as their conduct was inconsistent with the character which they had assumed, and with the precepts of that religion of which they professed to be the teachers and guardians. The horror hitherto felt at the name of heretic and Lutheran began to abate in Italy, and the minds of the people were prepared to listen to the teachers of the reformed doctrine, who, in their turn, were emboldened to preach and make proselytes in a more open manner than they had hitherto ventured to do. " In Italy also," says the historian of the council of Trent, speaking of this period, " as there had neither been Pope nor Papal court at Rome for nearly two years, and as most men looked on the calamities which had fallen on both as the execution of a divine judgment, on account of the corruptions of its government, many listened with avidity to the Reformation; in several cities, and particularly at Faenza, which was situated within the territories of the Pope, sermons were delivered in private houses against the Church of Rome; and the number of those named Lutherans, or, as they called themselves, Evangelicals, increased every day."* That these sermons were not entirely confined to private houses, and that the reformed doctrine was publicly preached in Italy before the year 1530, we learn from the highest authority. "From the report made to us," says Pope Clement VII., "we have learned with great grief of heart, that, in different parts of Italy, the pestiferous heresy of Luther prevails to a high degree, not only among secular persons, but also among ecclesiastics and the

* Fra Paolo, Hist. du Concile de Trente, vol. 1. p. 87, edit. Courayer. With this the statement of Giannone exactly agrees. (Hist. Civ. de Naples, tom. iv. p. 110.)

regular clergy, both mendicant and non-mendicant; so that some, by their discourses and conversation, and, what is worse, by their public preaching, infect numbers with this disease, greatly scandalize faithful Christians, who live under the obedience of the Roman Church and observe its laws, and contribute to the increase of heresies, the stumbling of the weak, and the no small injury of the Catholic faith."* These appearances, while they gave alarm to the friends of the papacy, excited hopes in the breasts of those who had espoused the cause of the Reformation. Both parties calculated on the national character of the Italians; and it was a common remark, that as the plague, aggravated by the intenser heat of the sky, was more virulent in Italy than in Germany, so Lutheranism, if it seized on the more susceptible and ardent minds of the Italians, would rage with an impetuosity and to an extent as yet unparalleled.†

CHAPTER III.

PROGRESS OF THE REFORMATION IN THE DIFFERENT STATES AND CITIES OF ITALY.

HAVING given a general account of the introduction of the reformed opinions into Italy, and the causes which led to this event, I now proceed to trace the progress which they made through the different states and cities of that country.

FERRARA is entitled to the first notice, on account of the protection which it afforded, at an early period, to the friends of the Reformation, who fled from various parts of Italy and from foreign countries. Under the government of its dukes of the illustrious house of Este, Ferrara had, for some time, vied with Flo-

* Raynaldi Annales, ad ann. 1530.
† Campegii Cardinalis Oratio ad ordines Imperii Norimberg.; apud Seckendorf, lib. i. p. 289. Busdragi Epistola; in Scrinio Antiquario, tom. i. par. ii. p. 325.

rence in the encouragement of learning and the fine arts. Ariosto lived at the court of Alfonso I., as did Bernardo Tasso, and, at a subsequent period, his more illustrious son, the author of *Jerusalem Delivered*, at the court of Ercole II.; and, in consequence of this, the genealogy and achievements of the dukes of Ferrara have been transmitted to posterity by the first poets of that age. Hercules had received a good education, and was induced, by personal judgment and feeling, to yield that patronage to learned men which contemporary princes paid as a tribute to fashion, and out of regard to their own fame.* The house of Este had, in several late instances, been but ill repaid for the devotion which they had shown to the interests of the see of Rome; but the reason already mentioned, as attaching the Italian princes to the Pope, overcame the sense of injury. Ippolito, a younger son of duke Alfonso, and afterwards his nephew Ludovico, were cardinals; and, from time immemorial, a branch of the family had occupied a place in the sacred college.†
Accordingly, Alfonso had proved a faithful ally to Clement during the humiliating disasters to which he was exposed; and his successor, though more liberal in his religious views than his father, avoided any thing which might give offence to the supreme pontiff.

In the year 1527, Hercules II. married Renée, or Renata, daughter of Louis XII. of France; and the countenance shown to the reformed opinions at the court of Ferrara is chiefly to be ascribed to the influence of this amiable and accomplished princess. Distinguished for her virtue and generosity, at once dignified and engaging in her manners, speaking the French and Italian languages with equal purity, and

* Cœlii Calcagnini Opera, p. 77, 116, 144, 175. The eulogium which Calcagnini has pronounced on him is justified by the account of a conversation between them respecting the choice of a tutor to the duke's son. (Ib. p. 168; conf. p. 160—162.)

† Black's Life of Tasso, i. 348. To this Ariosto alludes:—
'Twere long to tell the names of all thy race,
That in the conclave shall obtain a place,
To tell each enterprise their arms shall gain,
What conquests for the Roman Church obtain.
(Orlando Furioso, book iii.)

deeply versed in the Greek and Roman classics, she attracted the love and admiration of all who knew her.* Before leaving her native country she had become acquainted with the reformed doctrine, by means of some of those learned persons who frequented the court of the celebrated Margaret, queen of Navarre; and she was anxious to facilitate its introduction into the country to which her residence was now transferred. For some time she could only do this under the covert of entertaining its friends as men of letters, which the duke, her husband, was ready to encourage, or at least to wink at. The first persons to whom she extended her protection and hospitality on this principle, were her own countrymen, whom the violence of persecution had driven out of France.

Madame de Soubise, the governess of the duchess, had introduced several men of letters into the court of France during the late reign.† She now resided at the court of Ferrara, along with her son, Jean de Parthenai, sieur de Soubise, afterwards a principal leader of the Protestant party in France; her daughter, Anne de Parthenai, distinguished for her elegant taste; and the future husband of this young lady, Antoine de Pons, count de Marennes, who adhered to the reformed cause until the death of his wife.‡ In the year 1534, the celebrated French poet, Clement Marot, fled from his native country, in consequence of the persecution excited by the affair of the *placards*, and after residing for a short time at the court of the queen of Navarre, in Bearn, came to Ferrara.§ He

* Muratori, Antichità Estensi, tom. ii. p. 368. Tiraboschi, Storia, tom. vii. par i. p 37. Calcagnini Opera, p. 149, 150

† Oeuvres de Clement Marot, tom. ii. p. 182—184. A la Haye, 1731.

‡ Ibid. p 178—181. Bayle, Dict art. Soubise, J. de Parthenai.

§ In the biographical and critical preface to the Hague edition of Marot's works, by *Le Chevalier Gordon de Percel*, (under which name *Nicole Lenglet du Fresnoy* is supposed to have concealed himself,) it is stated, that the famous Diana of Poitiers, afterwards mistress of Henry II., instigated the persecution against Marot, in revenge for some satirical verses which he had written on her for deserting him. (Tom. i. p. 25, 76.)

was recommended by Madame de Soubise to the duchess, who made him her secretary;* and his friend, Lyon Jamet, finding it necessary soon after to join him, met with a reception equally gracious.† About the same time, the celebrated reformer, John Calvin, visited Ferrara, where he spent some months, under the assumed name of Charles Heppeville. He received the most distinguished attention from the duchess, who was confirmed in the Protestant faith by his instructions, and ever after retained the highest respect for his character and talents.‡ In the year 1536, the duke of Ferrara entered into a league with the pope and the emperor, by one of the secret articles of which he was bound to remove all the French from his court; and in consequence of this, the duchess was obliged reluctantly to part with Madame de Soubise and her family.§ Marot retired to Venice, from which he soon after obtained permission to return to his native country.‖ It is not improbable, that

* Oeuvres de Marot, tom. i. p. 75—79. Beze, Hist. Eccl. tom. i. p 22 Le Laboureur, Addit. aux Mem. de Castelnau, p. 716. Nolten, Vita Olympiæ Moratæ, p. 60—62, edit. Hesse.

† Nolten, p. 65—67.

‡ Beza, Vita Calvini. Muratori, Antichità Estensi, tom. ii. p. 389. Ruchat, Hist. de la Reform. de la Suisse, tom. v. p. 620. The misstatements of Varillas and Moreri, respecting Calvin's visit to Italy, are corrected by Bayle, Dict. art. Soubise

§ Epîtres de Rabelais, p 18. Marot has described with much tenderness the distress of mind which the duchess felt on this occasion, in an epistle to the queen of Navarre —

    Ha, Marguerite! escoute la souffrance
    Du noble cueur de Renée de France;
    Puis comme sœur plus fort que d'esperance
      Console-la.
    Tu sçais comment hors son pays alla,
    Et que parens et amis laissa là;
    Mais tu ne sçais quel traitement elle a
      En terre estrange.
    Elle ne voit ceux à qui se veult plaindre,
    Son œil rayant si loing ne peult attaindre,
    Et puis les monts pour se bien lui estaindre
      Sont entre deux.
        (Oeuvres, tom. ii. p 317, 318.)

‖ In the title to his twenty first *Cantique*, he is said to be " banni de France, depuis chassé de Ferrara, et de là retiré à Venise 1536." (Oeuvres, tom. ii. p. 316, comp. tom. i. p. 82, 83. Bayle, art. Marot, Clement.)

the poet was induced at first to take part with the Reformers from resentment at the opposition which the clergy made to every species of literature; but he appears to have conceived a real attachment to the Protestant doctrine during his residence at Ferrara, if we may judge from the strain of the letters and other pieces which proceeded from his pen at this time, and which breathe the spirit of martyrdom. He would probably have shrunk from the fiery trial, if he had been exposed to it; but it does not follow from this, either that the sentiments referred to are not noble, or that the author was not in earnest when he uttered them.* Lyon Jamet was allowed to remain with the duchess, probably as a person less known than Marot, and discharged the duty of secretary to Renée after the departure of his friend.† Hubert Languet, an accomplished scholar, and one of the first, or at least soundest, politicians of his age, embraced the reformed faith while residing in Ferrara.‡

Several persons, who were decidedly favourable to the Reformation, obtained a place in the university of Ferrara, which was now fast recovering its former lustre, after having suffered severely from the civil wars, in which the family of Este had, for many years, been involved.§ But the reformed doctrine

* The account which he gave of his faith, in his poetical epistle, addressed to his prosecutor, Mons. Bouchar, in 1525, differs widely from that which is contained in his epistle addressed to Francis I. in 1536. (Oeuvres, tom. ii. p. 39, comp. p. 167.) In the latter, his willingness to suffer martyrdom, which his biographer, after Bayle, laughs at, is expressed in the following lines:—

  Que pleust à l' Eternel,
 Pour le grand bien du peuple desolé,
 Que leur desir de mon sang fust saoulé,
 Ettant d'abus, dont ils se sont munis,
 Fussent à cler descouverts et punis,
 O quatre fois et cinq fois bien heureuse
 La mort, tant soit cruelle et rigoureuse!
 Qui feroit seule un million de vies
 Sous tels abus n'estre plus asservies?

† Oeuvres de Marot, tom. ii p. 159. Bayle, art. Marot, Clement.
‡ Langueti Epistolæ, lib. i. part. ii p. 111, 264. Halæ, 1699.
§ In the beginning of the sixteenth century, there were so many English students at the university of Ferrara, as to form a distinct nation in that learned corporation. (Bersetti Hist. Gymn. Ferrar. apud Tiraboschi, tom. vii. p. 119.)

was propagated chiefly by means of those learned men whom the duchess retained in her family for the education of her children. This was conducted on an extensive scale, suited to the liberality of her own views and munificence of her husband. Teachers in all branches of polite letters and arts were provided. In the galaxy of enlightened men which adorned the court of Ferrara, were Celio Calcagnini, Lilio Giraldi, Bartolomeo Riccio, Marzello Palingenio, and Marcantonio Flaminio, all of them men whose minds were elevated above the superstitions of their age, if they were not converts to the Protestant faith.* During a visit which the pontiff, Paul III. paid to Ferrara, in the year 1543, the Adelphi of Terence was acted by the youth of the family, and the three daughters of the duke, the eldest of whom was only twelve, and the youngest five years of age, performed their parts with great applause.† His holiness was not then aware of the religious sentiments of the masters, by whom the juvenile princesses had been qualified for affording him this classical amusement. Chilian and John Sinapi, two brothers from Germany, instructed them in Greek, and being Protestants, imbued their minds with sound views of religion.‡ Fulvio Peregrino Morata, a native of Mantua, and a successful teacher of youth in various parts of Italy, had been tutor to the two younger brothers of the duke, and having returned to Ferrara in 1539, was readmitted to his professorship in the university.§ Like most of his learned countrymen, Morata's mind had been engrossed with secular studies during the first part of

* Nolten, Vita Olympiæ Moratæ, p. 67—87, ed. Hesse.
† Muratori, Antich. Est. ii. 368.
‡ Opera Olympiæ Moratæ, p 76, 97, 203, 205.
§ Nolten, *ut supra*, p. 14—17. His works in Italian and in Latin are mentioned by Tiraboschi, (Storia, tom. vii. p. 1197—1200,) and by Schelhorn. (Amoen. Eccl. et Lit. tom. ii. p. 647.) A warm eulogium is passed on him by Calcagnini, (Opera, p. 156,) and by Bembo. (Epist. Famil. apud Schelhorn.) Bembo, in a letter " a M. Bernardo Tasso, Secretario della Signora Duchessa di Ferrara," May 27, 1529, speaks of " Maestro Pellegrino Moretto," as having said some injurious things of his prose works. (Lettere, tom. iii. p. 226. Milano, 1810.)

his life, but having met with Celio Secundo Curio, a refugee from Piedmont, he imbibed from him the knowledge of evangelical truth and a deep sense of religion.* Esteemed for his learning and integrity, he became still more celebrated as the father of Olympia Morata, the most enlightened female of the age, whom he educated with a zeal prompted by parental fondness and professional enthusiasm. In consequence of her early proficiency in letters, Olympia was chosen by the duchess to be the companion of her eldest daughter, Anne, with whom she improved in every elegant and useful accomplishment; and although she afterwards acknowledged that her personal piety suffered from the bustle and blandishments of a court, yet it was during her residence in the ducal palace that she first acquired that knowledge of the gospel which supported her mind under the privations and hardships which she afterwards had to endure.†

We have no means of ascertaining the number of Protestants at Ferrara, which probably varied at different times, according to the fluctuating politics of the duke, and the measures of religious constraint or toleration which were alternately adopted by the other states of Italy. One account mentions, that they had several preachers as early as the year 1528;‡ but whether they were permitted to teach publicly or not, we are not informed. That their labours were successful, is evident from the number of distinguished persons who either imbibed the Protestant doctrine, or were confirmed in their attachment to it, at Ferrara. The most eminent of the Italians who embraced the reformed faith, or who incurred the suspicions of the clergy by the liberality of their opinions, had resided for some time at the court of Ferrara, or

* Fulvio Morata calls Curio his "divine teacher—one sent of God to instruct him, as Ananias was sent to Paul." (Nolten, Vita Olympiæ Moratæ, p. 17, 18, ed. Hesse. Opuscula Olympiæ Moratæ, p. 94, 96, edit Basil 1580.)
† Cœlii Secundi Curionis Araneus, p. 153, 154. Basil. 1544.
‡ Tempe Helvetica, tom. iv. p. 138.

were indebted in one way or other to the patronage of Renée.*

Modena was also under the government of the house of Este, and most probably owed its first acquaintance with the reformed opinions to the same cause which introduced them into Ferrara. Some of the Modenese were among the early correspondents of Luther.† Few cities of Italy in that age could boast of having given birth to a greater number of persons eminent for talents and learning than Modena. It reckoned among its citizens four of the most accomplished members of the sacred college, (including Sadolet,) Sigonio, the celebrated antiquary, Castelvetro, a critic of great acuteness, and many others, whose names occur frequently in the history of Italian literature. Modena possessed one of those academies which sprung up in such great numbers in Italy during the sixteenth century, and threw into shade the old and endowed seminaries of science. It owed its origin to Giovanni Grillenzone, an enlightened physician, in whose house it met. The object of the associates was, at first, to promote their mutual improvement, by conversation and the reading of papers on literary and scientific subjects. But lectures were grafted on the original institution, which became so celebrated, especially after it procured the services of Franciscus Portus, a learned Greek, as to attract young men from all parts of Italy to Modena. The academy appears, at an early period, to have incurred the suspicion of being infected with the new opinions respecting religion. A writer, who has thrown great light on the history of Italy, is of opinion, that the proceedings against this society originated in one of those quarrels in which the literati of that age were

* Gerdes. Ital. Ref. p. 28, 29. One of these was Giovanni Francesco Virginio, a native of Brescia, and author of a paraphrase on the Epistles of Paul to the Romans, Galatians, and Hebrews; printed at Lyons in 1565. Speaking of Renee, Fontanini says, "Gianfrancesco Virginio Bresciano in dedicarle quegli le sue lettere, seminata di frasi Protestanti, e stampate in Venezia—nel 1548." (Della Eloq. Ital. p 306.)

† Gerdesii Italia Reformata, p. 61.

not unfrequently involved with the religious orders, and in the resentment of Annibale Caro against Castelvetro, a member of the academy, who had written a severe criticism on one of his poems;* but more accurate investigation has proved that they had a deeper foundation. It would seem that the priests looked upon the academy, from its commencement, with a jealous eye; while the academicians, in their turn, were not scrupulous in expressing their contempt of the priests, and especially of the monks, on account of their ignorance and hypocrisy; and, according to all accounts, the latter appear to have had good reason for the feelings which they indulged.† But the clergy had also reason for suspecting that their opponents had departed from the Romish faith. In December 1537, Serafina, a canon regular of St. Augustine, preaching in the cathedral church, told his audience that the Lutheran errors had begun to spread in Modena; and, in proof of his assertion, referred to a book, infected with heresy, which had come into his hands. He had found it in the chamber of Lucrezia Pica, widow of count Claudio Rangone, and had examined it, along with the inquisitor of heretical pravity and the vicar of the diocese, who had set on foot an inquiry into the author of the work, and the person who had brought it into the city. It was easily traced to Gadaldino, a printer and bookseller; the author could not be discovered, but it was strongly

* Muratori, Vita del Castelvetro; Opere Critiche, p. 17. In the former edition, I was guided chiefly by the account which Tiraboschi gives of the affair in his history of Italian Literature; but I have since had access to the *Biblioteca Modenese* of that author, in which he furnishes more ample details, supported by the most authentic documents It is in 6 vols. 4to, printed at Modena in 1781—1786.

† In 1530, a fiiar, preaching in the cathedral of Modena during Lent, produced and read to his audience a letter from Jesus Christ, drawn up in the style of a papal brief; beginning with "Jesus Episcopus," and ending with "Nulli ergo omnino hominum, &c. Datum in Paradiso Terrestri Creationis Mundi die sexto, Pontificatus nostri anno æterno," &c. (Biblioteca Modenese, dal Girolamo Tiraboschi, tom. i. p. 11) Grillenzone, in a letter to Sadolet, accounts for the informations which the monks had laid against him, by saying, "My nature is such, that I could never conceal my displeasure at the conduct of the idle, ignorant, and hypocritical." (Ib. tom. ii. p. 435.)

suspected he was one of the members of the academy, several of whom did not scruple to avow their approbation of the book, as containing doctrine which was both orthodox and edifying. The book was publicly burnt at Rome, and all the copies of it appear to have been carefully destroyed.* Soon after this occurrence, at the marriage of a daughter of Niccolo Machelli, a member of the academy, two persons in masks entered the place of entertainment, and recited a long satire on the preacher Serafina; and at the same time similar pasquinades were affixed to the pillars of the cathedral, the gate of the Dominican convent, and other public places in the city. Through the influence of the countess Lucrezia, who felt herself scandalized by the affair, the duke ordered two persons, tutors to two of the principal families of the city, to be thrown into prison, as the authors of this insult on the clergy; but they were soon after liberated, on the ground that they had not named any individual as the object of their raillery. As the clergy persevered in declaiming against the new opinions, the academicians had recourse to their former method of retaliation; and, irritated by the ignorant harangues to which they were obliged to listen, they, in some instances, rose up in the midst of the church, criticised the sermon, and held up the preacher to the derision of the audience. Fra Serafina, who had left the city for some time, having ventured to return in 1539, was driven from the pulpit in disgrace. So far indeed

* Bibl. Modenese, tom. i p. 8—10, 14 We are indebted for all our knowledge of this book to an honest chronicler who lived at that time in Modena. On hearing it denounced from the pulpit as heretical, he returned a copy of it, which he had lately purchased, and reclaimed his money; but his curiosity conquered his fears so far, that he previously inserted a description of it in his diary. It was in *mezzo quarto*, and consisted of ninety six pages, divided into thirty-one chapters. The following is the title:—" Il Summario de la Sancta Scriptura, & l'ordinario de li Christiani, qual demonstra la vere fede Christiana, mediante la quale siamo justificati, & de la vertu del baptismo secondo la doctrina de l'Evangelio & de li Apostoli, cum una informazione, como tutti li Stati debbono vivere secondo l'Evangelio." It had no name of author or printer, nor any date " Summarium Scripturæ" is mentioned in the Index Libr. Prohib. of 1559, sig. E. 7.

were the monks from being able to check the progress of the reformed doctrine in the city, that they could not prevent it from finding its way into their own cloisters. A friar, named Antonio della Catellina, having preached with great applause during the feast of Pentecost, was accused of heresy; but, instead of retracting, he appeared again in the pulpit, and defended the doctrine which he had taught.* This produced a papal rescript, charging the inquisitor to make a strict investigation into the opinions of the religious orders established in the city.†

Matters were in this state, when, in 1540, Paolo Ricio came to Modena.‡ He was a native of Sicily, obtained the degree of doctor of theology at Naples, and belonged to the order of Minor Conventuals; but having thrown off the cowl, that he might disseminate the gospel with greater freedom, took the name of Lisia Fileno. He was cordially welcomed by the members of the academy, and made it his business to seek out the friends of truth in the city, whom he persuaded to meet for worship in a private house. They were confirmed by his instructions, which were the means of adding to their numbers. A great sensation was produced in the city; the Scriptures became the common topic of conversation; and the subjects in dispute between the Church of Rome and the Reformers were freely and eagerly discussed. "Persons of all classes," says a contemporary historian of the popish persuasion, " not only the learned, but also the illiterate, and even women, wherever they met, in the streets, in shops, or in churches, disputed about faith and the doctrine of Christ, and all promiscuously tortured the sacred Scriptures, quoting Paul, Matthew, John, the Apocalypse, and all the doctors, whose writings they never saw."§ The news of this success of the gospel reached Germany, and drew from Bucer a letter of

* Bibl. Modenese, tom. i. p. 9—12.
† Spondani Annal. ad an. 1539.
‡ Riederer, Nachrichten zur Kirchen-gelehrten und Bucherges-chichte, tom. i. p. 172, 174; tom. iii. p. 444.
§ Cronaca di Alessandro Tassoni: Tiraboschi, Storia della Letter.

congratulation and advice to the Modenese disciples.*
Loud complaints were made by the priests to the Pope,
who remonstrated with the duke; and Ricio, who,
foreseeing the danger, had left Modena, was seized
at the neighbouring village of Staggio, and being conducted as a prisoner to Ferrara, chose to make a public recantation of his opinions, rather than be sent to
Rome, where he expected no mercy. But the seed
sown by him in Modena had taken too deep root to
be injured by his defection. With the view of preventing the renewal of the contentions, the duke had
issued orders that none should occupy the pulpit without the permission of the vicar of the diocese; but so
great was the avidity of the people to hear the Scriptures expounded, that some of the preachers were
bold enough to break through the restriction, in which
they were supported by the local magistrates, who
wrote in their favour to the ducal court. In the course
of the year 1540, the celebrated Ochino, of whom we
shall afterwards have occasion to speak largely, came
to Modena, and preached in the cathedral church, to
so great a crowd, that, according to the testimony of
one of the audience, "there was scarcely room to
stand." He resisted the entreaties of the academicians, who urged him to remain during Lent, promising that they would prevail on the preacher, whose
services had been engaged for that season, to yield
his place to him. Though the defection of Ochino
from the Catholic faith was not then known, the
clergy were displeased at a mode of preaching so
different from their own, and at the applause bestowed on it, especially by their adversaries of the
academy. One of the most obnoxious of these was
Giovanni di Politiano, called also de'Berettari. In
his youth he had been highly esteemed by Cardinals

Ital. tom. vii. p. 168. Ginguené has translated this passage into
good French, and given it as his own description of the fact, without
seeming to be aware that it was the common language of Roman
Catholic writers of that age, when they spoke of the reading of the
Scriptures, or conversation on religious topics, by the people.

* Buceri Scripta Anglicana, p. 687.

Bembo and Bibbiena for his poetical vein, and was, at this time, tutor to Camillo, a son of the celebrated Francesco Molza. Being in priest's orders, he expounded the Scriptures in the house of his patron; and to this exercise the citizens resorted in great numbers after the removal of Ricio. In consequence of information lodged against him by a spy, he was accused of having advanced, in his exposition of Paul's Epistles, three erroneous propositions; one of which was, that prayers in an unknown tongue are not pleasing to God. Berettari waited on the inquisitor, to whom he gave an explanation of his words; but this proving unsatisfactory, he was summoned, and, declining to attend, was excommunicated for contumacy. Upon this he appealed to the Pope, and, through the influence of Molza with Cardinal Farnese, the nephew of Paul III., the inquisitor was summoned to Rome. After a delay of some months, Berettari was acquitted, and, on the first of October 1541, returned, along with his pupil, in triumph to Modena; but his enemies were clamorous, and a new process having been commenced against him at Rome, he was found guilty, and sentenced to do penance privately in the presence of a few select persons.*

During these transactions, cardinal Morone, the bishop of Modena, was chiefly absent on missions from the pope to Germany. Reports of the progress of heresy in his diocese had repeatedly reached his ear, and they gave him the more uneasiness, that he was no stranger to the corruptions in the church, and felt an esteem for several of the persons who were principally inculpated. In a letter to the duke of Ferrara, dated 21st of November 1541, he says—" Eight days ago I came to Modena to make residence at my church, and to endeavour, with the divine assistance, to do all in my power, consistently with charity, to remove the bad fame which this city of your excellency has incurred, not only in Italy but abroad, in reference to the modern novelties of opinion. I had

* Bibl. Modenese, tom. i. p. 12—14, 230—234.

proceeded so far in this affair, and brought it to some issue, when I received an order from his holiness to repair to Rome."* On occasion of another visit to his diocese, he writes, on the 20th May, 1542, to his friend, cardinal Contarini—"I have found things which infinitely distress me, and, while I perceive the danger, am quite at a loss as to the means by which I can extricate myself in the affairs of this flock, which, with my blood, I would willingly secure to Christ, and clear from public infamy. Wherever I go, and from all quarters, I hear that the city is become Lutheran. Your suspicions are not without foundation, for it cannot be denied that much ignorance, joined with great audacity and little charity, reigns among the monks; but against the other side there are many violent suspicions, and even some proofs, which I mean to verify, with the view of adopting the remedies which God may direct."† And, on the 30th of July, he writes to the same person—"Yesterday a minister of that order frankly told me that their preachers would no longer go to Modena, on account of the persecution to which they were exposed from the academy, it being every where spread abroad that the city is Lutheran."‡

FLORENCE, the capital of Tuscany, rose to great distinction at the era of the revival of letters. No city in Italy could vie with it in the number of its enlightened citizens, the flourishing state of its academies, and the encouragement which it gave to every branch of science and liberal art. But the high cultivation of these studies has rarely been favourable either to pure religion or genuine liberty. Superstition, by appealing chiefly to the senses, allies itself with the fine arts; and the munificence with which letters were fostered at their first introduction into Europe, tended in many instances to corrupt both the patrons and their clients. The family of Medici, after raising their native city to renown, concluded by de-

* Ib. tom iii. p. 307.
† Quirini Diatrib. ad vol. iii. Epist. Card. Poli, p. cclxix.
‡ Ibid. p. cclxxxvi.

priving it of its liberties; and so true is the maxim, " men will praise thee when thou dost well to thyself," that their ambition has found apologists in those who have celebrated their early patriotism. Florence, in the course of a few years, felt herself honoured by seeing two of her sons exalted to the chair of St. Peter: during the pontificate of Leo X. the Lutheran schism broke out; and before the death of Clement VII., when it began to spread in Italy, Cosmo de' Medici had established himself as duke of Tuscany. In these circumstances, it was to be expected that the Reformation would encounter the most strenuous and powerful resistance in that city.

Notwithstanding these obstacles, we are assured that the reformed docrine had made its way into Florence before the year 1525, and was embraced by many of its citizens.* Among these was a person who has been already mentioned, but who deserves more particular notice on account of the invaluable services which he rendered to Italy by his writings. Antonio Brucioli was born about the end of the fifteenth century, and early distinguished himself among the members of the Platonic academy erected in his native city. Attached to popular government, he was induced by youthful ardour to embark in a design for expelling the house of Medici from Florence; but the conspiracy being discovered, he was obliged to fly, and after spending some time at Venice, retired into France, from which he went to Germany.† During the five years which he spent in exile, his political feelings were mellowed by the infusion of the spirit of religious liberty, and his studies assumed a graver cast. At Venice he applied to the study of Hebrew, in which he afterwards acquired great proficiency;‡ and in Germany he found the best helps

* Santes Pagnini, Præfat. in Bibl. Latin. anno 1528.
† Varchi, Storia Fior. lib. vii p 211 Giornali de' Letterati d'Italia, tom. xxxii p. 232—240.
‡ In a letter addressed to him in 1537, Aretino says, " Voi sete huomo senza pare nel' intelligentia de la lingua Hebraica, Græca, Latina, e Chaldea." (Colomesii Ital. Orient. p. 60.)

for understanding the Scriptures. In the year 1527, when the emperor had humbled Clement VII., and the authority of the Medici was suspended in Florence, Brucioli returned to his native city; but his late intercourse with Lutherans had brought upon him the suspicion of heresy, which was increased by the free manner in which he talked of the clergy. His friends warned him to be more guarded in his conversation, but he replied, "If I speak truth, I cannot speak wrong." The Dominicans of St. Marco were particularly galled with his censures; and one of their number, Fojano, then a popular preacher in Florence, denounced him one day from the pulpit as a heretic, and, in allusion to the meaning of his name, exclaimed, "Brucioli is fit for nothing but to be burned."*
He was soon after thrown into prison, and, in addition to the charge of heresy, was accused of corresponding with France to the prejudice of his native country; but, when his papers were examined, nothing suspicious was found among them, except specimens of a translation of the Bible, and a cypher which he had used in corresponding with his friend Alamanno. The monks pleaded hard for capital punishment, and Brucioli irritated the judge before whom he was tried by the boldness of his defence; but, through the influence of friends, his sentence was restricted to banishment for two years. It does not appear that he ever again entertained thoughts of returning to Florence, though he addressed one of his works to Cosmo de' Medici, in a respectful dedication, in which he praises the mildness of his administration, and, without asking any personal favour, exhorts him to encourage the reading of the Scriptures by his people, as calculated, above all other means, to make them devout men and dutiful subjects. Neither his dedications nor letters are dated from any place, probably from a prudential regard to his safety; but there can be no doubt that he resided ordinarily in Venice. He had to struggle at first with the privations attendant on

† *Brucioli*, in Italian, means twigs or shavings of wood.

exile,* but rather than become dependent on the bounty of a rich patron, he chose to live obscurely, and to support himself by the productions of his pen. For some time he acted as a corrector of the press, (no mean employment in those days,) until he was able, along with Francesco and Alessandro Brucioli, his brothers, or, as some say, his cousins, to establish a printing-office in the place of his sojourning. From 1530 to 1556, the probable year of his death, he published a variety of works of his own, including translations of the classics; but his biblical labours were the most valuable.

Besides his version of the Scriptures, already mentioned,† Brucioli produced a commentary on the whole Bible, extending to seven volumes in folio. Father Simon grants, that he translated from the original, and not, like the Roman Catholics from the vulgate; but says that, being imperfectly acquainted with Hebrew, he fell into a multitude of errors by following Pagnini. The charge has, however, been shown, by the most satisfactory proof, to be one of the rash judgments pronounced by this ingenious critic.‡ There is more truth in another remark of the same writer, that his version offends frequently against the purity of the Italian tongue, and abounds with Hebraisms; a fault which every one who resolves to give a literal translation must inevitably commit.§ We are pre-

* In his dedication of his translation and exposition of the book of Job, printed in 1534, he speaks of himself as " in bassa e povera fortuna locato."

† Schelhorn (Ergoetz. tom 1. p. 405—415, 648—670) has given a list of his works, (accompanied with a specimen of his hymns,) among which is the following :—" Ant. Brucioli Sermoni xxii.," to which is added, " Epistola a Renata di Francia, Duchessa di Ferrara, intorno a Christo Messia, Venezia per Alessandro Brucioli e fratelli, 1547."

‡ Simon, Hist. Crit. du V. Test. liv ii chap. 22. Anmerkung ueber des Urtheil P. Rich. Simons von des Brucioli Italianischen Bibel-Uebersetzung : Schelhorn, Ergoetzlichkeiten, tom. 11. p. 535—551.

§ It was the object of Rusticio to correct this fault in Brucioli's translation. But his version is very inferior in this respect to that of Diodati, an Italian refugee, published at Geneva in 1607, of which Dr. Geddes gives the following character :—" There is an elegance and ease in this translation that are extremely pleasing to the reader,

pared to expect, that the literary fame of Brucioli would suffer from his religious opinions, and that his countrymen would be cautious in the commendations which they bestow on his talents and erudition. "He was well acquainted," says one of them, "with Greek, Hebrew, and Latin, and endowed by nature with rare talents; but, trusting to his genius, he plunged into grievous errors, which are scattered over many of his writings; and he died without making any recantation."* His translations of the Bible were put into the first class of forbidden books, and all his works, on whatever subject, "published or to be published," together with all books which came from his press, even after his death, were strictly prohibited.† His commentary on the Scriptures is exceedingly rare, but a foreign writer who examined it, and was every way qualified to pronounce a correct judgment on the subject, has assured us, that it contains numerous and decisive proofs of the author's attachment to evangelical truth.‡ So far as the influence of the press is concerned, Brucioli is entitled to the name of the reformer of Italy. "Though Italy be the fortress and strength of the papal empire," say the Lucchese refugees at Geneva, "because the authority of the pope is most firmly established over the people of that country, this could not prevent the light from penetrating it in different quarters; in consequence of which, the scales fell from the eyes and the shackles from the hands of many who sat in darkness and captivity. This was effected by means of an Italian

joined with a conciseness which one would think hardly compatible with ease and elegance. F. Simon greatly injures him, when he says, he is rather a paraphrast than a translator; but this is not the only rash assertion which this father has made." (Prospectus, p. 86.)

* Negri, Istor. degli Scrittori Fiorentini, p 561. A similar character of him is given by Poccianti, Catal. Script Florent. p. 18.
† Ind. Libr. Prohib. sig A 4. F. 3, b., anno 1559.
‡ Schelhorn, Ergoetzlichkeiten. tom. i. p. 417. With this writer Tiraboschi agrees. He accounts for the opposition made to Brucioli, "per le molti eresie di cui egli imbratto la stessa versione, e piu ancora il diffusa commento in sette tomi in foglio, che poi diede in luce." (Storia, tom. vii p. 404. Conf. Scipio Maffei, Traduttori Ital. p. 32 Fontanini, Della Eloq. Ital. p. 305.)

translation of the Bible by Brucioli, which was published at that time, and which it was not judged prudent to stifle in its birth, by those violent measures which were afterwards employed for its suppression."*

The fact of three natives of Florence having at this time translated the Scriptures,† whether it be viewed in the light of a cause or an effect, affords the strongest presumptive proof that Scriptural knowledge was in request, and that the reformed doctrine had made no inconsiderable advances, in Tuscany. We may draw the same inference from the lamentations of the popish clergy, taken in connexion with the number of persons who, as we shall afterwards see, forsook this delightful country to escape the cruelties of the inquisition. "Oh, Florence!" exclaimed a friar of that day from the pulpit. "What is the meaning of *Florence?* The flower of Italy; and thou wast so, till these Ultramontanes persuaded thee that man is justified by faith and not by works."‡

BOLOGNA, in the sixteenth century, formed part of the territories of the church; and from it the supreme pontiffs issued some of the severest of their edicts against heresy. But this did not prevent the light, which was shining around, from penetrating into that city. The university of Bologna was one of the earliest, if not the very first, of the great schools of Europe; and the extensive privileges enjoyed by its members were favourable to liberal sentiments and the propagation of the new opinions in religion. The essential principles of liberty, equally obnoxious to political and ecclesiastical despots, were boldly avowed in public disputations before the students, at a time when they had fallen into disrepute in those states of Italy which still retained a shadow of their former freedom.§ John Mollio, a native of Montal-

---

* Lettre de M. Le Cardinal Spinola, Evêque de Luquez—Avec les Considerations, &c. p. 23. Genev. 1680.
† Brucioli, Marmochini and Teofilo.
‡ Gilles, Hist des Eglis. Ref. ou Vaud. p. 21.
§ Life of John Knox, vol. ii. p. 125 In the fifteenth century, the

cino, in the territory of Sienna, was a principal instrument of promoting the gospel at Bologna. He had entered in his youth into the order of Minorites; but instead of wasting his time, like the most of his brethren, in idleness or superstition, had devoted himself to the study of polite letters and theology. By the careful perusal of the Scriptures and certain books of the Reformers, he attained to clear views of evangelical truth, which his talents and his reputation for learning and piety enabled him to recommend, both as a preacher and an academical professor.* After acquiring great celebrity as a teacher in the universities of Brescia, Milan, and Pavia, he came, about the year 1533, to Bologna. Certain propositions which he advanced in his lectures, relating to justification by faith, and other points then agitated, were opposed by Cornelio, a professor of metaphysics, who, being foiled in a public dispute which ensued between them, lodged a charge of heresy against his opponent, and procured his citation to Rome. Mollio defended himself with such ability and address, that the judges appointed by Paul III. to try the cause were forced to acquit him, in the way of declaring that the sentiments which he had maintained were true, although they were such as could not be publicly taught at that time without prejudice to the apostolical see. He was therefore sent back to Bologna, with an admonition to abstain for the future from explaining the epistles of St. Paul. But, continuing to teach the same doctrine as formerly, and with still greater applause from his hearers, cardinal Campeggio procured an order from the pope to remove him from the university.†

Hussites, indignant at the burning of Wiclef's books, as contrary to the privileges of the university of Prague, having sent a deputy to the university of Bologna, to complain of this indignity, the latter had the boldness to condemn the deed—"on ne devait pas avoir brulé les livres de ce *Docteur*, de peur de s'attirer quelque ressentiment de la part de l'Angleterre." (L'Enfant, Hist. de Concile de Pise, tom. ii. p. 48.)

* Histoire des Martyrs, f. 264, edit. 1597, folio. Zanchii Epist. lib. ii col 278.

† Pantaleon, Rerum in Eccl. Gest. lib. ix. f. 263.

The state of religious feeling at Bologna is depicted in a letter, as singular in its style as in its matter, which some inhabitants of that city addressed, in 1533, to John Planitz, ambassador from the elector of Saxony to Charles V., who was then in Italy. Having mentioned the report that he was sent to entreat the emperor to use his influence with the pope to call a council for the reformation of the church, an object which had been long and earnestly expected by all good men, they proceed in the following manner:—
"If this be true, as we trust it is, then we offer our thanks to you all—to you for visiting this Babylonian land—to Germany for demanding a council—and especially to your evangelical prince, who has undertaken the defence of the gospel and of all the faithful, with such ardour, that not content with restoring the grace and liberty of Christ to his native Saxony and to Germany, he seeks to extend the same blessings to England, France, Spain, Italy, and the churches in every other country. We are quite aware that it is a matter of small consequence to you whether a council is assembled or not, seeing you have already, as becomes strenuous and faithful Christians, thrown off the tyrannical yoke of antichrist, and asserted your right to the sacred privileges of the free kingdom of Jesus Christ; so that you everywhere read, write, and preach at your pleasure, without any other restraint than the apostolic rule, that the spirits of the prophets be subject to the judgment of the prophets who mutually teach and hear. We are aware, also, that it gives you no uneasiness to know that you are loaded in foreign countries with the heavy charge of heresy, but that, on the contrary, you esteem it matter of joy and eternal gloriation to be the first to suffer reproaches, imprisonment, and fire and sword, for the name of Jesus. It is therefore plain to us, that, in urging the convocation of such a synod, you do not look to the advantage of the Germans, but that, obeying the apostolical injunction, you seek the advantage and salvation of other nations. On this account, all Christians profess themselves un-

der the deepest obligations to you, and especially we of Italy, who, in proportion to our proximity to the tyrannical court, (alas! we cherish the tyrant in our bosom,) are bound to give thanks for the divine blessing of your liberation. We beseech and obtest you, by the faith of Christ, (though you are sufficiently disposed to this already, and need not our admonitions,) to employ every means in your power with the religious emperor, and to leave no stone unturned to obtain this most desirable and necessary assembly, in which you can scarcely fail to succeed, as his gentle and gracious majesty knows that this is desired, demanded, expected, and loudly called for by the most pious, learned, and honourable men in the most illustrious cities of Italy, and even in Rome itself; many of whom, we have no doubt, will flock to you, as soon as they shall learn that this is the object of your embassy. In fine, we hope that this will be willingly granted, as a thing most reasonable in itself, and consonant to the constitutions of the apostles and holy fathers, that Christians shall have liberty to examine one another's confessions, since the just live not by the faith of others, but by their own, otherwise faith is not faith; nor can that persuasion which is not divinely produced in the heart be properly called persuasion, but rather a violent and forced impulse, which the simplest and most ignorant must perceive to be utterly unavailing to salvation. But if the malice of Satan still rages to such a degree that this boon cannot be immediately obtained, liberty will surely be granted in the mean time both to clergy and laity to purchase Bibles without incurring the charge of heresy, and to quote the sayings of Christ or Paul without being branded as Lutherans. For, alas! instances of this abominable practice are common; and if this is not a mark of the reign of antichrist, we know not what it is, when the law, and grace, and doctrine, and peace and liberty of Christ, are so openly opposed, trampled upon, and rejected."*

The number of persons addicted to Protestantism

* Seckendorf, lib. iii. p. 68, 69.

in Bologna continued to be great, many years after this period. In a letter written in the year 1541, Bucer congratulates them on their increasing knowledge and numbers;* and, in 1545, Baldassare Altieri writes to an acquaintance in Germany, that a nobleman in that city was ready to raise six thousand soldiers in favour of the evangelical party, if it was found necessary to make war against the pope.†

That the desire for ecclesiastical reform was as strongly and generally felt through Italy as is represented in the letter of the Bolognese Protestants, appears from a measure adopted by the court of Rome at this time. Averse to the holding of a general council, and yet unable to evade the importunities of those who demanded it, pope Paul III. in 1537, appointed four cardinals and five prelates‡ to meet at Bologna, and charged them, after due deliberation, to lay before him their advice as to the best method of reforming the abuses of the Church. The members of this commission, including some of the most respectable dignitaries of the Church, met accordingly, and presented their joint advice to his holiness. Though they touched the sores of the ecclesiastic body with a gentle hand, they acknowledged that both head and members "laboured under a pestiferous malady, which, if not cured, would prove fatal;" and, among the evils which called for a speedy remedy, they specified the admission of improper persons to the priesthood, the sale of benefices, the disposition of them by testaments, the granting of dispensations and exemptions, and the union of bishoprics, including "the incompatible offices of cardinal and bishop." Addressing the supreme pontiff, they say, "Some of your predecessors in the pontifical chair, having itching ears, have heaped to themselves teachers according to their own lusts, who, instead of instructing them what they ought to do, were expert in finding

---

* Buceri Scripta Anglican, p. 687. † Seckend. p. 579.
‡ These were cardinals Contarini, Caraffa, Sadolet, and Pole; Fregoso, archbishop of Salerno, Aleander of Brindisi, and Gibert of Verona, Cortese, abbot of St. George of Venice, and Badia, master of the Sacred Palace.

out reasons to justify what they wished to do, and encouraged them in their simoniacal practices, by maintaining their right to dispose, at their pleasure, of all ecclesiastical property."* No one acquainted with the politics of the court of Rome will suppose that it was serious in the proposal to reform these abuses. The Advice was approved of and printed by the order of Paul III.; but, instead of carrying it into execution, he glaringly transgressed its provisions in various instances.† Nor did the advisers themselves testify any forwardness to exemplify their own rules. The cardinals retained their bishopricks; Pole did not think it necessary to lay aside the purple when he became primate of all England; and Caraffa, when he afterwards ascended the papal throne, under the title of Paul IV. put the *Advice* which he had given to his predecessor into the list of prohibited books.‡ The protestants, however, did not overlook this document. A copy of the Advice being sent to Germany,§ it was published in Latin, with a prefatory epis-

---

* Wolfii Lect. Memorab. tom. ii. p. 398—449, where the *Consilium* is inserted at length, with a preface by Vergerio. It was reprinted, along with the letter to cardinal Quirini mentioned in the subsequent note, by Schelhorn, who added to it Sturmius' epistle, and the correspondence to which this gave rise between that learned man and Sadolet

† During the last century, cardinal Quirini took occasion, from this private council, to extol the exertions of the pope to reform ecclesiastical abuses, in his prefaces to his edition of cardinal Pole's Letters, and also in his *Diatriba de Gestis Pauli III Farnesii*, published at Brescia in 1745. To this two able replies were made; one by Joan. Rudolphus Kiesling, entitled, *Epistola de Gestis Pauli Tertii ad emendationem Ecclesiæ spectantibus*, Lipsiæ, 1747; and the other by Jo. Georg Schelhorn, entitled, *De Consilio de Emendanda Ecclesia, jussu Pauli Tertii, sed ab eodem neglecto*. Tiguri, 1748.

‡ In opposition to a statement by Schelhorn, cardinal Quirini maintained that Paul IV. did not condemn the *Consilium*, but only the commentaries which Sturmius and others wrote on it Schelhorn has refuted the arguments of the cardinal, and confirmed his original statement, in a tract, entitled, *De Consilio de Emendanda Ecclesia, auspiciis Pauli III. conscripto; ac a Paulo IV. damnato*. Tig. 1748. It is prohibited under the following title:—"Consiglio d'alcuni Vescovi congregati in Bologna." (Index Auct. et Lib. Prohib. sig. B 2. Romæ, 1559.)

§ Cardinal Quirini at first asserted that it was originally printed by the Protestants, but he afterwards found two copies of it printed at Rome in 1538, by the authority of the pope. (Ut supra, p. 9.)

tle by Sturmius, rector of the academy of Strasburg; and in German by Luther, accompanied with animadversions, in which among other satirical remarks, he says, that the cardinals contented themselves with removing the small twigs, while they allowed the trunk of corruption to remain unmolested, and like the Pharisees of old, strained at flies and swallowed camels. To set this before the eyes of his readers, he prefixed to the book a print, in which the pope is represented as seated on a high throne, surrounded by the cardinals, who hold in their hands long poles with foxes' tails fixed to them like brooms, with which they sweep the room. Pallavicini is displeased with this measure of the pope, who, "by ordering a reformation of manners, acknowledged the existence of corruptions, and countenanced the detracting speeches which heretics circulated among the vulgar."* The following was an article of the proposed reform:—"Since boys are now accustomed to read at schools the colloquies of Erasmus, in which are many things calculated to betray uninformed minds into impiety, the reading of that book or any other of the same kind shall be prohibited in seminaries of learning."† To this was affixed the name of Sadolet! Well might Melanchthon express a surprise, not unmingled with scorn, at this conclusion, and at the whole of the ridiculous affair. "I have not yet answered Sadolet," says he, in a letter to a friend. "I would certainly have written him, if I had leisure for it; but am of opinion, that the delay will not be without its utility, considering the way in which he is acting. My friends write me from Italy that he is offended at my silence, and that some persons have incensed him against me. He seems to have thought, that, by one letter sent into Germany,

* Storia Concil Trent lib iii sect 57, § 3.
† On the margin of that part of the Advice which relates to Erasmus, Luther wrote, *Wolte Gott er solte leben! O that he had been alive!* —an exclamation expressive of regret at the recent death of an illustrious antagonist, mingled with delight at the thought of the merited castigation which Erasmus, if he had been in life, would have bestowed on the mitred censors of his favourite work. (Seckend. lib. iii. p. 164)

he would, as with the music of Orpheus, charm, not only me, who, I confess, am weak, but all my countrymen, and induce us to abandon the cause. The only friend of peace at Rome was Schonberg, cardinal of Capua, who thought that some concessions ought to be made. I formerly looked upon him as a person of great moderation, and am confirmed in this opinion by the letters which I have received from my friends since his death, which has produced a great change of counsels. There has just been published a ridiculous consultation of the cardinals about the correction of abuses, at which the colloquies of Erasmus were forbidden to be used in schools; and to this consultation were called these heroes, *Aleander* and *Sadolet*."* What pigmies do mere men of letters appear in the eyes of a man, I say not of stern virtue, but of sterling principle!

FAENZA and IMOLA are both situated in that part of Italy which was called the patrimony of St. Peter, and acknowledged the popes as their temporal sovereigns. It has been already mentioned that the reformed doctrine was introduced into the former city. That it gained admission into the latter appears from an anecdote related in a letter of Thomas Lieber, a German, (better known, in the controversy respecting ecclesiastical discipline, by his Greek name of *Erastus*,) who was then prosecuting his medical studies at the neighbouring university of Bologna. An Observantine monk, preaching one day at Imola, told the people that it behoved them to purchase heaven by the merit of their good works. A boy, who was present, exclaimed, "That's blasphemy! for the Bible tells us that Christ purchased heaven by his sufferings and death, and bestows it on us freely by his mercy." A dispute of considerable length ensued between the youth and the preacher. Provoked at the pertinent replies of his juvenile opponent, and at the favourable reception which the audience gave

---

* Melanch. Epist coll. 752, 753 Sleidan's account of the sentiments and conduct of the cardinal of Capua is different from that of Melanchthon. (Comment. tom. ii. p 117.)

them, "Get you gone, you young rascal!" exclaimed the monk, "you are but just come from the cradle, and will you take it upon you to judge of sacred things, which the most learned cannot explain?"— "Did you never read these words, 'Out of the mouths of babes and sucklings God perfects praise?'" rejoined the youth; upon which the preacher quitted the pulpit in wrathful confusion, breathing out threatenings against the poor boy, who was instantly thrown into prison, "where he still lies," says the writer of the letter, which was dated on the 31st of December 1544.*

VENICE, of all the states of Italy, afforded the greatest facilities for the propagation of the new opinions, and the safest asylum to those who suffered for their adherence to them. Well apprized of the ambition and encroaching spirit of the Roman court, the senate had uniformly resisted the attempts made to establish the inquisition, and was cautious in allowing the edicts of the Vatican to be promulgated or carried into effect, within the Venetian territories. Political sagacity counteracted the narrow views of a proud and jealous aristocracy, and taught them to relax the severity of their internal police. Venice had risen to power and opulence by commerce; and the concession of a more than ordinary freedom of thinking and speaking was necessary to encourage strangers to visit her ports and markets. The Venetian republic was then among popish what Holland afterwards became among Protestant states. She was distinguished for the number of her printing presses;† and while letters were cultivated elsewhere for themselves, or to gratify the vanity of their patrons, they were encouraged here, from the additional consideration of their forming an important and not unproductive branch of manufacture and merchandise. The books of the German and Swiss Protestants were consigned to merchants at Venice, from which they were

* Schelhorni Amœnit Hist Eccles tom ii p 54
† See, besides the common typographic authorities, Le Brett Dissertatio de Ecclesia Græca hodierna in Dalmatia, &c p 22, 93.

circulated to the different parts of Italy;* and it was in this city that versions of the Bible and other religious books in the vulgar tongue were chiefly printed.

We have already had occasion to notice, that the first writings of Luther were read in Venice soon after they were published. In a letter written in the year 1528, the reformer says to a friend, "You give me joy by what you write of the Venetians receiving the word of God. To him be the thanks and glory."† In the course of the following year, he was in correspondence with James Ziegler, a learned man, who possessed great authority at Venice, and was favourable to the grand attempt to reform religion, though he never joined its standard.‡ Ziegler had sent from Venice to Wittenberg, his adopted brother, Theodore Veit,§ who acted for some time as secretary or amanuensis to Luther, and afterwards became minister of Nurenberg. This is the person so often mentioned under the name of Theodorus Vitus in the letters of Melanchthon, and through whom that Reformer chiefly received his intelligence respecting the Protestants in Italy.‖

An occurrence which took place in 1530, shows that there were then numbers in Venice who felt a deep interest in the cause of the Reformation. While car-

---

* "Bene vale; et si quando deest scribendi argumentum, vel de communibus studiis, vel si quid librorum Germani mancipes nuper Venetias invexerint, perscribe." (Cœl Calcagninus Peregrino Morato; Epist lib. xi p. 158.)

† Luther's Samtliche Schriften, tom xxi. p. 1092.

‡ Ibid. p 1163 Ziegler was the intimate friend of Celio Calcagnini, who has celebrated his talents and virtues in the warmest manner. (Calcagnini Opera, p 54—57, 67, 86) He was distinguished for his skill in mathematics, geography, and natural history, and published the principal works of the ancients on these subjects, with annotations Schelhorn published his *Historia Clementis VII.* and prefixed to it, a treatise *De Vita et Scriptis Jacobi Ziegleri*, which contains curious particulars concerning the learning and literati of that time. (Amœnit Hist Eccles et Liter. tom ii. p. 210, &c.)

§ Buddeus, in his Supplement to Luther's Letters, (p. 74,) reads, "misit ad me *virum*, (instead of *vitum*,) fratrem sibi adoptatum;" a mistake which has been corrected by Walch. He is also called *Veit Dietrich*, in the correspondence of Luther and Melanchthon.

‖ Melanch. Epist col. 598, 835, &c. Conf. Seckend. Index I. art. *Theodoricus.*

dinal Campeggio attended the imperial diet at Augsburg as papal legate, a report was widely spread that he had wrought so far on the yielding temper of Melanchthon, as to persuade him to submit to the judgment of the supreme pontiff. This excited great uneasiness in the breasts of the Venetians who favoured the gospel, one of whom, Lucio Paolo Rosselli, addressed a letter to that Reformer, conceived in a noble spirit. After expressing the high esteem which he felt for the character of Melanchthon, and the delight which he had received from his writings, he exhorts him, in respectful language, but with an honest freedom, to show himself a firm and intrepid defender of that faith to which he had been the honoured instrument of winning so many. "In this cause," continues he, "you ought to regard neither emperor, nor pope, nor any other mortal, but the immortal God only. If there be any truth in what the papists circulate about you, the worst consequences must accrue to the gospel, and to those who have been led to embrace it through your instrumentality and that of Luther. Be assured that all Italy waits with anxiety for the result of your assembly at Augsburg. Whatever is determined by it, will be embraced by Christians in other countries through the authority of the emperor. It behoves you and others, who are there for the purpose of defending the gospel, to be firm, and not to suffer yourselves to be either frightened from the standard of Christ by threats, or drawn from it by entreaties and promises. I implore and obtest you, as the head and leader of the whole evangelical army, to regard the salvation of every individual. Though you should be called to suffer death for the glory of Christ, fear not, I beseech you; it is better to die with honour than to live in disgrace. You shall secure a glorious triumph from Jesus Christ, if you defend his righteous cause; and in doing this, you may depend on the aid of the prayers and supplications of many who, day and night, entreat Almighty God to prosper the cause of the gospel, and to preserve you and its other champions through the blood of his Son. Fare-

REFORMATION IN ITALY. 105

well, and desert not the cause of Christ."* In the course of the same month, this zealous person wrote a second time to Melanchthon, enclosing a copy of the letter which the Reformer was said to have addressed to the legate. If unhappily he had been induced to write in a strain so unworthy of his character, Rosselli exhorts him to evince the more courage and constancy for the future; but if it was a fabrication, as many of his friends asserted, then he should lose no time in exposing such a malicious calumny, and maintain henceforth a declared and open warfare with men who sought to accomplish their ends by the base arts of stratagem and falsehood.†

Among those who contributed most to propagate the reformed opinions at Venice, were Pietro Carnesecchi, Baldo Lupetino, and Baldassare Altieri. With the first, we shall afterwards have occasion to meet among the martyrs of Italy. The second, who also obtained the crown of martyrdom, was a native of Albona, of noble extraction, and held in high esteem for his learning and worth. He was provincial of the Franciscans within the Venetian territories, and in that character, had the best opportunities of communicating religious instruction, and of protecting those who had received it.‡ It was by his advice that Matteo Flacio, a kinsman of his, altered his resolution of assuming the monastic garb, and retired into Germany, where he became distinguished for his learned writings, and the active though intemperate part which he took in the internal disputes which agitated the Lutheran church.§ Altieri, though a native of

* "Venetiis 8. 3 Kal. Augusti, anno 1530." Cælestini Act. Comit. August. tom. ii. f. 274.

† Cælestin. tom. iii. f. 18. Wolfii Lect. Memorab. tom. ii. p 344—345; where Melanchthon's letter to Campeggio is also inserted. If really written by him, it was sufficiently humble.

‡ Ritteri Vita Flacii Illyrici, p. 8. apud Gerdes. Ital. Ref. p. 58, 172—174.

§ He is usually called *Matthæus Flacius Illyricus*, and was the principal compiler of the Ecclesiastical History known by the title of *Centuriæ Magdeburgenses*, and of the *Catalogus Testium Veritatis*. An early and still valuable work on biblical interpretation, entitled, *Clavis Sacræ Scripturæ*, is the production of his pen. His account

8

Aquila in Naples, had fixed his residence at Venice, where he acted for some time as the secretary of the English ambassador, and afterwards as agent for the Protestant princes of Germany. He was distinguished for his ardent devotion to the reformed religion, which his official situations enabled him to advance, by the epistolary correspondence which he carried on with foreign courts, the books which he brought into Italy, and the advice and assistance which he was always ready to afford to such of his countrymen as had embraced or were inquiring after the truth.*

The evangelical doctrine had made such progress in the city of Venice between the years 1530 and 1542, that its friends, who had hitherto met in private for mutual instruction and religious exercises, held deliberations on the propriety of organizing themselves into regular congregations and assembling in public.† Several members of the senate were favourable to it, and hopes were entertained at one time that the authority of that body would be interposed in its behalf. In the beginning of the year 1538, Michele Bracchioli‡ came from Italy to Wittemberg to confer on religion with Melanchthon, who was greatly delighted with his manners and the elegance of his taste.§ Being called home unexpectedly, by information that his brother was in danger of proscription, he returned to Germany in the course of a year, charged with a message to Melanchthon, from

of his own life, under the title of *Historia Actionum et Certaminum*, which abounds in anecdotes of his time, is exceedingly rare.

* Laderchii Annal. Eccl. tom. xxii. f. 325. Seckendorf, lib. iii. p. 404, 578, 614. Schelhorn, Ergœtzlichkeiten, tom. i. p. 423.

† Gerdes. Ital. Ref. p. 57.

‡ Schelhorn thinks it probable that the translator, mistaking the handwriting of Melanchthon, which was not very legible, had read *Bracchiolus* instead of *Brucchiolus*, and that the person referred to might be a brother of Brucioli, the translator of the Bible. (Ergœtzlichkeiten, tom. i. p. 420—422.) There certainly is some mistake as to the name; for the person who is called *Bracchiolus* in one letter of Melanchthon, is called *Braccietus* in another.

§ "Est enim et ingenii suavitate summa præditus, et in versu scribendo elegans et venustus, seque ad imitationem Catulli comparavit, quem feliciter exprimit." (Epist. Melanchthonis ad Vitum, a. 1538. Collect. Joh. Sauberti, lib. iv. p. 46.)

the friends of reformation in Venice. This encouraged the Reformer to address a letter to the senate, in which he expressed the high satisfaction which he felt at hearing, that many honourable persons among them entertained a favourable opinion of the reform of ecclesiastical abuses which had been made in Germany. After a short statement of the cautious manner in which the Reformers had proceeded, by taking care to repress popular tumults and avoid dangerous innovations, and after suggesting some considerations to show that various corruptions had been introduced into the church, Melanchthon adds—"Such slavery surely ought not to be established, as that we should be obliged, for peace's sake, to approve of all the errors of those who govern the church; and learned men especially ought to be protected in the liberty of expressing their opinions and of teaching. As your city is the only one in the world which enjoys a genuine aristocracy, preserved during many ages and always hostile to tyranny, it becomes it to protect good men in freedom of thinking, and to discourage that unjust cruelty which is exercised in other places. Wherefore, I cannot refrain from exhorting you to employ your care and authority for advancing the divine glory, a service which is most acceptable to God."* Had Venice been then treated by the court of Rome in the same manner in which it was treated by it at the commencement of the seventeenth centu-

* Melanchthonis Epistolæ, Coll. 150—154, edit. Londini. Schelhorn (Amœn. Liter. tom. i. p. 422) suspects that Melanchthon was not on terms of such intimacy with the senators of Venice as to address a letter to them, and is of opinion that it was addressed *Ad Venetorum quosdam Evangelii studiosos*, under which title it appears in the *Selectæ Declamationes* of the author, published in 1541, p. 804. But the letter contains internal evidence of its having been intended for the magistrates of that republic; and Bock states, that he had seen, in the Royal Library of Kœnigsberg, a copy of the original edition, printed at Nurenberg, and bearing this title, *Epistola Philippi Melanchthonis ad Senatum Venetum*. It was a presentation copy to Prince Albert the elder, who had written on the title-page, "Accepi d. 17. Julii, a. 1538, per Eliam Plesse, Wratislauiensem;" which proves that the letter was written earlier than has been supposed. (Hist. Antitrin. tom. ii. p. 398.)

ry, it is highly probable that the republic would have declared in favour of the Reformation; and, in that case, it might at this day have possessed its political independence, if not also regained its ancient glory.

The gospel was introduced into the different territories belonging to the republic of Venice. At *Padua* it was embraced by many of the students and some of the professors in the university, which was celebrated at that period as a school of medicine.* At *Verona* and at *Brescia* there were converts to the reformed faith.† In the *Bergamasco*, the bishop, Vittore Soranzo, was favourable to evangelical doctrine, and exerted himself in reforming his clergy.‡ But the greatest number of Protestants were to be found in the *Vicentino* and *Trevisano*, situated in the neighbourhood of Venice. In the year 1535, the doge delivered up to the vicar-general of Vicenza a German, named Sigismund, to be punished for disseminating the Lutheran heresy in that diocese; for which act of filial obedience his excellency was formally thanked by Paul III. in a pontifical brief.§ This example of severity had not, however, the effect of arresting the progress of the reformed doctrine, which was patronized, or at least connived at and tolerated by the local magistrates; for, in a papal rescript addressed to the doge and senate ten years after, his holiness represents, that he had repeatedly notified to them, by letters and nuncios, that heresy had sprung up and been embraced by not a few in their city of Vicenza, and that the governor and magistrates of that place, though instructed by them to co-operate with their bishop in extirpating it, had hitherto refused to grant that assistance which was absolutely necessary to ac-

---

* Melanch. Epist coll. 373, 443, 758. Preface, by Cælio Secundo Curio, to the Life of Francis Spira, by Matteo Gribaldi, first printed in 1550.

† Gerdes. Ital. Ref. p. 274, 280, 338, 351.

‡ De Porta, Hist. Reformat. Ecclesiarum Rhæticarum, tom. ii p. 253. Laderchius introduces Victor Saranzius, bishop of Bergamo, among those whom he calls Valdesians, Lutherans, Zuinglians, and Calvinists. (Annales ad an. 1567.)

§ Raynaldi Annal. ad an. 1535.

complish this pious purpose: so that the heretics had been emboldened, and there was reason to fear that these pestilent tenets would take root and spread to adjoining cities, unless prompt measures were taken to apprehend and punish the guilty.*

A letter addressed to Luther, in the year 1542, by Altieri, "in the name of the brethren of the Church of Venice, Vicenza, and Treviso," is valuable, as evincing the excellent spirit of the writer, and throwing light on the state of the Protestant interest in that quarter, and in Italy at large. They felt ashamed, he said, and were unable to account for the fact, that they had so long failed to acknowledge the deep obligations which they lay under to him as the individual by whom they had been brought to the knowledge of the way of salvation; whether it was that the suddenness of their emancipation had astounded their minds, or whether a certain rustic bashfulness and servile dread had deterred them from addressing so grave and holy a personage. But now necessity, and the urgency of their circumstances, had driven them to that course which ingratitude and culpable negligence had hitherto prevented them from taking. Antichrist had begun to rage against them. Some of their number had been obliged to leave the country, others were thrown into prison, and the rest were in a state of trepidation. As members of the same body, they looked for the sympathy and assistance of their brethren in Germany, at whose call they had come forth and espoused that cause for the sake of which they were now exposed to such imminent danger. What they begged of him was, to use his influence with the evangelical princes of Germany to write in their behalf, requesting the senate of Venice to abstain from that violence which the ministers of the pope urged it to employ against the poor flock of Christ, and to permit them to enjoy their own manner of worship, at least until the meeting of a general council, in the way of adopting measures to prevent all sedition and

* Raynaldi Annal. ad an. 1545.

disturbance of the public peace. "If God grant," continues he, "that we obtain a truce of this kind, what accessions will be made to the kingdom of Christ in point of faith and charity! How many preachers will appear to announce Christ faithfully to the people! How many prophets, who now lurk in corners, exanimated with undue fears, will come forth to expound the Scriptures! The harvest is truly great, but there are no labourers. You know what a great increase your churches had, and what a wide door was opened for the gospel, by the truce which, as we understand, you have enjoyed for three years. Exert yourselves to procure the same favour for us; cherish the common cause; do your endeavour, that by this means the consolation which is by Christ may be imparted to us, who daily suffer for Christ; for it is our fervent desire that the word of God may be spread abroad, but we have none to feed us, unless our want be supplied out of your abundance."*

The MILANESE, as early as the year 1542, contained adherents to the reformed doctrine.† Several causes contributed to its propagation in this interesting portion of Italy. The struggle which Milan, the capital of Lombardy, had anciently maintained for its ecclesiastical independence, continued to be remembered long after its submission to the see of Rome; a circumstance which, joined to the natural advantages of the country, drew to it those who dissented from the doctrines or declined the communion of the general Church. The Milanese bordered on Switzerland, in which the reformed doctrine established itself at an early period, and on Piedmont, where the Vaudois had for centuries fixed their residence. To these causes may be added the political state of the duchy, and the protracted contest for its sovreignty between Francis I. and Charles V., with its alternate occupation by the armies of the contending monarchs; in consequence of which, the efforts of the Reformers to

* Seckendorf, lib. iii. p. 401.
† Erasmi Epistolæ: Gerdes. Hist. Ref. tom. iv. p. 30.

spread their sentiments were for a time overlooked. In a brief addressed to the bishop of Modena, in the year 1536, Paul III. states that he was informed that there had been lately discovered, in the religious and illustrious state of Milan, conventicles, consisting of noble persons of both sexes, belonging to a sect holding and observing the tenets of one friar Batista de Crema, by which many heresies, condemned by the ancient Church, were fostered. His holiness therefore commands the bishop, who was then at Milan, to make inquisition after these conventicles and heretics, and to see that condign punishment was inflicted on the guilty, so that the pravity sown by the devil might be extirpated before it had time to shoot up and strengthen.* Though the "impure tenets of ancient heretics" are imputed to these "innovators," according to the usual language of the Church of Rome, there can be little doubt that they held the common opinions of Luther and Zuingle.

This part of our history is closely connected with some interesting facts in the chequered life of a man who had great influence in promoting the cause of the Reformation in Italy. Celio Secundo Curione, or Curio, was born at Turin in 1503, and was the youngest of twenty-three children. When only nine years of age he was left an orphan, but being allied to several noble families in Piedmont, received a liberal education at the university of his native city. In his youth, he was induced to read the Bible with more than ordinary attention, in consequence of his father having bequeathed him a copy of that book beautifully written; and when he reached his twentieth year, he had the writings of the Reformers put into his hands, by means of Jeronimo Negri of Fossano, who, along with some others in the Augustinian monastery of Turin, had come to the knowledge of the truth. This inflamed him with a desire of visiting Germany, to which he set out, accompanied by Giacomo Cornello and Francesco Guarino, who afterwards became distinguished ministers of the reformed

* Raynaldi Annales, ad an. 1536.

church. Having, on their journey, entered incautiously into dispute on the controverted heads of religion, they were informed against, seized by the spies of the cardinal bishop of Ivrée, and thrown into separate prisons. Curio was released through the intercession of his relations; and the cardinal, pleased with his talents, endeavoured to attach him to himself by the offer of pecuniary assistance in his studies, and by placing him in the neighbouring priory of St. Benigno, with the administration of which he had been intrusted by the late pope Leo X. In this situation Curio exerted himself in enlightening the monks and freeing their minds from the influence of superstition. He one day opened a box, placed on the altar of the chapel, and having abstracted the relics from it, substituted a copy of the Bible, with the following inscription, "This is the ark of the covenant, which contains the oracles of God, the true relics of the saints." When the relics were required on the next solemn festival, the trick was discovered, and suspicion having fallen on Curio, he fled and made his escape to Milan. This happened about the year 1530. After visiting Rome and several cities in Italy, he returned to the Milanese, where he married a lady belonging to the illustrious family of the Isacii, and devoted himself to the teaching of polite letters, by which he gained great reputation in the city and vicinity of Milan. The ravages committed by the Spanish troops obliging him to quit the Milanese, he embraced an invitation from the count of Montferrat, under whose protection he resided for some years in tranquillity at Casale.*

Being persuaded to visit his native country, with the view of recovering his patrimony, he found it seized by one of his sisters and her husband, who unnaturally preferred a charge of heresy against him, as the most effectual way of defeating his legal claims. Upon this he retired to a village in the territories of the duke of Savoy, where he was employed in teaching the children of the neighbouring gentlemen. Hav-

* Stupani Oratio de Cæli Secundi Curionis Vita atque Obitu; in Schelhorni Amœn. Liter. tom. xiv. p. 328—336.

ing gone one day, in company with some of his patrons, to hear a Dominican monk from Turin, the preacher, in the course of his sermon, drew a frightful picture of the German Reformers, and, in proof of its justness, gave false quotations from a work published by Luther. Curio went up to the friar after sermon, and, producing the book, which he happened to have in his possession, read the passages referred to in the presence of the most respectable part of the audience, who, indignant at the misrepresentations which had been impudently palmed on them, drove their ghostly instructor, with disgrace, from the town. Information was immediately given to the inquisitor, and Curio was apprehended and carried a prisoner to his native city, when his meditated journey to Germany and his abstracting of the relics at St. Benigno, were produced as aggravations of his crime and strong presumptions of heretical pravity. As his friends were known to possess great influence, the administrator of the bishopric of Turin went to Rome to secure his condemnation, leaving him under the charge of a brother of cardinal Cibo, who, to prevent any attempt at rescue, removed him to an inner room of the prison, and ordered his feet to be made fast in the stocks. In this situation a person of less fortitude and ingenuity would have given himself up for lost; but Curio, having in his youth lived in the neighbourhood of the jail, devised a method of escape, which, through the favour of Providence, succeeded. His feet being swoln by confinement, he prevailed on his keeper to allow him to have his right foot loosed for a day or two. By means of his shoe, together with a reed and a quantity of rags which lay within his reach, he formed an artificial leg, which he fastened to his right knee, in such a manner as that he could move it with ease. Having obtained permission to have his other foot relieved, he inserted the artificial limb into the stocks. Both his feet being thus at liberty, he, during the following night, forced the door of his apartment, felt his way through the dark passages, dropped from a window, and having scaled the walls of his prison with difficulty, made his escape into Italy. As he had extracted the fictitious limb from the stocks, and taken it to pieces, before leaving the prison, his persecutors could not account for his escape, and circulated the report that he had effected it by magic; upon which he published an account of the whole affair, in the form of a dialogue, interspersed with humorous and satirical strictures upon some of the popish errors.* After remaining some months with his family at Sale, a remote village in the territory of Milan, he was drawn from his retirement by his former friends and placed in the university of Pavia. As soon as this was known, orders were sent from Rome to apprehend him; but so great was the favour in which he was held by the principal inhabitants of the place, and by the students, many of whom had come from other seminaries to attend his lectures, that he was protected for nearly three years from the attempts of the inquisitors; a guard, composed of his scholars, accompanying him to and from his house every day, during a great part of that time. At last, the pope threatening the senate of the town with excommunication, he was forced to retire to Venice, from which he removed to Ferrara. The labours of Curio were blessed for opening the eyes of many to the errors and corruptions of the Roman church, during his journeys through Italy, and the residence which he made in several parts of it, especially in the Milanese.†

NAPLES and SICILY had for some time belonged to the crown of Spain, and were now governed by separate viceroys under the emperor Charles V. In Calabria, which formed one of the departments of the kingdom of Naples, the Vaudois still existed; and the doctrine of Luther and the other Reformers now spread extensively in the Neapolitan territory, and

* It is entitled "Cœlii Secundi Curionis Pasquillus Ecstaticus, una cum aliis etiam aliquot sanctis pariter et lepidis Dialogis;" without date or place of printing. The book was reprinted at Geneva in 1667, which is the edition I have used. The Dialogue, so far as it relates to his escape from Turin, is inserted by Schelhorn in the second volume of his Amœnitates Hist. Eccles. et Hist. p. 759—776.
† Stupani Oratio, p. 342.

especially in its capital. It is supposed to have been first introduced by the German soldiers, who, after the sack of Rome, obliged Lautrec, the French general, to raise the siege of Naples, and continued to garrison that city for some time.* A rigorous edict, published by Charles V. in the year 1536, by which he charged Don Pedro de Toledo, his viceroy at Naples, with the punishment of all who were infected with heresy, or who inclined to it, was intended to extirpate the seeds which had been sown by these foreigners.†

The Germans were succeeded by a person who, according to the account of a contemporary popish historian, "caused a far greater slaughter of souls than all the thousands of heretical soldiery."‡ This was Juan Valdes, or as he is sometimes called, Valdesso, a Spanish gentleman, who had gone to Germany along with his sovereign, Charles V. by whom he was knighted and sent to Naples, where he acted as secretary to the viceroy, don Pedro de Toledo. In tracing the progress which the Reformation made in Spain, we shall have an opportunity of showing how the religious opinions of Valdes were formed.§ His character was admirably adapted to produce an impression favourable to the new opinions. Possessed of considerable learning and of superior address, fervent in his piety and gentle in his dispositions, polite in manners and eloquent in conversation, he soon became a favourite with the principal nobility and with all the enlightened men, who, at a certain season of the year, resorted in great numbers to the Neapolitan metropolis. Valdes did not take on him the office of a preacher, and he is an example of the extensive good which may be done by one who confines himself to the sphere within which Providence has placed him. By his private instructions, he not only imbued the minds

* Anton Caraccioli, Collect. de Vita Pauli IV. p. 239.
† Giannone, Hist. Civ. de Naples, liv. xxxii. chap. 5.
‡ Caraccioli, Collect. ut supra.
§ History of the Progress and Suppression of the Reformation in Spain.

of many distinguished laymen with the knowledge of evangelical truth, but contributed materially to advance the illumination and to stimulate the zeal of others, whose station gave them an opportunity of preaching the gospel to the people, or of instilling its doctrines into the minds of the ingenuous youth whose studies they superintended.* Among these were Ochino and Martyr, two persons of whom it is proper to give an account, as they produced a strong sensation in their native country, and distinguished themselves afterwards in the reformed churches on this side the Alps.

Bernardino Ochino, or, as he is sometimes called, Ocello, was born in the year 1487, at Sienna, a city of Tuscany, of obscure parents. Feeling, from his earliest years, a deep sense of religion, he devoted himself, according to the notions of that age, to a monastic life, and joined the Franciscan Observantines, as the strictest of all the orders of the regular clergy. For the same reason he left them, and, in 1534, became a member of the Capuchin brotherhood, which had been recently established according to the most rigid rules of holy living, or rather voluntary humility and mortification.† During his monastic retirement, he acknowledges that he escaped those vices with which his life might have been tainted if he had mixed with the world; and from the studies of the cloister, barren and unprofitable as they were, reaped a portion of knowledge which was afterwards of some use to him;‡ but he failed completely in gaining, what was the great thing which induced him to choose that unnatural and irksome mode of life, peace of mind and assurance of salvation. But let us hear his own

---

* Caraccioli, ut supra. Giannone, ut supra. Schelhorni Amœnit. Hist. Eccl. tom. ii. p. 49. Simleri Oratio de Vita Martyris, sig. b. iij.

† De Vita, Religione, et Fatis Bernardini Ochini Senensis; published in Observ. Select. Liter. Halens. tom. iv. p. 409—414. The author of this Life of Ochino was Burch. Gottlieb Struvius. Some popish writers had incautiously stated that Ochino was the founder of the Capuchins, a heretical blot which their successors were eager to remove.

‡ Ochini Dialogi, tom. ii. p. 374. Basil 1563.

account of his feelings, and of the manner in which a change was first wrought on his sentiments concerning religion. "When I was a young man, I was under the dominion of the common error by which the minds of all who live under the yoke of the wicked Antichrist are enthralled; so that I believed that we were to be saved by our own works, fastings, prayers, abstinence, watchings, and other things of the same kind, by which we were to make satisfaction for our sins, and purchase heaven, through the concurring grace of God. Wherefore, being anxious to be saved, I deliberated with myself what manner of life I should follow, and believing that those modes of religion were holy which were approved by the Roman Church, which I regarded as infallible, and judging that the life of the friars of St. Francis, called *de observantia*, was above all others severe, austere, and rigid, and, on that account, more perfect and conformable to the life of Christ, I entered their society. Although I did not find what I had expected, yet no better way presenting itself to my blinded judgment, I continued among them until the Capuchin friars made their appearance, when, being struck with the still greater austerity of their mode of living, I assumed their habit, in spite of the resistance made by my sensuality and carnal prudence. Being now persuaded that I had found what I was seeking, I said to Christ, 'Lord, if I am not saved now, I know nothing more that I can do.' In the course of my meditations, I was often perplexed and felt at a loss to reconcile the views on which I acted with what the Scriptures said about salvation being the gift of God through the redemption wrought by Christ; but the authority of the Church silenced these scruples, and in proportion as concern for my soul became more intense, I applied myself with greater diligence and ardour to those bodily exercises and mortifications which were prescribed by the doctrine of the Church, and by the rules of the order to which I had submitted. Still, however, I remained a stranger to true peace of mind, which at last I found by searching the

Scriptures, and such helps for understanding them as I had access to. I now came to be satisfied of the three following truths:—*First,* that Christ, by his obedience and death, has made a plenary satisfaction and merited heaven for the elect, which is the only righteousness and ground of salvation; *secondly,* that religious vows of human invention are not only useless but hurtful and wicked; and, *thirdly,* that the Roman Church, though calculated to fascinate the senses by her external pomp and splendour, is unscriptural and abominable in the sight of God."*

In Italy it was not the custom, as in Germany, for the secular clergy to preach: this task was performed exclusively by the monks and friars. The chapters of the different orders chose such of their number as possessed the best pulpit talents, and sent them to preach in the principal cities during the time of Lent, which was almost the only season of the year in which the people enjoyed religious instruction. Ochino attained to the highest distinction in this employment, to which he was chosen by his brethren at an early period. His original talents compensated for his want of erudition. He was a natural orator; and the fervour of his piety and the sanctity of his life gave an unction and an odour to his discourses which ravished the hearts of his hearers. "In such reputation was he held," says the annalist of the Capuchins, after Ochino had brought on them the stigma of heresy, "that he was esteemed incomparably the best preacher of Italy; his powers of elocution, accompanied with the most admirable action, giving him the complete command of his audience, and the more so that his life corresponded to his doctrine."† His external appearance, after he had passed middle age, contributed to heighten this effect. His snow-white head, and his beard of the same

* Bernardini Ochini Responsio, qua rationem reddit discessus ex Italia. Venet. 1542. Ep. Dedic.: Observat. Select. Halenses, tom. iv. p. 412—414. Epistre aux Magnifiques Seigneurs de Siene—par Bernardin Ochin. Avec un autre Epistre à Mutio Justinopolitain, 1544. The epistle to Mutio is a translation of the work first mentioned. M Aug. Beyeri Memor. Libr. Rariorum, p. 259—261.
† Bzovius, apud Bock, Hist. Antitrin. tom. ii. p. 485.

colour flowing down to his middle, added to a pale countenance, which led the spectators to suppose that he was in bad health, rendered his aspect at once venerable and deeply interesting.* He never rode on horseback or in a carriage, but performed all his journeys on foot; a practice which he continued after he was advanced in years. When he paid a visit to the palaces of princes or bishops, he was always met and received with the honours due to one of superior rank, and accompanied, on his departure, with the same marks of distinction; yet, wherever he lodged, he retained all the simplicity and austerity of the religious order to which he belonged.† As a preacher, he was admired and followed equally by the learned and illiterate, by the great and the vulgar. Charles V., who used to attend his sermons when in Italy, pronounced this high encomium on him—" That man would make the stones weep!"‡ Sadolet and Bembo, who were still better judges than his imperial majesty, assigned to Ochino the palm of popular eloquence.§ At Perugia, he prevailed on the inhabitants, by his discourses, to bury all their animosities and bring their lawsuits to an amicable settlement; and in Naples, he preached to so numerous an assembly and with such persuasive eloquence as to collect at one time, for a charitable purpose, the almost incredible sum of five thousand crowns.‖

The fame of the devout and eloquent Capuchin was so great, that the most respectable inhabitants of Venice, in the year 1538, employed cardinal Bembo to procure him to preach to them during the ensuing Lent. The cardinal wrote to Vittoria Colonna, marchioness of Pescaro, begging her to intercede with

* Graziani, Vita Card. Commendoni, lib. ii. cap. 9.
† Ibid.
‡ Schrœkh, Christliche Kirchengeschichte seit der Reformation, tom. ii. p. 780.
§ Sadoleti Epist. in Oper. Aonii Palearii, p. 558. edit. Halbaueri. Quirini Diatrib. præfix. Epp. Reg. Poli, tom. iii. p. 86.
‖ Annali de' Fratri Minori Capuccini composti dal P. Zaccaria Boverio da Saluzzo, e tradotti en volgare dal P. F. Benedetto Sanbenedetti da Milano, tom. i. p. 411. Venet. 1643.

Ochino, over whom she had great influence, to visit Venice, where he would find all the inhabitants inflamed with the most passionate desire to hear him.* He went accordingly, and the reception he met with is thus described by the elegant pen of Bembo, in a letter to the marchioness, dated from Venice, the 23d day of February, 1539:—" I send your highness the extracts of our very reverend Frate Bernardino, to whom I have listened, during the small part of this Lent which is over, with a pleasure which I cannot sufficiently express. Assuredly I never heard so edifying and holy a preacher, and do not wonder that your highness esteems him as you do. He discourses very differently from any other that has mounted the pulpit in my day, and in a more Christian manner; bringing forth truths of superior excellence and usefulness, and enforcing them with the most affectionate ardour. He pleases every body above measure, and will carry the hearts of all with him when he leaves this place. From the whole city I send your highness immortal thanks for the favour you have done us; and I especially will ever feel obliged to you."† In another letter to the same lady, dated the 15th of March, he says—"I talk with your highness as I talked this morning with the reverend father, Frate Bernardino, to whom I have laid open my whole heart and soul, as I would have done to Jesus Christ, to whom I am persuaded he is acceptable and dear. Never have I had the pleasure to speak to a holier man than he. I should have been now at Padua, both on account of a business which has engaged me for a whole year, and also to shun the applications with which I am incessantly assailed in consequence of this blessed cardinalate;‡ but I was unwilling to deprive myself of the opportunity of hearing his most excellent, holy, and edifying sermons."§ And on the

* Lettere di Pietro Bembo, vol. iv. p. 108. Opere, vol. viii. Milano, 1810.
† Lettere di Pietro Bembo, vol iv. p. 109
‡ Bembo had lately received a cardinal's hat from Rome.
§ Lettere, ut supra, p. 112.

14th of April he writes—"Our Frate Bernardino, whom I desire henceforth to call mine as well as yours, is at present adored in this city. There is not a man or woman who does not extol him to the skies. Oh, what pleasure! Oh, what delight! Oh, what joy has he given! But I reserve his praises until I meet your highness, and, in the meantime, supplicate our Lord to order his life so as that it may endure longer to the honour of God and the profit of men, than it can endure according to the way in which he now treats himself."* The following letter, addressed by the cardinal to the parson of the church of the Apostles, is still more descriptive of the deep interest which was felt for Ochino at Venice:—"I pray you to entreat and oblige the reverend father, Frate Bernardino, to eat flesh, not for the gratification and benefit of his body, about which he is indifferent, but for the comfort of our souls—that he may be able to preach the gospel to the praise of our blessed Saviour. For he cannot continue his exercises, nor bear up under them, during the present Lent, unless he leave off the diet of the season, which, as experience proves, always brings on him a catarrh."†

These extracts will be considered as sufficient to establish the character of Ochino for piety and eloquence; but there is another reflection which they can scarcely fail to suggest. How deceitful are the warmest feelings excited by hearing the gospel! and how do they vary with the external circumstances in which the truth is presented to the mind! Bembo was delighted with the sentiments which he heard, as well as the eloquence with which the preacher adorned them; and yet the future conduct of the cardinal leaves us at no loss in determining, that he would have felt and spoken very differently, had he been told that the doctrine to which he listened with such devout ravishment was essentially protestant. Names

---

* Lettere, ut supra, p. 112.
† "Ali 12 di Maizo, 1539." This letter was first published, from the archives of the Marquis Ugolino Barisone, by Chevalier Jacopo Morelli, in his late edition of Bembo's works. (Tomo. ix. p. 497.)

exert great influence over mankind; but let not those who can laugh at this weakness flatter themselves that they have risen above all the prejudices by which the truth is excluded or expelled. The love of the world outweighs both names and things. Provided men could enjoy the gospel within the pale of their own church, within the circle of that society in which they have been accustomed to move and shine, and without being required to forego the profits, honours, or pleasures of this life, "all the world" might be seen wondering after Christ, as it once "wondered after the beast."

In a general chapter of his order, held at Florence in the year 1538, Ochino was chosen general or chief director of the Capuchins. And three years after, in another chapter, held at Whitsuntide, 1541, in the city of Naples, he was, as an unexampled mark of respect, and in opposition to his own earnest request, unanimously re-elected to the same office.* Before Ochino was advanced to these honours, or had acquired such extensive popularity as a preacher, the change in his religious sentiments, already described, had taken place.† It produced a corresponding change on his strain of preaching, which, for some time, was felt rather than understood by his hearers. He appealed directly to the Scriptures in support of the doctrines which he delivered, and exhorted the people to rest their faith on the infallible authority of the word of God, and to build their hopes of salvation on the obedience and death of Christ alone. But a prudential regard to his own safety, and to the edifica-

---

* Boverio, Annali Capuccini ad ann. 1539, 1541. His official designation is expressed in the title of one of his first publications—"Dialogi Sacri del Rev Padre Frate B Ochino da Siena, Generale de i Frati Capuzzini. Venetio, 1542" (De Bure, Partie Theologique, p. 432)

† Observ. Select Hallens. tom iv. p. 416. Caraccioli, Collect p. 239. Giannone, liv. xxxvii chap v Bock, Hist Antitrin. tom. ii. p. 489—491. Caraccioli says, that Ochino's adoption of the Protestant tenets was discovered as early as the year 1536 This error has been corrected by Bock, who has himself fallen into a mistake in stating that Ochino was drawn over to the evangelical party by Valdes in the year 1541, whereas the latter died in 1540.

tion of his hearers, whose minds were not prepared
for the discovery, prevented him for some time from
exposing the errors and superstition by which Christianity had been corrupted. When he came to preach
at Naples, the sagacious eye of Juan Valdes quickly
detected the protestant under the patched rocket and
sharp-horned cowl of the Capuchin; and, having
gained his friendship, he introduced him to the private meetings held by the converts to evangelical
doctrine in that city.

Pietro Martire Vermigli* was born in the year
1500, of an honourable family in Florence, and received that liberal education which had been denied to
Ochino. In his youth he was taught Latin by his
mother; and having, when he arrived at the age of
sixteen, entered, in opposition to the will of his parents,
among the canons regular of St. Augustine, he passed
his noviciate in their convent at Fiezoli, which the
liberality of the Medici had furnished with an excellent library. From this he was sent to the university
of Padua, where he made great proficiency in philosophy and the Greek language. He afterwards visited
the most celebrated academies of his native country.
At Vercelli, by the persuasion of his intimate friend
Cusano, he interpreted Homer; and at Bologna he
acquired the knowledge of Hebrew from a Jewish
physician, named Isaac. Being selected by the Augustinians as one of their public preachers, he distinguised himself by the solidity and eloquence of his
discourses at Rome, Bologna, Fermo, Pisa, Venice,
Mantua, Bergamo and Montferrat. Having thus
recommended himself to those of his order by his
talents and labours, he was unanimously elected
abbot of Spoleto, and soon after provost of the college

* His father's name was *Stefano Vermigli*, from whom he is ordinarily designated Petrus Martyr *Vermilius*, to distinguish him from
Petrus Martyr *Mediolanensis*, a martyr after whom he was named,
in consequence of a vow of his parents; and also to distinguish him
from a learned countryman and contemporary of his own, Petrus
Martyr *Anglerius*, (of Anghiera,) whose epistles are known to the
learned as throwing great light on the history of the early part of
the sixteenth century.

of St. Pietro *ad aram*, in the city of Naples, a situation of dignity and emolument. This was about the year 1530, and in the thirtieth year of his age. It was at this time, and when he had the prospect of certain and rapid advancement in the Romish church, that a change took place on his religious sentiments, which gave a complete turn to his future life. From his youth, as he himself has told us, he had a decided preference for sacred studies; and having access to the Scriptures in the convent to which he belonged, applied himself to read them with great care, and not altogether without profit to himself and others.* At a subsequent period he fell in with the treatises of Zuingle on True and False Religion, and on Providence, and with some of Bucer's commentaries on Scripture, which left impressions in his mind. These were now confirmed and deepened by the conversation of Valdes, Flaminio, and others, with whom he became acquainted at Naples.†

Martyr excelled as much in judgment and learning, as Ochino did in popular eloquence. To their exertions in diffusing evangelical truth were added those of Mollio, formerly mentioned, who now filled the station of lecturer to the monastery of St. Lorenzo at Naples. While Ochino employed his persuasive eloquence in the pulpit, Martyr and Mollio read lectures, chiefly on Paul's epistles, which were attended by the monks of different convents, by many of the nobility, and by individuals of the episcopal order. The three friends did not fail to meet with opposition from the strenuous adherents of the established religion, who were supported by the authority of the viceroy; but such was the prudence with which they conducted themselves, and the countenance which they received from persons of the first consideration in the city, that they were able to maintain their

* Oratio quam Tiguri primum habuit: Martyris Loc. Commun. p. 744.
† Simleri Oratio de Vita et Obitu Petri Martyris Vermilii, præfix. ad Loc. Commun. Martyris, sig. b. ij. b iij Genev. 1624. This funeral oration was republished by Gerdes, in his *Scrinium Antiquarium*, tom. iii. par. ii.

ground, and for a time to triumph over their adversaries. The favourite doctrine of Ochino was justification by faith in Christ, which, as appears from his printed sermons, he perfectly understood, and explained with much Scriptural simplicity. Purgatory, penances, and papal pardons, fell before the preaching of this doctrine, as Dagon of old before the ark of Jehovah. An Augustinian monk of Trevigio, as much perhaps with the view of recommending himself to his superiors as from any hopes of success, challenged Ochino and his colleagues to a dispute on these points; but he was woisted and put to silence by their superior talents and acquaintance with Scripture. The church of Rome had long relied on the third chapter of the first epistle to the Corinthians,* as one of the main pillars of purgatory; and from this passage the monks were accustomed to draw their most popular arguments in favour of that lucrative doctrine. Martyr did not directly attack the doctrine; but, in the course of his lectures on that epistle, he gave a quite different interpretation of the words, which he confirmed by arguments drawn from the text and context, and by appeals to the writings of the most learned and judicious among the fathers. This view of the passage occasioned great speculation; and the monks, provoked by the favourable reception which it met with, and dreading that the most fertile source of their gain would be dried up, moved heaven and earth against the daring innovator. By the influence of the viceroy, and their own representations, they obtained an order interdicting him from preaching and lecturing. Martyr enjoyed the favour of Gonzago, cardinal of Mantua and protector of his order; and he was well known to cardinals Contarini, Pole, Bembo, and Fregoso, all men of learning, and some of them favourable to ecclesiastical reform. Relying on their patronage, he carried his cause by appeal to Rome, and succeeded in obtaining the removal of the interdict.†

* Ver. 13—15.
† Simler, Vita Martyris, sig. b. iij.

By the blessing of God on the labours of these men, a reformed Church was established in Naples, which included persons of the first rank in the kingdom, both male and female. Among these were Galeazzo Caraccioli, the eldest son of the marquis of Vico; his noble relation, Gianfrancesco de Caserta, by whom he was first induced to attend the discourses of Martyr;* and Bernardino Bonifacio, marquis of Oria, a nobleman equally distinguished by his learning and piety, who after travelling through various countries, settled at last in Nurenberg.†

It would be improper to omit here the name of another Neapolitan nobleman, who acquired a taste for the reformed doctrine in Italy, though he did not profess it until he had left his native country. This was Antonio Caraccioli, the son of the prince of Melphi, and who was usually known by his father's title. Having gone to France, he was made abbot of St. Victor in Paris, and afterwards bishop of Troyes, in Champagne. He had been long acquainted with the writings of the reformers, especially those of Calvin; and on his advancement to the bishoprick, in 1551, began to inveigh with great boldness and eloquence against the abuses of the Church of Rome. Multitudes flocked to his sermons, attracted by curiosity to hear a bishop preach, or by love to the truth; but being summoned to answer for his conduct, he disappointed the hopes of many by making a public recantation in his own cathedral. In 1557, his zeal for the reformed faith was rekindled by an interview which he had with Calvin and Beza, at Geneva, on his return from a visit to Italy.‡ After the conference between the Catholics and Protestants at Poissy, in 1560, at which he was present, he was accompanied to Troyes by his countryman, Peter Martyr, to whom he ex-

---

* Simler, ut supra. Life of Galeas Caraccioli, p. 3—5.

† Vita Philippi Camerarii, per Schelhornium, p 142. Micrelii Syntag p. 313. Fontanini, p 498. Some of his poems are included in *Deliciæ Poetarum Italorum*.

‡ Beze, Hist. des Eglis Reform. de France, tom. i. p 83, 86. Martene et Durand, Collect. Vet. Script. et Monument. tom. i. col. 1615.

pressed his resolution, at all hazards, to avow and abide by the truth, of which he was now thoroughly convinced in his conscience. Accordingly, he met with the Protestants in that city, and having made a profession of his faith, and stated his scruples as to the validity of his episcopal orders, declared his willingness to serve them, provided they gave him a call to the pastoral office; upon which they unanimously made choice of him as their minister.* It is unnecessary to add, that this step led to his degradation by the popish clergy. Subsequently, the reformed bishop gave offence to his new friends, by deserting his Church and attaching himself to the court, but he did not desist altogether from preaching, and persevered in the Protestant religion to his death.†

While the church at Naples was enjoying peace and daily increasing in numbers, it was deprived of Valdes, to whom it chiefly owed its plantation. He died in the year 1540, deeply lamented by many distinguished persons, who owned him as their spiritual father. "I wish we were again at Naples," says Bonfadio, in a letter to Carnesecchi. "But when I consider the matter in another point of view, to what purpose should we go there, now when Valdes is dead? His death truly is a great loss to us and to the world; for Valdes was one of the rarest men in Europe, as the writings left by him on the Epistles of St. Paul, and the Psalms of David abundantly demonstrate.‡ He was, beyond all doubt, a most accomplished man in all his words, actions, and counsels. Life scarcely supported his infirm and spare body;

* Langueti Epist. ep. 63, 64. Martyris Epistolæ, in Loc. Commun. p. 582. Thuani Hist. ad an. 1561

† Beze, vol. ii. p 148, 246. Prosper Marchand, art. *Caraccioli*. Colomies says, that he wrote a defence of the count de Montgomery, who mortally wounded Henry II. (Colomesiana, edit. De Maiseaux, tom. i. p. 585.)

‡ These works must have been then in manuscript. His commentary on the Romans was published in Spanish, at Venice in 1556, and his commentary on the Psalms at the same place in the following year. His countryman and friend, Juan Perez, the translator of the New Testament into Spanish, prefixed an epistle dedicatory to each. (Baumgarten, apud Gerdes. Ital. Ref. p. 344.)

but his nobler part and pure intellect, as if it had been placed without the body, was wholly occupied with the contemplation of truth and divine things. I condole with Marco Antonio, (Flaminio,) for, above all others, he greatly loved and admired him."* The fervent piety of Valdes, and the unspotted purity of his life, are universally acknowledged. The charge of heterodoxy of sentiment, brought against him after his death, rests chiefly on the very questionable ground that some of those who were intimate with him ultimately inclined to the sect denominated Socinian; for it cannot be pleaded that their tenets are to be found in his writings, which, it must be allowed, contain some other opinions which are either untenable or unguardedly expressed.†

The doctrines of the gospel were most eagerly received in the capital, but they spread also through the kingdom of Naples, and even reached *Sicily*, which was at that period an appendage to the crown of Spain. Occupied in defending the coasts against the Turk, the viceroys who governed that island under Charles V. were not involved in the intrigues of Italian policy; and those who fled from persecution on the continent, found protection under their compara-

---

* Lettere volgari di diversi nobilissimi huomini, p. 33 Ald. 1543.

† Sandius (Bibl. Antitrin. p. 2.) claims him as an anti-trinitarian; but that writer puts in the same claim to Wolfgang, Fabricius Capito, and others, who are known to have entertained opposite sentiments. (Schelhorni Amœni. Liter. tom. xiv p. 386. Amœnit. Eccles. tom. ii. p. 51—53) If Ochino ever embraced that creed, (which some have denied,) it was unquestionably long after he left Italy. (Observ. Sel. Hal. tom. iv. obs. 20. tom. v. obs. 1, 2.) Beza, while he expresses his dissatisfaction with some things in the *Divine Considerations* of Valdes, declares that he meant nothing disrespectful to the author, and does not insinuate, in the slightest degree, that he erred as to the doctrine of the Trinity. (Epistolæ, p. 43, 276.) Some remarks on the peculiar opinions of Valdes will be found elsewhere. (Hist. of the Progr. and Suppress. of the Reformation in Spain. The following is the title of the *Considerations* in the Italian, which appears to have been the original edition, and published by Celio Secundo Curio:—" Le Cento e Dieci Considerationi de Signore Valdesso, nelle quale si ragiona cose più utile, più necessarie, et più perfette della Christiana Religione. In Basilea, 1550." 8vo. In the French translation of the *Considerationi* the author is called *Jan de Val d'Esso.*

tively mild administration. Benedetti, surnamed Locarno, from the place of his birth, a minister of great sanctity, having gained the favour of the viceroy, preached the truth under his patronage to crowded audiences in Palermo, and other parts of that island.* The seeds of his doctrine which afterwards sprung up, gave ample employment to the inquisitors; and, for many years, persons charged with the Lutheran heresy were produced in the public and private *autos de fe* celebrated in Sicily.†

LUCCA, the capital of a small but flourishing republic, lying on the east coast of the gulf of Genoa, had the honour to reckon among its inhabitants a greater number of converts to the reformed faith than perhaps any other city in Italy. This was chiefly owing to the labours of Martyr. Finding, after a trial of several years, that the climate of Naples was injurious to his health, he left it with the consent of his superiors, and was chosen visitor general of the Augustinians in Italy. The rigid inspection which he exerted over them, and the reform which, with the concurrence of cardinal Gonzaga, he sought to introduce into their monasteries, created alarm among the monks, who contrived to rid themselves of their troublesome visitor, by getting him appointed prior of St. Fridiano at Lucca, an honourable situation, which invested him with episcopal powers. His adversaries hoped that he would be unacceptable in his new situation, as a Florentine, on account of an ancient grudge between the Lucchese and the inhabitants of Florence; but with such prudence did he conduct himself, that he was as much esteemed as if he had been a native of Lucca. One object which engaged the particular attention of Martyr was the education of the novices in the priory, whose minds he was

* Jo. de Muralto, Oratio de Persecutione Locarnensi, sec. iii et append. no. ii. iii. Tempe Helvetica, tom. iv. p. 142, 184, 186. Two viceroys of Naples, Don Pedro Cordova, and the marquis de Terranova, one of the grandees of Spain, were forced to do penance for interfering with the Inquisition. (Llorente, ii. 82—88.)

† Llorente, ii. 123, 129.

anxious to imbue with the love of sacred literature. For this purpose he established a private college or seminary, to which he drew such teachers as he knew to be both learned men and lovers of divine truth.* Paolo Lacisio, a native of Verona, taught the Latin language; Celso Martinengho, of the noble family of the counts of that name, taught Greek; and Emanuel Tremellio, of Ferrara, who afterwards distinguished himself as an oriental scholar, gave instructions in Hebrew. Martyr himself applied the literary knowledge which the young men imbibed from these sources to the elucidation of the Scriptures, by reading lectures to them on the New Testament and the Psalter, which were attended by all the learned men and many of the patricians of Lucca. He also preached publicly to the people, confining himself to the gospels during Advent and Lent, according to the usual custom of the monks, but taking his subjects from the epistles during the rest of the year. By means of these labours a separate church was formed in that city, of which Martyr became pastor; and many, including persons of the first respectability in the place, gave the most decided proofs of genuine piety and ardent attachment to the reformed faith.†

While these things were going on, pope Paul III. paid a visit to Lucca, accompanied by the emperor, who was at that time in Italy. It was feared that the enemies of Martyr would embrace that opportunity to inform against him, and that his life would be brought into danger; but he was not molested, probably because it was deemed impolitic and premature to attack a teacher whose reputation and authority were then so high among the inhabitants. About the same time, Martyr received a visit from cardinal Contarini, as he passed through Lucca, on his return from Germany, where he had been in the character

* Celio Secundo Curio resided for some time at Lucca, where he taught in the university, having been recommended to the senators by the duchess of Ferrara. (Stupani Oratio, p. 343, 344.)
† Simler, ut supra, sig. b iij.

of papal legate. They had a confidential conversation on the state of the church, and on the sentiments of the German reformers.*

The PISANO received the knowledge of evangelical doctrine from Lucca, and was supplied, for some time, by preachers from that place; but, in the year 1543, the Protestants in the city of Pisa formed themselves into a church, and had the sacrament of the Lord's supper celebrated among them.†

The SIENNESE contained many converts to the reformed doctrine. Ochino, in the course of his preaching tours, frequently visited Sienna, which was his native place. But the person to whom the inhabitants of this city were most indebted for their illumination was Aonio Paleario, a native of Veroli in Campagna di Roma, who was on a footing of intimacy with the most learned men in Italy. He was first a tutor in the house of Belanti; and, about the year 1534, was nominated public teacher of Greek and Latin by the senate of Sienna,‡ where he afterwards read lectures on Philosophy and Belles Lettres. Having studied the Scriptures, and read the writings of the German reformers, his lectures on moral philosophy were distinguished from those of his colleagues by a liberal tone of thinking. This was not more gratifying to the students than it was offensive to those who adhered obstinately to the old ideas.§ Cardinal Sadolet, in the name of his friends, set before him the danger of his giving way to novelties, and advised him, in consideration of the times, to confine himself to the safer task of clothing the peripatetic ideas in elegant language.‖ This prudential advice was not altogether congenial to the open mind of Paleario, and the devotion which he felt for truth. The freedom with which he censured vain pretenders to learning and religion irritated a class of men who scruple at no means to oppress and ruin an adversary, and who eagerly

* Simler, ut supra, sig b iiij. † Ibid.
‡ Galluzzi, Istoria del Granducato di Toscano, tom ii. p. 203.
§ Palearii Opera, p. 527. edit. Halbaueri, Jenæ, 1728.
‖ Ibid. p. 536, 559.

seized the opportunity to fasten on him the charge of heresy.* His private conduct was watched; and expressions which had dropped from him in the unsuspecting confidence of private conversation were circulated to his prejudice. He had laughed at a rich priest who was seen every morning kneeling at the shrine of a saint, but refused to pay his debts.† "Cotta asserts," says he, in one of his letters, " that, if I am allowed to live, there will not be a vestige of religion left in the city. Why? Because, being asked one day what was the first ground on which men should rest their salvation, I replied, Christ; being asked what was the second, I replied, Christ; and being asked what was the third, I still replied, Christ."‡ But Paleario gave the greatest offence by a book which he wrote on the Benefit of the death of Christ,§ of which he gives the following account in his defence of himself, pronounced before the senate of Sienna:—" There are some persons so sour, so morose, so censorious, as to be displeased when we give the highest praise to the author and God of our salvation, Christ, the king of all nations and people. When I wrote a treatise this very year, in the Tuscan language, to show what great benefits accrue to mankind from his death, this was made the ground of a

* Palearii Opera, p. 88, 99, 523—531, 538—543.
† Ibid p. 545.   ‡ Ibid. p. 519.
§ This book was printed in 1543 in Italian, under the title *Il Beneficio di Christo*, and was afterwards translated into Spanish and French. (Schelh. Amœnit. Eccl. tom. i p. 155—159. Ergotzlichkeiten, vol. v. p 27.) An account of its contents is given in Riederer, Nachrichten zur kirchen-gelehrten, tom iv. p. 121, 235—241. Vergerio says of it, "Many are of opinion that there is scarcely a book of this age, or at least in the Italian language, so sweet, so pious, so simple, so well fitted to instruct the ignorant and weak, especially in the doctrine of justification. I will say more—Reginald Pole, the British cardinal, and the intimate friend of Morone, was esteemed the author of that book, or partly so; at least, it is known that he, with Flaminio, Priuli, and his other friends, defended and circulated it." (Amœnit. Eccl ut supra, p.158) Laderchio asserts that Flaminio wrote an apology for the *Beneficio*. (Annal. tom. 22. f 326) That it was translated into English, and read in Scotland, appears from the following notice:—" Item, foure Benefite of Christ, the piece 2 sh." (Testament of Thomas Bassinden, printer in Edinburgh, who deceased 18 October 1577.)

criminal accusation against me! Is it possible to utter or conceive any thing more shameful? I had said, that since he in whom the divinity resided, has poured out his life's blood so lovingly for our salvation, we ought not to doubt of the good will of heaven, but might promise ourselves the greatest tranquillity and peace. I had affirmed, agreeably to the most unquestionable monuments of antiquity, that those who turn with their souls to Christ crucified, commit themselves to him by faith, acquiesce in the promises, and cleave with assured confidence to him who cannot deceive, are delivered from all evil, and enjoy a plenary pardon of their sins. These things appeared so grievous, so detestable, so execrable to the twelve—I cannot call them men, but—inhuman beasts, that they judged the author worthy of being committed to the flames. If I must undergo this punishment for the foresaid testimony, (for I deem it a testimony rather than a libel,) then, senators, nothing more happy can befall me. In such a time as this I do not think a Christian ought to die in his bed. I am not only willing to be accused, to be dragged to prison, to be scourged, to be hung up by the neck, to be sewed up in a sack, to be exposed to wild beasts—let me be roasted before a fire, provided only the truth be brought to light by such a death."* Addressing his accuser, he says— " You accuse me of being of the same sentiments with the Germans. Good God, what an illiberal charge! Do you mean to bind up all the Germans in one bundle? Are they all bad? Though you should restrict your charge to their divines, still it is ridiculous. Are there not many excellent divines in Germany? But your accusation, though full of trifling, has nevertheless a sting, which, as proceeding from you, is charged with poison. By Germans, you mean Ecolampade, Erasmus, Melanchthon, Luther, Pomeran, Bucer, and others who have incurred suspicion. But surely there is not a divine among us so stupid as not to perceive and confess, that the writings of these men contain many things worthy of the highest praise—many

* Palearii Opera, p. 101, 102.

things gravely, accurately, and faithfully stated, repeated from the early fathers, who have left us the institutes of salvation, and also from the later commentaries of the Greeks and Latins, who, though not to be compared with those pillars, are still of use for interpretation. 'But do not you approve of all that the Germans have done?" This, Otho, is like the rest of your questions; yet I will answer it. I approve of some things; of others I disapprove. To pass by many things, I praise the Germans, and consider them as entitled to public thanks, for their exertions in restoring the purity of the Latin language, which, till of late, was oppressed by barbarism and poverty of speech. Formerly sacred studies lay neglected in the cells of idlers, who retired from the world to enjoy their repose, (and yet, amidst their snoring, they contrived to hear what we said in cities and villages;) now these studies are, in a great measure, revived in Germany. Chaldaic, Greek, and Latin libraries, are erected; books are beautifully printed; and honourable stipends are assigned to divines. What can be more illustrious than these things? what more glorious? what more deserving of perpetual praise? Afterwards arose civil discords, intestine wars, commotions, seditions, and other evils, which, for the sake of charity and brotherly love among Christians, I deplore. Who does not praise the former? who is not displeased with the latter?"*

The eloquent defence of Paleario, in which boldness and candour were tempered by prudence and address, triumphed over the violence and intrigues of his adversaries. He was, however, obliged soon after to quit Sienna; but though he changed the place of his residence, he did not escape from the odium which he had incurred; and we shall afterwards find him enduring that martyrdom which he early anticipated, and for which it appears to have been his object all along to prepare his thoughts. Some idea may be formed of the extent to which the reformed opinions had spread in Sienna, from the number of individuals

* Palearii Opera, p. 92—95.

belonging to it, who, at a subsequent period, submitted to a vountary exile on their account, among whom were Lanctantio Ragnoni, Mino Celso,* and the Soccini, who became celebrated by giving their name to a new sect.

MANTUA, which, in the sixteenth century, gave birth to several persons of distinguished talents, did not shut out the light of the Reformation. In the capital, and throughout the duchy, there were many who sighed under the tyranny which oppressed the human mind, and made a generous effort to break asunder its chains. To this they were not a little encouraged by their countryman, Gianbattista Folengo, a liberal and pious Benedictine, who was anxious to heal the schism which afflicted the church, by introducing an extensive reform among both secular and regular clergy.† Cardinal Gonzaga, bishop of Mantua, evinced the same disposition, and extended his protection to those who swerved from the established faith, as far as was consistent with the station which he held in the church. On this ground he appears to have given offence at Rome; and on the 7th of February, 1545, Paul III. addressed a brief to him, with the view of stimulating his slumbering zeal. His holiness states, that he had heard of certain illiterate clergymen and artizans, in the city of Mantua, having, to the ruin of their own souls and the great scandal of others, rashly dared to dispute and even to doubt of matters belonging to the catholic doctrine, the articles of belief, and the rites of the holy Roman Church; he therefore exhorts the bishop to persevere in the pious ' vigilance which he had begun to show, and by himself or his deputies to proceed against all suspected of heresy, including the clergy, secular and regular, of every order, in the city of Mantua and throughout the whole diocese; to inquire if they have read or possess any heretical books, or if they have taught any opinion condemned by the church; to take the deposition of

---

* Giannone, Hist de Naples, tom. iv. p. 149. Schelhorn, Diss. de Mino Celso, p. 18, 61.
† Thuani Hist. ad an. 1559.

witnesses, seize the persons of the accused or suspected, examine them by the torture, and, having brought the processes as far as the definitive sentence, to transmit the whole in an authentic shape to Rome for judgment.* The reigning duke for some time screened his subjects from the effects of this persecuting edict, and incurred, as we shall afterwards see, the indignation of the pope by this humane interference.

Locarno is a city of Italy, and the capital of a province or bailiwick of that name, situate on the lake Maggiore, in the southern confines of the Alps. It was one of four provinces which Maximilian Sforza, duke of Milan, in the year 1513, gave to the Swiss cantons as a remuneration for the military aids which they had furnished him; and was governed by a prefect, whom the cantons sent by turns every two years. Though the territory was small, its inhabitants were possessed of considerable wealth, derived from the riches of the country in their neighbourhood, and from their being carriers in the trade which was maintained between Italy and Switzerland. So early as the year 1526, the reformed opinions were introduced into it by Baldassare Fontana, whom we have already had occasion to mention.† The number of converts was for some time small. "There are but three of us here," says that zealous and devoted servant of Christ, in a letter to Zuingle, "who have enlisted and confederated in the cause of propagating the truth. But Midian was not vanquished by the multitudes of brave men who flocked to the standard of Gideon, but by a few selected for that purpose by God. Who knows but he may kindle a great fire out of this inconsiderable smoke? It is our duty to sow and plant: the Lord must give the increase."‡ Twenty years elapsed before the fruit of the prayers and labours of these good men sprung up; and it is not improbable that, before this happened, they had all gone to receive their reward in a better world. In the year

---

* Raynaldi Annales, ad an. 1545. † See before, p. 54.
‡ Jo. de Muralto, Oratio de Persecutione Locarnensium. in Tempe Helvetica, tom. iv. p. 141.

1546, Benedetto Locarno returned to his native place, after he had been employed in preaching the gospel in various parts of Italy, and in the island of Sicily. His exertions to enlighten the minds of his townsmen were zealously seconded by Giovanni Beccaria, commonly called the apostle of Locarno, a man of excellent character and good talents, who, by reading the Scriptures without the aid of a teacher or any human writings, had discovered the principal errors and corruptions of the Church of Rome. To these were soon added four individuals of great respectability, and animated by the true spirit of confessors—Varnerio Castiglione, who spared neither time nor labour in promoting the truth; Ludovico Runcho, a citizen; Taddeo de Dunis, a physician, who, as well as Runcho, was a young man of genius and undaunted resolution; and Martino de Muralto, a doctor of laws, and a person of noble birth, who had great influence in the bailiwick. In the course of four years the Protestants of Locarno had increased to a numerous church, which was regularly organized, and had the sacraments administered in it by a pastor whom they called from the church of Chiavenna.* The daily accessions which it received to its numbers excited the envy and chagrin of the clergy, who were warmly supported by the prefect appointed, in the year 1549, by the popish canton of Underwald. A priest belonging to the neighbouring bailiwick of Lugano, who was employed to declaim from the pulpit against the Locarnese Protestants, loaded them with calumnies of all kinds, and challenged their preacher to a public dispute on the articles controverted between the two churches. He was completely silenced on the day of trial; and, to revenge his defeat, the prefect ordered Beccaria into prison. This step excited such indignation in the city, that the prisoner was immediately enlarged, and the enemies of the Protestants were obliged to wait for a more favourable opportunity of attack.†

ISTRIA, a peninsular district on the Gulf of Venice,

---
* Muralto, Oratio, ut supra, p. 142—144; conf. p. 150.
† Ibid. p. 144—148 ; conf. p. 150.

belonged to the Venetian republic. It is mentioned separately, and in this place, because it was the last spot which the light of the reformation visited in its progress through Italy, and because it gave birth to two distinguished Protestants, both of whom were bishops of the Roman Catholic Church, and one of them a papal legate. Pierpaolo Vergerio was a native of Capo d'Istria, and sprung from a family which had shared in the literary reputation of the fifteenth century. We have already had occasion to notice him as a young man of promising talents and excellent character, who felt a desire to visit Wittenberg for the purpose of finishing his studies.* Having devoted himself to the study of law, he obtained the degree of doctor from the university of Padua, where he acted for some time as a professor, and as vicar to the Podesta, and afterwards distinguished himself as an advocate at Venice.† Such was his fame for eloquence and address, that pope Clement VII. sent him into Germany as legate to Ferdinand, king of the Romans, at whose court he remained for some years, advancing the interests of the court of Rome, and opposing the progress of Lutheranism.‡ On the death of Clement, his successor Paul III. recalled Vergerio, but, after receiving an account of his embassy, sent him back to Germany, where he treated with the German princes, and had more than one interview with Luther, respecting the proposed general council. On his return to Italy in 1536, he was advanced to the episcopal dignity, being made first bishop of Modrusium in Croatia, a see in the patronage of Ferdinand, and afterwards of Capo d'Istria, his native place. Having gone into France, he appeared, in 1541, at the conference of Worms, in the name of his Christian Majesty, but, as was believed, with secret instructions from the pope.§ It is certain, that he

* See before, p. 50.
† Tiraboschi, Storia, vii. 375, 376.
‡ Sleidan (lib. vii. tom i. p. 395) represents Vergerio as sent to Ferdinand in 1530; Tiraboschi says it was in 1532. (Tom. vii p. 377.)
§ This is asserted by Father Paul, (lib. i.) and Sleidan, (lib. xiii. tom. ii. 204,) but contradicted by Pallavicini, (lib. iv. cap. 12,) and

drew up at this time an oration on the unity of the Church, in opposition to the idea of a national council, which was desired by the Protestants.

His mind appears, however, to have received a bias in favour of the Reformation during his residence in Germany. Protestant writers assert, that the pope intended to confer a cardinal's hat on him at his return, but was diverted from this by the suspicions raised against his soundness in the faith. This is denied by Pallavicini and Tiraboschi; but they allow that his Holiness was informed, that Vergerio had cultivated undue familiarity with the German heretics, and spoken favourably of them; and that, on this account, means were used to oblige him to return to Italy, and to convince him that he had incurred the displeasure of his superiors. This is confirmed by the letters of cardinal Bembo. In a letter to his nephew, who appears to have held a high official situation in the Istrian government, the cardinal signifies that the bishop of Capo d'Istria had urged him "to intercede for some of his relations, who had been unjustly thrown into prison." This was on the 24th of September 1541; and on the 1st of February following, Bembo expresses his satisfaction that his request had not been granted, adding, "I hear some things of that bishop which, if true, are very bad—that he not only has portraits of Lutherans in his house, but also that, in the causes which come before him, he is eager to favour, in every way, the one party, whether right or wrong, and to bear down the other."*

It was no easy matter for a person in Vergerio's circumstances to relinquish the honourable situation which he held, and to sacrifice the flattering prospects of advancement which he had long cherished. Besides, his convictions of the truth were still imperfect and unsteady. When he first retired from the bustle of public life to his diocese, he set about finishing a work which he had begun, "against the apostates of

Tiraboschi (Ut sup. p 380) Courayer supports the former opinion, in his notes on Father Paul's History.

* Bembo, Opere, tom. ix. p. 288, 294.

Germany," by the publication of which he expected to remove the suspicions which he had incurred; but, in the course of writing, and of examining the books of the Reformers, his mind was so struck with the force of the objections which it behoved him to answer, that he threw away the pen, and abandoned the work in despair. He now sought relief by unbosoming himself to his brother, Gianbattista, bishop of Pola in the same district. The latter was thrown into great distress by this communication; but, upon conference with his brother, and hearing the reasons of his change of views, especially on the head of justification, he became himself a convert to the Protestant doctrine. The two brothers now concerted a plan for enlightening their dioceses, by conveying instruction to the people on the leading articles of the gospel, and withdrawing their minds from those ceremonial services and bodily exercises in which they were disposed to place the whole of religion. This they were able to effect in a good degree by means of their own personal labours, and the assistance of some persons who had previously received the knowledge of the truth; so that, before the year 1546, a great part of the inhabitants of that district had embraced the reformed faith and made considerable advances in the knowledge of Christian doctrine.*

ANCONA deserves to be mentioned here, if it were for no other reason than its having given birth to Matteo Gentilis, and his two accomplished sons, Alberic and Scipio. The father left his native country for the sake of the reformed doctrine, and settled in Carniola, where he followed his profession as a physician. The two sons became eminent civilians. Alberic, the eldest, came to England, and was made professor of laws at Oxford.† His brother held the same situation at Altorf, and, in addition to his legal

* Sleidan, lib. xxi. tom. iii. p. 150—152. Ughelli Italia Sacra, tom. v. p. 341, 391.

† Wood's Athenæ Oxon. vol. ii. p. 90, edit Bliss. Albericus Gentilis, doctor of the civil law of the university of Perugia, was incorporated at Oxford, March 6, 1580. (Fasti Oxon. 217.)

knowledge, was distinguished for his poetical talents and skill in biblical criticism.*

Besides the places which have been specified, adherents to the reformed opinions were to be found at this time in Genoa, in Verona, in Cittadella, in Cremona, in Brescia, in Civita di Friuli, in various parts of the Roman territories, and in Rome itself.†

CHAPTER IV.

MISCELLANEOUS FACTS RESPECTING THE STATE OF THE REFORMED OPINIONS IN ITALY.

THERE are a number of facts which could not well be interwoven with the preceding narrative, but which are of too great importance in themselves, and as throwing light on the progress of the Reformation in Italy, to be omitted in this history. I shall therefore collect them in this chapter, under the following heads:—The disputes which unhappily arose among the Italian Protestants; the illustrious females who embraced the new opinions; and the learned men who favoured the views of the Reformers, though they declined embarking in their cause.

I. It is well known that a controversy arose at an early period between the two principal Reformers respecting the presence of Christ in the sacrament of the supper; Luther insisting that the words of institution ought to be understood in a literal sense, while Zuingle interpreted them figuratively. At a conference held at Marburg in the year 1529, and procured chiefly by the influence of Philip, landgrave of Hesse,

* Scipionis Gentilis in Epist. ad Philem. Comment. Norim. 1574. The charge of Photinianism brought against him by Crenius has been wiped off by Zeltner. (Hist. Crypto-Sociniani Altorfini, tom. i. p. 71, 357.)
† Gerdesii Specimen Italiæ Reformatæ. Martyris Epistolæ. Zanchii Epistolæ. Melanchthonis Epistolæ.

the two parties, after ascertaining that their sentiments harmonized on all other points agreed to bear with each other, and to cultivate mutual peace and good will, notwithstanding their different views of this single article. But the controversy broke out afresh, chiefly through the ill offices of some forward and injudicious friends of Luther, and being inflamed by publications on both sides, laid the foundation of a lasting division between the churches of Switzerland and Upper Germany. After the death of Zuingle, his opinions were vigorously defended by Ecolampade, Bullinger, and Calvin.

The Protestants of Italy had been equally indebted to the two Reformers for the knowledge which they had obtained of the truth. If the circumstance of the works of Zuingle having been chiefly composed in Latin gave an advantage to his opinions, by contributing to their more extensive circulation, this was counterbalanced by the celebrity of Luther's name, and the numbers of his countrymen who frequented Italy and carried his opinions along with them. It would appear, however, that the Italian Protestants were generally favourable to the views of the Swiss Reformer. This may be concluded from their writings, and from the fact, that by far the greater part of those who were obliged to leave their native country sought an asylum in the Protestant cantons of Switzerland.*

That this dispute was warmly agitated among the Protestants of Modena, Bologna, and other parts of Italy in 1541, we learn from three letters addressed to them in the course of that year by Bucer. This Reformer had all along been a strenuous friend to peace and concord between the contending parties. It seems to have been his sincere belief that there was

* Vergerio had more connection with the Germans than most of his countrymen; and yet we find Paulus Eberus, a professor of Wittenberg, writing of him as follows, in a letter dated June 21, 1556: —" Jam cœnabimus cum Petro Paulo Vergerio, qui fuit Justinopolitanus episcopus, et nunc vocatus a duce Alberto proficiscetur in Borussiam. Eum audio non dissimulanter probare sententiam Calvini." (Scrinium Antiquarium, tom. iv. p. 713.)

no real difference of sentiment between them; and although he evidently inclined to the explications given by the Swiss divines, yet in his efforts for pacification, he alternately employed the phrases of both sides; a method which threw an obscurity over his writings, and is not the best calculated for promoting conciliation between men of enlightened understanding. However, the advice which he imparted on the present occasion was in the main sound, and does great honour to his heart. In a letter "to certain friends of the truth in Italy,"* he says—"I hear, my good brethren, that Satan, who has afflicted us long, and with great defection in religion, has begun to disturb you also; for it is said, that a dispute has arisen among you respecting the eucharist. This grieves me exceedingly. For, what else can you expect from this controversy than what we have experienced, to the great damage of our churches? Dear brethren, let us rather seek to embrace Christ in the eucharist, that so we may live in him and he in us. The bread and the wine are symbols, not things of such great mystery. This all confess; but God forbid that, on the other hand, any should imagine that empty symbols are exhibited in the supper of the Lord; for the bread which we break is the participation of the Lord's body, and not bread only. Avoid strifes of words: support the weak. While our confidence is placed in Christ, all is well; all men cannot at once see the same things. Studiously cultivate concord: the God upon whom we call is not the God of division. Thus live, and advance, and overcome every evil."† In another letter to the same persons,‡ after giving his views of the subject, this amiable man adds—"This is my opinion on the whole matter in dispute. If I have not explained myself with sufficient perspicuity, the reason is, that from constitution, and owing to the defects of my education, I am apt to be obscure and perplexed, and also

* "Augusti 17, 1541." † Buceri Scripta Anglicana, p. 686.
‡ "Anno 1541. 23. Decemb."

that I write in haste, and without the helps necessary for discussing such a subject; which, indeed, appears too evidently in all my writings. I desire to avoid giving offence, whenever it is lawful; yet, were I able, I would wish to explain as clearly as possible those things which it concerns the church to know. I exhort you, beloved brethren, to avoid in these questions, with all possible care, a spirit of curiosity and contention. Let those who are strong in knowledge bear with the weak; and let the weak pay due deference to the strong. We ought to know nothing but Christ and him crucified. All our exertions ought to be directed to this, that he may be formed more fully in us, and portrayed in a more lively manner in the whole of our conduct. You ascribe too much to me; I know my own weakness. Express your love by praying to God for me, rather than by praising me."*
In a letter to the Protestants at Bologna and Modena, he says—" The too sharp contention which has taken place among us in Germany respecting this sacrament was a work of the flesh. We thought, that Luther fixed Christ glorified to earthly signs by his too strong language; he and his friends, on the contrary, thought that we acknowledged and gave nothing in the supper but bread and wine. At length, however, the Lord has brought us to a happy agreement, both in words and as to the matter; which is to this purpose, that both parties should speak honourably of these mysteries, so that the one should not appear to ascribe to Christ what is unworthy of him, nor the other to celebrate the Lord's supper without the Lord. I beseech you, keep this agreement along with us; and if, in any instance, it has been injured, restore it, imitating our conduct so far as it is according to Christ, and not wherein it is according to the flesh. This should be the only dispute and contest among saints."†

But the controversy was carried on with the greatest heat within the Venetian territories, where the Pro-

---

* Buceri Scripta Anglicana, p. 690.
† Ibid. p. 689.

testants had all along kept up a close correspondence with the divines of Wittenberg, and where there were individuals not disposed to yield implicit submission to the authority of any name, however high and venerated. We learn this fact from the letter which the excellent Baldassare Altieri addressed, in the name of his brethren, to Luther, and from which I have already made a quotation.* The following extract contains some additional particulars as to the state of the reformed cause in that quarter of Italy, at the period when it was written:†—" There is another affair which daily threatens our churches with impending ruin. That question concerning the Lord's Supper, which arose first in Germany, and subsequently has been introduced among us, alas! what disturbances has it excited! what dissensions has it produced! what offences to the weak, what losses to the Church of God, has it caused! what impediments has it thrown in the way of the propagation of the glory of Christ! For if in Germany, where there are so many churches rightly constituted, and so many holy men, fervent in spirit and eminent for every kind of learning, its poison has prevailed so far as to form two parties through mutual altercation, (for although it behoved such things necessarily to happen, yet are they to be guarded against as dire, dreadful, and abominable before God,) how much more is the prevalence and daily increase of this plague to be dreaded with us? With us, where there are no public assemblies, but where every one is a church to himself, acting according to his own will and pleasure; the weak exalting themselves above the strong beyond the measure of their faith, and the strong not receiving the weak and bearing with them in the spirit of meekness and gentleness, mindful that they are themselves encompassed with the same infirmity and sin, instead of which they proudly neglect and despise them. All would be teachers, instead of disciples, although they know nothing, and are not led by the Spirit of God. There are many teachers who do not understand what

* See before, p. 109. † " Kal. Dec. 6, 1542."

they say or whereof they affirm; many evangelists who would do better to learn than to teach others; many apostles who are not truly sent. All things here are conducted in a disorderly and indecorous manner." Altieri goes on to state, that Bucer had written them that the two parties in Germany had come to a happy agreement, of which Melanchthon was about to publish a defence; and had exhorted the friends of truth in Italy to lay aside their contentions, and with one mouth to glorify him who is the God of peace and not of confusion. This intelligence, Altieri says, had filled them with joy, and on a sudden all was harmony and peace among them. But of late again, at the instigation of the great adversary of the truth, certain foolish and unreasonable men had embroiled matters, and raised new disputes and animosities. He therefore begs Luther to write to them; for, though they were not ignorant of his opinion on the disputed question, (to which they meant to adhere, as most consonant to the words of Christ and Paul,) and although they relied on and rejoiced at the information of Bucer, yet they were anxious to be certified of the mode of conciliation from Luther himself, to whose opinion they paid a higher deference than to that of any other person, and to receive from him the above-mentioned defence, or any other books lately published relating to that subject or to the general cause. The letter contains the warmest professions of regard for the Reformer, and of solicitude for the success of the Reformation in Germany; "for," says the writer, "whatever befalls you, whether prosperous or adverse, we consider as befalling ourselves, both because we have the same spirit of faith, and also because on the issue of your affairs depends our establishment or overthrow. Be mindful of us, most indulgent Luther, not only before God in your fervent prayers, that we may be filled with the knowledge of him through the Spirit of Christ, but also by the frequency of your learned, pleasant, and fruitful writings and letters; that so those whom you have begotten by the word of truth may the sooner grow up to the stature of a perfect man in Christ. We labour here under a great and painful scarcity of the word of God, not so much owing to the cruelty and severity of the adherents of antichrist, as to the almost incredible wickedness and avarice of the booksellers, who, after bringing your writings here, conceal them with the view of raising the price to an exorbitant rate, to the great loss of the whole church. The brethren, who are numerous here, salute you with the kiss of peace."*

Luther had it in his power to do much at this time for the advancement of the evangelical cause in Italy. The flames of persecution were just ready to burst upon its friends, while they were unhappily become a prey to intestine dissensions. It appears that the greater part of the Protestants in the Venetian states were favourable to the opinion of the German Reformer as to the eucharist; but it is also evident, that they, or at least the leading men among them, were inclined to moderation, and willing to live in harmony with such of their brethren as thought in a different manner from themselves on the controverted article, and to wait till God, who had wonderfully brought them to the knowledge of many great truths of which they had been profoundly ignorant, should "reveal this also to them." Feeling the highest veneration for the character of Luther, they were disposed to pay a deference almost implicit to his advice, and a single word from him would either allay or inflame the dissension which had arisen. Unhappily he adopted that method which naturally produced the last of these effects. In his answer to the letter from the Venetian Protestants, he not only dissipated the pleasing delusion which they were under as to a reconciliation having been effected, but inveighed, in the most bitter terms, against the sacramentarians and fanatics, as he abusively denominated the Swiss divines; and asserted that "the popish tenet of transubstantiation was more tolerable than that of Zuingle."† Nor was

---

* Seckendorf, lib. iii. p. 402.

† Hospiniani Hist. Sacrament part. ii. p. 184. The letter is published in Hummelii Neue Bibliotheck von seltenen Buchern, tom. i. p. 239—246 Nurnb. 1775.

he a whit more moderate in another letter written by
him in the course of the following year, in which he
stimulated the Italians to write against the opinions
of Zuingle and Ecolampade, whom he did not scruple
to stigmatize as "poisonous teachers" and "false prophets," who "did not dispute under the influence of
error, but opposed the truth knowingly, at the instigation of Satan."* In addition to this, he caused
some of his controversial writings against the Zuinglians to be translated and sent into Italy.

Alas! what is man! What are great men, those
who would be thought, or are represented by their
fond admirers, to be gods! Lighter than vanity—a
lie. Willingly would I have passed over this portion
of history, and spared the memory of a man who has
deserved so much of the world, and whose character,
notwithstanding all the faults which attach to it, will
never cease to be contemplated with admiration and
gratitude. But the truth must be told. The violence
with which Luther acted in the dispute that arose
between him and his brethren respecting the sacrament is too well known; but never did the character
of the Reformer sink so much into that of the leader of
a party, as it did on the present occasion. Some excuse may be found for the manner in which he treated
those who opposed his favourite dogma in Germany,
and even in Switzerland; but one is utterly at a loss
to conceive the shadow of an apology for his conduct
in reference to the Italians. Surely he ought to have
considered that the whole cause of evangelical religion was at stake among them, that they were few
in number and rude in knowledge, that there were
many things which they were not yet able to bear,
that they were as sheep in the midst of wolves, and
that the only tendency of his advice was to set them
by the ears, to divide, and scatter, and drive them into
the mouths of the wild beasts which stood ready to devour them. This was foreseen by the amiable and
pacific Melanchthon, who had always written in a
very different strain to his correspondents in Italy,

* Luther's Sammtliche Schriften, tom. xvii. p. 2632. edit. Walch.

and who deplored this rash step of his colleague; although the mildness and timidity of his disposition prevented him on this, as on some other occasions, from adopting those decisive measures which might have counteracted in a great degree its baneful effects.*

But another controversy had arisen among the Italian Protestants, bearing on points of vital importance to Christianity, and calculated, if it had become general, to inflict a deeper injury on the interests of religion than the dispute to which I have just adverted. This related primarily to the doctrine of the Trinity, and by consequence to the person and atonement of Christ; and it extended to most of the articles which are peculiar and distinguishing in the Christian faith.

It has been supposed by some writers, that persons attached to the opinions of Arius had remained concealed in Italy down to the sixteenth century; and that the fame of the Reformation begun in Germany drew them from their lurking places.† Some have even asserted that the mind of the well-known Michael Servetus was first tainted by intercourse with Italian heretics ‡ But there is no good evidence for either of these opinions. It is much more probable that the Spaniard acquired his peculiar views, so far as they were not the offspring of his own invention, in Germany, subsequently to the visit which he paid to Italy at a very early period of his life. Before his name had been heard of, and within a few years after the commencement of the Reformation, certain confused notions, sometimes approaching to the ancient tenets of Arius and Pelagius, and at other times assuming a form which bore a nearer resemblance to those afterwards called Socinian, were afloat in Germany, and vented by some of those who went by the common name of anabaptists. Among these were

* In a letter to Vitus Theodorus, written in 1543, Melanchthon complains, "quod horridiùs scripserit Lutherus ad Italos." (Hospin. ut supra)
† Bock, Hist. Antitrinit. tom. ii. p. 414.
‡ L'Abbé d'Artigny, Nouveaux Mémoires, tom. ii. p. 58, 59.

Hetzer and Denck, who published translations of parts of Scripture before Luther.* In the conference held at Marburg, in 1529, between the Saxon and Swiss Reformers, it was stated by Melanchthon, as matter of complaint, or at least of suspicion, that the latter had among them persons who entertained erroneous opinions concerning the Trinity. Zuingle cleared himself and his brethren from this imputation, without denying, however, that there might be individuals lurking among them who cherished such tenets.† It is not improbable, that, on his return, means were taken to discover these concealed heretics, and that, being expelled from Switzerland, some of them travelled into Italy. We know that the reformed church at Naples was, in its infancy, disturbed by Arians and anabaptists;‡ but this appears to have happened at a later period, and the persons referred to might be disciples of Servetus. He began to publish against the Trinity in the year 1531, and there is ground to believe that his books were soon after conveyed to Italy.§ Though he had not formed his peculiar opinions when he was in that country, yet he contracted, during the visit which he paid to it, an intimate acquaintance with several persons with whom he maintained an epistolary correspondence to a late period of his life; and it is known that he was as zealous in propagating his notions by private letters as by the press.‖ Upon the whole, it is highly probable that the antitrinitarian opinions were introduced into Italy by means of the writings of Servetus.

When the minds of men have been suddenly emancipated from implicit subjection to human authority, and disentangled from the errors into which it had

---

* Zuinglii et Œcolampadii Epistolæ, f. 82, 197. Bock, Hist. Antitrin. tom. ii. p. 134—136. Ruchat, Histoire de la Reform. de la Suisse, tom. ii. p. 509. Hetzer and Denck retracted their sentiments.

† Zuinglii et Œcol. Epist. f. 24. Ruchat, ut supra, p. 461, 483.

‡ Life of Galeacius Caracciolus, Marquesse of Vico, p. 13. Lond. 1635.

§ Sandii Nucleus Hist. Eccl. append. p. 90. Boxhornii Hist. Univ. p. 70.

‖ Calvini Opera, tom viii. p. 517.

betrayed them, they are in great danger of overleaping the boundaries prescribed to them by that authority which is divine, and of plunging rashly into inquiries, which reason, as well as revelation, pronounce to be impracticable and pernicious. The genius of the Italians led them to indulge in subtle and curious speculations, and this disposition was fostered by the study of the eclectic and sceptical philosophy, to which many of them had of late years been addicted.* Crude and indigested as the new theories respecting the Trinity and collateral topics were, they fell in with this predisposition; and not a few Protestants found themselves entangled, before they were aware, in the mazes of an intricate and deceitful theology, into which they had entered for the sake of intellectual exercise and amusement. These speculations appear to have commenced at Sienna, whose inhabitants were proverbial among their countrymen for levity and inconstancy of mind;† and from it they were transferred to the Venetian territories, where the friends of the Reformation were numerous, but not organized into congregations, nor placed under the superintendence of regular teachers.‡

The letter addressed by Melanchthon to the Senate of Venice in the year 1538, and from which a quotation has already been made, shows that the antitrini-

* Illgen, Vita Lælii Socini, p. 7. Lips. 1814. Melanchthon speaks repeatedly of the "Platonic and sceptical theories" with which he found the minds of his Italian correspondents and acquaintance enamoured. (Epist. coll 852, 941.) And Calvin, speaking of that vain curiosity and insatiable desire of novelty which leads many into pernicious errors, says—"In Italis, propter rarum acumen, magis eminet" (Opera, tom. viii. p. 510.)

† ——————— Was ever race
Light as Sienna's? Sure not France herself
Can show a tribe so frivolous and vain'
                    DANTE, *Inf. c.* xxix.

‡ Altieri's letter, as quoted above, p. 145—147. Bock (Hist Antitrin. ii. 405) refers to the academy at Venice, and its form and constitution, which allowed great liberty in starting doubts, and canvassing opposite opinions, as confirming the accounts of the rise of Socinianism in that state. But that learned writer does not appear to have been aware, that academies of this description, and founded on the same principles, were, in that age, common throughout Italy.

tarian tenets had then gained admission into that state.*
"I know," says he, "that very different judgments have always prevailed in the world respecting religion, and that the devil has been intent from the beginning on sowing impious doctrines, and inciting men of curious and depraved minds to corrupt and overthrow the truth. Aware of the dangers arising from this quarter to the church, we have been careful to keep within proper bounds; and while we reject certain errors more recently introduced, do not depart from the apostolical writings, from the Nicene and Athanasian creeds, nor even from the ancient consent of the Catholic church. I understand there has lately been introduced among you a book of Servetus, who has revived the error of Samosatenus, condemned by the primitive church, and who seeks to overthrow the doctrine of the two natures in Christ by denying that 'the word' is to be understood of a person, when John says, 'In the beginning was the word.' Although my opinion on that controversy is already in print, and I have condemned the tenet of Servetus by name in my Common Places, yet I think it proper at present to admonish and obtest you to use your utmost exertions to persuade persons to avoid, reject and execrate that impious opinion." Having advanced some considerations in support of the orthodox doctrine on that head, he adds—"I have written these things more largely than the bounds of a letter admit, but too briefly for the importance of the subject. My object was merely to let you know my opinion, not to enter at length into the controversy; but, if any one desires it, I shall be ready to discuss the question more copiously."† The representations of Melanchthon, though they might check, failed in arresting the progress of these opinions. In a letter to Camerarius,

* Bock, in giving an account of this letter, has expressed himself in such a way as may lead his readers to think that Melanchthon had signified his having heard that above forty persons in the city and territories of Venice, distinguished by their rank and talents, had embraced Servetianism. (Hist. Antitrin. ii. 407.) Nothing of that kind appears in the copy of the letter which is now before me.
† Melanch. Epist. coll. 150—154.

written in 1544, he says—" I send you a letter of Vitus, and another written from Venice, which contains disgraceful narratives; but we are admonished, by these distressing examples, to preserve discipline and good order with the greater care and unanimity."*
And, in another letter to the same correspondent, dated on the 31st of May 1545, he writes—" I yesterday returned an answer to the theological question of the Italians, transmitted by Vitus last winter. Italian theology abounds with Platonic theories; and it will be no easy matter to bring them back from that vainglorious science of which they are so fond, to truth and simplicity of explanation."†

Socinian writers have fixed the origin of their sect at this period. According to their account, upwards of forty individuals of great talents and learning were in the habit of meeting in private conferences, or "colleges," as they have called them, within the territories of Venice, and chiefly at Vicenza, to deliberate on the plan of forming a purer faith, by discarding a number of opinions held by Protestants as well as papists; but these meetings, being discovered by the treachery of an individual, were dispersed in the year 1546; some of the members having been thrown into prison, and others forced to flee into foreign countries. Among the latter they mention Lælius Socinus, Camillus Siculus, Franciscus Niger, Ochino, Alciati, Gentilis, and Blandrata. These writers have gone so far as to present us with a creed or system of doctrine agreed upon by the collegiates of Vicenza, as the result of their joint inquiries and discussion.‡

Historians distinguished for their research and discrimination, as well as their impartiality, have rejected this narrative, which, it must be confessed, rests on very doubtful and suspicious authority.§ It was first

* Melanch. Epist. coll. 835. † Ibid. 852.
‡ Lubieniecii Hist. Reform. Polonicæ, p. 38, 39. Sandii Bibl. Antitrin. p. 18, et Wissowatii Narratio adnex. p. 209, 210.
§ Mosheim, (Eccles Hist cent. xvi. sect. iii. part ii. chap. iv. § 3,) and Fueslin, (Beytrage zur Erlauterung der Kirchen-reform. Geschichten des Schweizerlandes, tom. iii. p. 327,) do not consider the narrative as entitled to credit. Bock, (Hist. Antitrin. tom. ii. p. 404

published a century after the time to which it refers, and by foreigners and persons far removed from the sources of information. No trace of the Vicentine "colleges" has been found, after the most accurate research, in the contemporary history of Italy, or in the letters and other writings of learned men, popish, Protestant, or Socinian, which have since been brought to light. No allusion is made to the subject by Faustus Socinus in any part of his works, or by the Polish knight who wrote his life.* The ambitious designation of colleges, applied to the alleged meetings, is suspicious, while the mistakes respecting the persons who are said to have composed them, give to the whole narrative the air of, at best, a story made up of indistinct and ill-understood traditionary reports. Ochino, Camillo, and Negri, had left Italy before these assemblies are represented as having existed, and the writings which the first of these continued for many years after that period to publish, coincided exactly with the sentiments of the first Reformers. Lælius

—416,) and Illgen. (Vita Lælii Socini, p. 8—14) admit its general truth, while they acknowledge its incorrectness as to particular facts. A modern writer has pronounced Mosheim's reasons "extremely weak," and "extremely frivolous;" and maintains the opposite opinion on the grounds which Bock has laid down in his History of the Antitrinitarians. (Rees's Historical Introduction to the Racovian Catechism, p. 20—24.) Bock was an industrious and trustworthy collector, but very inferior in critical acumen to Mosheim, and he has brought forward no fact in support of his opinion which was not known to his predecessor.

* Lubieniecius professes to have taken the account "ex Lælii Socini vitæ Curriculo, et Budzinii comment. MSS." But he does not quote the words of these documents, which were never given to the world. Mr Rees says—" Andrew Wissowatius may himself be regarded in the light of an original authority." (Ut supra, p. 22.) But how a writer, who was born in 1608, could be an original authority for what happened in 1546, it is difficult to comprehend; nor does Wissowatz pretend to have taken his statement from any original documents of his grandfather, Faustus Socinus, which, if they had existed, would undoubtedly have been communicated to Samuel Pryzcovius, when he undertook to write the life of the founder of the sect.—The work of Pryzcovius was translated into English, and published under the following title.—" The Life of that incomparable man, *Faustus Socinus Senensis*, described by a Polonian Knight. London, printed for Richard Moone, at the Seven Stars, 1653." The epistle to the reader is subscribed "J. B.;" *i. e.* John Biddle.

Socinus belonged to Sienna; there is no evidence of his having resided at Venice; and, although we should suppose that he visited that place occasionally, it is not probable that a young man of twenty-one could possess that authority in these assemblies which is ascribed to him by the narrative we are examining. Besides, the part assigned to him is at variance with the whole of his conduct after he left his native country. Though it is evident that his mind was tinctured with the tenets afterwards called Socinian, yet so far was he from courting the honours and dangers of a heresiarch, that he uniformly propounded his opinions in the shape of doubts or difficulties, which he was anxious to have removed; and he continued till his death, notwithstanding the suspicions of heterodoxy which he had incurred, to keep up a friendly intercourse, not only with his countrymen, Martyr and Zanchi, but with Melanchthon, Bullinger, and even Calvin. The assemblies suppressed within the Venetian territories in the year 1546, were those of the Protestants in general; and it was as belonging to these, and not as forming a distinct sect, that the friends of Servetus were at that time exposed to suffering. Such are the reasons which incline me to reject the narrative of the Socinian historians.

But while there is no good ground for thinking that the favourers of the antitrinitarian tenets in Italy had formed themselves into societies, or digested a regular system of belief, it is undeniable that a number of the Italian Protestants were, at the time referred to, infected with these errors; and it is highly probable that they were accustomed to confirm one another in the belief of them when they occasionally met, and perhaps to introduce them as topics of discussion into the common meetings of the Protestants, and by starting objections, to shake the convictions of such as adhered to the commonly received doctrines. This was exactly the line of conduct pursued by them after they left their native country, especially in the Grisons, where the expatriated Italians first took refuge. Soon after their arrival, disputes arose in the

Grison churches respecting the Trinity, the merit of Christ's death, the perfection of the saints in this life, the necessity and use of the sacraments, infant baptism, the resurrection of the body, and similar articles, in which the chief opponents of the common doctrine, both privily and openly, were natives of Italy, several of whom afterwards propagated their peculiar opinions in Transylvania and Poland.* Subsequently to the year 1546, adherents to antitrinitarianism were still to be found in Italy. Such of them as had fled, maintained a correspondence with their friends at home, and made converts to their opinions by means of their letters.† About the year 1553, the learned visionary, William Postel, published at Venice an apology for Servetus, in which he mentions, that this heresiarch had many favourers among the Italians.‡ And in the year 1555, pope Paul IV. issued a bull against those who denied the doctrine of the Trinity, the proper divinity of Christ, and redemption by his blood.§ I close this part of the subject with the words of a judicious Italian, who left his native country for the gospel, and laboured with great zeal, and not without success, in opposing the spread of this heresy. "It is not difficult to divine," says he, "whence this evil sprung, and by whom it has been fostered. Spain produced the hen; Italy hatched the eggs; and we in the Grisons now hear the chicks pip."‖

II. Another class of facts which I have thought deserving of a place in this chapter, relates to illustrious females who favoured the new opinions, although their names are not associated with any public transaction in the progress which the Reformation made through Italy. The literary historians of Italy have dwelt with enthusiasm and pride on such of their

---

* De Porta, Hist. Ref. Eccles. Rhæticarum, tom. i. p. 63. Bock, Hist. Antitrin. tom. ii. p. 410, 411. Schelhornii Dissert. de Mino Celso Senensi, p. 34—36, 44—47.
† Illgen, Vita Lælii Socini, p. 58
‡ Bock, ut supra, p. 539—542.
§ Bullarium Romanum, ab Angel. Mar Cherubino, tom. i. p 590.
‖ Zanchius, apud Bock, ut supra, p. 415. I have not observed these words in the writings of Zanchi.

countrywomen as distinguished themselves by patronizing or cultivating literature and the fine arts. Their proficiency in sacred letters and in the practice of piety, is certainly not less to their honour. It has been mentioned by a modern historian, that any piety which existed in Italy at the close of the fifteenth century, was to be found among the female part of the population.* A writer who flourished in the middle of the following century, and whose religion was of a more enlightened kind than that which usually prevails in the cloister, gives the following account of what he had observed:—" In our age we behold the admirable spectacle of women (whose sex is more addicted to vanity than learning) having their minds deeply imbued with the knowledge of heavenly doctrine. In Campania, where I now write, the most learned preacher may become more learned and holy by a single conversation with some women. In my native country of Mantua, too, I found the same thing, and were it not that it would lead me into a digression, I could dilate with pleasure on the many proofs which I received, to my no small edification, of an unction of spirit and fervour of devotion in the sisterhood, such as I have rarely met with in the most learned men of my profession."† The female friends of the truth in Italy, whose names have come down to us, were chiefly of the higher ranks, and such as had not taken the veil.

The first place is due here to Isabella Manricha of Bresegna, who embraced the reformed doctrine at Naples under Valdes, and exerted herself zealously in promoting it. Having given proofs of invincible fortitude, by resisting the solicitations and threats of her friends, this lady, finding that it behoved her either to sacrifice her religion or her native country, retired into Germany, from which she repaired to Zurich, and finally settled at Chiavenna in the Grisons, where she led a life of poverty and retirement, with as much

* Sismondi, Hist. des Rép. d'Italie, tom. vii. p. 238.
† Folengius in Psalmos; apud Gerdesii Ital. Ref. p. 261.

cheerfulness as if she had never known what it was to enjoy affluence and honours.*

One of the greatest female ornaments of the reformed Church in Italy was Lavinia della Rovere, daughter-in-law to the celebrated Camillo Orsini, "than whom I know not a more learned, or, what is still higher praise, a more pious woman in Italy," says Olympia Morata. The epistolary correspondence carried on between these two female friends is highly honourable to both. We learn from it the interesting fact, that Lavinia, while she resided at the court of Rome, not only kept her conscience unspotted by idolatry, but employed the influence of her father-in-law, which was great, with the pope and catholic princes, in behalf of the Protestants who fell into the hands of the inquisition. From various hints dropped in the course of the correspondence, it is evident that she felt her situation extremely delicate and painful, apparently from the importunities of her husband, and the ruder attempts of her other relations, to induce her to conform to the established religion; but these served only to call forth her patience and magnanimity.† It requires both reflection and sensibility to form a proper estimate of the trials which a distinguished female must endure when placed in the circumstances of Lavinia della Rovere. A cup of cold water, or even a kind message, sent to a prisoner in the cells of the inquisition, a word spoken in behalf of the truth, or a modest refusal to be present at a superstitious festival, afford, in such cases, a stronger and more unequivocal proof of a devoted soul, than the most flaming professions, or a fortune expended for religious purposes, by one who lives in a free country, and is surrounded by persons who are friendly to the gospel.

* Simleri Oratio, ut supra, sig. b iij. Bock, ii. 524. To this lady Celio Secundo Curio dedicated the first edition of the works of Olympia Fulvia Morata. (Noltenius, Vita Olympiæ, p. 8, 119. edit. Hesse.) Ochino's work, *De Corporis Christi Præsentia in Cœnæ Sacramento*, is also dedicated " Illustri et piæ fœminæ Isabellæ Manrichæ Bresegnæ."

† Opera Olympiæ F. Moratæ, p. 89—92, 105, 107, 121, 123

By the same letters we are authorized to record, among the friends of the reformed doctrine, two females of the Orsini family, Madonna Maddelena, and Madonna Cherebina;* as also Madonna Elena Rangone of Bentivoglio,† who appears to have belonged to the noble family of that name in Modena, which had long been distinguished, both on the male and female side, for the cultivation and patronage of literature.‡

Julia Gonzago, duchess of Trajetto, and countess of Fondi, in the kingdom of Naples, is ranked among "illustrious women, suspected of heretical pravity."§ She was the sister of Luigi II. conte di Sabioneta, a nobleman celebrated for his knowledge of letters, as well as for his valour, and who was surnamed Rodomonte, from his having killed a Moorish champion in battle. Julia Gonzago is commemorated, by Ortensio Landi, among the learned ladies of Italy; and her name often occurs in writings of that age.‖ After the death of her husband, Vespasiano Colonna, she remained a widow, and exhibited a pattern of the correctest virtue and piety. She was esteemed one of the most beautiful women in Italy; and Brantome relates, that Solyman, the Turkish emperor, having given orders to Hariadan Barbarossa, the commander of his fleet, to seize her person, a party of Turks landed during the night, and took possession of the town of Fondi; but the duchess, though at the risk of her

* Opera Olympiæ F. Moratæ, p. 92, 212—222.
† Ibid. p. 102.
‡ The letters of Girolamo Muzio, the great opponent of heresy in his time, throw light on what is mentioned in the text. In a letter to Lucrezia, the wife of Count Claudio Rangone, he expresses his apprehensions lest that lady should suffer herself to be ensnared by the new heresy, and points to an enemy whom she had in her house. In another letter he expresses the joy which he felt at hearing that his fears were unnecessary. Both letters were written in 1547. (Muzio, Lettere; apud Tiraboschi, tom vii. p. 100) The families of Rangone and Bentivoglio were allied by frequent intermarriages. (Ibid. p. 90, 93, 96)
§ Thuani Hist. lib. xxxix. cap. 2.
‖ Tiraboschi, Storia, tom. vii. p 1195. Ab. Bettinelli, Delle Lettere ed Arte Montovane, p. 89.

life, eluded their search, and made her escape.* She was a disciple of Valdes,† and continued, after his death, to entertain and protect the preachers of the new doctrine; on which account she incurred the displeasure of the pope to such a degree, that the fact of having corresponded with her by letters was made a ground of criminal charge on trials for heresy.‡

I place Vittoria Colonna last, because the claims of the Protestants to the honour of her name have been strongly contested. She was the daughter of Fabrizio Colonna, grand constable of Naples, and of Anna de Montefeltro, daughter of Federigo, duke of Urbino; and having been deprived of her husband, the celebrated commander Fernando Davalos, marquis of Pescara, in the flower of youth, she dedicated her life to sacred studies, and retirement from the gay world, without however entangling herself with the vow. The warmest tribute of praise was paid to the talents and virtues of this lady by the first writers of her age.§ "In Tuscan song," says one of them, "she was inferior only to Petrarch; and in her elegiac poems on the death of her husband, she has beautifully expressed her contempt of the world, and the ardent breathings of her soul after the blessedness of heaven." ‖ The marchioness associated with the Reformers at Naples, and was regarded as one of their most distinguished disciples.¶ When Ochino,

* Vies des Dames Illustres, p 282.
† The Commentaries of Valdes on the Psalms, and on the Epistle to the Romans, were dedicated to this lady.
‡ Laderchii Annales, tom. xxii. p 325. Thuanus, ut supra.
§ Schelhorn has collected a number of these testimonies in his Amœnit. Hist. Eccles. tom. ii. p. 132—134. See also Tiraboschi, Storia, tom. vii p. 1179—1181.
‖ Toscanus, in Peplo Italiæ.
¶ Giannone, l. xxxii. c. 5. Thuani Hist. ad an. 1566. The testimony of these writers is confirmed by a letter concerning her, written in 1538, by Casper Cruciger, to Theodorus Vitus, and published in Hummelii Neue Bibliotheck von seltenen Buechern, Band ii. p. 126. To an Italian version of Beza's Confession of Faith, printed (probably at Geneva) in 1560, the translator, Francesco Cattani, prefixed "Sonetto della Illustriss Marchesana di Pescara xxxiii. nel suo libro stampato, col quale sfida i Papisti al combattere, mostranda la lor mala causa."

for whom she felt the deepest veneration,* deserted the Church of Rome, great apprehensions were entertained that she would follow his example; and cardinal Pole, who watched over her faith with the utmost jealousy, exacted from her a promise that she would not read any letters which might be addressed to her by the fascinating ex-capuchin, or, at least, would not answer them without consulting him or cardinal Cervini. This appears from a letter to Cervini, afterwards pope Marcellus II., in which Vittoria says, that, from her knowledge of "Monsegnor d'Inghelterra," she was convinced she could not err in following his advice, and had therefore obeyed his directions, by transmitting a packet sent her from Bologna by "Fra Belardin." Her highness adds, in a postscript, (which may be considered as a proof that her new advisers had succeeded in alienating her mind from Ochino, and confirming her attachment to the Church of Rome,) "I am grieved to see, that the more he thinks to excuse himself, he condemns himself the more, and the more he believes he will save others from shipwreck, the more he exposes himself to the deluge, being out of the ark which saves and gives security."†

III. The last class of miscellaneous facts which I have to state, as throwing light on the progress of the Reformation in Italy, relates to those learned men who never left the communion of the church of Rome, but were favourable, in a greater or less degree, to the views and sentiments of the Reformers. These may be subdivided into three classes. The first consisted of persons who were convinced of the great corruptions which reigned not only in the court of Rome, but generally among all orders in the catholic church; and who, though they did not agree with the Reformers in doctrinal articles, yet cherished the hope

* See before, p. 120, &c
† This letter was first published by Tiraboschi, (Storia, tom. vii. p. 118,) from the archives of the noble family of Cervini at Sienna, as a confirmation of the statement of cardinal Quirini, in his Diatrib. ad vol. iii. Epist. Card. Poli, p. 58, &c.

that their opposition, and the schism which it threatened, would force the clergy to correct abuses which could no longer be either concealed or defended. The second class comprehended those who were of the same sentiments with the Reformers as to the leading doctrines of the gospel which had been brought into dispute, but who wished to retain the principal forms of the established worship, purified from the grosser superstitions, and to maintain the hierarchy, and even the papacy, after its tyranny had been checked, as a necessary or at least useful means of preserving the unity of the catholic church. The third class consisted of those who were entirely of the sentiments of the Reformers, but were restrained from declaring themselves, and taking that side which their consciences approved, by lukewarmness, dread of persecution, love of peace, or despair of success, in a country where the motives and the means to support the established religion were so many and so powerful. It is not meant that the persons included under these classes were formed into parties; but by keeping this distinction in our eye, we shall be the better able to form a correct judgment of the views and conduct of certain individuals, who have been claimed as friends both by Papists and Protestants.

The instances which I shall produce, belong chiefly to the second of these classes. That there were many persons in Italy, eminent for their talents and station, whose creed differed widely from that which received the sanction of the council of Trent, is etablished on the best evidence, though it has been denied by the later historians and apologists of the church of Rome. It is proved by the fact, that their names and writings were suppressed, or stigmatized as heretical or as suspected, by the authorized censors of the press. And it was acknowledged by writers who had the best opportunities of information, and were under no temptation to misrepresent the fact. "Those who at that time were disposed to exert themselves seriously for the reformation of the church," says the enlightened and impartial De Thou, "had frequent conferences about faith, works, grace, free-will, election, and glorification; and many of them, entertaining opinions on these subjects different from what were publicly taught, availed themselves of the authority of St. Augustine to support their sentiments."*

Pier Angelo Manzolli was principal physician to Hercules II. duke of Ferrara. Under the anagrammatical name of Marcellus Palingenius, he published an elegant Latin poem, in which he describes human life in allusion to the twelve signs of the zodiac.† This poem abounds with complaints of the corrupt manners of the clergy; nor are there wanting in it passages which prove the alienation of the author's mind from the church of Rome, and his satisfaction at the growing success of the new opinions.‡ It was put into the index of prohibited books, and the bones of the author, after his death, were taken out of their grave, and burnt to ashes as those of an impious heretic.§

The claims of the Protestants to rank Marc-antonio Flaminio among their converts, have been keenly

---

* Thuani Historia ad ann. 1551.

† It is generally allowed, that the author of the *Zodiacus Vitæ* concealed himself under a fictitious name. Flaminio, Fulvio Peregrino Morata, and several other learned men, have been supposed to be the real author; but the most probable opinion is that which is stated in the text, and which was first suggested by Facciolati. (Heumanni Pœcile, tom. i. p. 259—266; ii. p. 175.) Whether Facciolati replied to the queries which Heumann proposed to him, with the view of obtaining fuller information respecting his countryman, I do not know. (Conf. Nolten, Vita Oylmpiæ Moratæ, p. 82, edit. Hesse.)

‡ The following passage may serve as a specimen.—

Atque rogant quidnam Romana ageretur in urbe.
Cuncti luxuriæ, atque gulæ, furtisque dolisque,
Certatim incumbunt, nosterque est sexus uterque,
Respondit. sed nunc summus parat arma sacerdos,
Clemens, Martinum cupiens abolere Lutherum,
Atque ideo Hispanas retinet nutritque cohortes.
Non disceptando, aut subtilibus argumentis
Vincere, sed ferro mavult sua jura tueri.
Pontifices nunc bella juvant, sunt cætera nugæ.
Nec præcepta patrum, nec Christi dogmata curant:
Jactant se dominos rerum, et sibi cuncta licere.
                    Zodiacus Vitæ—*Capricornus*.

§ Lil. Greg. Gyraldus, De Poetis sui ævi, dial. ii. Opera, p. 569.

contested. It is undeniable, that, at one period of his life at least, he cultivated the friendship of the leading persons in his native country who were favourable to the new opinions—that he was an admirer of Valdes, encouraged Martyr and Ochino, and induced several individuals of rank to attend their sermons and embrace their doctrine.* So early as the year 1536, he had, with his natural sincerity and love of truth, professed his doubts as to certain articles of the received faith, and been called to an account for the freedom of his language and his familiarity with the writings of heretics. In a letter quoted by Tiraboschi, Cortese requests Contarini to obtain for him the pope's permission to read certain books of the heretics; "for," says he, "I would not have that happen to me which befel Marc-antonio in the holy week, especially if M. di Chieti (cardinal Caraffa) should know of it."† Nor is this all. His writings prove, beyond all reasonable doubt, that he entertained sentiments, on the principal points of controversy, which coincided with the Protestant creed, and were at variance with the decisions of the council of Trent. It would be easy to establish this fact by a multiplicity of extracts; but the following may suffice:—" Human nature," says he, "was so depraved by the fall of Adam, that its corruption is propagated to all his posterity, in consequence of which we contract, in our very conception, a stain and an incredible proneness to sin, which urges us to all kinds of wickedness and vice, unless our minds are purified and invigorated by the grace of the Holy Spirit. Without this renovation, we will always remain impure and defiled, although to men, who cannot look into the inward dispositions of others, we may appear to be pure and upright."‡ " In these

* Moncurtius, in Vita Flaminii, præfix. ejus Carmin p. 28. Diss. de Religione M. Flaminii, in Schelhornii Amœn. Eccles. tom. ii. p. 3—179. Epistolæ Flaminii, edit. a Joach. Camerario. Schelhornii Amœnit Liter. tom. x. p. 1161.

† Barnard's Mem. of Marc-antonio Flaminio, prefixed to Imitation of his Select Poems, p. 15, 16

‡ Flaminii in Librum Psalmorum brevis Explanatio, f. 198, 199. Parisiis, 1551.

words, (Ps. xxxii. 1.) the psalmist pronounces blessed, not those who are perfect and free from the spot of sin, (for no man is so in this life,) but those whose sins God has pardoned in his mercy; and he pardons those who confess their sins, and sincerely believe that the blood of our Lord Jesus Christ is an expiation for all transgressions and faults."*—" God, for the sake of Christ his Son, adopted them as his sons from all eternity: those whom he adopted before they were born he calls to godliness; and having called them, he confers on them first righteousness and then everlasting life."†—" The creature, considered in itself, and in the corruption of its nature, is an impure mass; and whatever is worthy of praise in it is the work of the Spirit of Christ, who purifies and regenerates his elect by a living faith, and makes them creatures by so much the nobler and more perfect that they are disposed to count themselves as nothing, and as having nothing in themselves but all in Christ."‡—" Christian faith consists in our believing the whole word of God, and particularly the gospel. The gospel is nothing else than the message of good news announced to the whole world by the apostles, telling us, that the only begotten Son of God, having become incarnate, hath satisfied the justice of his Father for all our sins. Whosoever gives credit to these good tidings of good, he believes the gospel, and having faith in the gospel, which is the gift of God, he walks out of the kingdom of this world into that of God, by enjoying the fruit of a general pardon; from a carnal he becomes a spiritual creature, from a child of wrath a child of grace, from a son of Adam a son of God; he is governed by the Holy Spirit; he feels a sweet peace of conscience; he studies to mortify the affections and lusts of the flesh, acknowledging that he is dead with his head Jesus Christ; and he studies to vivify the spirit, and lead a heavenly life, acknow-

* Flaminii in Librum Psalmorum brevis Explanatio, f. 143, b.
† Ibid. f. 288, a.
‡ Flaminii Epist. ad quandam principem fœminam. Schelhornii Amœn. Eccles. tom. ii. p. 103.

ledging that he is risen with the same Jesus Christ. A lively faith in the soul of a Christian man produces all these and other admirable effects."* But the clear views of the gospel entertained by Flaminio are nowhere more decidedly made known than in a letter to a friend, in which he pronounces a most discriminating judgment on the writings of Thomas à Kempis, and furnishes an important caution against the spirit of slavish fear which they have a tendency to foster in the breasts of devotional persons.† Such were the sentiments of one who lived in the heart of Italy during the heat of the controversy between the Papists and Protestants—the sentiments of a poet, whose writings discover " the simplicity and tenderness of Catullus without his licentiousness," and " melt the heart of the reader with sweetness." If there be any truth in the maxim laid down by a most catholic historian of the council of Trent,‡ " that the doctrine of justification is a test by which catholics may be distinguished from heretics, and the root from which all other doctrines, true or false, germinate," then Flaminio was unquestionably a Protestant.

On the other hand, there is a letter from him, in which he strenuously defends, in opposition to his friend Carnesecchi, the doctrine of the real presence and commemorative oblation of Christ in the eucharist, and expresses himself with considerable acrimony in speaking of the Reformers.§ To reconcile these ap-

---

* Flaminii Epist. ad quandam principem fœminam: Schelhornii Amœn. Eccles, tom. ii. p. 115. This last extract is taken from a letter to Theodora, or Theodorina Sauli, a lady belonging to a noble family in Genoa, whose name Gerdes has added to his list of female Protestants, merely upon the authority of this letter. (Ital. Reform. p. 158.)

† See this letter in the appendix. ‡ Pallavicini.

§ This letter, dated from Trent, January 1, 1543, and Carnesecchi's reply to it, were inserted in a collection of Italian letters, published by Ludovico Dolci in 1555, and republished in Latin by Schelhorn, in his Amœnitates Ecclesiasticæ, tom. ii. p 146—179. Some writers have denied the genuineness of the letter of Flaminio, while others suppose that Carnesecchi's reply induced him to retract his opinion. (Hesse, Not. ad Nolten. Vit. Olympiæ Moratæ, p. 73.) A desire to add a celebrated name to the Protestant roll appears to have led to the adoption of these hypotheses.

parently contradictory statements, we must attend to the different periods in the life of Flaminio. During the flower of his age he was entirely engrossed with secular literature, as his juvenile poems evince. In middle life he applied his mind to sacred letters, made the Scriptures his chief study, and derived his highest pleasure from meditating on divine things. It was at at this time that he composed his paraphrases on the Psalms in prose and verse, and lived in the society of Valdes, Martyr, the duchess of Ferrara, and other persons addicted to the reformed opinions. The third period of his life extends from the time that the court of Rome adopted decisive measures for suppressing the reformed opinions in Italy, to the year 1550, in which he died. His letter on the eucharist was written immediately after some of his most intimate acquaintances had been forced to fly from their native country, to avoid imprisonment or a fiery death. The mild and yielding disposition of Flaminio was more fitted for contemplation and retirement than for controversy and suffering. Like many others, he might not have made up his mind to separate formally from the Church of Rome; and the fate of those who had ventured on that step would not help forward his resolution. His friends in the sacred college were anxious to retain him; and the article of the real presence, from which many Protestants could not extricate themselves, was perhaps the means best fitted for entangling the devout mind of Flaminio, and reconciling him to remain in the communion of a church whose public creed was at variance with some of the sentiments which were dearest to his heart. But two years after the time now referred to, he refused the honourable employment of secretary to the council of Trent; "because," says Pallavicini, "he favoured the new opinions, and would not employ his pen for an assembly by which he knew these opinions would be condemned."[*] The cardinal indeed adds, that Flaminio had the happiness to be brought subsequently to acknowledge his errors

[*] Istor. Conc. Trent. ad an. 1545.

through his acquaintance with Pole, and died a good Catholic. But there is no evidence that he ever retracted his former sentiments; and in none of his writings, earlier or later, do we read any thing of purgatory, prayers for the dead or to saints, pilgrimages, penances, or any of those voluntary services which were so much insisted on by all the devoted adherents to Rome; but every where we find the warmest piety and purest morality, founded on Scriptural principles, and enforced by the most evangelical motives. We know, that the court of Rome, after it was awakened to its danger, was eager to engage the pens of the learned in its defence against the Reformers.* If the advisers to whom Flaminio committed himself during the last years of his life, could have prevailed on him to write any thing of this kind, it would have been triumphantly proclaimed; but it was a sufficient victory for them to be able to retain such a man in their chains, and to publish the solitary letter on the eucharist, which was written seven years before his death, as if it had been his dying testimony, and as a proof that he was not alienated from the catholic faith. Even this was the opinion only of a few of his private friends; for the verdict of the Vatican was very different. The report that it was intended to disinter his body, after his death, might be groundless;† but it is certain that his writings were inserted in the prohibitory index, though care was taken afterwards to wipe off this disgrace, by expunging from that record the name of a man who had lived on terms of intimacy with the chief dignitaries

---

* It is well known what solicitations were used with Erasmus before he drew his pen against Luther. Christopher Longolius, in a letter to Stefano and Flaminio Sauli, mentions, with an air of no small vanity, that he had been solicited from Germany to write in defence of Luther, and from Italy to write against him; that both parties had furnished him with memorials; that he thought himself qualified for either task, and that he had already, by way of essay, (like a wise and prudent procurator,) drawn up a pleading for and against the accused heretic. (Longolii Epist. lib. ii. p 139.) The cautious orator chose the safer side, and sent forth a Ciceronian Philippic against Luther.

† Manlii Collect. p. 116. Georg. Fabricii Poem. Sacr. P. i. p. 264.

of the church, and whose genius and piety must always reflect credit on the society to which he belonged.*

The preceding account of the sentiments of Flaminio materially agrees with that of a contemporary author who appears to have possessed good means of information. The following quotation is long, but it deserves a place here, as serving to throw light on the state of religious opinion in Italy, and on the character of an Englishman, who makes but too conspicuous a figure in the history of his native country. Referring to the letter to Carnesecchi, of which he had stated the substance, that writer goes on to say—" This at least we gain from the letter of Flaminio, that, while he professes to differ from us on those heads which I have pointed out, he makes no such professions as to transubstantiation, and the oblation for the living and dead, which we reject; he agrees with us in giving the cup to the laity; and I am persuaded that, had he lived longer, he would have made further progress, and come over to us completely. But cardinal Pole kept him under restraint, and prevented him from freely avowing his sentiments, as he did many others. It is dreadful to think what injury Satan did to the resuscitated gospel, by the instrumentality of this crafty Englishman, who acknowledged, or at least professed to acknowledge, that we are justified by faith in Christ alone, and laboured, along with those who resided in his house, among whom was Flaminio, to instil this doctrine into the minds of many. Not to name others, it is well known that John Morell, late minister of the foreign church in Frankfort on the Maine, a man of great piety and learning, imbibed this doctrine in that school, and was drawn by Pole into the society of those who had a relish for the gospel, and were said to agree with us. The cardinal laboured, by all the influence of his character and reputation, to persuade others to rest satisfied with a

* The article in the Index of Rome for 1559 runs thus.—" Marci Antonii Flaminii Paraphrases et Comment. in Psal. Item literæ et carmina omnia." Sig. D 8.

secret belief of the truth, and not think themselves answerable for the errors and abuses of the church,* alleging that we should tolerate, and even give our consent to these, in the expectation that God, at the fit time, would afford a favourable opportunity for having them removed. It is unnecessary to say, that this is a doctrine very agreeable to those who would have Christ without the cross. If Luther and other faithful servants of God, by whose means the truth has been clearly brought to light in our days, had chosen in this manner to conceal and wink at errors and abuses, how could they have been extirpated? How could the pure voice of the gospel ever have been heard in that case, when we see with what difficulty it has prevailed to a very limited extent, through great contention and profusion of blood, in opposition to the predominating power and cruelties of antichrist? Pole, however, did not hesitate to assert, that he could advance the pure doctrine by concealment, dissimulation, and evasion. And not only so, but when some individuals more ardent than the rest, threatened to break through these restraints, his agents were always ready to urge the propriety of waiting for the fit season, and discovering their sentiments gradually; in consequence of which some persons were so credulous as to believe that, at a future period, the cardinal and his confidential friends would openly profess the truth before the pope and the whole city of Rome, and by the general attention which this must excite, would singularly advance the glory of God. After waiting for this until they were wearied out, how did the matter issue? I cannot relate it without tears. O wretched cardinal! O miserable dupes of his promises! The purity of religion had been restored in England: the doctrines of justification by faith, the assurance of salvation, true repentance, scriptural absolution, the right use of the sacraments, and the sole headship of Christ over the church, were taught in that kingdom. Pole went there; and what was the consequence?

* "L'huomo si havesse a contentare di quella secreta cognitione, senza tener poi conto se la chiesa havea degli abusi et degli errori."

He absolved the whole kingdom, including the nobles, and the king and queen, on their knees, from the crimes which they had committed against the church of Rome. And what were these? The teaching of those very doctrines which he himself had favoured, and the triumph of which he had promised to secure by the arts of moderation and prudent delay. Nor did he rest, until, in his desire to gratify the pope and cardinals, he had restored all the abuses, superstitions, and abominations which had been removed; and had sent a printed account of his deeds through every country in Europe."*

Gasparo Contarini was one of the distinguished persons whom Paul III., aware of the necessity of conciliating public favour, had judiciously advanced to the purple. It is impossible to read the treatise on justification,† drawn up by him when he acted as legate at the diet and conference held at Ratisbon in 1541, together with the letters which passed between him and Pole at that time, without being convinced that both these prelates agreed with the Reformers on this article, and differed widely from Sadolet and others, whose sentiments were afterwards sanctioned by the council of Trent. Pole tells him, that "he knew long ago what his sentiments on that subject were;" that he rejoiced at the treatise which Contarini had composed, "because it laid not only a foundation for agreement with the Protestants, but such a foundation as illustrated the glory of Christ—the foundation of all Christian doctrine, which was not well understood by many;" that he and all who were with him at Viterbo, joined in giving thanks to God "who had begun to reveal this sacred, salutary, and necessary doctrine;" and that its friends ought not to

* Giudicio sopra le lettere di tredeci huomini illustri publicate da Dionigi Atanagi, Venet. 1554; Schelhornii Amœnit. Eccles. tom. ii. p. 11—15; conf. tom. i. p. 144—155. Colomesii Italia Orientalis, p. iii. Sleidani Com. lib. x. tom. ii. p. 54; lib. xxi. tom. iii. p. 190. edit. Am Ende. To these may be added the testimony of Aonio Paleario. (Opera, p. 561, 562.)

† This was republished, from Contarini's works, by cardinal Quirini, in his collection of Pole's Letters, vol. iii. p. cic.

be moved by the censures which it met with at Rome, where it was "charged with novelty," although "it lies at the foundation of all the doctrines held by the ancient church."*—That cardinal Morone was of the same sentiments appears, not only from the articles of charge brought against him, but from his known agreement in sentiment with Pole and Contarini.†— To these members of the sacred college, we have to add Federigo Fregoso, a prelate equally distinguished by his birth, learning, and virtues.‡ He gave great scandal, by declining to appear at the court of the Vatican, after the pope had honoured him with the purple.§ Disgusted with the manners of that court, he had divested himself of the archbishoprick of Salerno, and retired to the diocese of Gubbio, of which he was administrator; and perceiving that the people conceived the whole of religion to lie in pronouncing, at stated hours and with the prescribed gesticulations, the pater noster, ave maria, and hymns in honour of the saints, he, with the view of initiating them into a more rational and scriptural devotion, composed in Italian a treatise on the method of prayer, which had the honour of being prohibited at Rome.¶ The

* See Pole's letters to Contarini, of the 17th May and 16th July, 1541, and 1st May 1542. (Epistolæ Reginal Poli, vol. III. p. 25, 27—30, 53.) Quirini, besides what is contained in his dissertations prefixed to Pole's Letters, attempted to defend Contarini's orthodoxy, in a separate tract, entitled "*Epistola ad Gregorium Rothfischerum, Brixiæ* 1752; to which Jo. Rud. Kieslingius replied, in his *Epistola ad Eminent. Princ. Angelum Mariam Quirinum, de Religione Lutherana amabili, Lips.* 1753.

† Wolfii Lect. Memor. tom. II. p. 655. When the articles were afterwards published, with scholia, by Vergerio, the inquisitors did not insert the book in their index, lest it should call the attention of the public to the fact, that a cardinal had been accused of holding such opinions. (Vergerii Oper. tom. I. p 262. Schelhornii Amœnit. Liter. tom. XII. p. 546, &c.)

‡ He was the nephew of Guidubaldo, duke of Urbino, and the brother of Ottaviano Fregoso, doge of Genoa, a name celebrated in the annals of that republic. (Tiraboschi, VII 1076.) " Egli è tutto buono, e tutto santo, e tutto nelle sacre lettere, e Latine, e Greche, e Ebraiche," says Bembo. (Opere, tom. VII. p. 267.)

§ Bembo, Lettere, tom. I. p. 139.

¶ An account of this book is given by Riederer, in the third volume of his Nachrichten. Conf. Wolfii Lect. Memorab. tom. II. p. 698

same honour was reserved for the elegant commentaries of the learned and pious abbot, Giambattista Folengo, which abound with sentiments similar to those which have been quoted from the writings of Flaminio, accompanied with severe strictures on the superstitious practices which the priests and friars recommended to the people.*

Angelo Buonarici, general of the canons regular at Venice, is another example of the extent to which the leading opinions of the reformed had spread in Italy. In his exposition of the apostolical epistles, he has stated the doctrine of justification by faith with as much clearness and accuracy as either Luther or Calvin. "This passage of Scripture," says he, "teaches us, that if we are true Christians, we must acknowledge that we are saved and justified, without the previous works of the law, by means of faith alone. Not that we are to conclude, that those who believe in Christ are not bound and obliged to study the practice of holy, devout, and good works; but no one must think or believe that he can attain to the benefit of justification by good works, for this is indeed obtained by faith, and good works in the justified do not precede but follow their justification." Similar sentiments pervade this work, which appeared with the privilege of the inquisitors of Venice; a circumstance which might have excited our astonishment, had we not known that still greater oversights have been committed by these jealous and intolerant, but ignorant and injudicious, censors of the press.†—Still more remarkable were the sentiments of Giovanni Grimani, a Venetian of noble birth, and patriarch of

and Index Auct Prohibit Romæ, 1559. There is a curious letter, written in 1531, by Bembo to Fregoso, about a treatise in manuscript, which the latter had sent to him, on the subject of free will and predestination. Bembo promises not to allow it to go into improper hands, but refuses to burn it, as Fregoso had urged him to do (Bembo, Opere, tom. v. p. 165, 166.)

* See the extracts from his Commentary on the Psalms, in Gerdes. Ital. Ref. p 257—261. Comp. Ginguene, Hist. Liter. d'Italie, tom. vii. p. 58. Teissier, Eloges, tom. i. p. 170. Tiraboschi, Storia, vii. 400.

† Gerdesii Ital. Ref. p. 198—200.

Aquileia. A Dominican monk of Udina, in Friuli, had given offence by teaching, in a sermon, that the elect cannot incur damnation, but will be recovered from the sins into which they may fall; and that salvation and damnation depend upon predestination, and not on our free-will. The patriarch undertook the defence of this doctrine, first in a letter to the general of the Dominicans, and afterwards in a treatise which he wrote expressly on the subject. This was subsequent to the decrees of the council of Trent which determined the doctrine of the church on these points. Grimani was not at first troubled for his opinions, but having, at a subsequent period, irritated his clergy by attempting to reform their manners, he was delated to the inquisitors: and at the very time that pope Pius IV., at the request of the senate of Venice, was about to advance him to the purple, he was accused of holding Lutheran and Calvinistic errors on seven different articles. The republic of Venice procured an order from the pope, to take the cause out of the hands of the inquisitors, and commit it to the judgment of the fathers, who, in the year 1563, were still assembled at Trent, and who, after an examination which lasted twenty-four days, came at last to the determination that the writings of the patriarch were not heretical, though they ought not to have been made public on account of certain difficult points which were treated in them, and not explained with sufficient accuracy. So great was the influence of the Senate of Venice with the pope and council!*

Of the mode of thinking, or rather feeling, among a numerous class of enlightened Italians, we have an

---

* Raynaldi Annal. ad ann. 1549, 1563. Pallavicini, apud Gerdes. Ital. Ref. p. 91—93. I have not adduced the examples of Foscarari, bishop of Modena, and San Felicio, bishop of Cava, with several others, who have been ranked among the favourers of the reformed opinions by Schelhorn, (Amœn. Eccles. tom. 1. p. 151;) because I am not aware that he had any other ground for doing this than the moderation of these distinguished prelates, and the fact of their having been thrown into the prisons of the Inquisition by that violent pontiff, Paul IV.

example in Celio Calcagnini, "one of the most learned men of that age."* His friend Peregrino Morata had sent him a book in defence of the reformed doctrine, and requested his opinion of it. The reply of Calcagnini was cautious, but sufficiently intelligible: —"I have read (says he) the book relating to the controversies so much agitated at present;† I have thought on its contents, and weighed them in the balance of reason. I find in it nothing which may not be approved and defended, but some things which, as mysteries, it is safer to suppress and conceal than to bring before the common people. Though suitable to the primitive and infant state of the church, yet now, when the decrees of the fathers and long usage have sanctioned other modes, what necessity is there for reviving antiquated practices which have for ages fallen into desuetude, especially as neither piety nor the salvation of the soul is concerned with them? Let us then, I pray you, allow these things to rest. Not that I disapprove of their being embraced by scholars and lovers of antiquity; but I would not have them communicated to the vulgar and those who are fond of innovations, lest they give occasion to strife and sedition. There are illiterate and unqualified persons who having, after long ignorance, read or heard certain new opinions respecting baptism, the marriage of the clergy, ordination, the distinction of days and of food, and public penitence, instantly conceive that these things are to be stiffly maintained and observed; wherefore, in my opinion, the discussion of these points ought to be confined to the initiated, lest the seamless coat of our Lord should be rent and torn. It was this consideration, I suppose, which moved those good men who lately laid before pope Paul a plan of reforming Christianity, to advise that the colloquies of Erasmus should be banished from our republic, as Plato formerly banished the poems of Homer from his." Having made some observations of a simi-

---

* Tiraboschi, Storia, vii. 163.
† Tiraboschi thinks that Morata was himself the author of the book, (vii. 1199.)

lar kind on the doctrine of predestination, taught by the author of the book, he concludes thus:—" Saint Paul says, 'Hast thou faith? have it to thyself before God.' Since it is dangerous to treat such things before the multitude and in public discourses, I deem it safest to 'speak with the many and think with the few.'"* In this manner did the learned apostolical protonotary satisfy his conscience; and very probably he was not aware, or did not reflect, how much weight self-interest threw into one of the scales of "the balance of reason." The temporizing maxim in which he at last takes refuge was borrowed from his former friend Erasmus; and it is curious to find it here employed to justify the sentence pronounced against one of the most useful works of that elegant and accomplished scholar. It will always be a favourite maxim with those who are determined, like Erasmus, to escape suffering, or who, as he expressed it, " feel that they have not received the grace of martyrdom;" a mode of speaking, by the way, which shows that those who are most shy to own the doctrine of predestination and grace are not the most averse to avail themselves of it, in its least defensible sense, as an apology for their own weakness. Let us not, however, imagine that this plea was confined to one age or one description of persons. An attentive observation of the conduct of mankind will, I am afraid, lead to the humiliating conclusion, that the greater part, including those who lay claim to superior intelligence and superior piety, are but too apt, whenever a sacrifice must be made or a hardship endured, to swerve from the straight path of duty which their unbiassed judgment had discerned, and to act on the principle, which, though glossed over with the specious names of expediency, prudence, and regard to peace, amounts to this, when expressed in plain language, " Let us do evil, that good may come."

The preceding narrative sufficiently shows that the reformed opinions, if they did not take deep root, were at least widely spread in Italy. The number of

* Cælii Calcagnini Opera, p. 195.

those who, from one motive or another, desired a reformation, and who would have been ready to fall in with any attempt to introduce it which promised to be successful, was so great as to warrant the conclusion that, if any prince of considerable power had placed himself at their head, or if the court of Rome had been guilty of such aggressions on the political rights of its neighbours as it committed at a future period, Italy would have followed the example of Germany, and Protestant cities and states would have risen on the south as well as the north of the Alps.* The prospect of this filled the friends of the papacy with apprehension and alarm. In a letter to the nephew of pope Paul III., Sadolet complains that the ears of his holiness were so pre-occupied with the false representations of flatterers, as not to perceive that there was " an almost universal defection of the minds of men from the church, and an inclination to execrate ecclesiastical authority."† And cardinal Caraffa signified to the same pope, "that the whole of Italy was infected with the Lutheran heresy, which had been extensively embraced both by statesmen and ecclesiastics."‡ "There was scarcely a city of Italy," says a late writer belonging to that country, "into which error had not attempted to insinuate itself, and everywhere almost it had its partizans and followers. The name of reform, the reproach of ignorance which, not without some reason, was attached to the theologians of that day, and the imposing apparatus of erudition with which the new opinions were invested, might easily deceive honest people as well as the learned; and, accordingly, many suffered themselves to be seduced, especially before the meeting of the council of Trent, who afterwards discovered their error and returned to a good way of thinking."§

No wonder, in these circumstances, that the ardent friends of the Reformation should at this period have

* Bayle, Dict. art. Acontius; addition in English translation.
† Raynaldi Annal. ad an. 1539.
‡ Spondani Annal. ad an. 1542.
§ Tiraboschi, Bibl. Modenese, tom. i. p. 20

cherished the sanguine hope that Italy would throw off the papal yoke. "See," says one, "how the gospel advances even in Italy, where it is so much borne down, and exults in the near prospect of bursting forth, like the sun from a cloud, in spite of all opposition."*
"Whole libraries (writes Melanchthon to George, prince of Anhalt) have been carried from the late fair into Italy, though the pope has published fresh edicts against us. But the truth cannot be wholly oppressed: our captain, the Lord Jesus Christ, the Son of God, will vanquish and trample on the dragon, the enemy of God, and will liberate and govern us."†
This issue of the religious movement in his native country was hailed with still more rapturous feelings by Celio Secundo Curio, in a dialogue composed by him at the period now referred to, and intended to prove that the kingdom of God and his elect is more extensive than that of the devil and the reprobate. He introduces his interlocutor, Mainardi, as saying—
"If the Lord shall continue, as he has begun, to grant prosperous success to the gospel, the delectable embassy of reconciliation and grace, we shall behold the whole world thronging, more than it has ever done at any former period, to this asylum and fortified city, to Jesus Christ, its prince, and to its three towers, faith, hope, and charity; so that, with our own eyes, we may yet see the kingdom of God of much larger extent than that which the enemy of mankind has acquired, not by his own power, but by the providence of God."—"O blessed day! O that I might live to see the ravishing prospect realized!" exclaims Curio.—"You shall live, Celio, be not afraid; you shall live to see it. The joyful sound of the gospel has within our own day reached the Scythians, Thracians, Indians, and Africans. Christ, the king of kings, has taken possession of Rhœtia and Helvetia: Ger-

* Gabrieli Valliculi, De liberali Dei Gratia, et servo hominis Arbitrio. Norimb. 1536; apud Bock, Hist. Antitrin. ii. 396.

† Epistolæ, col. 303. This letter has no date; but, from comparing its contents with Sleidan, Comment. tom. ii. p. 187, it appears to have been written in 1540.

many is under his protection: he has reigned, and will again reign in England: he sways his sceptre over Denmark and the Cymbrian nations: Prussia is his: Poland and the whole of Sarmatia are on the point of yielding to him: he is pressing forward to Pannonia: Muscovy is in his eye: he beckons France to him: Italy, our native country, is travailing in birth: and Spain will speedily follow. Even the Jews, as you perceive, have abated their former aversion to Christianity. Since they saw that we acknowledge one God, the creator of heaven and earth, and Jesus Christ whom he sent; that we worship neither images, nor symbols, nor pictures; that we no longer adore mystical bread or a wafer, as God; that they are not despised by us as they formerly were; that we acknowledge we received Christ from them; and that there is access for them to enter into that kingdom from which they have been secluded, as we once were,—their minds have undergone a great change, and now at last they are provoked to emulation."*

The striking contrast between this pleasing picture and the event which soon after took place, admonishes us not to allow our minds to be dazzled by flattering appearances, or to build theories of faith on prospects which fancy may have sketched on the deceitful horizon of public opinion; and we should recollect, that though persecution is one means, it is not the only one, by which the march of Christianity has been, and may yet again be, checked and arrested.

CHAPTER V.

SUPPRESSION OF THE REFORMATION IN ITALY.

It was in the year 1542, that the court of Rome first became seriously alarmed at the progress of the

* Cœlius Secundus Curio, De Amplitudine Regui Dei; in Schelhornii Amœn. Liter. tom. xii. p. 594, 595.

new opinions in Italy. Engrossed by foreign politics, and believing that they could at any time put down an evil which was within their reach, the pope and his counsellors had either disregarded the representations which were made to them on this head as exaggerated, or contented themselves with issuing prohibitory bulls and addressing to the bishops of the suspected places monitory letters, which were defeated by the lukewarmness of the local magistrates, or the caution of the obnoxious individuals. But in the course of the year referred to, the clergy, and particularly the friars, poured in their complaints from all parts of the country, as to the danger to which the catholic faith was exposed from the boldness of the Reformers and the increase of conventicles. At the head of these was Pietro Caraffa, commonly called the Theatine cardinal,* a prelate who made high pretensions to sanctity, but distinguished himself by his ambition and violence, when he afterwards mounted the pontifical throne, under the name of Paul IV. He laid before the sacred college the discoveries he had made as to the extent to which heresy had spread

---

* Caraffa founded a religious order called the *Theatine*, from Civita di *Chieti*, a city in Naples, of which he was bishop. In his youth he was a patron of letters; and Erasmus mentioned him in very flattering terms, in the dedication of his edition of the works of Jerome, published at Basle in 1516. "Nam ad trium linguarum haud vulgarem peritiam, ad summam cum omnium disciplinarum tum præcipue theologicæ rei cognitionem, tantum homo juvenis, (Rev. in Christo pater Joan Pet. Caraffa, episcopus Theatinus,) adjunxit integritatis et sanctimoniæ, tantum modestiæ, tantum mira gravitate conditæ comitatis, ut et sedi Romanæ magno sit ornamento, et Britannis omnibus absolutum quoddam exemplar exhibeat, [the bishop of Chieti was then in England as ambassador from Leo X. to Henry VIII.] unde omnes omnium virtutum formam sibi petere possint." The bishop discharged this obligation, when he was afterwards advanced to the pontifical chair, by prohibiting the *Jerome*, and all the other works of Erasmus. It may not be improper to give the words of the discharge in full, as a lesson to all literary flatterers. Of others, whose whole works were interdicted, the names are merely given, but he is introduced at full length with all the honours:—" Desiderius Erasmus Roterdamus cum universis commentariis, annotationibus, scholiis, dialogis, epistolis, censuris, versionibus, libris et scriptis suis, etiam si nil penitus contra religionem vel de religione contineant." (Index Auct. et Lib. Proh. sig b. 3. Romæ, 1559.)

in Naples, and various parts of Italy; and convinced them of the necessity of adopting the speediest and most vigorous measures for its extermination.* It was resolved to proceed, in the first place, against such of the ecclesiastics as were understood to favour the new opinions. Among these Ochino and Martyr were the most distinguished; but as they were in possession of great popularity, and had not yet made open defection from the catholic faith, spies were placed round their persons, while a secret investigation was made into their past conduct, with the view of procuring direct evidence of their heretical opinions.

Such a deep impression had the sermons delivered by Ochino made on the minds of the citizens of Venice, that they joined in an application to the pope to grant them an opportunity of hearing him a second time. His holiness accordingly directed the cardinal of Carpi, who was protector of the order of Capuchins, to send him to Venice during Lent in the year 1542; but, at the same time, gave instructions to the apostolical nuncio to watch his conduct. The whole city ran in crowds to hear their favourite preacher. It does not appear that he used greater freedom in his discourses on the present occasion than he had used on the former; but a formal complaint was soon made against him, of having advanced doctrines at variance with the catholic faith, particularly on the head of justification.† On his appearance before the nuncio, however he was able to defend himself so powerfully against his accusers, that no plausible pretext could be found for proceeding against him. Perceiving that he was surrounded by spies, he for some time exerted a greater circumspection over his words in the pulpit; but having heard that Julio Terentiano, a convert of Valdes, with whom he had been intimate at Naples, was thrown into prison, he could no longer restrain himself. In the course of a sermon, at which the

* Caracciolus, de Vita Pauli IV. p. 240.
† Palearii Opera, p. 294. The same thing is stated by Ochino himself in his Apology to the Magistrates of Sienna, republished at the end of the second volume of his *Prediche.*

senators and principal persons of the city were present, he introduced that subject, and broke out in these words—"What remains for us to do, my lords? And to what purpose do we fatigue and exhaust ourselves, if those men, O noble Venice, queen of the Adriatic—if those men, who preach to you the truth, are to be thrown into prisons, thrust into cells and loaded with chains and fetters? What place will be left to us? what field will remain open to the truth? O that we had but liberty to preach the truth! How many blind, who now grope their way in the dark, would be restored to light!" On hearing of this bold appeal, the nuncio instantly interdicted him from preaching, and reported the matter to the pope. But the Venetians were so importunate in his behalf, that the interdict was removed within three days, and he again appeared in the pulpit.* Lent being ended, he went to Verona, where he assembled those of his order who were engaged in studies preparatory to the work of preaching, and commenced reading to them a course of lectures on the Epistles of Paul; but he had not proceeded far in this work, when he received a citation from Rome to answer certain charges founded on his lectures, and on the informations of the nuncio at Venice.† Having set out on his journey to the capital, he had an interview at Bologna with cardinal Contarini, then lying on his death-bed, who assured him that he agreed with the Protestants on the article of justification, though he was opposed to them on the other points of controversy.‡ In the month of August, Ochino went to Florence, where he received information that his death was resolved on at Rome, upon which he retired hastily to Ferrara, and being assisted in his flight by the duchess Renée, escaped the hands

* Boverio, Annali de Capuccini, tom. i. p. 426.
† Ibid. p. 427.
‡ Ochino, Prediche, tom. i. num. 10. This fact has been strongly denied by Boverio, (ut supra,) and by Card Quirini. (Diatrib. ad vol. iii Epist. Poli, cap. ix.) Beccatello says he was present at the interview, and that the cardinal, who was very weak, merely requested a share in Ochino's prayers. (Ibid. p. 137.)

of the armed men who had been despatched to apprehend him, and reached Geneva in safety.*

The defection and flight of Ochino struck his countrymen with amazement, proportioned to the admiration in which they had held him.† Claudio Tolomeo, esteemed one of the best epistolary writers of his age, says, in a letter which he addressed to him, that the tidings of his defection from the Catholic to the Lutheran camp, had completely stunned him, and appeared for some time utterly false and incredible.‡ The lamentations of the Theatine cardinal were still more tragical, and may be quoted as a specimen of that mystical and sublimated devotion, which, at this period, was combined with a spirit of ambition and bigotry, in a certain class of the defenders of the papacy. "What has befallen thee, Bernardino? What evil spirit has seized thee, like the reprobate king of Israel of old? My father, my father! the chariot and the charioteer of Israel! whom, a little ago, we with admiration beheld ascending to heaven in the spirit and power of Elias, must we now bewail thy descent to hell with the chariots and horsemen of Pharaoh? All Italy flocked to thee; they hung upon thy breast: thou hast betrayed the land; thou hast slain the inhabitants. O doting old man, who has bewitched

---

* Ochino has himself given an account of his departure from Italy and the reasons of it, in his answer to Muzio, which is reprinted at the end of the second volume of his *Prediche*. Lubieniecius and Sandius represent him as having gone to Rome, and, in the presence of the pope, reproved from the pulpit the tyranny, pride, and vices of the pontifical court. The latter adds, that, in a sermon, he brought forward a number of arguments against the doctrine of the Trinity, deferring the answer to them till another time, under the pretence that the hour had elapsed; but, as soon as he left the pulpit, he mounted a horse which was ready for him, and, quitting Rome and Italy, eluded the inquisitors. This is a ridiculous story, evidently made up from the manner in which Ochino brought forward the antitrinitarian sentiments a little before his death.

† In a letter to Melanchthon, dated from Geneva on the 14th of Feb. 1543, Calvin says—"Habemus hic Bernardinum Senensem, magnum et præclarum virum, qui suo discessu non parum Italiam commovit. Is, ut vobis suo nomine salutem ascriberem, petiit." (Sylloge Epist. Burman. tom. ii. p. 230.)

‡ Tolomeo, Lettere, p. 237. Venez. 1565. Schelhorn, Ergoetzlichkeiten, tom. iii. p. 1006.

thee to feign to thyself another Christ than thou wert taught by the catholic church? Ah! Bernardino, how great wert thou in the eyes of all men! Oh, how beautiful and fair! Thy coarse but sacred cap excelled the cardinal's hat and the pope's mitre, thy nakedness the most gorgeous apparel, thy bed of wattles the softest and most delicious couch, thy deep poverty the riches of the world. Thou wert the herald of the highest, the trumpet sounding far and wide; thou wert full of wisdom and adorned with knowledge; the Lord placed thee in the garden of Eden, in his holy mount, as a light above the candlestick, as the sun of the people, as a pillar in his temple, as a watchman in his vineyard, as a shepherd to feed his flock. Still thy eloquent discourses sound in our ears; still we see thy unshod feet. Where now are all thy magnificent words concerning contempt of the world? Where thy invectives against covetousness? Thou that didst teach that a man should not steal, dost thou steal?"* In this inflated style, which cardinal Quirini calls "elegant and vehement," did Caraffa proceed until he had exhausted all the metaphors in the *Flowers of the saints*.

Ochino was not silent on his part. Beside an apologetical letter to the magistrates of his native city of Sienna, and another to Tolomeo, he published a large collection of his sermons, and various polemical treatises against the church of Rome, which, being written in the Italian language and in a popular style, produced a great effect upon his countrymen, notwithstanding the antidotes administered by writers hired to refute and defame him.† His flight was the signal for the apprehension of some of his most intimate friends, and a rigorous investigation into the sentiments of the religious order to which he belong-

* Bock, Hist. Antitrin. tom. ii. p. 495. Quirini Diatr. ad vol. iii. Epist. Poli, p. 86.
† A list of Ochino's works is to be found in Haym, Biblioteca, tom. ii. p. 616, &c.; in Observat Halens. tom. v. p. 65. &c.; and in Bock, ii. p. 515, &c. His principal antagonists were Girolamo Muzio, the author of *Le Mentite Ochiniane*, and Ambrogio Catarino, who wrote *Remedio a la pestilente dottrina di Bernardo Ochino*.

ed; some of whom made their escape, and others saved their lives by recanting their opinions. The pope was so incensed by the apostasy of Ochino, and the number of Capuchins who were found implicated in his heresy, that he proposed at one time to suppress the order.*

Martyr, in the mean time, was in equal danger at Lucca. The monks of his order, irritated by the reformation of manners which, as general visitor, he had sought to introduce among them, were forward to accuse him, and acted as spies on his conduct. For a whole year he was exposed to their secret machinations and open detraction, against which he could not have maintained himself, if he had not enjoyed the protection of the Lucchese.† With the view of trying the disposition of the citizens, his enemies obtained an order from Rome to apprehend Terentiano, one of his friends, who was confessor to the Augustinian convent, as a person suspected of heresy. Some noblemen, who admired the confessor's piety and were convinced of his innocence, forced the doors of his prison and set him at liberty; but having fallen and broken a limb in his flight, he was again taken and conveyed to Rome in triumph. Encouraged by this success, they lodged a formal accusation against Martyr before the papal court; messengers were sent through the different convents to exhort the monks not to neglect the opportunity of recovering "their ancient liberty," by inflicting punishment on their adversary; and a general congregation of the order being convened at Genoa, he was cited instantly to attend. Aware of the prejudice which had been excited against him, and warned by his friends that snares were laid for his life, he resolved, after deliberation, to avoid the danger, by withdrawing himself from the

* Bock, ii p. 496.
† In the course of the inquiries which he had instituted, several individuals had been deprived of their offices on account of gross delinquencies, and the rector-general of the order with some others, were condemned to perpetual confinement in the islands of Tremiti. (Simler, Oratio de Martyre, sig. b iij.)

rage and craft of his enemies. After allotting a part of his library to the convent, he committed the remainder to Cristoforo Trenta, a patrician of Lucca, with the view of its being sent after him to Germany; and having set the affairs of the institution in order, and committed the charge of it to his vicar, he left the city secretly, accompanied by Paolo Lacisio, Theodosio Trebellio, and Julio Terentiano, who had been released from prison. At Pisa he wrote letters to cardinal Pole, and to the brethren of the monastery at Lucca, which he committed to trusty persons with instructions not to deliver them until a month after his departure. In these he laid open the grievous errors and abuses which attached to the popish religion in general, and the monastic life in particular, to which his conscience would no longer allow him to give countenance; and, as additional grounds for his withdrawing, referred to the odium which he had incurred, and the plots formed against his life. At the same time, he sent back the ring which he had been accustomed to wear as the badge of his office, that it might not be said that he had appropriated the smallest part of the property of the convent to his private use. Having met with Ochino at Florence, and settled with him their respective routes, he set out, and, travelling cautiously and with expedition by Bologna, Ferrara, and Verona, reached Zurich in safety, along with his three companions.* They had not been long there when they received an invitation from Bucer to repair to Strasburg, where they obtained situations as professors in the academy. From that place Martyr wrote to the reformed church of Lucca, of which he had been pastor, stating the reasons which had induced him to quit his native country, and encouraging them to persevere in their adherence to the gospel which they had embraced.†

* Simler, Oratio de Martyre, sig. b iiij.

† Martyris Epist. universis Ecclesiæ Lucensis fidelibus, 8 Calend. Jan. 1543, in Loc. Commun p. 750—752 He, about the same time, published an Exposition of the Apostles' Creed in Italian, "to render to all an account of his faith." (Simler, Orat. de Martyre, sig. cj.)

It was no sooner known that Martyr had fled, than a visitation of the monastery over which he had presided was ordered, with the view of ascertaining the extent to which it was tainted with his heretical opinions. A great many of the monks were thrown into prison; and, before a year elapsed, eighteen of them had deserted Italy and retired to Switzerland.* The Protestant church which had been formed in the city, though discouraged by the loss of its founder, and exposed to the threats of its adversaries, was not dispersed or broken up. Under the protection of some of the principal persons of the state, it continued to hold its meetings in private, enjoyed the instruction of regular pastors, and increased in knowledge and even in numbers. In a letter addressed to them, more than twelve years after he left Lucca, and on the back of a disastrous change in their situation, Martyr says— " Such progress have you made for many years in the gospel of Jesus Christ, that it was unnecessary for me to excite you by my letters; and all that remained for me to do, was to make honourable mention of you every where, and to give thanks to our Heavenly Father for the spiritual blessings with which he had crowned you. To this I had an additional motive, from reflecting that my hand was honoured to lay the foundations of this good work, in weakness I confess, but still, by the grace of Christ, to your no small profit. My joy was increased by learning that, after my labours among you were over, God provided you with other and abler teachers, by whose prudent care and salutary instructions the work begun in you was advanced."†

One of the teachers to whom Martyr refers was Celio Secundo Curio, who had obtained a situation in the university. The senate protected him for some

* Martyris Epist. ut supra. Lettre de M le cardinal Spinola, Evêque de Luques—Avec les Considerations, p. 24. It appears, from the remarks which the refugees make upon the cardinal's letter, that Jerom Zanchi was one of the learned men whom Martyr drew to Lucca.

† Martyris Epistola ad fratres Lucenses, anno 1556; in Loc. Commun. p. 771.

time in spite of the outcries of the clergy;* but the pope having, in the year 1543, addressed letters to the magistrates complaining of this, and requiring them to send him to Rome to answer charges which had been brought against him from various quarters, they gave him private intimation to consult his safety. Upon this he retired to Ferrara, whence, by the advice of the duchess Renée, who furnished him with letters of recommendation to the magistrates of Zurich and Berne, he quitted Italy, and took up his residence at Lausanne. In the course of the same year he returned for his wife and children, whom he had left behind him; on which occasion he made one of those narrow escapes which, though well authenticated, throw an air of romance over the narrative of his life. The familiars of the inquisition, who were scattered over the country, had tracked the route of Curio from the time he entered Italy. Not venturing to appear in Lucca, he stopped at the neighbouring town of Pessa, until his family should join him. While he was sitting at dinner in the inn, a captain of the papal band, called in Italy barisello, suddenly made his appearance, and entering the room, commanded him, in the pope's name, to yield himself as a prisoner. Curio, despairing of escape, rose to deliver himself up, retaining unconsciously in his hand the knife with which he had been carving his food. The barisello seeing an athletic figure approaching him with a large knife, was seized with a sudden panic, and retreated to a corner of the room; upon which Curio, who possessed great presence of mind, walked deliberately out of the room, passed, without interruption, through the midst of the armed men who were stationed at the door, took his horse from the stable, and made good his flight.†

* In a letter, dated "Lucæ, 1542, quarto Idus Junii," Curio says, "I meant to have added more, but a message has been just sent me, that I am in danger of my life, by the information of certain adversaries of the truth, who plot, and think, and dream of nothing else but abolishing the memory of Christ from the earth" (Coelii Secundi Curionis Araneus, p. 161. Bas 1544.)

† Stupani Oratio de S. C. Curione, ut supra, p. 344, 345.

The inquisition, from the first establishment of that court in the twelfth century, had been introduced into Italy, and was placed under the management of the conventual friars of the order of St. Francis. Its arbitrary and vexatious proceedings could not, however, be long borne by the free states of which that country was then composed; and, about the middle of the fourteenth century, measures were generally adopted to restrain its exorbitant power, in spite of the opposition made by Clement VI. and the censures which he fulminated. The right of the bishops to take part with the inquisitors in the examination of heretics was recognized; they were restricted to the simple cognizance of the charge of heresy, and deprived of the power of imprisonment, confiscation, fine, and corporal punishment, which was declared to belong solely to the secular arm.* Such a mode of procedure was found to be ineffectual for suppressing free inquiry, and maintaining the authority of the church, after the new opinions began to spread in Italy. The bishops were, in some instances, lukewarm; they were accessible to the claims of humanity or friendship; their forms of process were slow and open; and the accused person often escaped before the necessary order for his arrest could be obtained from the civil power. On these accounts, the erection of a court, similar to the modern inquisition of Spain, had been for some years eagerly pressed by the more zealous Romanists, with cardinal Caraffa at their head, as the only means of preserving Italy from being overrun with heresy. Accordingly, pope Paul III. founded at Rome the Congregation of the Holy Office, by a bull dated the 1st of April 1543, which granted the title and rights of inquisitors-general of the faith to six cardinals, and gave them authority, on both sides of the Alps, to try all causes of heresy, with the power of apprehending and incarcerating suspected persons, and their abettors, of whatsoever estate, rank, or order, of nominating officers under them, and appointing

* Galluzzi, Istor. del Granducato di Toscano, tom. i. p. 142, 143.

inferior tribunals in all places, with the same or with limited powers.*

This court instantly commenced its operations within the ecclesiastical states; and it was the great object of the popes, during the remainder of this century, to extend its power over Italy. The greatest resistance was made to it in Venice. After long negotiation, the inquisitors were authorized to try causes of heresy within that state, on the condition that a certain number of magistrates and lawyers should always be present at the examination of witnesses, to protect the citizens from prosecutions undertaken on frivolous grounds or from mercenary views, and that the definitive sentence should not, at least in the case of laics, be pronounced before it was submitted to the senate.† The popes found less opposition in the other states and cities of Italy. In Tuscany it was arranged, that three commissioners, elected by the congregation at Rome, along with the local inquisitor, should judge in all causes of religion, and intimate their sentence to the duke, who was bound to carry it into execution.‡ One would have thought that such provisions would have satisfied the Holy Office; but, in addition, it was continually soliciting the local authorities to send such as were accused, especially if they were either ecclesiastical persons or strangers, to be tried by the inquisition at Rome; and even the senate of Venice, jealous as it was of any interference with its authority, yielded in some instances to requests of this kind.§

No court ever knew so well as that of Rome how to combine policy with violence, to temporize without relinquishing its claims, and dexterously to avail itself of particular events which crossed its wishes, for the purpose of advancing its general designs. The Nea-

* Limborch's Hist. of the Inquisition, vol. i. p. 151; Chandler's transl. Llorente, Hist. de l'Inquis. tom ii p. 78.
† Busdragi Epistola: Scrinium Antiquar. tom. i. p. 321, 326, 327. Thuani Hist. ad an. 1548.
‡ Galluzzi, i. 143.
§ Bezæ Icones, sig Hh. iij. Hist. des Martyrs, f. 444, 446. Geneve, 1597.

politans had twice successfully resisted the establishment of the inquisition in their country, at the beginning of the sixteenth century. In 1546, the emperor Charles V., with the view of extirpating the Lutheran heresy, renewed the attempt, and gave orders to set up that tribunal in Naples, after the same form in which it had long been established in Spain. This measure created the greatest discontent, and one day as the officers of the inquisition were conducting some persons to prison, the inhabitants, having released the prisoners, rose in arms, and broke out into open tumult. The revolt was suppressed by military force, but it was judged prudent to abandon the design. Nothing could be conceived more agreeable to the court of Rome than this formidable tribunal; yet they took the part of the people against the government of Naples, and encouraged them in their opposition, by telling them that they had reason for their fears, because the Spanish inquisition was extremely severe, and refused to profit by the example of that of Rome, of which none had had reason to complain during the three years in which it had existed.* They pursued the same line of policy when Philip II., at a subsequent period, endeavoured to establish his favourite tribunal in the duchy of Milan. The reigning pontiff, Pius IV., was at first favourable to that scheme, from which he anticipated effectual aid to his measures for keeping down the reformed opinions; but finding that the Milanese were determined to resist the innovation, and had engaged the greater part of the Italian bishops on their side, his holiness told the deputies who came to beg his intercession in their favour, that "he knew the extreme rigour of the Spanish inquisitors," and would take care that the inquisition should be maintained in Milan as formerly in dependence on the court of Rome, "whose decrees respecting the mode of process were very mild, and reserved to the accused the most entire liberty of defending themselves."† This language was glaringly

* Limborch, vol. i. p. 143. Llorente, tom. i. p. 332; ii. 118, 121.
† Limborch and Llorente, ut supra.

hypocritical, and quite irreconcilable with the conduct of the reigning pontiff, as well as that of his predecessors, who had all supported the Spanish inquisition, and given their formal sanction to the most cruel and unjust of its modes of procedure. But it served the purpose of preserving the authority of the holy see, and of reconciling the minds of the Italians to the court which had been lately erected at Rome. The Roman inquisition was founded on the same principles as that of Spain, nor did the forms of process in the two courts differ in any essential or material point; and yet the horror which the inhabitants of Italy had conceived at the idea of the latter induced them to submit to the former: so easy is it, by a little management and humouring of their prejudices, to deprive the people of their liberties.

The peaceable establishment of the inquisition in Italy was decisive of the unfortunate issue of the movements in favour of religious reform in that country. This iniquitous and bloody tribunal could never obtain a footing either in France or in Germany. The attempt to introduce it into the Netherlands was resisted by the adherents of the old as well as the disciples of the new religion; and it kindled a civil war, which, after a sanguinary and protracted struggle, issued in rending seven flourishing provinces from the Spanish crown, and establishing civil and religious liberty. The ease with which it was introduced into Italy, showed that, whatever illumination there was among the Italians, and how desirous soever they might be to share in those blessings which other nations had secured to themselves, they were destitute of that public spirit and energy of principle which were requisite to shake off the degrading yoke by which they were oppressed. Popish historians do more homage to truth than credit to their cause, when they say that the erection of the inquisition was the salvation of the catholic church in Italy.* No sooner was this engine of tyranny and torture erected, than those who had rendered themselves obnoxious to it by the pre-

* Pallavicini, Istor. Concil. Trent, lib. xiv. c. 9.

vious avowal of the their sentiments, fled in great numbers from a country in which they could no longer look for protection from injustice and cruelty. The prisons of the inquisition were every where filled with those who remained behind, and who, according to the policy of that court, were retained for years in dark and silent durance, with the view of inspiring their friends with dread, and of subduing their own minds to a recantation of their sentiments. With the exception of a few places, the public profession which had been made of the Protestant religion was suppressed. Its friends, however, were still numerous; many of them were animated by the most ardent attachment to the cause; they continued to encourage and edify one another in their private meetings; and it required all the activity and violence of the inquisitors, during twenty years, to discover and exterminate them.

The proceedings of the inquisition excited indignation and terror in the breasts of others besides those who were the immediate objects of its vengeance; and these feelings, acting on the disturbed state of the public mind, gave rise to a conspiracy, which, if it had been organized with greater secresy and foresight, might have given a favourable turn to the affairs of the Protestants in Italy. Great discontent had been caused by the overthrow of republican government in different cities; and numerous exiles from Florence, Pisa, and Sienna, had taken refuge in Lucca, where they confirmed one another in resentment against the pope and emperor, as the authors of their wrongs, and in the hopes of being able, on some emergency, and in concert with their friends at home, to recover their ancient liberties. Francesco Burlamacchi, gonfalomere or captain of the forces at Lucca, a man of ardent and enterprising mind, conceived the bold design of uniting the political and religious malcontents in an attempt to revolutionize the country. By means of the troops, of which he had the command, added to the exiles in the city, he proposed to surprise Pisa, to call on the inhabitants to assert their independence, and, having reinforced his army, to rear the standard of liberty, and, with the assistance of Pietro Strozzi and France, to effect a change in the government and religion of the Italian states.* The time chosen for executing this project was not unpropitious, and held out a flattering prospect of success to persons of a sanguine mind. After employing in vain every method of policy, for many years, to dissolve the Smalcaldic league, Charles V. determined, in 1546, to suppress it by force, and, for this purpose, drew the flower of his army to Germany, from various parts of his dominions, including Naples and Milan. The pope and the grand duke of Tuscany had sent reinforcements to the emperor,† while other states had contributed money for carrying on this war of religion; so that Italy was, in a great degree, stripped of that military defence by which it had been kept in a state of subjection to the dominant authorities. It is not improbable, that some correspondence had taken place between the projector of the insurrection and the Protestant princes of Germany, as they had solicited the duke of Tuscany to make a diversion in their favour by attacking the states of the pope, with whom he was at variance. That secret negociations were carried on with the court of France through Strozzi, there can be little doubt. But Francis I. was approaching the end of his active reign; age and ill success had rendered him cautious and inert; and the same reasons which led him to permit the German princes to be crushed by his rival, would prevent him from lending open or efficient aid to the undertaking of an obscure individual in Italy. The affair, however, did not come to a trial of arms: the conspiracy was revealed at the same time to the senate of Lucca and the grand duke of Tuscany, and Burlamacchi was instantly seized and sent a prisoner to Milan.‡ Though the Protes-

* Galluzzi, Istoria del Granducato di Toscano, tom. i. p. 79.
† Sleidan, Comment tom. ii. p. 515, 516, edit. Am. Ende.
‡ Galluzzi, ut supra, p. 80. This author does not assert, that Burlamacchi had adopted the reformed opinions. Several distinguished individuals of that name, however, are to be found among the Lucchese, who afterwards took refuge in Geneva. A descendant of that

tants do not appear to have taken an active part in this plot, its discovery could not fail to operate to their prejudice, by awakening the jealousy of the civil authorities, and stimulating the vigilance of the inquisition.

It was natural for the Protestants, when overtaken by the storm, to retreat to the court of Ferrara, where they had found shelter at an early period; but the pope had taken the precaution of gaining over the duke, and securing his co-operation in his measures against the Reformers. The effects of this change were first felt at Modena. In consequence of the unfavourable reports made of the sentiments of the members of the Academy, consultations had been repeatedly held at Rome; and Paul III. would have proceeded to the highest censure of the church against them, had not some of their personal friends in the conclave interposed, and averted his displeasure. In the month of June, 1542, it was proposed to cite some of the most influential persons among them to Rome or Bologna; but cardinal Sadolet requested permission, in the first place, to try the effect of a friendly letter upon them. Accordingly, he wrote in the most conciliatory spirit to Lodovico Castelvetro, informing him of what had passed in the consistory, and begging that he and his colleagues would give assurances of their attachment to the Catholic faith, and desist from every practice which gave rise to suspicions against them. Castelvetro and his companions answered this letter to the satisfaction of the cardinal, who insisted, however, that they should write to the pope himself, protesting that they were faithful sons of the Roman Church.* This they appear to have declined; upon

family, Fabrice, called by Bayle the Photius of his age, was minister of the Italian church there; and another, Jean-Jaques, was professor of law, and author of a celebrated treatise on that science. (Fragmens Extraits des Registres de Geneve, p. 131, 436. Senebier, Hist. Litt. de Geneve, ii. 27. iii. 87.)

* Sadoleti Epist. Famil. vol. iii. p. 317, 319. The answers by Grillenzoni, Portus, Castelvetro, and Alessandro Milano, are inserted in Bibl. Modenese, tom. iii. p. 433—441.

which a resolution was taken to draw up certain articles of faith, to be subscribed by all the members of the academy. The report of this produced a great sensation in Modena. Portus, the Greek lecturer, and two of his companions, left the place on different pretexts, and the rest complained loudly of the manner in which they were treated. If the proposed measure was carried into effect, they said, there was an end to all freedom of inquiry: they might sell their books and renounce the study of the sacred Scriptures, for no ingenuous person would consent to think or write under such fetters. So great was the ferment, that Morone, tender of the peace of his see and the honour of the academy, repented of the consent he had given to a measure which, it would seem, had not originated with him; and he is said to have written to the pope, praying him to suspend the subscription of the formulary, as the academicians had already given sufficient pledges of their catholicism, and declined to subscribe, because it would lead the world to believe that they had been justly suspected of heresy. But the court of Rome was resolute in carrying the measure into execution. Much light is thrown on these transactions by a document, preserved in the ducal archives at Ferrara, which contains the secret instructions given by the governor of Modena to his chancellor, whom he sent, on the 2d of August, 1542, to advise with Hercules on this perplexing affair. It states, that the academicians showed themselves averse to subscription, and urged, that though they were ready to affix their names to some of the articles of the formulary, yet these were matters which should be referred to the determination of a council; that the bishop had proceeded in this affair with all possible dexterity, and acted in concert with the governor, whom he had reminded that, through the harshness of cardinal Cajetan, the papal legate, to the Lutherans, a small spark had burst into a conflagration, which continued still to rage, and that he was afraid lest God, for the sins of the world, should permit so many men of genius, spirit, and subtlety to be driven to despair, and thereby another such flame should be kindled in Italy: that the pope, thinking that Morone proceeded with too great gentleness, had committed the affair to six cardinals in Rome, one of whom had already come to Modena to inquire after heretics; and that the bishop, offended at this step, had signified that he would interfere no more in the business, but was prevailed upon, by the entreaties of the governor, to lend his aid in accommodating the parties, and to receive the subscriptions.*

In the beginning of September, cardinals Sadolet and Cortese met with the bishop at Modena, as commissioners from the pope to see the formulary subscribed. It had been drawn up with great moderation by Contarini, at the request of Morone, and the objections made to it related chiefly to the sacraments. The members of the academy, when called, refused to subscribe until the conservators of the city had set the example. Three of these were with difficulty induced to affix their names; and to encourage them still further, the cardinals agreed to add their own signatures. But still the academicians continued to demur, and the negotiation would have broken off, had it not been for the exertions of Morone. He had already held interviews with them individually, particularly with Berettari, to whose scruples on the subject of the mass and collateral topics he had listened with much forbearance and candour.† He now assembled them, and spoke with such earnestness and affection, that they yielded to his request; and their brethren who had withdrawn having returned upon a friendly invitation, the formulary was subscribed by the whole body, together with the official men in the city, to the great joy of the commissioners.‡

* Bibl. Modenese, tom. i. p. 15—17.
† Beccatelli, Vita del Card. Contarini, sect. 33. Muratori, Vita del Castelvetro; Opere Crit p. 18. Bibl. Modenese, tom. i. p. 234, 235 Letter from Morone to Contarini, 3d July 1542. (Poli Epist. vol. iii p. 285.) In this letter Morone says—"Ben priego V S. Reverendiss non lascia che questi mie lettere vadino in mano d'altre, che delli suvi fedeli secretari."
‡ Bibl. Modenese, tom. i. p. 17—19. Muratori. p. 19, 20. The

It was not to be expected that an arrangement so eagerly pressed on the one side, and so reluctantly acceded to on the other, would be productive of real or lasting concord. The members of the academy retained their former sentiments, and took every opportunity of mortifying the clergy, whom they looked upon as the prime instigators of the late proceedings against their body. On the first Sunday of Advent, 1543, there was no sermon in Modena; because, as one who lived in the city at that time expresses it in his journal, "every preacher, how excellent soever, was criticised by certain literati, and none would come to contest with them on their own ground." In the following year, the bishop sent a minor-conventual friar, named Bartolommeo della Pergala, of whose preaching the journalist just quoted gives the following account, in his style of homely humour:— "All the members of the academy went to hear him, to the number of more than twenty-five, including the bookseller, Antonio, who first introduced the prohibited books in the vulgar language, which were afterwards burnt at Rome as heretical. The said friar did not preach the gospel,* nor did he make mention of any saint, male or female, nor of any doctor of the Church, nor of lent, or fasting. This was to the taste of the academicians. Many believed that they would go to paradise in their stocking soles;† for, said they, Christ has paid for us." Disappointed in his expectations from the preacher, the bishop

---

formulary, with the subscriptions, is printed in the first volume of the works of cardinal Cortese. When it was first submitted to the revisal of Cortese, he suggested a number of alterations, with the view of making the test stricter, on the heads of justification, free will, and the eucharist; but Morone, who knew they would defeat the object, took care that they should not be adopted. (Bibl. Moden. tom. vi. p. 1—3.) It is to the termination of this affair that cardinal Pole refers, when, in a letter to Contarini, he says, that the marchioness of Pescaro gives thanks to God; "per il gran dono di charita, il qual risplende più in quella santo negozio di Modena." (Poli Epist. vol. iii. p. 58.)

* The meaning is, that the preacher took his text from the epistles, and not from the gospels.

† "Molti credono andare in Paradiso in calze solate."

caused Pergala to be apprehended and delivered over to the inquisition, which condemned forty-six propositions in his doctrine, and ordered him to retract them publicly in the Church in which he had preached. The retractation was made for form's sake; and it was no sooner over, than an address was presented to him, signed by the most respectable citizens, and bearing an honourable testimony to his character and talents. In the course of the same year, Pontremolo, another monk of the same order, who preached at Modena, was condemned for teaching heretical doctrines.*

In the year 1545, a prosecution was commenced against the academicians, which had for its immediate object Filippo Valentino, a young man of great precocity of intellect and versatility of genius.† Pellegrino Erri, or Heri, a member of the academy having received an affront from some of his colleagues, went to Rome, and gave information to the Holy Office that the literati of his native city were generally disaffected to the Catholic Church, and that some of them were industrious in disseminating their heretical sentiments in private ‡ In consequence of this, the pope addressed a brief to the duke of Ferrara, stating, that he had received information that the Lutheran

---

* Bibl. Modenese, tom. i. p. 18, 19.

† Castelvetro says, that at seven years of age Valentino composed letters in a style worthy of Cicero, and sonnets and canzoni which would have done honour to a poet of mature age He could repeat verbatim sermons or lectures which he had heard only once; and had the principal poets in Latin and Italian by heart. (Muratori, ut supra, p. 21, 22.)

‡ That Erri was a scholar, and acquainted with Hebrew, appears from the following work:—"I Salmi di David, tradotti con bellissimo e dotissimo stile dalla lingua Ebrea, nella Latina e volgare, dal S. Pellegrino Heri Modenese." The dedication by the author, to Conte Fulvio Rangone, is dated "Di Modena il 1 de Gennaio 1568;" but the work was published at Venice in 1573, with a preface by Giordan Ziletti. Riederer, who has given extracts, both from the translations and notes, says—"I am certain, that any person who examines this book narrowly, will find in it many traces of a concealed Protestant, who continued in external communion with the Roman church, and did not choose to expose himself to the inquisition." (Nachrichten, tom. iv. p. 28.) This confirms the account given in the text, of Erri's motives in informing against his colleagues.

heresy was daily gaining ground in Modena, and that the author and prime cause of this was that son of wickedness, Filippo Valentino; on which account his holiness, knowing how grieving this must be to a person of the duke's piety, requires him to cause the said Filippo to be immediately seized, his books and papers to be examined, and his person detained at the instance of the pope; so that, the ringleader being quelled, his accomplices might be reduced to obedience, and a stop put to the alarming evil.* Erri returned to Modena in the character of apostolical commissary; and, attended by an armed force which he procured from the civil power, came one night to the house of Filippo to apprehend him. The latter having received warning of the design, had made his escape; but his books and papers were seized by the inquisition, which proved the occasion of great trouble to many of his fellow-citizens, and especially to those who had lived on terms of the greatest intimacy with him. On the following morning a ducal edict was published. It forbade any to have heretical or suspected books, or to dispute in public or private on any point of religion, under the penalty, for the first offence of a hundred crowns of gold, or of being subjected to the strappado, if unable to pay that sum; for the second offence two thousand crowns, or banishment from the state; and for the third offence, confiscation of goods, or death. The proclamation of this severe edict spread dismay through the city, and dispersed the academy, of which we hear no more afterwards.†

There were still many persons attached to the reformed opinions in Modena, and, within a short time, an arrangement was made, through the good offices of the duke, which permitted Valentino to return to his native city. During the pontificates of Julius III. and Marcellus II., matters continued quiet; but no

* Raynaldi Annal. ad an. 1545. The letter is inserted by Tiraboschi, in his Biblioteca Modenese, tom v p. 312, 313

† Bibl. Modenese, tom. 1 p 19. Muratori, Vita del Castelvetro, p. 21—23.

sooner had Paul IV. mounted the papal throne, than violent measures were adopted. By orders from Rome, a secret inquiry was instituted into the sentiments of some of the principal citizens, without the knowledge either of the governor, or of Foscarari, who was now bishop of Modena, both of whom were offended at a step which they regarded as at once unnecessary and an ungracious interference with their authority.* On being made acquainted with the fact, the duke, through his minister at Rome, endeavoured to put a stop to the proceedings, and to prevent the fire, which it had cost so much pains to suppress, from being again kindled; but he was forced to yield to the solicitations of the pope, and granted permission to execute a summons publicly at Modena, on the 6th of July 1556, by which Castelvetro, Filippo Valentino, his cousin Bonifacio, provost of the cathedral church, and Gadaldino the printer and bookseller, were cited to appear before the inquisition at Rome.

The city was greatly agitated by this citation, and the conservators, having met on the 17th of the same month, addressed a strong remonstrance to the duke. It was, they said, a thing altogether unusual and strange that laics should be cited to Rome, and that citizens should be subjected to so great inconvenience and expense; the charge of heresy was calculated to bring infamy upon a city, which, as they were assured by their officials, was in a state of the greatest quietness; the only tendency of reviving suspicions which had been buried, and prosecuting upon vague rumors, was to add scandal to scandal; the persons cited were highly respectable, and universally esteemed as virtuous men, who did not deserve to be disgraced in such a manner; there was reason to think that the prosecution had originated in spleen and prejudice on the part of men, of whom his excellency knew there were not a few in that country who, under the cloak of zeal for the faith, sought to gratify

* Letters from Clemente Tiene to duke Hercules II., 26th of Oct. 1555. Bibl. Modenese, tom. i. p. 446, 447

their personal revenge; it was impossible to foresee an end to the affair, after so many expedients had already been tried, without pacifying the authorities at Rome; the cardinals had put the whole city to the test of subscription, his excellency had interposed his authority, the local inquisitors had used their office without any impediment, and their diocesan, a man of great sanctity, was vigilant in such matters: what could they discover at Rome which nobody could discover at Modena? The conservators afterwards sent one of their number to urge the duke to interpose in behalf of their fellow-citizens, and the governor wrote in support of their application. Thus urged, the duke again applied to the pope, requesting that the trial should be suspended, or, if this could not be granted, that it should take place at Modena. Both of these requests were refused. With the view of softening the rigour of the pontiff, Hercules informed him, by another communication, that he had caused the bookseller, Gadaldino, to be imprisoned; and though he doubted if he could be conveyed to Bologna on account of the decrepitude of age, yet he should be sent if his holiness required it. But, soon after, the vice-legate of Bologna made his appearance at the court of Ferrara, and demanded, in the name of his master, that the three Modenese gentlemen and the bookseller, accused of heresy, should be sent to Rome. The duke consented to send the provost Valentino, who, being a priest, was under greater obligations than the rest to obey the pope; having first obtained the vice-legate's promise that the process should be so conducted as not to affect the prisoner in his person or honour. This promise was, however, disregarded. After being detained a whole year in prison, the provost was obliged to make public recantation of the errors imputed to him in the Church of Minerva at Rome, and afterwards to repeat the ceremony in his own Church at Modena, on the 28th of May 1558. The poor printer, who had also been carried to Rome, was detained still longer in prison, though upwards of eighty years old. Filippo Valentino and

Castelvetro not having made their appearance at the time appointed, were excommunicated for contumacy and orders were sent to the bishop to cause the sentence to be intimated at Modena. Foscarari consulted the duke, who, irritated by the treatment which he had received, forbade the intimation.*

We are not informed where Valentino took refuge from the fury of the implacable pontiff, but his friend Castelvetro appears to have lived secretly in Ferrara. The year 1559 proved fatal to pope Paul IV. and Hercules II. of Ferrara; and Alfonso II., who succeeded his father in the dukedom, hoping to find the new pontiff more tractable, applied for a commission to try the cause of Castelvetro within his own territories. This having been refused, Castelvetro, confiding in the interest of the duke, and in the promises made him by persons connected with the papal court, was persuaded to go to Rome. At his first arrival, he was treated with great courtesy, and, instead of being committed to prison, had the convent of Santa Maria *in Via* assigned to him as a place of residence, with liberty to receive his friends; but, after his third appearance before the inquisitors, finding that they had obtained possession of strong evidence against him, or dreading that they would put him to the torture, he suddenly left Rome, along with his brother Giammaria. On the 26th of November 1560, the cardinals of the congregation published their final sentence, declaring him a fugitive and impenitent heretic, who had incurred all the pains, spiritual and temporal, decreed against such criminals, and calling upon every person who might have it in his power, to arrest his person and send him as a prisoner to Rome. His effigy was publicly burnt; and pressing letters were written to the duke of Ferrara to seize the fugitive brothers and confiscate their property.† One of the leading charges against Castelvetro was, that he had translated into Italian a work of Melanchthon on the Authority of the Church and the Fathers, a copy of

---
* Bibl Modenese, tom. 1 p. 446—452.
† Bibl. Modenese, tom. 1. p 452—455.

which, said to be in his own hand-writing, was produced on his trial.*

While these measures were taken at Modena, the papal court was still more intent on extirpating the reformed opinions in Ferrara, which it regarded as the nursery and hotbed of heresy in Italy. In the year 1545, his holiness addressed a brief to the ecclesiastical authorities of that place, requiring them to institute a strict investigation into the conduct of persons of every rank and order, who were suspected of entertaining erroneous sentiments, and, after having taken the depositions, applied the torture, and brought the trial as far as the definitive sentence, to transmit the whole process to Rome for judgment.† The distress caused by the execution of this mandate was greatly increased by a base expedient lately adopted for discovering those who wavered in their attachment to the Church of Rome. A horde of commissioned spies were dispersed over Italy, who, by means of the recommendations with which they were furnished, got admission into private families, insinuated themselves into the confidence of individuals, and conveyed the secret information which they obtained in this way to the inquisitors. Assuming a variety of characters, they haunted the company of the learned and illiterate, and were to be found equally in courts and cloisters.‡ A number of excellent persons

---

* Bibl. Modenese, tom. i. p. 457—460. Pallavicini had mentioned the charge, but did not give the name of the book. (Storia del Concil. di Trento, l. xv. c. x.) Fontanini assumed that it was the Common Places of Melanchthon, (see before, p. 51,) which led Muratori to call in question the truth of the whole charge. But the book—the identical *corpus delicti* which was verified before the inquisition—has since been discovered in the archives of St. Angelo. It is a MS. in 4to, with the following title.—" Libricciulo di Phi. M. dell' autorita della Chiesa, e degli Scritti degli Antichi, volgarizzato per Reprigone Rheo con l'aggiunto di alquanto chiose." The translator, in a short epistle to the reader, states that he had added a few notes, chiefly in explanation of certain Greek words used in "this noble little work." Tiraboschi is of opinion, that the style of this book corresponds perfectly with that of the undoubted works of Castelvetro.

† Raynaldi Annal. ad an. 1545.

‡ Calcagnini Opera, p. 169. Olympiæ Moratæ Opera, p. 102.

at Ferrara were caught in the toils spread by these pests of society. They succeeded in alienating the mind of the duke from the accomplished Olympia Morata, who, having left the palace, on the death of her father,* to take charge of her widowed mother and the younger branches of the family, was treated in a harsh and ungrateful manner by the court; and she would have suffered still worse treatment, had not a German student of medicine married her, and carried her along with him to his native country.† The persecution became more severe, when, on the death of Paul III., the papal chair was filled by cardinal De Monte, under the title of Julius III. While this indolent pontiff wallowed in voluptuousness,‡ he signed, without scruple or remorse, the cruel orders which were dictated by those to whom he intrusted the management of public affairs. In the year 1550, the reformed Church, which had subsisted for a number of years at Ferrara, was dispersed; many were thrown into prison, and one of their preachers, a person of great piety, was put to death.§ Olympia Morata writes on this subject‖—"We did not come here with the intention of returning to Italy; for you are not ignorant how dangerous it is to profess Christianity in that country where antichrist has his throne. I hear that the rage against the saints is at present so violent, that former severities were but child's play compared with those which are practised by the new pope, who cannot, like his predecessor, be moved by entreaties and intercession." And, in another letter

111. In writings of that time, these spies are called *Corycæans*, Vide Suidæ Lex. voc. κωρυκαιος.

* He died in 1548.
† Olympiæ Moratæ Opera, p. 93—95. Noltenii Vita Oympiæ, p. 122—125. Her husband's name was Andrew Grunthler, whose life is to be seen in Melch. Adam. Vit. Medic. Germ. Conf. Englerti. Franconic. Acta, vol. ii. p. 269. Nolten says that the duchess also was alienated from her; but Olympia herself gives no hint of this in her letters.
‡ Bayle, Dict. art. Julius III. Tiraboschi, vii. 27
§ Olympiæ Moratæ Opera, p. 102 Actiones et Monimenta Martyrum, f. 163. Joan. Crispin. 1560, 4to.
‖ To Celio Secundo Curione: Olympiæ Moratæ Oper. p. 101.

she says*—"I learn, from letters which I have lately received out of Italy, that the Christians are treated with great cruelty at Ferrara; neither high nor low are spared; some are imprisoned, others banished, and others obliged to save their lives by flight."

The success of these measures in abolishing the face of a reformed church, and silencing all opposition to the established faith, in Ferrara, did not however give satisfaction at Rome. All this availed nothing in the eyes of the clergy, so long as there remained one person, occupying the place nearest the prince, who scrupled to yield obedience to their authority. The high rank and distinguished accomplishments of the duchess of Ferrara aggravated, instead of extenuating, the offence which she had given to the clergy, who resolved to humble her pride, if they could not subdue her firmness. Renée, who for some time had not concealed her partiality to the reformed sentiments, testified great dissatisfaction at the late persecution, and exerted herself in every way within her power to protect those who were exposed to its violence. This led to repeated and strong representations from the pope to the duke, her husband. He was told that the minds of his children and servants were corrupted, and the most pernicious example held out to his subjects; that the house of Este, which had been so long renowned for the purity of its faith and its fealty to the holy see, was in danger of contracting the indelible stain of heresy; and that if he did not speedily abate the nuisance, he would expose himself to the censures of the church, and lose the favour of all catholic princes. In consequence of these remonstrances, Hercules pressed the duchess to avert the displeasure of his holiness by renouncing the new opinions, and conforming herself to the rites of the

* To Chilian Sinapi; Ibid. p. 143 In another letter, addressed to Vergerio, (p. 158,) after deploring the weakness of some of her acquaintance, who had renounced their faith, she speaks with satisfaction of the constancy of her mother; "Matrem vero meam constantem fuisse in illis turbis, Deo gratias agimus, eique totum acceptum referimus. Eam oravi, ut ex illa Babylonia una cum sororibus ad nos proficiscatur."

established worship. As she persisted in refusing to sacrifice her convictions, recourse was had to foreign influence. Whether it was with the view of overcoming the reluctance which her husband testified to proceed to extremities, or of affording him a decent excuse for adopting those severe measures which he had previously agreed to, it is certain that the pope procured the interference of the king of France, who was nephew to the duchess. Henry II. accordingly sent Oritz,* his inquisitor, to the court of Ferrara. His instructions bore, that he was to acquaint himself accurately with the extent to which the mind of the duchess was infected with error; he was then to request a personal interview with her, at which he should inform her of the great grief which his most Christian Majesty felt at hearing that "his only aunt," whom he had always loved and esteemed so highly, had involved herself in the labyrinth of these detestable and condemned opinions; if, after all his remonstrances and arguments, he could not recover her by gentle means, he was next, with the concurrence of the duke, to endeavour to bring her to reason by rigour and severity: he was to preach a course of sermons on the principal points on which she had been led astray, at which she and all her family should be obliged to attend, "whatever refusal or objection she might think proper to make:" if this proved unsuccessful in reclaiming her, he was next, in her presence, to entreat the duke, in his majesty's name, to "sequester her from all society and conversation," that she might not have it in her power to taint the minds of others; to remove her children from

* This appears to have been the same person of whom we read at an earlier period of the history of France. "Notre Maitre Oris," the inquisitor of the faith, was, in the year 1534, sent to Sancerre to search for heretics; but the inhabitants, aware of his fondness for good cheer, treated him with such hospitality, that he reported them to be a very good sort of people His depute, Rocheli, returned with the same report. Upon which the *Lieutenant Criminel*, chagrined at missing his prey, said, that "good wine would at any time make all these fellows quiet." (Beze, Hist. des Eglises Ref. de France, tom. i. p. 20) But "Notre Maitre" was then but young, and had not yet tasted blood.

her, and not to allow any of the family, of whatever nation they might be, who were accused or strongly suspected of heretical sentiments, to approach her; in fine, he was to bring them to trial, and to pronounce a sentence of exemplary punishment on such as were found guilty, only leaving it to the duke to give such directions as to the mode of process and the infliction of punishment, as that the affair might terminate, so far as justice permitted, without causing scandal, or bringing any public stigma on the duchess and her dependents.*

The daughter of Louis XII., whose spirit was equal to her piety, spurned these conditions; and on her refusal to violate her conscience, her children were taken from under her management, her confidential servants proceeded against as heretics, and she herself detained as a prisoner in the palace.† Renée could have borne the insolence of Oritz, but felt in the keenest manner the upbraidings of her husband, who, without listening to her exculpations, told her she must prepare herself to conform unconditionally and without delay to the practices of the Roman church—an unnatural demonstration of zeal on the part of Hercules, which the court of Rome rewarded, at a subsequent period, by depriving his grandson of the dukedom of Ferrara, and adding it to the possessions of the Church.‡ The duchess continued for some time to bear with fortitude this harsh treatment from her husband, aggravated as it was by certain low intrigues to which he descended; but in the year 1555, on the accession of that truculent pontiff, Paul IV., the persecution began to rage with greater violence; and it would seem, that the threats with which she was anew assailed, together with the desire which she felt to be restored to the society of her children, induced her to relent and make concessions.§ On the

* Le Laboureur, Additions aux Memoires de Michel de Castelnau, tom. i. p. 717.
† Ibid. p. 718.
‡ Giovannandrea Barotti, Diffesa degli Scrittori Ferraresi, p. 112. Muratori, Annali d'Italia, tom. x. p. 553—558.
§ Calvin, in a letter to Farel, says—" De Ducissa Ferrariensi

death of the duke in 1559, she returned to France, and took up her residence in the castle of Montargis, where she made open profession of the reformed religion, and extended her protection to the persecuted Protestants. The duke of Guise, her son-in-law, having one day come to the castle with an armed force, sent a messenger to inform her that, if she did not dismiss the rebels whom she harboured, he would batter the walls with his cannon; she boldly replied, "Tell your master, that I shall myself mount the battlements, and see if he dare kill a king's daughter."* Her eldest daughter, Anne of Este, "whose integrity of understanding and sensibility of heart were worthy of a better age,"† was married to the first Francis, duke of Guise, and afterwards to James of Savoy, duke of Nemours, two of the most determined supporters of the Roman Catholic religion in France; and if she did not, like her mother, avow her friendship to the reformed cause, she exerted herself in moderating the violence of both her husbands against its friends.‡

Next to the dominions of the duke of Ferrara, the papal court felt most anxious for the suppression of the reformed doctrine within the territories of the Venetian republic. On the flight of Ochino, a rigor-

tristis nuncius, et certius quam vellem, minis et probris victam cecidisse. Quid dicam nisi rarum in proceribus esse constantiæ exemplum." (Senebier, Catalogue des Manuscrits dans la Bibliotheque de Geneve, p. 274, 275) Mons. Senebier states, that this letter is dated, "du 1 Novembre," and he places it under the year 1554; but as Calvin informs his correspondent that he had written a defence of the *Consensus,* or agreement among the Swiss churches respecting the sacrament of the Supper, and as the dedication of that work is dated, Nonis Januarii 1556, the letter to Farel was most probably written in 1555. (Conf. Calvini Opera, tom viii. p. 660.)

* Bayle, Dict art. *Ferrara,* note F.
† Condorcet, Eloge de Chancelier d'Hopital.
‡ Bayle says, that she became zealous against the Hugonots during the League, which he imputes to the remembrance of the assassination of her first husband by Poltrot; but he produces no authority for his assertion. Calcagnini, Riccio, Paleario, Rabelais, St. Marthe, De Thou, and Condorcet, have vied with each other in extolling this amiable princess. There is a beautiful letter of Olympia Morata, addressed, " Annæ Estensi, principi Guisianæ," in the printed works of the former, p. 130—133.

ous inquisition was made into the sentiments of the Capuchins residing in that part of Italy.* For several years after this, the pope ceased not to urge the senate, both by letters and nuncios, to root out the Lutheran heresy, which had been embraced by many of their subjects, especially in Vicenza. Cardinal Rodolfo, who was administrator of the bishoprick of Vicenza, showed great zeal in this work; but the local magistrates, either from personal aversion to the task, or because they knew that their superiors did not wish the orders which they had publicly given to be carried into execution, declined lending the assistance of the secular arm. Information of this having been conveyed to Rome, the pope in 1546, addressed a long and earnest brief to the senate, in which, after complimenting them on their former zeal for religion and fidelity to the holy see, and telling them that innovation in religion would lead to civil dissentions and sedition among them, as it had done elsewhere, he complains loudly of the conduct of the podesta and capitano of Vicenza, who, instead of obeying the commands which had been repeatedly given them, allowed the Lutheran doctrines to be openly professed before the eyes of their masters, and of the ecumenical council which had been called and was now sitting at Trent, chiefly for the purpose of extirpating these heresies; on which account his holiness earnestly requires the doge and senators to enjoin these magistrates peremptorily to compensate for their past negligence, by yielding every assistance to the vicars of the diocese in seizing and punishing the heretics.† The senate complied with this request, and issued orders which led to the dissipation of the Church at Vicenza.‡

* Bock, Hist. Antitrin. tom. ii. p. 496.
† Raynaldi Annales, ad an 1546.
‡ Ibid. This is the persecution by which Socinian writers say that their colleges were dispersed. But the only heresy mentioned in the apostolical brief, or by the annalist, is the Lutheran; and it is reasonable to suppose, that, if it had been known that antitrinitarians existed in that place, they would have been specified, as we find they were in a subsequent bull.

They adopted similar measures in the rest of their dominions. In the year 1548, an edict was published, commanding all who had books opposed to the catholic faith to deliver them up within eight days, at the risk of being proceeded against as heretics; and offering a reward to informers.* This was followed by great severities against the Protestants in the city of Venice, and in all the territories of that republic. "The persecution here increases every day," writes Altieri. "Many are seized, of whom some have been sent to the galleys, others condemned to perpetual imprisonment, and some, alas! have been induced, by fear of punishment, to recant. Many have been banished along with their wives and children, while still greater numbers have fled for their lives. Matters are brought to that pass, that I begin to fear for myself; for though I have frequently been able to protect others in this storm, there is reason to apprehend that the same hard terms will be proposed to me; but it is the will of God that his people be tried by such afflictions."† Altieri continued to exert himself with the most laudable and unwearied zeal in behalf of his brethren. He not only procured letters in their favour from the elector of Saxony and other German princes, for whom he acted as agent with the Venetian republic; but he undertook a journey into Switzerland, with the express view of persuading the Protestant cantons to exert their influence in the same cause. On his way home he attended an assembly of the deputies of the Grison confederation at Coire, where he pleaded the cause of his persecuted countrymen. In both places he succeeded so far as to obtain letters interceding for lenity to the Protestants; but he was disappointed in his expectations of procuring a public commission to act for these states, which would have given additional

* Thuani Hist. ad an. 1548. Surius, apud Bock, Hist. Antitrin. tom. ii. p. 416.
† Alterius ad Bullingerum, d. 24. Mart. 1549, Venetiis: De Porta, Hist. Reform. Eccles. Rhæticarum, tom. ii. p. 32. Curiæ Rhæt. 1774, 4to.

weight to any representations which he might make to the doge and senate. The authorities of Switzerland and the Grisons might have good reasons for refusing his request; but we cannot help sympathizing with the disappointment, and even with the complaints of this good man, as well as admiring the rare example which he gave of disinterested devotion to the cause of truth and the best interests of his country, at a time when the greater part either knew them not or cared not for them. In a letter from Coire to Bullinger, a distinguished minister of Zurich, he says— "I have delivered your letter and that of Myconius to the ministers of this Church; I have also conversed with them on my business, but find them rather lukewarm, either because this is their natural disposition, or because they think the matter too difficult to be obtained, especially after your friends in Switzerland have refused it. They, however, give me some hopes of success."* In another letter to the same correspondent, he writes—"From the assembly of the Grison states, which has been held here, I have only been able to obtain commendatory letters; had it not been for the opposition made by some enemies of religion, I would have also obtained a public commission. They have concluded a treaty with France; the emperor's ambassador was present, but could do nothing."† After mentioning the discouragements he had met with from those of whom he had hoped better things, he exclaims—"Thus do the minds of men now cleave to the world! If the Spirit of the Lord had not long ago taken possession of my heart, I would have followed the common example, and, hiding myself in some secret corner, attended to my own private affairs, instead of taking an active part in the cause of Christ. But God forbid that I should entertain the blasphemous thought of desisting to labour for him, who never ceased to labour in my cause until he had endured the reproach of the cross. Therefore I return to Italy, ready, as before, to encounter

* Curia, ult. Jan. 1549 : De Porta. tom. ii. p. 34.
† Julii 22, 1549: Ibid.

whatever may befall me, and willing to be bound for the name of Christ."* Before leaving the Grisons he received intelligence that the persecution was daily waxing hotter at Venice. "It is not, therefore without danger that I return," says he in another letter; "for you know how much I am hated by the papists and wicked. I do not undertake the journey rashly: God will preserve me from all evil: do you pray for me."† On his arrival at Venice, he found that his enemies had succeeded in incensing the magistrates against him; and he was ordered either to renounce his religion, or instantly to quit the territories of the republic. Without hesitation he chose the latter; but being unwilling to despair of the reformation of his native country, and anxious to be at hand to lend succor to his suffering brethren, he lingered in Italy, wandered from city to city, and, when he durst no longer appear in public, sought an asylum in a retired place for himself and his family. Soon after his banishment from Venice he wrote to Bullinger:—"Take the following particulars concerning my return to Italy. I am well with my wife and little child. As to other things, all the effect of my commendatory letters was an offer, on the part of the senate, that I should be allowed to remain in safety among them, provided I would yield conformity to their religion, that is, the Roman; otherwise it behoved me to withdraw without delay from their dominions. Having devoted myself to Christ, I chose exile rather than the enjoyment of pleasant Venice, with its execrable religion. I departed accordingly, and went first to Ferrara, and afterwards to Florence."‡ In another letter, written from his place of hiding, somewhere in the territory of Brescia, he says—"Know that I am in great trouble and danger of my life, nor is there a place in Italy where I can be safe with my wife and boy. My fears for myself increase daily, for I know

* Sangallo, 28 Jan. 1549; De Porta, tom. ii. p. 34.
† Curia, 28 Jul. 1549: Ibid p. 96.
‡ Epist. ad Bulling Ex itinere, 25 Aug. 1549: De Porta, ut supra, p. 35.

the wicked will never rest till they have swallowed me up alive. I entreat a share in your prayers."*
These are the last accounts we have of this excellent person. It is probable that he never escaped from Italy, and that his fate will remain a secret, until the horrid mysteries of the Roman inquisition shall be disclosed.

When the Protestants were treated in this manner in the capital, we need not be surprised to find the magistrates of Venice permitting the greatest severities to be used against them in the more distant provinces. This was particularly the case in Istria, where the agents of Rome were irritated beyond measure by the more than suspected defection of the two Vergerii, the bishops of Capo d'Istria and Pola. Annibale Grisone, who was sent into these dioceses as inquisitor, in the year 1546, spread distress and alarm among the inhabitants. He read every where from the pulpits the papal bull, requiring all, under the pain of excommunication, to inform against those whom they suspected of heresy, and to deliver up the prohibited books which might be in their possession. Those who confessed and supplicated forgiveness he promised to treat with lenity, but threatened to condemn to the fire all who, concealing their crime, should be convicted on information. Not satisfied with public denunciations, he entered into every house in search of heretical books. Such as confessed that they had read the New Testament in the vulgar tongue, he charged to abstain from that dangerous practice for the future, under the severest pains. The rich he subjected to private penance, and obliged the poor to make a public recantation. At first, only a few individuals of weaker minds were induced to inform against themselves or their acquaintances; but at last consternation seized the multitude, and every one became afraid that his neighbour would get the start of him. The ties of consanguinity and gratitude were disregarded: the son informed against his father, the wife against her husband, the client against his patron.

* Ad Bulling. Ex agro Brixiano, prid. Kal. Nov. 1549. Ibid.

Taking advantage of the agitated state of the public mind, Grisone ascended the pulpit, in the cathedral of Capo d'Istria, on a high festival day, and after celebrating mass, harangued the crowded assembly. "You see," said he, "the calamities which have befallen you for some years past. At one time your fields, at another your olive trees, at another your vines have failed; you have been afflicted in your cattle, and in the whole of your substance. To what are all these evils to be ascribed? To your bishop and the heretics whom he protects; nor can you expect any alleviation of your distress until they are punished. Why do you not rise up and stone them?" So much were the ignorant and frightened populace inflamed, that Vergerio found it necessary to conceal himself.

In the midst of this confusion, the bishop of Pola died, not without suspicion of having been carried off by poison.* His brother withdrew, and took refuge at Mantua with his patron, cardinal Gonzaga, who soon dismissed him, in consequence of the representations made by the noted Della Casa, the papal nuncio, resident at Venice. Upon this Vergerio went to the council of Trent, with the view of vindicating himself, or, as some state, of demanding his seat in that assembly. The pope would have ordered him to be arrested, but was afraid of giving any reason for asserting that the council was not free, at a time when he professed to wish the attendance of the German Protestants. In order to obtain the removal of so dangerous a person from Trent, the papal legates agreed to supersede the summons which had been given him to appear at Rome, and remitted the trial of the charges exhibited against him to the nuncio and patriarch of Venice. Vergerio managed his defence with such address as to protract the trial for two years, at the end of which he was prohibited from returning to his diocese.† At that time Fran-

---

* A work by the bishop was afterwards published by his brother, with this title —" Esposizione e Parafrasi sopra il Salmo cxix. di M. Gio. Battista Vergerio Vescovo di Pola, data d. 6. Gennajo, 1550." (De Porta, tom. ii. p. 151.)

† Pallavicini, lib. vi. cap. 13. Tiraboschi, vii. 380.

cesco Spira, a lawyer of Padua, died in a state of great mental horror, in consequence of his having been induced, by the terrors of the inquisition, to recant the Protestant faith. Vergerio, who had come from Venice to Padua, saw him on his death-bed, and joined with some other learned and pious persons in attempting to comfort the wretched penitent.* The scene made such a deep impression on the mind of Vergerio, that he determined to relinquish his bishopric and native country, and to seek an asylum in a place where he could with safety make a public profession of the truth which he had embraced. "To tell the truth," says he, "I felt such a flame in my breast, that I could scarcely restrain myself at times from going to the chamber-door of the legate at Venice, and crying out, 'Here I am: where are your prisons and your fires? Satisfy your utmost desire upon me; burn me for the cause of Christ, I beseech you, since I have had an opportunity of comforting the miserable Spira, and of publishing what it was the will of God should be published.'"† In the end of the year 1548, he carried his purpose into execution, by retiring into the Grisons, to the surprise equally of those whom he deserted and of those whom he joined.‡

* The History of Spira was compiled by Vergerio, with the assistance of letters from Celio S. Curio, Matthæus Gribaldus, a native of Padua, Sigismundus Gelous, a Pole, and Henricus Scotus. The last named was our countryman, Henry Scrimger. In the library of the University of Leyden, I met with a manuscript volume, containing, among others, a letter from Calvin to Bullinger, dated "15th August 1549," in which he writes:—" I received lately a letter from Paulus Vergerius, along with a history of Franciscus Spira, which he wishes printed here. He says the chief cause of his being obliged to leave his native country was, that the pope, irritated by this book, laid snares for his life. At present he is residing in the Grisons, but expresses a strong desire to see me. I have not yet read the history, but, so far as I can judge from a slight glance, it is written with somewhat more prudence and gravity than in the letters translated by Celio. When I have read the work more carefully, I shall think of the preface which he urges me to write to it." The history was printed in 1550, with a preface by Calvin. (Miscell. Groningana, tom. iii. p. 109.)

† Historia Spiræ: De Porta, tom. ii. p. 144.

‡ Sleidan, lib. xxi. tom. iii. p 123, 124. Bayle, Dict. art. Vergier. (Pierre Paul.) Ughelli Italia Sac tom. v. p. 391.

The inquisitor Grisone was succeeded by Tommaso de Santo Stella, who, after irritating the inhabitants by his vexatious proceedings, endeavoured to persuade the senate of Venice to put garrisons into their principal cities, under the pretext that Vergerio meditated an invasion of Istria.* This gave the latter an occasion to publish a defence of his conduct, addressed to the doge and senate, in which besides complaining of the insidious and violent methods adopted by the fire-brands of persecution through Italy,† he states several facts as to their conduct in the Venetian dominions. "Nothing," says he, "can be more shameful than what this pope has done. He has conferred honours and rewards on such of your prelates as are unprofitable and godless; but the bishop of Bergamo, your countryman of the house of Soranzo, he has thrown into prison, for no other reason than that he opposed non-residence and superstition, and testified a regard for the doctrine of the gospel. What is it to exercise oppression and tyranny over you, if this is not? Is it possible that this should not awaken you?"‡ The senate, about this time, showed a disposition to check the violent proceedings of the papal agents, by opposing a strong barrier to their encroachments on criminal jurisdiction. "The news from Italy is," says Vergerio, "that the senate of Venice have made a decree, that no papal legate, nor bishop, nor inquisitor, shall proceed against any subject, except in the presence of a civil magistrate; and that the pope, enraged at this, has fulminated a bull, interdicting, under the heaviest pains, any secular prince from

---

* Al Sereniss. Duce e alla Eccelsissima Rep. di Venezia, Orazione e Defensione del Vergerio, di Vico Suprano, A x Aprile, 1551; Da Porta, tom. ii. p. 152.

† Girolamo Muzio, who had fomented the persecution in Istria, and afterwards wrote against Vergerio, he thus characterizes:—"Un certo Muzio, le cui professione è di dettar cartello, e condurre gli uomini ad ammazzarsi negli steccati, è fatto Teologo papesco in tre giorni, e di più Barigello de' papisti." In another work, (Giudicio sopra le Lettere di XIII. Uomini Illustri,) he names, as the leading persecutors, at a period somewhat later, the Archinti, Buldragi, Todeschini, Falzetti, and Crivelli.

‡ Orazione e Defensione, ut supra, p. 253.

interposing the least hinderance to trials for heresy. It remains to be seen whether the Venetians will obey."* But the court of Rome, by its perseverance and intrigues, ultimately triumphed over patrician jealousy. Even foreigners who visited the republic in the course of trade, were seized and detained by the inquisition. Frederic de Salice, who had been sent to Venice from the republic of the Grisons, to demand the release of some of its subjects, gives the following account of the state of matters in the year 1557:—" In this commonwealth, and in general throughout Italy, where the pope possesses what they call spiritual jurisdiction, the faithful are subjected to the severest inquisition. Ample authority is given to the inquisitors, on the smallest information, to seize any one at their pleasure, to put him to the torture, and (what is worse than death) to send him to Rome; which was not wont to be the case until the time of the reigning pontiff. I am detained here longer than I could wish, and know not when I shall be able to extricate myself from this labyrinth."† Scarcely had this ambassador returned home, after accomplishing his object, when another of his countrymen, a merchant, was thrown into prison by the inquisition at Vicenza. To procure his release, it was necessary to despatch Hercules de Salice, late governor of the Grisons. His remonstrances, though seconded by the influence of the French ambassador, were for some time disregarded by the senate, who sought to evade the terms of the treaty between the two countries, and the concessions which they had made during the preceding year; until, having demanded a public audience, he inveighed, amidst the murmurs of the elder patricians, with such intrepid eloquence, against the intolerable arrogance of the papal claims, that the majority of the senate voted for the instant discharge of the prisoner.‡ As a reward for the zeal which

* Vergerio a| Gualt On. Pratello, di Samadeno in Agnedina, a' 24 April. 1551. De Porta, tom. ii. p. 252.
† De Porta, tom. ii. p. 299.
‡ Ibid. p. 299—301. The ambassador was afterwards thanked by

they had displayed against the doctrine of Luther, the pope, in 1559, conferred on the senate of Venice the perpetual right of electing their own patriarch.*

In spite of the keen search made for them, many Protestants still remained in the city of Venice. In the year 1560, they sent for a minister to form them into a church, and had the Lord's Supper administered to them in a private house. But soon after this, information having been given of their meetings by one of those spies whom the court of Rome kept in its pay, all who failed in making their escape were committed to prison. Numbers fled to the province of Istria; and after concealing themselves there for some time, a party of them, amounting to twenty-three, purchased a vessel to carry them to a foreign country. When they were about to set sail, an avaricious foreigner, who had obtained a knowledge of their design, preferred a claim before the magistrates of the place against three of them for a debt which he alleged they owed him, and failing in his object of extorting the money, accused them as heretics who fled from justice; in consequence of which they were arrested, conveyed to Venice, and lodged in the same prisons with their brethren.† Hitherto the senate had not visited the Protestants with capital punishment; though it would appear that, before this period, the inquisitors had, in some instances, prevailed on the local magistrates of the remoter provinces to gratify them to that extent.‡ But now the senators yielded to those counsels which they had so long resisted; and acts of cruelty commenced which continued for years to disgrace the criminal jurisdiction of the republic. Drowning was the mode of death to which they doomed the Protestants, either because it was less cruel and odious than committing them to the flames, or because it accorded with the customs of

several of the senators, who admired the boldness with which he, being a foreigner, and formerly in the military service of Venice, had dared to state what would have cost a patrician his life.
* Puffendorf, Introd. p. 574.
† Histoire des Martyrs, f. 630, à Geneve, 1597, folio.
‡ Calvini Epist. p. 85: Oper. tom. ix.

Venice. But if the *autos de fé* of the Queen of the Adriatic were less barbarous than those of Spain, the solitude and silence with which they were accompanied were calculated to excite the deepest horror. At the dead hour of midnight, the prisoner was taken from his cell, and put into a gondola or Venetian boat, attended only, beside the sailors, by a single priest, to act as confessor. He was rowed out into the sea, beyond the Two Castles, where another boat was in waiting. A plank was then laid across the two gondolas, upon which the prisoner, having his body chained, and a heavy stone affixed to his feet, was placed; and, on a signal given, the gondolas retiring from one another, he was precipitated into the deep.*

The first person who appears to have suffered martyrdom at Venice, was Julio Guirlauda, a native of the Trevisano.† When set on the plank, he cheerfully bade the captain farewell, and sank into the deep calling on the Lord Jesus.‡ Antonio Ricetto, of Vicenza, was held in such respect, that, subsequently to his conviction, the senators offered to restore him not only to his liberty, but also to the whole of his property, part of which had been sold, and the rest promised away, provided he would conform to the Church of Rome. The firmness of Ricetto was put to a still severer test; his son, a boy of twelve years of age, having been admitted into the prison, fell at his feet, and supplicated him, in the most melting strains, to

---

* Histoire des Martyrs, f. 681. De Porta, tom. ii. p. 33.

† The Socinian historians, formerly quoted, in giving an account of the suppression of their colleges at Vicenza in 1546, say that two individuals holding their sentiments, "Julius Trevisanus and Franciscus de Ruego, were strangled at Venice." This could not have happened at that time; for it is a well authenticated fact, that none were capitally punished for religion at Venice before the year 1560. (Busdragi Epist. ut supra, p. 326. Histoire des Martyrs, f. 680.) I have little doubt, that the two persons referred to were Julio Guirlauda of the Trevisano, and Francesco Sega of Rovigo, mentioned in the text as drowned, and the Martyrology represents them as of the common Protestant faith. The author of that work, speaking of their death, uses the phrase, "persecutée par nouveaux Ebionites." Did the Socinian historians read *pour* instead of *par*?

‡ On the 19th October 1562. He was in his fortieth year. (Hist. des Martyrs, f. 680.)

accept of the offers made him, and not leave his child an orphan. The keeper of the prison having told him one day, with the view of inducing him to recant, that one of his companions had yielded, he merely replied, "What is that to me?" And in the gondola, and on the plank, he retained his firmness; praying for those who ignorantly put him to death, and commending his soul to his Saviour.* Francesco Sega, a native of Rovigo, composed several pious works during his confinement, for the comfort of his fellow-prisoners, part of which was preserved after his death.† Francesco Spinula, a native of the Milanese, being a priest, was more severely questioned than his brethren. He was thrice brought before the judges, and on one of these occasions the papal legate and a number of the chief clergy attended. In their presence, and when threatened with a fiery death, he professed openly the articles of the Protestant faith, and bore an explicit testimony against the usurpations of the pope, the doctrine of purgatory, and the invocation of saints. During a fit of sickness, brought on by the length and rigour of his confinement, some concessions were extorted from him, but, on his recovery, he instantly retracted them, and being formally degraded from the priesthood, obtained the same watery grave with his brethren.‡ But the most distinguished of those who suffered death at Venice, was the venerable Fra Baldo Lupetino. The following account of him by his nephew, in a book now become very rare, deserves to be preserved entire. "The reverend Baldus Lupetinus, sprung from a noble and ancient family, was a learned monk and provincial of the order to which he belonged. After having long preached the word of God in both the vulgar languages, (the Italian and Sclavonian,) in many

---

* He died on the 15th of February 1566. (Ibid.)
† He was drowned ten days after Ricetto. (Ibid.)
‡ He suffered on the 31st of January, 1567. (Ibid. p. 681.) Gerdes makes Spinula, the martyr, the same individual who composed the Latin poetical version of the Psalms, which has been several times printed along with that of Flaminio. (Spec. Italiæ Ref p. 336.)

cities, and defended it by public disputation in several places of celebrity with great applause, was at last thrown into close prison at Venice, by the inquisitor and papal legate. In this condition he continued, during nearly twenty years, to bear an undaunted testimony to the gospel of Christ; so that his bonds and doctrine were made known, not only to that city, but to the whole of Italy, and even to Europe at large, by which means evangelical truth was more widely spread. Two things among many others, may be mentioned as marks of the singular providence of God towards this person during his imprisonment. In the first place, the princes of Germany often interceded for his liberation, but without success. And, secondly, on the other hand, the papal legate, the inquisitor, and even the pope himself, laboured with all their might, and by repeated applications, to have him, from the very first, committed to the flames, as a noted heresiarch. This was refused by the doge and senate, who, when he was at last condemned, freed him from the punishment of the fire by an express decree. It was the will of God that he should bear his testimony to the truth for so long a time; and that, like a person affixed to a cross, he should, as from an eminence, proclaim to all the world the restoration of Christianity, and the revelation of antichrist. At last, this pious and excellent man, whom neither threatenings nor promises could move, sealed his doctrine by an undaunted martyrdom, and exchanged the filth and protracted tortures of a prison for a watery grave."*

We have good reason to think that many others, whose names have not come down to us, suffered the same death at Venice,† beside those who perished by

---

* Matth. Flacius, De Sectis, Dissensionibus, &c. Scriptorum Pontificiorum; Præfat. ad Ducem et Senat. Venet. p 43. Conf. Vergerio, Lettere al Mons. Delfino, Vescovo de Lesina · De Porta, tom. ii. p. 33.

† " Veneti in sua ditione persecutionem satis gravem Christo faciunt Bergomi, Brixiæ, Veronæ, Patavii. Omnia bona Ulixi comitis (nempe Martinengi) ad fiscum redacta sunt Brixiæ. Comes Ulys-

diseases contracted during a tedious and unwholesome imprisonment. Among the latter was Jeronimo Galateo, who evinced his constancy in the faith by enduring a rigorous confinement of ten years.* It may naturally be supposed that these violent measures would dissipate the Protestants in Venice; and yet we learn that they had secret meetings for worship in the seventeenth century, distinct from those which the ambassadors of Protestant states were permitted to hold.†

Every where throughout Italy, during the period under consideration, those suspected of favouring the new opinions were sought out with equal keenness, and treated with at least equal cruelty, as in the Venetian territories. As the archives of the inquisition are locked up, we are left in general to judge of its proceedings in the interior states, whose political or commercial relations with Protestant countries were slender, from collateral circumstances and incidental notices. From the number of those who escaped, we may form some idea of the still greater number which must have been caught in the fangs of that vigilant and insatiable tribunal; and there was not a city of any note in Italy from which there were not refugees in some part of Protestant Europe. The execution done by the inquisition at Cremona may be conjectured from the notice bestowed on it by the popish historians, who often refer with peculiar satisfaction,

---

ses mihi tuas legit." (Aug. Maynardus ad Fabritium, 7 Mart 1563: De Porta, ii. 459.) "Veneti, cæterique Italiæ Principes sævam adversus pios persecutionem prosequuntur." (Ulysses Martinengus, Comes à Barcho, ad Bullingerum, idib. Decembr. 1563; Ibid. p. 486.)

* Eusebius Captivus, per Hieronymum Marium, p. 249, Basil. 1553. Curionis Pasquillus Ecstaticus, p. 34.

† Jacobi Grynæi Epistola ad Hippolytum a Collibus 1609 scripta; in Monument. Pietatis, tom ii. p. 157. Franc. ad Mœn. 1701. Conf. Gerdes. Ital. Ref. p. 93. Scaliger says, that Mons. Dolot (C. de Harlay, brother to the first president of Paris) told him that he had carried the writings of Calvin to the lords of Venice, and that there were many persons there who were previously acquainted with the Protestant doctrine and books. (Secunda Scaligerana, art. Dolot.) See also the letters of Diodati to Scaliger. Epistres Françoises à M. de la Scala, p. 68, 235—237.)

to the superior strictness of its regulations and celerity of its movements.* At Faenza, a nobleman, revered for his high birth and distinguished virtues, fell under the suspicion of the inquisitors of that city as a Lutheran. After being long detained in a foul prison, he was put to the torture. Not being able to extort from him what they wished, the inquisitors ordered the infernal operation to be repeated, and the victim expired among their hands. The report of this barbarous deed spreading through the city created a tumult, in which the house of the inquisition was attacked, its altars and images torn down, and some of the priests trodden to death by the incensed multitude.† The persecution was also severe in the duchy of Parma; the duke having entered into a treaty with that violent pontiff, Paul IV., by which he delivered up the properties and lives of his innocent subjects to the mercy of the inquisition.‡

The flourishing church at Locarno was a great eyesore to the popes, distant as it was from Rome. In the measures taken for its suppression it was necessary to proceed with caution, as it included persons of wealth and respectability, and as the sovereignty of the place belonged to the Swiss cantons, some of which were Protestant, and all of them jealous of their authority. From the year 1549, when the disputation formerly mentioned took place, every means was taken to excite odium against the Protestants in the minds of their fellow-citizens, and to involve them in a quarrel with the inhabitants of the neighbouring districts and with the government of Milan. Beccaria, their most zealous advocate, though dismissed from prison, was exposed to such personal danger, that he deemed it prudent, by the advice of his friends, to banish himself and retire to Chiavenna.§ Next to him, the individual most obnoxious, from his talents

---

* Limborch's History of the Inquisition, part ii. passim.
† Eglinus ad Bullingerum, 29 Mart. 1568: De Porta, tom. ii. p. 487, 488
‡ Fridericus Saliceus ad Bullingerum, 10 Jan. 1558: Ibid. p. 295.
§ Muralti Oratio, in Tempe Helvetica, tom. iv. p. 165.

and activity, was Taddeo de Dunis. His fame as a physician having made his advice to be sought for throughout the adjacent country, he found it necessary to remove to a more central place within the Milanese. No sooner was it known that he was without the protection of the Swiss confederacy, than his old antagonist, the priest of Lugano, gave information against him, as a ringleader of the heretics, to the inquisitor at Milan, who sent a party to intercept and seize him on one of his professional journeys. Being warned of his danger, he secured himself by retreating hastily to the mountains. Trusting, however, to his innocence, or to the powerful interest of the families which he attended, he afterwards appeared voluntarily before the inquisitor, and was so fortunate as to be dismissed, on condition of his quitting the Milanese, and confining his medical aid for the future to the inhabitants of his native district.*

During four years the Protestants at Locarno were subjected to every species of indignity short of open violence. They had for some time desisted from employing the priests to confess their sick, and from burying their dead after the popish manner, with torches and the cross; and they had their children baptized by ministers whom they brought for that purpose from Chiavenna, when they had no pastor of their own. The increase of the Protestants lessened in this way the gains of the mercenary priesthood, who endeavoured to move heaven and earth against the innovators, as at once sacrilegious and unnatural. They circulated the base report that the Protestants were guilty of the most licentious practices in their secret meetings; and such calumnious rumours, while they met with easy credit from the ignorant and superstitious multitude, were encouraged by others who were too enlightened not to know their falsehood. In the mean time, a deep plot was laid by one Walther, a native of the popish canton of Uri, who was at that time town-clerk of Locarno, and who, some years after, was banished for holding a treasonable corres-

* Ibid. p. 149.

pondence with the duke of Alva, governor of Milan. He forged a deed, purporting that the senators, citizens, and other inhabitants of the town and bailiwick of Locarno, bound themselves by oath, to the seven popish cantons, that they would adhere to the pope and the Roman religion until the meeting of a general council. This paper he dated several years back, and sent it as a genuine deed to an assembly of the seven cantons, held in March 1554, who, without making any inquiries, immediately passed a decree, that all the Locarnese should, agreeably to their bond, make confession to the priests during the ensuing Lent, that they should give their names to the superior of the church, and that the rites of sepulture should be denied to those who had not received mass on their death-bed.* The promulgation of this decree at Locarno came on the Protestants as a thunder-bolt. They instantly despatched a commissioner to the Protestant cantons, with instructions to represent the utter falsehood of the allegation on which the decree proceeded, and to entreat them, as their joint temporal superiors, and as professors of the same faith, to exert their influence to avert the ruin which threatened two hundred heads of families, who had never swerved from their allegiance, and against whom no occasion or fault had been found, except concerning the law of their God. In consequence of this representation, the deputies of the Protestant cantons assembled at Arau, and wrote to those of the popish persuasion, desiring them not to proceed further in the affair of Locarno until the meeting of the next diet of the confederacy, nor to take any step which would infringe the rights of the Protestant cantons in that territory. To defeat this interposition, the enemies of the persecuted Locarnese industriously circulated through Switzerland that they were not entitled to the protection of the Protestant cantons, inasmuch as they were infected with Servetianism, anabaptism, and other fanatical opinions.† Being informed of this by their commis-

---

* March 10, 1554 Muralti Oratio, p. 150—152.
† This report has misled a modern Swiss historian, who, speaking of

sioner, they transmitted to Zurich a confession of their faith, in which they avowed their agreement with the Reformed churches concerning the trinity, the incarnation and mediatory work of Christ, justification, and the sacraments; which had the effect of silencing this unfounded calumny. Two general diets were held in the end of the year 1554, for discussing this subject. The fictitious bond was unanimously set aside; but when they came to the main point, the enemies of the reformed at Locarno insisted that it should be decided by the majority of votes in the diet, contrary to the rule usually observed in questions relating to religion. Riverda, bishop of Terracino, who had been sent as papal nuncio to the diet, stimulated the popish deputies to violent measures, while those of the Protestant cantons were influenced, partly by jealousy of one another, and partly by dread of interrupting the peace of the confederacy. The matter was referred at last to arbiters chosen from the two mixed cantons, who gave it as their judgment, that the inhabitants of Locarno, who were free from crime, should either embrace the Roman Catholic religion, or leave their native country, taking with them their families and property; that they should not return thither, nor be permitted to settle in the territories of the seven catholic cantons; that those chargeable with reproaching the Virgin Mary, with anabaptism, or other opinions contrary to both confessions, should be punished; that this sentence should be intimated to the prefect of Locarno, and that it should be carried into effect by deputies sent by the seven catholic cantons, provided those of the four Protestant ones refused to take part in the affair, or absented themselves. Against this decision the deputies of Zurich

Locarno, says—"Lelius et Faustus Socin avoient répandu dans cette contrée une doctrine beaucoup plus libre encore que celle de Zwingli et de Calvin. Mais ils furent chassés, et leurs adhérens punis par l'exil ou par la mort Après eux, Beccaria devint à Locarno," &c. (Histoire de la Nation Suisse, par Hen Zschokke, trad. par Ch. Monnard, p. 207.) Faustus Socinus was only born in 1539; and there is not the least evidence that his uncle Lelius ever saw Locarno.

protested, declaring that, though they were resolved to abide by the league, and not to excite any commotion, they could not agree to have this sentence intimated in their name, and still less to take any share in carrying it into execution. This protest was afterwards formally approved of by their constituents. It was no small part of the indignity offered to the Protestants by this decree, that Locarno was that year under the government of Isaiah Reuchlin, the prefect appointed by the canton of Zurich. This excellent man, who had already experienced repeated vexations, in the discharge of his office, from the violence of the Roman catholics, was thrown into great perplexity by the intelligence of what was concluded at the diet; from which, however, he was relieved, by instructions from home to regulate his conduct by the protest taken by the deputies of his native city.*

So bent were the popish cantons on the execution of their edict, and so much were they afraid lest any thing should intervene to prevent it, that they ordered their deputies to cross the Alps in the depth of winter. On their arrival at Locarno, the latter assembled the inhabitants, and, in a threatening harangue, told them, that, as they had, by their rebellious and perverse innovations in religion, disturbed the peace and nearly broken the union of the Helvetic body, they might justly have been visited with exemplary punishment, but that the diet, graciously overlooking their past faults, had ordained a law by which their future conduct should be imperiously regulated. The decree having been read, the municipal authorities immediately ratified it by their subscriptions: the inhabitants, being divided in sentiment, were allowed till next day to give in their answer. On the following morning such as were resolved to adhere to the popish religion appeared before the deputies, and begging forgiveness for any thing in their past conduct which might have been offensive, promised an entire obedience and conformity to the laws for the future. In the afternoon, the Protestants, drawn up in regular order, two men,

* Muralti Oratio, p. 152—160.

followed by their wives, walking abreast, the women carrying their infants in their arms, the men leading their children, and those who were most respectable for their rank taking the lead, proceeded to the council room, where they were received by the deputies with marks of indecent levity, instead of that respect and sympathy to which their appearance and prospects entitled them. One of their number addressed the deputies in the name of his brethren. Being heavily accused of embracing novelties and dangerous opinions, they begged leave, he said, humbly to declare that they professed that faith which was prefigured under the Old Testament, and more clearly revealed by Christ and his apostles: after searching the Scriptures, and comparing the Latin and Italian translations, with prayer for divine illumination, they had embraced that doctrine which was summarily comprehended in the apostles' creed, and rejected all human traditions contrary to the word of God: they disclaimed Novatianism and all novel opinions, and held in abhorrence every thing that favoured licentiousness of manners, as they had often protested to the seven popish and four Protestant cantons: committing themselves to Providence, they were prepared to suffer any thing rather than foment strife, or be the occasion of war in the confederation: they had always preserved their allegiance to the confederate cantons inviolate, and were willing to spend their blood and treasure in their defence: they threw themselves on the generosity and mercy of the lords of the seven cantons, and supplicated them, in the bowels of Jesus Christ, to take pity on such a number of persons, including delicate females and helpless infants, who, if driven from their native country, must be reduced to the greatest distress: but whatever resolution might be come to respecting this request, they entreated that a rigorous investigation should be made into the crimes, affecting their honour and the credit of their religion, with which they had been charged; and that if any of them were found guilty, they should be punished, according to their demerit, with the utmost severity. With hearts as rigid and haughty as the Alps which they had lately passed, the deputies replied to this touching and magnanimous appeal—"We are not come here to listen to your faith. The lords of the seven cantons have, by the deed now made known to you, declared what their religion is, and they will not suffer it to be called in question or disputed.* Say, in one word, are you ready to quit your faith, or are you not?" To this the Protestants with one voice replied—" We will live in it, we will die in it;" while the exclamations—" we will never renounce it"—" it is the only true faith"—" it is the only holy faith"—" it is the only saving faith,"—continued for a considerable time to resound from different parts of the assembly, like the murmurs which succeed the principal peal in a thunder storm. Before leaving the room, they were required individually to give their names to the clerk, when two hundred persons immediately came forward with the greatest alacrity and with mutual congratulations.†

Perceiving that they could look for no favour from the deputies, who sternly refused them permission to remain till the rigour of winter was over, the Protestants made preparations for their departure, and sent Taddeo de Dunis before them to request an asylum from the magistrates of Zurich. But they had still to suffer greater trials. Riverda, the papal nuncio, following up his success at the diet in Switzerland, made his appearance at Locarno. Having obtained an audience of the deputies, and thanked them in the pope's name for the care they had testified for the catholic faith, he requested, first, that they should require the Grison league to deliver up the fugitive preacher Beccaria, that he might be punished for the daring crime which he had committed in corrupting the faith of his countrymen; and, secondly, that they would not permit the Locarnese emigrants to carry along with them their property and children; but that the former should be forfeited, and the latter retained

* " Das wöllen sie unarguieret und ungedisputieret haben."
† Muralti Oratio, p. 160—164.

and brought up in the faith of the church of Rome. The deputies readily acceded to the first of these requests, but excused themselves from complying with the second, with which their instructions did not warrant them to interfere. They begged the nuncio, however, to grant power to the priests of Locarno to receive such of the Protestants as might be induced to return into the bosom of the Church. This Riverda not only granted, but also offered his own services, along with those of two Dominican doctors of theology, whom he had brought along with him, to convince the deluded heretics. But though he harassed the Protestants, by obliging them to listen to harangues delivered by the monks and to wait on conferences with himself, he did not succeed in making a single convert. Having heard of three ladies of great respectability, Catarina Rosalina, Lucia di Orello, and Barbara di Montalto, who were zealous Protestants, the nuncio felt a strong inclination to enter the lists of controversy with them; but they parried his attacks with so much dexterity, and exposed the idolatry and abuses of the Romish church with such boldness and severity, as at once to mortify and irritate his eminence. Barbara di Montalto, the wife of the first physician of the place, having incurred his greatest resentment, he prevailed on the deputies to issue an order to apprehend her for blasphemies which she had uttered against the sacrifice of the mass. Her husband's house, which had been constructed as a place of defence during the violent feuds between the Guelphs and Ghibellines, was built on the Lake Maggiore, and had a concealed door, requiring the strength of six men to move it, which opened upon the water, where a boat was kept in waiting to carry off the inmates upon any sudden alarm. This door he had caused his servants to open that night in consequence of an alarming dream, which led him to apprehend danger, not to his wife indeed, but to himself. Early next morning the officers of justice entered the house, and bursting into the apartment where the lady was in the act of dressing herself, presented a warrant from the deputies to convey her to prison. Rising up with great presence of mind, she begged them, with an air of feminine delicacy, to permit her to retire to an adjoining apartment, for the purpose of putting on some article of apparel. This being granted, she descended the stairs, and, leaping into the boat, was rowed off in safety, before the eyes of her enemies, who were assembled in the court-room to receive her. Provoked at this disappointment, the nuncio and deputies wreaked their vengeance upon the husband of the lady, whom they stripped of his property. Not satisfied with this, they amerced in a large sum two members of the reformed church who had refused to have their children baptized after the popish forms. But the severest punishment fell on a poor tradesman, named Nicolas. He had been informed against, some time before, for using, in a conversation with some of his neighbours, certain expressions derogatory to the Virgin Mary, who had a celebrated chapel in the vicinity, called Madonna del Sasso; and the prefect Reuchlin, with the view of silencing the clamours of the priests, had punished his imprudence by condemning him to an imprisonment of sixteen weeks. The poor man was now brought a second time to trial for that offence, and, after being put to the torture, had sentence of death passed upon him, which was unrelentingly executed by order of the deputies, notwithstanding the intercession of the Roman catholic citizens in his behalf.*

The Protestants had fixed on the 3d of March 1555, for setting out on their journey; and so bitter had their life been for some time, that, attached as they were to their native place, they looked forward to the day of their departure with joy. But before it arrived, the government of Milan, yielding to the instigations of the priesthood, published an edict, prohibiting the Locarnese exiles from remaining above three days within the Milanese territory, under the pain of death; and imposing a fine on those who should afford them any assistance, or enter into conversation with them,

* Muralti Oratio, p. 157, 164—170.

especially on any matter connected with religion. Being thus precluded from taking the road which led to the easiest passage across the Alps, they set out early on the morning of the day fixed, and, after sailing to the northern point of the Lake Maggiore, passed the Helvetian balliages, by the way of Bellinzone, and reached Rogoreto, a town subject to the Grison league. Here the Alps, covered with snow and ice, presented an impassable barrier, and obliged them to take up their winter quarters, amidst the inconveniences necessarily attending the residence of such a number of persons among strangers. After two months, the thaw having opened a passage for them, they proceeded to the Grisons, where they were welcomed by their brethren of the same faith. Being offered a permanent residence, with admission to the privileges of citizenship, nearly the half of their number took up their abode in that country; the remainder, amounting to a hundred and fourteen persons, went forward to Zurich, the inhabitants of which came out to meet them at their approach, and, by the kind and fraternal reception which they gave them, consoled and revived the hearts of the sad and weary exiles.*

In the meantime, the city of Locarno rejoiced at the expulsion of the Reformed, as if it had been the removal of a plague; but this exultation was of short continuance. The most industrious part of the community being expelled, the trade of the place began to languish. As if visibly to punish the cruelty with which they had treated their brethren, their lands were laid waste during the succeeding year by a tempest, while the pestilence raged with still more destructive violence among the inhabitants. To these calamities were added intestine animosities and dissensions. The two powerful families of the Buchiachi

---

* Muralti Oratio, p. 171, 172. Sleidan, tom iii lib. xxvi. p 506 Schelhorn makes the number of those who reached Zurich one hundred and thirty-three. (Ergoetzlichkeiten, tom. iii. p 1162.) A few persons, attached to the Reformed doctrine, still remained at Locarno. (De Porta, tom. ii p. 346.)

and Rinaldi, who had been leagued against the Protestants, now became competitors for the superiority of the neighbouring village of Brisago, vacant by the expulsion of the Orelli; and, in support of their claims, they raised bands of armed men, attacked each other, and committed depredations on the peaceable inhabitants; in consequence of which, the Swiss government was obliged to maintain a garrison at great expense in Locarno.*

Hard as was the fate of the Locarnese Protestants, it was mild compared with that of their brethren in the interior of Italy, who had no friendly power to save them from the vengeance of Rome, and no asylum at hand to which they could flee, when refused the protection of their own governments. To retire in a body was impossible; they were obliged to fly singly; and when they ventured to return for the purpose of carrying away their families or recovering the wreck of their fortunes, they were often seized by the familiars of the inquisition, and lodged in the same prisons with their brethren whom they had left behind them. While the profession of the truth exposed persons to such hardships and perils, we need not wonder that many were induced to recant, while still greater numbers, with the view of avoiding or allaying suspicion, gave external countenance to a worship which they inwardly detested as superstitious and idolatrous. This was the case at Lucca. Averse to quit their native country, and to relinquish their honours and possessions, trusting in their numbers and influence, and deceived by the connivance of the court of Rome at their private meetings for a course of years, the Protestants in that republic became secure, and began to boast of their superior courage in maintaining their ground, while many of their brethren had timidly deserted it, and suffered the banner of truth, which had been displayed in different quarters

* Muralti Oratio, p. 174, 175. Another account of the persecution of the Locarnese, besides that of Muralto, is given in a letter from Simon Sultzer, minister at Basle, to J. Marbach. (Fechtius, Epist. Marbach, p. 46, &c.)

of Italy, to fall to the ground. But this pleasing dream was soon to be dissipated. Scarcely had Paul IV. mounted the papal throne, when orders were issued for the suppression of the Lucchese conventicle; according to a preconcerted plan, its principal members were in one day thrown into the dungeons of the inquisition; and, at the sight of the instruments of torture, the stoutest of them lost their courage, and were fain to make their peace with Rome on the easiest terms which they could purchase. Martyr, whose apology for his flight they had with difficulty sustained, and whose example they had refused to follow when it was in their power, felt deeply afflicted at the dissipation of a church in which he took a tender interest, and at the sudden defection of so many persons in whose praises he had often been so warm. In a letter which he addressed to them on this occasion, he says—" How can I refrain from lamentations, when I think that such a pleasant garden as the Reformed Church at Lucca presented to the view, has been so completely laid waste by the cruel tempest, as scarcely to retain a vestige of its former cultivation. Those who did not know you, might have entertained fears that you would not be able to resist the storm; it never could have entered into my mind that you would fall so foully. After the knowledge you had of the fury of antichrist, and of the danger which hung over your heads, when you did not choose to retire, by availing yourselves of what some call the common remedy of the weak, but which, in certain circumstances, I deem a wise precaution, your friends were disposed to say, 'These tried and brave soldiers of Christ, will not fly, because they are determined, by their martyrdom and blood, to open a way for the progress of the gospel in their native country, emulating the noble examples which are given every day by their brethren in France, Belgium, and England.' Ah, how much have these hopes been disappointed! What matter of boasting has been given to our antichristian oppressors! But this confounding catastrophe is to be deplored with tears, rather than words."*

Notwithstanding these severities, the seeds of the reformed doctrine were not extirpated in Lucca. In the year 1556, some of the best families in that city, with the view of enjoying the free exercise of religion, transferred their families and wealth to Switzerland and France. The Micheli, Turretini, Calendrini, Burlamacchi, Diodati, Balbani, and Minutoli, who have made so great a figure in the state and church of Geneva, came originally from Lucca. Irritated by their departure, the government barbarously offered three hundred crowns to the person who should kill one of them in Italy, France, or Flanders. The council of Geneva wrote to Lucca requesting the recall of this proclamation, but all their solicitations were in vain, though it does not appear that the refugees were molested any further than by being put in fear of their lives.† We find the popish writers complaining that, in the year 1562, the heretics in Lucca kept up a correspondence with their countrymen in foreign countries, and, by means of merchants, procured Protestant books from Lyons and Geneva.‡ In 1556, more families from Lucca arrived at Geneva;§ and, in the following year, a severe ordinance came from the Lucchese authorities, prohibiting all intercourse, by speech or letters, with those who had been denounced "rebels for the cause of religion."‖

The refugees from Lucca appear to have been allowed to remain in quietness until 1679, when an unexpected occurrence showed that they were not

---

* Martyris Loc. Com. p. 771, 772.
† Picot, Histoire de Geneve, tom. ii. p. 110.
‡ Raynaldi Annales, ad an. 1562.
§ Leti, Historia Genevrina, parte iii. p. 162
‖ Bibl. Modenese, tom. v p. 125. Among the persons named in this ordinance as rebels, is "Messer Simoni Simone, Medico." This ingenious but versatile man resided at Geneva, Heidelberg, Leipsic, Prague, and Cracow, and was as unsettled in his religious creed as in his place of residence, having been successively a Calvinist, Lutheran, Arian, Jesuit, and (if we may believe his countryman Squarcialupo) Atheist. (Bezæ Epist. ep. 53, 56. Brucker, Hist. Philos. iv. 286. Bock, i. 834, 910.)

altogether forgotten in the land of their fathers. This was a letter addressed to them by cardinal Spinola, at that time bishop of Lucca, in which his eminence declared that, in his paternal solicitude for the diocese over which Innocent XI. had placed him, he had learned with grief that, during the troubles of the bygone century, multitudes, remarkable for the nobility of their extraction and the superiority of their talents, had left a city in which they filled the highest offices, to repair to Geneva; that the affection he felt for the descendants of these men would not allow him to rest until he had taken this step, with the view of prevailing with them to return to the bosom of their mother church, for the success of which he had ordered a public supplication throughout the whole of his diocese; and that he trusted they would remember, that there was nothing more glorious nor more conducive to their safety than to yield to God, and betake themselves to the only sanctuary of truth. The refugees at first thought it most prudent to return no answer to this letter, lest truth should oblige them to say things unpleasant to a prelate who had spoken of their ancestors in such flattering terms; but being aware that there was, at that time, a general concert among the Roman catholic powers to make proselytes of the Protestants, and hearing that reports unfavourable to their steadfastness were abroad, and that the cardinal was actually applying to the pope for their absolution, they felt it incumbent on them to publish to the world their real sentiments. After giving a sketch of the progress which the reformed religion had made at Lucca, they, in their answer, analyze the cardinal's letter, and conclude with an affectionate and forcible appeal to their "kinsmen according to the flesh," who were still groping in the darkness of popish Lucca.* When the reply came into the hands of Spinola, he sent one copy of it to the pope and

* Lettre de M. le Cardinal Spinola, évêque de Luques aux originaux Luquois qui demeurent à Geneve. Avec les Considerations qu'ils ont fait à ce sujet. A Geneve, 1680. The cardinal's letter was dated the 19th of May 1679.

another to the Congregation of the Holy Office, who ordered him to cause all the copies to be burnt by the executioner.*

Two facts are sufficient to establish the severity of persecution in the duchy of Mantua. In the year 1566, Guglielmo, duke of Mantua, respecting the rights of his subjects as well as his own authority, refused to send certain persons accused of heresy to Rome for trial. This drew down upon him the indignation of Pius V., who threatened him with excommunication and a declaration of war, as one who had made Mantua a nest of heretics; and his holiness would have carried his threats into execution, had not the princes of Italy prevailed on him to pardon the duke on his submission.† Two years after, a person, allied to the duke, having been seized by the inquisition on suspicion of heresy, his highness begged the chief inquisitor to release the prisoner. This request was refused by the haughty monk, who replied, that though he acknowledged the duke as his temporal lord, yet, in the present case, he acted for the pope, who possessed a power paramount to that of any secular prince. Some days after, the duke sent a second message, pressing his former request, when the inquisitor, holding out the keys of the dungeon, told the messengers insolently they might release the prisoners at their peril.‡

In no quarter of Italy were more cruel methods employed to extirpate the new opinions than in the Milanese, especially after it fell under the dominion of Philip II. of Spain. Galeazzo Trezio, a nobleman of Lodi, while attending the university of Pavia, had imbibed the reformed doctrines from Maynardi, who acted at that time as an Augustinian preacher, and was afterwards confirmed in them by the instructions of Curio. Having fallen into the hands of the inqui-

* Leti, Historia Genevrina, parte v. p 351—366. The reply was written by the pastor Burlamacchi, from materials furnished by the pastor Turretini.

† Bzovii Annales, ad an. 1566.

‡ Epist Tob. Eglini ad H. Bullingerum, 2 Mart. 1568: De Porta, tom. ii. p. 486.

sition in 1551, and retracted some concessions which he had been induced to make at his first apprehension, he was sentenced to be burned alive, a punishment which he bore with the utmost fortitude.* The persecution became more general when the duke of Alva was made governor. In the year 1558 two persons were committed alive to the flames. One of them, a monk, being forced by an attending priest into a pulpit erected beside the stake to make his recantation, confessed the truth with great boldness, and was driven into the fire with blows and curses. During the course of the following year, scarcely a week elapsed without some individual being brought out to suffer for heresy; and, in 1563, eleven citizens of rank were thrown into prison. The execution of a young priest in 1569 was accompanied with circumstances of peculiar barbarity. He was condemned to be hanged and dragged to the gibbet at a horse's tail. In consequence of earnest intercessions in his favour, the last part of the sentence was dispensed with; but, after being half-strangled, he was cut down, and, refusing to recant, was literally roasted to death and his body thrown to the dogs.†

Persecution was also let loose within the territories of Tuscany. In 1547, a law was proclaimed at Florence, calling upon all who possessed heretical books, particularly those of Ochino and Martyr, to deliver them up within fifteen days, under the pain of a hundred ducats, and ten years' confinement in the galleys; threatening a personal visit to the houses of suspected persons after the expiry of the limited time; and forbidding, under heavy penalties, the printing of such books. After the establishment of the inquisition, more decisive measures were adopted by the commissioners of the Holy Office, the vicar of the archbishop, the provost of the metropolitan church, and the spedalingo or director of the hospital of Santa Maria Nuova. In December 1551, an *auto de fé* was cele-

* The account of this martyr was furnished by Celio S Curio to Pantaleon. (Rerum in Eccl. Gest p. 247—249. Conf. Hieronymi Marii Eusebius Captivus, f. 105.)
† De Porta, tom. ii. p. 295, 296, 486, 488.

brated in the city of Florence, in which twenty-two persons walked in procession as penitents, among whom was Bartolommeo Panchiarichi, a wealthy citizen, who had served the duke in the capacity of ambassador to the court of France. They were clothed in caps and cloaks painted with crosses and devils, and were publicly "reconciled" in the cathedral church, while the books found in their possession were burned in the piazza. At the same time a number of females went through this ceremony privately in the church of San Simone. The zeal of the inquisitorial commissioners was soon after signalized in the case of a native of Piacenza, who had come to Florence in 1547, and having dedicated to the duke a translation of Xenophon, continued his literary pursuits in that city. The record of his process, which has been preserved, bears, " that Ludovico Domenichi, a learned man of about thirty years of age, had translated, from Latin into the vulgar tongue, the Nicodemiana of Calvin, caused it to be printed, and corrected it, the book being most dishonest, and printed in Florence, not at Basle, as it falsely pretended, on which account he was suspected of heresy, though he denied having ever held any dangerous opinions: that he should therefore abjure, as one violently suspected, having a copy of the book translated by him hung from his neck, and be afterwards condemned to the galleys for ten years, less or more, for transgressing the laws which regulated the press."* These severities increased at a subsequent period. Under the pretext that it was dangerous to entrust to a number of persons the secrets which transpired in the course of examination, Pius V. discharged the three commissaries who had hitherto taken part in trials for heresy, and committed the whole business to a single inquisitor, which was the same thing as transferring the power to the congregation at Rome, by whose directions he was regulated. This, together with the facile conduct of Cosmo in delivering up to the pope Carnesecchi, whose fate will afterwards be recorded,

* Galluzzi, i. 143, 144.

spread terror and discontent over the city. Numbers betook themselves to flight, and others were sent to Rome. The inquisitor, fond of displaying his power, and anxious to recommend himself by his activity, harassed the inhabitants incessantly, interrogating the unlearned on the profoundest mysteries of religion, and converting into heresy what proceeded from mere ignorance. In the year 1567, the regent remonstrated with the pope against these iniquitous proceedings, and insisted that the archbishop and nuncio should be associated with the inquisitor; but all that could be obtained was the removal of the latter, and the substitution of one less indiscreet and ignorant. The consequence was, that Florence, which had long been the resort of enlightened men from all parts of the world, was shunned by foreigners; and as the minds of the inquisitors were filled with the notion that emissaries were sent from Germany and France to disseminate the new opinions in Italy, persons coming from these countries, unless they were furnished with the most unexceptionable testimonials, were subjected to infinite trouble and vexation.*

These proceedings drove many persons, eminent for their talents and rank, from Tuscany. Michael Angelo Florio, a popular preacher in his native country, became pastor to a congregation of Italian Protestants, first in the Grisons and afterwards in London.† The name of Nardi, so familiar to those acquainted with Italian literature, appears in the catalogue of those who forsook Florence from love to the

* Galluzzi, ii. 203, 204.

† Florio is the author of a very rare and curious work, including a life of the unfortunate and accomplished Lady Jane Gray:—"Historia de la Vita e de la morte de l'illustriss. Signora Giovanna Graia, gia Regina eletta e publicata d'Inghilterra: e de la cose accadute in quel Regno dopo la morte del Re Edoardo VI nella quale secondo le Divine Scritture si trata de i principali articoli de la Religione Christiana. Con l'aggiunto d'una doctiss. disputa Theologica fatta in Ossonia, l'anno 1554. L'Argumento del tutto si dechiaro ne l'Auuertimento sequente, e nel' Proemio de l'Authore, M. Michel-angelo Florio Fiorentino, gia Predicatore famoso del Sant Evangelio en piu cita d'Italia, et en Londra.—Stampate appressi Richardo Pittore ne l'anno di Christo 1607."

gospel.* Pietro Gelido, a native of Samminiato, was an ecclesiastic of great learning, who having been educated in his youth at the court of Clement VII. took up his residence in Florence.† He had served the duke in the character of secretary at the court of France, and acted as his resident in Venice from 1552 to 1562, during which period he acquitted himself equally to the satisfaction of the republic and of his prince. During the visits which he paid to Ferrara, Gelido had imbibed the doctrines of the Reformation, and gave great offence to the clergy by the intercourse which he held with Germans, and the protection which he extended to those who were suspected of heresy. This induced him to retire to France, and to take up his abode with the duchess Renée of Ferrara. But he was not permitted to enjoy this retirement. A spy of his former master gave false information against him to the Florentines who surrounded queen Catharine; and being accused at court, he found it necessary to retreat to Geneva, where he joined the Italian congregation already erected in that city. From that place he addressed a letter to Cosmo, vindicating his own conduct, and urging the duke to use his influence with the pope to assemble a council in the heart of Germany, and to attend it in person.‡ The example of Gelido was followed, at a later period, by Antonio Albizio, who belonged to one of the noblest families in Tuscany. He was the founder of the academy of Alterati at Florence, and had been sent by the grand duke as ambassador to the emperor Maximilian II.; but having discovered the truth by reading the Scriptures, he made a voluntary sacrifice of his honours, and retired to Kempten in Suabia, where he divided his time, until his death in 1626, between devotional exercises and literary studies.

* Joannes Leo Nardus, Florentinus, Tabularum duarum Legis Evangelicæ, Gratiæ, Spiritus, et Vitæ, Libri quinque, Bas. 1553.
† We learn from Galluzzi, that he was commonly called " il Pero," and he is no doubt the person mentioned by that name in a letter from Paulus Manutius to Carnesecchi. (Lettere di Tredeci, p. 294, edit. 1565.)
‡ Galluzzi, ii. 77, 78.

Great influence was used by his friends to recover him to the ancient faith, but without effect; and his process was going on before the inquisition at Rome when he died.*

Similar proceedings took place in Sienna, which had now fallen under the dominion of the grand duke of Tuscany. During a number of years after the discovery of the defection of Ochino, the Soccini, and Paleario, from the Roman faith, the clergy and inquisitors alarmed the government with reports of the spread of heresy in the city and territories of Sienna. In 1560 the bishop of Bologna was sent to conduct a process, which was deemed of greater importance; it was that of Cornelio Soccini, who was accused of having adopted the peculiar opinions of his relation, Faustus Socinus. As all that could be drawn from him by examination was, that he believed whatever was contained in the Scriptures, he was, with the consent of the duke, transferred to Rome. In the year 1567 the persecution became severer, and many were driven from the country, subjected to process, or delivered up to the Holy Office. Even Germans, who had come, under the security of the public faith, to study at the university of Sienna, were seized and placed in the hands of the pope.†

At Naples, the Protestants enjoyed a reprieve from persecution during the dissensions excited by the renewed attempt to introduce the Spanish Inquisition.‡ But the people were satisfied with the abandonment of that measure by the government, which, in its turn, not only forgave the pope for fomenting the late opposition to its measures, but entered into a treaty with him, in which it was agreed to take common measures for rooting out the new opinions. Lorenzo Ro-

* Mazzuchelli, Scrittori Italiani, tom. i. part i p. 337. He was the author of Stemmata Principum Christianorum, Aug. Vind. 1612, and of Exercitationes Theologicæ, Campoduni, 1616 An account of his conversion was published by Jac. Zeamann in 1692, and his life by F. D. Haeberlin in 1740.

† Galluzzi, ii. 202, 203.

‡ Gonçalo de Illescas, Historia Pontifical y Catholica, parte ii. f. 418, a.—420, b. Burgos, 1578.

mano, a native of Sicily, had, at a former period,
instilled the doctrine of Zuingle into the minds of
many of the inhabitants of Caserta, a town lying
about fifteen miles north of Naples. Having gone to
Germany, where he was more fully instructed in the
truth, he returned to the Neapolitan territory in 1549,
and, having opened a class for logic, took occasion to
expound the Scriptures to his scholars. But the jealousy of the clergy was awake, and he was soon delated to the Inquisition. Romano did not possess the
firmness of a martyr: alarmed at the danger which
he had incurred, he sought an interview with the
Theatine cardinal, confessed his errors, and informed
him of the numbers, including persons of the first
rank, male and female, who had embraced heresy,
both in the capital and in other parts of the kingdom.
He was condemned to abjure his opinions publicly in
the cathedral churches of Naples and Caserta, and to
undergo certain other penances at Rome; after which
he obtained his liberty.* In consequence of his information, the inquisitors sent by the pope commenced
a rigorous search after heretics in the city of Naples,
which was afterwards extended over the kingdom.
Many were thrown into prison, and not a few sent to
Rome to undergo the fiery ordeal. These severities
continued, with intervals of relaxation, during several
years. On the 24th of March, 1564, two noblemen,
Giovan-Francesco d'Alois, of Caserta, and Giovan-
Bernardino, di Gargano, of Avarsa, after being convicted of heresy, were beheaded in the market-place,
and their bodies consumed to ashes in the sight of the
people.†

The prosecutions for heresy, together with the
dread in which the inhabitants were kept of the introduction of the court of inquisition, had a fatal influence on the interests both of trade and literature.
Whole streets in the city of Naples were deserted by
their inhabitants. The academies of the Sireni, Ardenti, and Incogniti, lately erected for the cultivation

* Giannone, Hist. Civ. de Naples, b. xxxii. chap. v. sect. 1.
† Ibid. sect. 11.

of poetry, rhetoric, and astronomy, were shut up by the viceroy, under the pretext that the members, after giving out a question on some branch of secular learning, dropped it, and entered on discussions respecting the Scriptures and divinity.*

Two things conspired with this violence to ruin the reformed cause in Naples. The first was, the coming of certain adherents of anabaptism and arianism, who got introduced to the secret meetings of the Protestants, and made disciples to their peculiar tenets.† The second was the practice which some of them indulged of attending the popish worship, partaking of mass, and conducting themselves in public in every respect as if they had been papists. These have been called Valdesians by some writers, because they justified themselves by appealing to the example of Valdes, and to the advice which he gave those whom he had instructed in the doctrine of justification, but whose minds were yet fettered by prejudices in favour of the church of Rome and the ancient rites. This practice, which became more general as the persecution increased, not only offended those conscientious individuals who shunned the popish worship as idolatrous, but it gradually wore off from the minds of the conformists the impressions of that faith which they had embraced, and prepared them for sacrificing it on the slightest temptation. Notwithstanding all their caution, not a few of them were seized as suspected persons, and purchased their lives by recanting those truths which they had professed to hold in the highest estimation. But this was not all: having once incurred the jealousy of the inquisitors, and exposed themselves to the malice or avarice of informers, some of them were seized a second time, and subjected to tortures and a cruel death, as relapsed heretics.‡ Afraid of incurring the same punishment, or actuated by a desire to enjoy the pure worship of God, a considerable number of Protestants agreed to quit Italy;

* Giannone, lib. xxxii. chap v. sect. 1.
† Life of the Marquis of Vico, chap. vii. p 13. Lond. 1635.
‡ Life of the Marquis of Vico, chap. vii. p. 14.

but when they came to the Alps, and stopped to take a last view of their beloved country, the greater part, struck with its beauties, and calling to mind the friends and the comforts which they had left behind, burst into a flood of tears, and, abandoning their purpose, returned to Naples. They had scarcely arrived there, when they were thrown into prison, and, having submitted to penance, spent the remainder of their lives distrusted by those around them, and preyed upon by remorse and a consciousness of self-degradation.*

When the reformed opinions had been suppressed in the capital, the Neapolitan government permitted the inquisitors to roam through the country like wild beasts let loose, and to devour its innocent subjects. Of all the barbarities of which Rome was guilty at this period, none was more horrible than those which were inflicted on the descendants of the ancient Waldenses. It would seem as if she wished to exceed the cruelties committed during the dark ages, in the crusades which Simon de Montfort, of bloody memory, had conducted against the ancestors of that people, under the consecrated banners of the church.

The Waldensian colony in Calabria Citeriore had increased in the sixteenth century to four thousand persons, who possessed several towns in the neighbourhood of Cosenza, of which the principal were Santo Xisto, belonging to the duke of Montalto, and La Guardia, situate on the sea-coast. Cut off from intercourse with their brethren of the same faith, and destitute of the means of education for their pastors, this simple people, at the same time that they observed their own forms of worship, had gradually become habituated to attend on mass, without which they found it difficult to maintain a friendly intercourse with the original inhabitants of the place. Their curiosity was awakened by hearing that a doctrine bearing a strong affinity to that of their fathers was propagated in Italy; they eagerly sought to become acquainted with it, and being convinced that they had

* Life of the Marquis of Vico, chap. x. p. 21.

erred hitherto in countenancing the popish worship, they applied to their brethren in the valleys of Pragela, and to the ministers of Geneva, to obtain teachers who should instruct them more perfectly, and organize their churches after the Scripture pattern.* By diligent preaching and catechizing, these missionaries not only promoted the knowledge of the truth among those to whom they were sent, but propagated it in the neighbouring towns, and in the province of Basilicata.†

No sooner was this known at Rome, than the sacred college sent two monks, Valerio Malvicino and Alfonso Urbino, into Calabria, to suppress the churches of the Waldenses, and reduce them to the obedience of the holy see. On their first arrival, the monks assumed an air of great gentleness Having assembled the inhabitants of Santo Xisto, they told them, that they had not come with the view of hurting any person, but merely to warn them in a friendly manner to desist from hearing any teachers but those appointed by their ordinary: that if they would dismiss those men who had led them astray, and live for the future according to the rules of the Roman church, they had nothing to fear; but that, if they acted otherwise, they would expose themselves to the danger of losing their lives and property, by incurring the punishment of heretics. They then appointed a time for celebration of mass, which they required all present to attend. Instead of complying with this injunction, the inhabitants, in a body, quitted the town and retired into the woods, leaving behind them only a few aged persons and children. Concealing their chagrin, the monks immediately went to La Guardia, and having caused the gates to be shut, assembled the inhabitants, and told them that their brethren of Santo Xisto had renounced their erroneous opinions, and gone to mass, exhorting them to imitate so dutiful and wise an example. The poor simple people, crediting the report

* Zanchii Epistolæ, lib ii. p 360. Leger, Hist. des Eglises Vaud. part ii p. 333.
† Giannone, lib. xxxii. chap. v. sect. ii.

of the monks, and alarmed at the danger which they held out, complied; but no sooner did they ascertain the truth, than, overwhelmed with shame and vexation, they resolved instantly to leave the place with their wives and children, and to join their brethren who had taken refuge in the woods; a resolution from which they were with difficulty diverted by the representations and promises of Salvatore Spinello, the feudatory superior of the town. In the meantime, the monks procured two companies of foot soldiers to be sent into the woods, who hunted the inhabitants of Santo Xisto like beasts of prey, and, having discovered their lurking place, fell on them with cries of *Ammazzi, ammazzi,* "Murder them, murder them." A part of the fugitives took refuge on a mountain, and having secured themselves among the rocks, demanded a parley with the captain. After entreating him to take pity on them, their wives, and children, they said, that they and their fathers had inhabited that country for several ages, without having given any person cause to complain of their conduct; that if they could not be allowed to remain in it any longer without renouncing their faith, they hoped they would be permitted to retire to some other country; that they would go, by sea or land, to any place which their superiors were pleased to appoint; that they would engage not to return; and that they would take no more along with them than what was necessary for their support on the journey, for they were ready to part with their property rather than do violence to their consciences by practising idolatry. They implored him to withdraw his men, and not oblige them reluctantly to defend themselves, as they could not answer for the consequences, if reduced to despair. Instead of listening to this reasonable offer, and reporting it to his superiors, the captain ordered his men to advance by a defile, upon which those on the hill attacked them, killed the greater part, and put the rest to flight.*

* Perrin, Hist des Vaudois, part. i. p 199—202. Perrin relates this under the year 1560, and speaks of it as having taken place after

It was immediately resolved to avenge on the whole body this unpremeditated act of resistance on the part of a few. The monks wrote to Naples that the country was in a state of rebellion, upon which the viceroy despatched several companies of soldiers to Calabria, and, to gratify the pope, followed them in person. On his arrival, listening to the advice of the inquisitors, he caused a proclamation to be made, delivering up Santo Xisto to fire and sword, which obliged the inhabitants to remain in their concealments. By another proclamation, he offered a pardon to the *bannitti*, or persons proscribed for crimes, (who form a numerous class in Naples,) on the condition of their assisting in the war against the heretics. This brought a number of desperate characters to his standard, who, being acquainted with the recesses of the woods, tracked out the fugitives, the greater part of whom were slaughtered by the soldiers, while the remainder took refuge in the caverns of the high rocks, where many of them died of hunger. Pretending to be displeased with the severity of military execution, the inquisitors retired to some distance from the place, and cited the inhabitants of La Guardia to appear before them. Encouraged by the reports which they had heard, the people complied; but they had no sooner made their appearance, than seventy of them were seized and conducted in chains to Montalto.* They were put to the question by the orders of the inquisitor Panza, to induce them not only to renounce their faith but also to accuse themselves and their brethren of having committed odious crimes in their religious assemblies. To wring a confession of this from him, Stefano

Louis Paschal came to Calabria. But I suspect he has placed it too late. At least the author of *Busdragi Epistola*, which is dated 15th December, 1558, speaking of the progress of the reformed doctrine in Italy, says—" Nam quotidie aliquid novi sentitur, nunc in hac civitate, nunc in illa. Calabria nuper ferè tota tumultuata est." (Scrin. Antiq. tom. i. p. 322.)

* Giannone says, that the heretics had fortified Guardia; and that Scipio Spinelli, finding he could not reduce it by force, had recourse to deceit, and, under pretext of an exchange of prisoners, introduced soldiers into the castle, and gained possession of the town. Hist. de Naples, b. xxxii. c. v. sect. ii.

Carlino was tortured until his bowels gushed out. Another prisoner, named Verminel, having, in the extremity of pain, promised to go to mass, the inquisitor flattered himself that, by increasing the violence of the torture, he could extort a confession of the charge which he was so anxious to fasten on the Protestants. But though the exhausted sufferer was kept during eight hours on the horrid instrument called *the hell*, he persisted in denying the atrocious calumny. A person of the name of Marzone was stripped naked, beaten with iron rods, dragged through the streets, and then felled with the blows of torches. One of his sons, a boy, having resisted the attempts made for his conversion, was conveyed to the top of a tower, from which they threatened to precipitate him, if he would not embrace a crucifix, which was presented to him. He refused; and the inquisitor, in a rage, ordered him instantly to be thrown down. Bernardino Conte, on his way to the stake, threw away a crucifix which the executioner had forced into his hands; upon which Panza remanded him to prison, until a more dreadful mode of punishment should be devised. He was conveyed to Cosenza, where his body was covered with pitch, in which he was burnt to death before the people.* The manner in which persons of the tender sex were treated by this brutal inquisitor, is too disgusting to be related here. Suffice it to say, that he put sixty females to the torture, the greater part of whom died in prison in consequence of their wounds remaining undressed. On his return to Naples, he delivered a great number of Protestants to the secular arm at St. Agata, where he inspired the inhabitants with the utmost terror; for, if any individual came forward to intercede for the prisoners, he was immediately put to the torture as a favourer of heresy.†

Horrid as these facts are, they fall short of the bar-

---

* Perrin, ut supra, p. 202—204. Leger, Hist. des Eglises Vaudoises, tom ii. p. 335.

† Perrin, p. 205, 206. A priest named Anania, who had taken an active part in the persecution of that innocent people, wrote an account of it in *Latin verse*. (Giannone, ut supra.)

barity perpetrated on the same people at Montalto in the year 1560, under the government of the marquis di Buccianici, to whose brother, it is said, the pope had promised a cardinal's hat, provided the province of Calabria was cleared of heresy. I shall give the account in the words of a Roman Catholic, servant to Ascanio Caraccioli, who witnessed the scene. The letter in which he describes it was published in Italy, along with other narratives of the bloody transaction: "Most illustrious sir—Having written you from time to time what has been done here in the affair of heresy, I have now to inform you of the dreadful justice which began to be executed on these Lutherans early this morning, being the 11th of June. And, to tell you the truth, I can compare it to nothing but the slaughter of so many sheep. They were all shut up in one house as in a sheepfold. The executioner went, and, bringing out one of them, covered his face with a napkin, or *benda*, as we call it, led him out to a field near the house, and, causing him to kneel down, cut his throat with a knife. Then, taking off the bloody napkin, he went and brought out another, whom he put to death after the same manner. In this way, the whole number, amounting to eighty-eight men, were butchered. I leave you to figure to yourself the lamentable spectacle, for I can scarcely refrain from tears while I write; nor was there any person who, after witnessing the execution of one, could stand to look on a second. The meekness and patience with which they went to martyrdom and death are incredible. Some of them at their death professed themselves of the same faith with us, but the greater part died in their cursed obstinacy. All the old men met their death with cheerfulness, but the young exhibited symptoms of fear. I still shudder while I think of the executioner with the bloody knife in his teeth, the dripping napkin in his hand, and his arms besmeared with gore, going to the house and taking out one victim after another, just as the butcher does the sheep which he means to kill. According to orders, wagons are already come to carry away the dead bodies, which are appointed to be quartered, and hung up on the public roads from one end of Calabria to the other. Unless his holiness and the viceroy of Naples command the marquis di Buccianici, the governor of this province, to stay his hand and leave off, he will go on to put others to the torture, and multiply the executions until he has destroyed the whole. Even to-day; a decree has passed that a hundred grown up women shall be put to the question, and afterwards executed; in order that there may be a complete mixture, and we may be able to say, in well-sounding language, that so many persons were punished, partly men and partly women. This is all that I have to say of this act of justice. It is now eight o'clock, and I shall presently hear accounts of what was said by these obstinate people as they were led to execution. Some have testified such obstinacy and stubbornness as to refuse to look on a crucifix, or confess to a priest; and they are to be burnt alive. The heretics taken in Calabria amount to sixteen hundred, all of whom are condemned; but only eighty-eight have as yet been put to death. This people came originally from the valley of Angrogna, near Savoy, and in Calabria are called Ultramontani. Four other places in the kingdom of Naples are inhabited by the same race, but I do not know that they behave ill; for they are a simple unlettered people, entirely occupied with the spade and plough, and, I am told, show themselves sufficiently religious at the hour of death."* Lest the reader should be inclined to doubt the truth of such horrid atrocities, the following summary account of them, by a Neapolitan historian of that age, may be added. After giving some account of the Calabrian heretics, he says—"Some had their throats cut, others were sawn through the middle, and others thrown from the top of a high cliff: all were cruelly but deservedly put to death. It was strange to hear of their obstinacy; for while the father saw his son put to death, and the

* Pantaleon, Rerum in Eccles Gest. Hist. f. 337, 338. De Porta, tom. ii. p. 309, 312.

son his father, they not only exhibited no symptoms of grief, but said joyfully, that they would be angels of God: so much had the devil, to whom they had given themselves up as a prey, deceived them."*

By the time that the persecutors were glutted with blood, it was not difficult to dispose of the prisoners who remained. The men were sent to the Spanish galleys; the women and children were sold for slaves; and, with the exception of a few who renounced their faith, the whole colony was exterminated.† "Many a time have they afflicted me from my youth," may the race of the Waldenses say—" many a time have they afflicted me from my youth. My blood— the violence done to me and to my flesh—be upon" Rome!

While the popes exerted themselves in the suppression of the reformed doctrine in other parts of Italy, it may be taken for granted that they were not idle within the territories of the church. It has been stated by some writers, that the procedure of the inquisition was milder in Italy than in Spain: but both the statement of the fact, and the reasons by which it is usually accounted for, require to be qualified. One of these reasons is, the policy with which the Italians, including the popes, have always consulted their pecuniary interests, to which they postponed every other consideration. This, however, will be found to hold true as to their treatment of the Jews, rather than of the Lutherans. The second reason is, that the popes being temporal princes in the states of the church, had no occasion to employ the inquisition to undermine the rights of the secular authorities in them, as in other countries. This is unquestionably true; and it accounts for the fact, that the court of inquisition, long after its operations had been suspended in Italy, continued to be warmly supported by papal influence in Spain. But at the time of which I write, and during the remainder of the

* Tommaso Costo, Seconda Parte del Compendio dell' Istoria di Napoli, p 257.
† Perrin. ut supra, p. 206, 207. Hist. des Martyrs, f. 516, a.

sixteenth century, it was in full and constant operation, and the popes found that it enabled them to accomplish what would have baffled their power as secular sovereigns. The chief difference between the Italian and Spanish inquisitions at that period, consisted in their policy respecting the mode of punishment. The latter sought to inspire terror by the solemn spectacle of a public act of justice, in which the scaffold was crowded with criminals. Except in the case of the remote and friendless Calabrians, it was the object of the former to avoid all unnecessary publicity and eclat. With this view, the mode of punishment usual at Venice was sometimes adopted at Rome, as in the case of Bartolommeo Fonzio.* In other cases the victims were brought to the stake singly or in small numbers, and often strangled before being committed to the flames. The report of the *autos de fé* of Seville and Valladolid blazed at once over Europe: the executions at Rome made less noise in the city, because they were less splendid as well as more frequent, and the rumour of them died away before it could reach the ear of foreigners.

Paul III. threw many of the Protestants into the prisons of Rome; they were brought forth to execution by Julius III.; and Paul IV. followed in the bloody track of his predecessor. Under the latter, the inquisition spread alarm every where, and created the very evils which it sought to allay. Princes and princesses, clergy and laity, bishops and friars, entire academies, the sacred college, and even the holy office itself, fell under the suspicion of heretical pravity.

---

* De Porta, tom. ii. p. 33. Heidegger states, that Fonzio was drowned along with thirteen preachers of the gospel. (Diss. de Miraculis Eccles. Evang. § 45.) I conjecture that this writer was misled by a cursory inspection of a letter, (then probably unprinted,) from Frechtus to Bullinger, dated July 24, 1538, which says—"Bartholomæum Fontium Venetum, publica fide sibi a Romano Pontifice data, Romam pervenisse et fidei suæ rationem dedisse, ac statim ab Antichristo sacco impositum et Tiberi immersum, in Domino mortuum, in hujus locum XIII. *emersisse* evangelicos prædicatores, qui Romæ, invito etiam Antichristo, Christum annuncient." (Fueslin, Epist. Reform. Helvet. p. 177.) It is rather a serious mistake to confound *emergo* with *immergo*.

The conclave was subjected to an expurgatory process. Cardinals Morone and Pole, with Foscarari, bishop of Modena, Luighi Priuli, and other persons of eminence, were prosecuted as heretics. It was at last found necessary to introduce laymen into the inquisition, "because (to use the words of a contemporary writer) not only many bishops, and vicars, and friars, but also many of the inquisitors themselves, were tainted with heresy."* Much of the extravagance displayed at this time is, no doubt, to be ascribed to the personal fanaticism and jealousy of the pontiff, who sent for some of the cardinals to his death-bed, and recommended the inquisition to their support with his latest breath. Such was the frenzied zeal of this infallible dotard, that, if his life had been spared a little longer, the poet's description of the effects of superstition would have been realized, "and one capricious curse enveloped all." Irritated by his violent proceedings, and by the extortion and rapine with which they had been accompanied, the inhabitants of Rome, as soon as the tidings of his death transpired, rose in tumult, burnt the house of inquisition to the ground, after having liberated all the prisoners, broke down the statue which Paul had erected for himself, and dragging its members with ropes through the streets, threw them into the Tiber.†

Pius IV. was naturally of a mild disposition, and put a stop to the violent and arbitrary proceedings of his predecessor.‡ But he was unable to control the cardinal placed at the head of the inquisition; and, accordingly, his pontificate was disgraced by the massacres in Calabria, and by executions in various parts of Italy. In the room of the edifice which had been demolished in the tumult, a house beyond the Tiber, which belonged to one of the cardinals, was appro-

* Bernini, Istoria di tutte l'Heresia, secol. xvi. cap. vii.: Puigblanch's History of the Inquisition, i. 61, 62.
† Natalis Comes, Hist. sui Temporis, lib. xii f. 263, 269.
‡ Galluzzi, tom. ii. p. 71. "Du temps de Pie IV. on parloit fort librement à Rome; j'y etois du regne de Pie IV. et V." (Secunda Scaligerana, Collect. des Maiseaux, tom. ii. p. 504.)

priated to the inquisitors, and cells were added to it for the reception of prisoners. This was commonly called the Lutheran prison, and is said to have been built on the site of the ancient Circus of Nero, in which so many Christians were delivered to the wild beasts. It was in this prison that Philip, the son of the learned Joachim Camerarius, and Peter Rieter de Kornburg, a Bavarian gentleman, were confined for two months during the year 1565; having been seized, when visiting Rome on their travels, in consequence of the information of a Jew, who mistook Rieter for another German with whom he had quarrelled. But although the mistake was acknowledged by the informer himself, they were detained as heretics, and obtained their liberty only through the interference of the imperial ambassador, accompanied with a threat from the Protestant princes that the agents of Rome should be treated in the same manner in travelling through Germany.* Pompeio di Monti, a Neapolitan nobleman, who had been seized by the familiars of the inquisition, as he was crossing the bridge of St. Angelo on horseback, along with his relation, Marc-antonio Colonna, was lodged in the same apartment with Camerarius, who derived from his conversation much Christian comfort, as well as useful counsel, to avoid the snares which the inquisitors were in the habit of spreading for their prisoners.† During the subsequent year, Di Monti was sentenced to be burnt alive; but, in consideration of a sum of seven thousand crowns being advanced by his friends, he was

* Schelhorn, Vita Philippi Camerarii, p. 86—101. Relatio de Captivitate Romana Philippi Camerarii et Petri Rieteri, p. 7—30, 54—64. This last work was published by Camerarius himself, and contains a particular account of the examinations which he underwent, and of the causes of his release, accompanied with documents.

† Relatio, ut supra, p. 73, 74. They shared together the use of a Latin Bible, which the baron had procured and kept concealed in his bed. Camerarius having applied for a Psalter to assist him in his devotions, the noted Jesuit, Petrus Canisius, by whom he was visited, pressed on him the *Office of the Holy Virgin*, as more conducive to edification, and, when it was declined, sent him *Amadis de Gaul*, and Cæsar's Commentaries. (Ibid. p. 14, 15.)

only strangled, and his body afterwards committed to the flames.*

The flames of persecution were rekindled under Pius V., who was created pope in the year 1566. The name of this inexorable pontiff was Michele Ghisleri; and the cruelties committed during the two preceding pontificates are in no small degree to be ascribed to his influence, as president of the inquisition, a situation which he had held, under the designation of the Alexandrine cardinal, since the late establishment of that tribunal.† His elevation to the popedom was followed by a hot persecution in Rome and the states of the church. It raged with great violence in Bologna, where "persons of all ranks were promiscuously subjected to the same imprisonment, and tortures, and death."‡ "Three persons (says a writer of that time) have lately been burnt alive in that city, and two brothers of the noble family of Ercolani seized on suspicion of heresy, and sent bound to Rome." At the same time, many of the German students in the university were imprisoned, or obliged to fly.§ The following description of the state of matters in the year 1568 is from the pen of one who was residing at that time on the borders of Italy:—" At Rome some are every day burnt, hanged, or beheaded: all the prisons and places of confinement are filled, and they are obliged to build new ones. That large city cannot furnish gaols for the numbers of pious persons who are continually apprehended. A distinguished person, named Carnesecchi, formerly ambassador to the duke of Tuscany, has been committed to the flames. Two persons of still greater distinction, baron Bernardo di Angole, and count di Petigliano, a genuine and brave Roman, are in prison. After long resistance, they were at last

* Relatio, ut supra, p. 7, 8.
† Thuani Hist. lib. xxxix. ad an. 1566. Vita Philippi Camerarii. p. 102. Galluzzi, tom ii. p. 75.
‡ Thobias Eglinus ad Bullingerum, 29 Decem. 1567: De Porta, tom. ii p. 460.
§ Epistola Joachimi Camerarii, 16 Feb. 1566, et Epist. Petri Rieteri, prid. Id. Maii 1567: Vita Phil. Camerarii, p. 174, 197.

induced to recant, on a promise that they should be set at liberty. But what was the consequence? The one was condemned to pay a fine of eighty thousand crowns, and to suffer perpetual imprisonment; and the other to pay one thousand crowns, and be confined for life in the convent of the Jesuits. Thus have they, by a dishonourable defection, purchased a life worse than death."* The same writer relates the following anecdote, which shows the base stratagems which the Roman inquisition employed to get hold of its victims:—" A letter from Genoa to Messere Bonetti states, that a rich nobleman at Modena, in the duchy of Ferrara, was lately informed against as a heretic to the pope, who had recourse to the following method of getting him into his claws. The nobleman had a cousin at Rome, who was sent for to the castle of St. Angelo, and told, ' Either you must die, or write to your cousin at Modena, desiring him to meet you in Bologna at a certain hour, as if you wished to speak to him on important business.' The letter was despatched, and the nobleman having ridden in haste to Bologna, was seized as soon as he had dismounted from his horse. His friend was then set at liberty. This is dragon's game."† Speaking of the rigour of the inquisition in Italy, and the suddenness of executions at this period, Muretus said to De Thou—" We know not what becomes of people here: I am terrified every morning when I rise, lest I should be told that such and such a one is no more; and, if it should be so, we durst not say a word."‡

Furious as this pope was, he felt himself sometimes forced to yield to a power which he durst not brave. Galeas de San Severino, count de Caiazzo, was a favourite of Charles IX. of France, and held a high rank in his army. Having occasion to go into Italy on his private affairs about the year 1568, he was thrown into the inquisition as a Hugonot. Charles

* Thobias Eglinus ad Bullingerum, 2 Mart. 1568. De Porta, tom. ii. p. 486.
† Ibid. 20 Mart 1568: De Porta, tom. ii. p. 487.
‡ Thuana, Collect. des Maiseaux, tom. i. p. 16.

instantly despatched the marquis de Pisano with instructions to insist on the liberation of the count as a French subject. The pope requested time to deliberate. After repeated delays, the marquis demanded the release of the prisoner within eight days; and, that time having elapsed, he obtained an audience of his holiness, and told him peremptorily, that, if the count was not delivered to him next day, the ambassador of France should be instantly recalled, and a stop put to all the ordinary intercourse with Rome as to ecclesiastical benefices in the kingdom. By the advice of the cardinals, Pius was prevailed on to give up the prisoner, but with great reluctance, saying, that the king had sent him an *imbriacone*.*

It is not my intention to write a martyrology; but I cannot altogether pass over the names of those men who intrepidly displayed the standard of truth before the walls of Rome, and fell within the breach of the antichristian citadel.

Faventino Fanino, or Fannio, a native of Faenza, within the states of the Church, is usually, though not correctly, said to be the first who suffered martyrdom for the Protestant faith in Italy.† Having received the knowledge of the truth by reading the Bible and other religious books in his native language, he began to impart it to his neighbours, and was soon thrown into prison. Through the persuasion of his friends, he purchased his liberty by recantation, which threw him into great distress of mind. On recovering from this dejection, he resolved to exert himself more zealously than before in discovering to his countrymen the errors by which they were deluded, and in ac-

---

* A *drunkard*. De Thou received this anecdote from the marquis himself. (Thuana, Collect. des Maiseaux, tom. 1 p. 3, 4.) It was the same nobleman who, when ordered by Sixtus V. to quit his territories within eight days, replied—"Your territories are not so large, but that I can quit them within twenty-four hours." (Ibid. p. 5.)

† According to Scaliger, a person named Jacobin was the first martyr in Italy. The civilian Cujas, who was present at his execution, says he was not a Protestant, but merely differed in some things from the Roman church; for, adds he, "in those days they burnt for a small matter." (Scaligerana Secunda, art. *Hæretici*.)

quainting them with the way of salvation. For this
purpose he commenced travelling through the province of Romagna. His plan was, after succeeding
with a few individuals, to leave them to instruct others,
while he removed to another place; by which means
he, within a short time, disseminated extensively the
knowledge of evangelical doctrine. He was at last
seized at a place called Bagnacavallo, and conducted
in chains to Ferrara. Neither threats nor solicitations
could now move him to waver in his confession of the
truth. To the lamentations of his wife and sister,
who came to see him in prison, he replied, "Let it
suffice you, that, for your sakes, I have *once* denied
my Saviour. Had I then had the knowledge which,
by the grace of God, I have acquired since my fall, I
would not have yielded to your entreaties. Go home
in peace." Of Fannio's imprisonment, which lasted
two years, it may be said, that it fell out "to the fur-
therance of the gospel, so that his bonds in Christ
were manifest in all the palace." He was visited by
the princess Lavinia della Rovere, by Olympia Morata, and other persons distinguished for rank or intelligence, who were edified by his instructions and prayers, and took a deep interest in his fate. When orders
were issued to prevent strangers from having access
to him, he employed himself in teaching his fellow-
prisoners, including several persons of rank, confined
for state crimes, upon whom his piety, joined with
uncommon modesty and meekness, produced such an
effect, that they acknowledged, after their enlargement, that they never knew what liberty and happiness was until they found it within the walls of a
prison. Orders were next given to put him in solitary confinement, when he spent his time in writing
religious letters and essays, which he found means of
conveying to his friends, and several of which were
published after his death. So much were the priests
afraid of the influence which he exerted over those
who approached him, that his prison and his keeper
were repeatedly changed. In the year 1550, Julius
III., rejecting every intercession made for his life,

ordered him to be executed. He was accordingly brought out to the stake at an early hour in the morning, to prevent the people from witnessing the scene, and being first strangled, was committed to the flames.*

At the same time and in the same manner did Domenica della Casa Bianca suffer death. He was a native of Basano in the Venetian states, and acquired the knowledge of the truth in Germany, when a soldier in the army of Charles V. With the zeal of a young convert he endeavoured, on his return to Italy, to disabuse the minds of his deluded countrymen. After labouring with success in Naples and other places, he was thrown into prison at Piacenza, and, refusing to retract what he had taught, suffered martyrdom with much fortitude, in the thirtieth year of his age.†

We have already met repeatedly with Molho, the Bolognese professor, who was held in such high esteem through Italy for his learning and holy life.‡ After the flight of his brethren, Ochino and Martyr, in 1542, he was frequently in great danger, and more than once thrown into confinement, from which he had always providentially escaped. But after the accession of pope Julius III. he was sought for with great eagerness, and being seized at Ravenna, was conducted, under a strong guard, to Rome, and lodged in a strait prison.§ On the 5th of September 1553, a public assembly of the inquisition was held with great pomp, which was attended by the six cardinals and their episcopal assessors, before whom a number of prisoners were brought with torches in their hands. All of them recanted and performed penance, except

* Olympiæ Moratæ Opera, p. 90, 102, 107. Nolten, Vita Olym. Moratæ, p. 127—134. Hist. des Martyrs, f. 186, 187. Bezæ Icones, sig Hh ij.
† Hist. des Martyrs, f. 487, b The following work I have not seen :—"De Fannii Faventini ac Dominici Bassanensis morte, qui nuper ob Christum in Italia Rom. Pontificis jussu impie occisi sunt, brevis historia, Fran. Nigro Bassanensi auctore. 1550."
‡ See before p. 94, 124.
§ During his imprisonment he composed a commentary on Genesis, which is praised by Rabus, the German martyrologist. (Gerdesii Italia Reform. p. 302.)

Mollio, and a native of Perugio, named Tisserano. When the articles of accusation against Mollio were read, permission was given him to speak. He defended the doctrines which he had taught respecting justification, the merit of good works, auricular confession, and the sacraments; pronounced the power claimed by the pope and his clergy to be usurped and antichristian; and addressed his judges in a strain of bold and fervid invective, which silenced and chained them to their seats, at the same time that it cut them to the quick. "As for you, cardinals and bishops," said he, "if I were satisfied that you had justly obtained that power which you assume to yourselves, and that you had risen to your eminence by virtuous deeds, and not by blind ambition and the arts of profligacy, I would not say a word to you. But since I know, on the best grounds, that you have set moderation, and modesty, and honour, and virtue at defiance, I am constrained to treat you without ceremony, and to declare that your power is not from God but the devil. If it were apostolical, as you would make the poor world believe, then your manner of life would resemble that of the apostles. But when I perceive the filth, and falsehood, and profaneness with which it is overspread, what can I think or say of your Church but that it is a receptacle of thieves and a den of robbers? What is your doctrine but a dream—a lie forged by hypocrites? Your very countenances proclaim that your belly is your god. Your great object is to seize and amass wealth by every species of injustice and cruelty. You thirst without ceasing for the blood of the saints. Can you be the successors of the holy apostles, and vicars of Jesus Christ—you who despise Christ and his word, you who act as if you did not believe that there is a God in heaven, you who persecute to the death his faithful ministers, make his commandments of no effect, and tyrannize over the consciences of his saints? Wherefore I appeal from your sentence, and summon you, cruel tyrants and murderers, to answer before the judgment-seat of Christ at the last day, where your pompous titles and gorgeous trappings will not dazzle, nor your guards and torturing apparatus terrify us. And in testimony of this, take back that which you have given me." In saying this, he threw the flaming torch which he held in his hand on the ground and extinguished it. Galled and gnashing upon him with their teeth, like the persecutors of the first Christian martyr, the cardinals ordered Mollio, together with his companion, who approved of the testimony he had borne, to instant execution. They were conveyed, accordingly, to the Campo del Fior, where they died with the most pious fortitude.*

Pomponio Algieri, a native of Nola, in the kingdom of Naples, was seized when attending the university of Padua, and after being examined in the presence of the podesta, was sent bound to Venice. His answers, on the different examinations which he underwent, contain a luminous view of the truth, and form one of the most succinct and nervous refutations of the principal articles of popery, from Scripture and the decretals, which is anywhere to be found. They had the effect of spreading his fame through Italy. From regard to his learning and youth, the senators of Venice were anxious to set him at liberty, but as he refused to abandon his sentiments, they condemned him to the galleys. Yet, yielding to the importunities of the nuncio, they afterwards sent him to Rome, as an acceptable present to the newly-elected pope, Paul IV., by whom he was doomed to be burnt alive, in the twenty-fourth year of his age. The Christian

* Hist. des Martyrs, f. 264, 265. Gerdesii Ital. Reform. p. 104. Zanchi gives the following anecdote of this martyr, in a letter to Bullinger.—" I will relate what (Mollio of) Montalcino, the monk, who was afterwards burnt at Rome for the gospel, once said to me respecting your book, *De origine errorts*. As I had not read or seen the work, he exhorted me to purchase it; 'and,' said he, 'if you have not money, pluck out your right eye to enable you to buy it, and read it with the left.' By the favour of providence, I soon after found the book, without losing my eye, for I bought it for a crown, and abridged it in such a character as that not even an inquisitor could read it; and in such a form, that, if he had read it, he could not have discovered what my sentiments were." (Zanchii Epist. lib. ii. p. 278.)

magnanimity with which this youthfnl martyr bore that cruel death, terrified the cardinals who attended to grace the spectacle. A letter written by him, in his prison at Venice describes the consolations by which his spirit was refreshed and upheld under his sufferings, in language to which I scarcely know a parallel. It appears from this interesting document, that the friends of evangelical truth were still numerous in Padua.*

Equally distinguished was the constancy of Francesco Gamba, a native of Como. He was in the habit of visiting Geneva for the sake of conversation with the learned men of that city. Having on one of these occasions, participated along with them of the Lord's Supper, the news of this fact reached home before him, and he was seized on the Lake of Como, thrown into prison, and condemned to the flames. By the interposition of the imperial ambassador and some of the Milanese nobility, his execution was prevented for some days, during which interval his firmness was assailed by the sophistry of the monks, the entreaties of his friends, and the interest which many of his townsmen of the popish persuasion took in his welfare. He modestly declined the last services of the friars, expressed his gratitude to those who had testified a concern for his life, and assured the judge, who lamented the necessity which he was under of executing the law, that he forgave him, and prayed God to forgive him. His tongue having been perforated to prevent him from addressing the spectators, he kneeled down and prayed at the place of execution; then rising, he looked round the crowd, which consisted of several thousands, for a particular friend, to whom he waved his right hand, which was loose, as the appointed sign that he died in peace and confidence; after which he stretched out his neck to the executioner, who had been authorized, by way of

* The autograph of this letter, together with the facts respecting the writer, were communicated by Curio to the historian Henry Pantaleon. (Rerum in Eccles. Gest. part. ii. app. 329—332. Conf. Bezæ Icones, sig. Hh iij)

favour, to strangle him before committing his body to the fire.*

Godfredo Varaglia, though a Piedmontese, and put to death in his native country, deserves a place here from his intimate connexion with Italy. He belonged to the order of Capuchins, and acquired great celebrity as one of their preachers. Inheriting from his ancestors a strong antipathy to the Waldenses, he had received an appointment to labour as a missionary in their conversion, and the highest hopes of success were entertained from his zeal and eloquence; but the issue turned out very different, for he became a convert to the opinions of his opponents, and, like another Paul, began to preach the faith which he had sought to destroy.† From that time he acted in concert with Ochino.‡ When the latter left Italy, he and twelve others of his order were apprehended and conveyed to Rome. The suspicions against them being slight, or their interest powerful, they were admitted to make an abjuration of heresy in general terms, and confined to the capital on their parole for five years. At the end of that period Varaglia was persuaded to lay aside the cowl, and enter into secular orders. His talents had procured him the friendship of a dignitary of the church, from whom he enjoyed a pension for some time; and his patron being appointed papal legate to the king of France in the year 1556, he accompanied him to that country. But his conscience not permitting him any longer to conceal his sentiments, he parted from the legate at Lyons, and repaired to Geneva, where he accepted an appointment to preach the gospel to the Waldenses in the valley of Angrogna.§

* This account is taken from a letter written by a gentleman of Como to the martyr's brother. (Acta et Monim. Martyrum, f. 270—272. Wolfii Lect. Memorab. tom. ii. p. 686.) Gamba suffered on the 21st of July 1554.

† Leger, Histoire des Eglises Vaudoises, p. 29. Hospinian, by mistake, makes Varaglia to have been the founder of the Capuchins. (De Orig. Monach. cap. ix. p. 297.) This order of monks was instituted by Matteo de Baschi. (Observationes Halenses, tom. iv. p. 410.)

‡ Gerdesii Hist. Ref. tom. iv. p. 360.

§ This is the account which he gave of himself, on his examina-

He had not laboured many months among that people, when he was apprehended, conveyed to Turin, and condemned to death, which he endured with great fortitude on the 29th of March 1558, in the fiftieth year of his age. When interrogated on his trial as to his companions, he told his judges that he had lately been in company with twenty-four preachers, who had mostly come from Geneva; and that the number of those who were ready to follow them was so great, that the inquisitors would not find wood wherewith to burn them.*

Ludovico Paschali was a native of Cuni in Piedmont, and having acquired a taste for evangelical doctrine at Nice, left the army to which he had been bred, and went to study at Lausanne. When the Waldenses of Calabria applied to the Italian church at Geneva for preachers, Paschali was fixed upon as eminently qualified for that station. Having obtained the consent of Camilla Guerina, a young woman to whom he had previously been affianced, he set out along with Stefano Negrino. On their arrival in Calabria, they found the country in a state of agitation; and after labouring for some time to quiet the minds of the people and comfort them under persecution, they were both apprehended at the instance of the inquisitor. Negrino was allowed to perish of hunger in his prison. Paschali, after being kept eight months in confinement at Cosenza, was conducted to Naples, from which he was transferred to Rome. His sufferings were great, and he bore them with the most uncommon fortitude and patience, as appears from the letters, equally remarkable for their noble sentiments and pious unction, which he wrote from his prisons to the persecuted flock in Calabria, to his afflicted spouse, and to the church of Geneva. Giving an ac-

tion before the supreme court of justice at Turin. (Hist. des Martyrs, f. 4186.)

* The account of Varaglia was transmitted to Pantaleon by Curio, (Rerum in Eccl. Gest. p. 334, 335. Hist. des Martyrs, f. 418—421.) In 1563, the nuncio Visconti wrote to cardinal Borromeo, that more than the half of the Piedmontese were Hugonots. (Epist. apud Gerdes. Ital. Ref. p. 94)

count of his journey from Cosenza to Naples, he says —" Two of our companions had been prevailed on to recant, but they were no better treated on that account; and God knows what they will suffer at Rome, where they are to be conveyed, as well as Marquet and myself. The *good* Spaniard, our conductor, wished us to give him a sum of money to be relieved from the chain by which we were bound to one another; and, with the view of extorting a bribe, he put on me a pair of handcuffs so strait that they entered into the flesh and deprived me of all sleep; but I found that nothing would satisfy him short of all the money I had, amounting to two ducats, which I needed for my support. At night the beasts were better treated than we, for their litter was spread for them, while we were obliged to lie on the hard ground without any covering; and in this condition we remained for nine nights. On our arrival at Naples, we were thrust into a cell, noisome in the highest degree, from the damp and the ordure of the prisoners."

His brother, Bartolomeo, who had come from Cuni, with letters of recommendation to endeavour to procure his liberty, gives an interesting account of the first interview which, after great difficulty, he obtained with him at Rome, in the presence of a judge of the inquisition. "It was quite hideous to see him, with his bare head, and his arms and hands lacerated by the small cords with which he was bound, like one about to be led to the gibbet. On advancing to embrace him, I sank to the ground. 'My brother!' said he, 'if you are a Christian, why do you distress yourself thus? Do you not know, that a leaf cannot fall to the earth without the will of God? Comfort yourself in Christ Jesus, for the present troubles are not worthy to be compared with the glory to come.'— 'No more of that talk!' exclaimed the inquisitor. When we were about to part, my brother begged the judge to remove him to a less horrid prison. 'There is no other prison for you than this,' was the answer. —'At least show me a little pity in my last days, and

God will show it to you.'—'There is no pity for such obstinate criminals as you,' replied the hardened wretch. A Piedmontese doctor who was present joined me in entreating the judge to grant this favour; but he remained inflexible. 'He will do it for the love of God,' said my brother, in a melting tone.— 'All the other prisons are full,' replied the judge, evasively.—'They are not so full but that a small corner can be spared for me.'—'You would infect all who were near you by your smooth speeches.'—'I will speak to none who does not speak to me.'—'Be content; you cannot have another place.'—'I must then have patience,' replied my brother, meekly." How convincing a proof of the power of the gospel do we see in the confidence and joy displayed by Paschali, under such protracted and exhausting sufferings! "My state is this," says he, in a letter to his former hearers—" I feel my joy increase every day as I approach nearer to the hour in which I shall be offered as a sweet-smelling sacrifice to the Lord Jesus Christ, my faithful Saviour; yea, so inexpressible is my joy, that I seem to myself to be free from captivity, and am prepared to die for Christ, not only once, but ten thousand times, if it were possible; nevertheless, I persevere in imploring the Divine assistance by prayer, for I am convinced that man is a miserable creature when left to himself, and not upheld and directed by God." A short time before his death, he said to his brother— "I give thanks to my God, that, in the midst of my long-continued and severe affliction, I have found some kind friends; and I thank you, my dearest brother, for the tender interest you have taken in my welfare. But as for me, God has bestowed on me that knowledge of our Lord Jesus Christ which assures me that I am not in an error, and I know that I must go by the narrow way of the cross, and seal my testimony with my blood. I do not dread death, and still less the loss of my earthly goods; for I am certain of eternal life and a celestial inheritance, and my heart is united to my Lord and Saviour." When his brother was urging him to yield a little, with the view of saving his life and property, he replied, "Oh! my brother, the danger in which you are involved gives me more distress than all that I suffer, or have the prospect of suffering, for I perceive that your mind is so addicted to earthly things as to be indifferent to heaven." At last, on the 8th of September 1560, he was brought out to the conventual church of Minerva, to hear his process publicly read; and next day he appeared, without any diminution of his courage, in the court adjoining the castle of St. Angelo, where he was strangled and burnt, in the view of the pope and a party of cardinals assembled to witness the spectacle.*

Passing over others, I shall give an account of two persons of great celebrity for their talents and stations, but whose names, owing to the secrecy with which they were put to death, have not obtained a place in the martyrology of the Protestant church.

Pietro Carnesecchi was a Florentine of good birth and liberally educated.† From his youth it appeared that he was destined to "stand before kings and not before mean men." Possessing a fine person and a quick and penetrating judgment, he united affability with dignity in his manners, and was at once discreet and generous. Sadolet praises him as "a young man of distinguished virtue and liberal accomplishments;"‡ and Bembo speaks of him in terms of the highest respect and affection.§ As he had followed the fortunes of the Medici, he was made secretary, and afterwards apostolical protonotary, to Clement VII., who bestowed on him two abbacies, one in Naples and the other in France; and so great was his influence with that pope, that it was commonly said, "that the Church was governed by Carnesecchi rather than by Clem-

* Hist. des Martyrs, f. 506—516. Leger, Hist. des Eglises Vaudoises, part. i. p. 204.
† Camerarius says, that Francesco Robertello was his preceptor. (Epistolæ Flaminii, &c. apud Schelhornii Amœnit. Literarias, tom. x. p. 1200.) If this was the case, the master must have been as young as the scholar (Tiraboschi, tom. vii. p. 841.)
‡ Epist. Famil. vol. ii. p. 189.
§ Lettere, tom. iii. p. 437—439.

ent." Yet he conducted himself with so much modesty and propriety in his delicate situation, as not to incur envy during the life of his patron, and to escape disgrace at his death. His career of worldly honour, which had commenced so auspiciously, was arrested by a very different cause. Being deeply versed in Greek and Roman literature, an eloquent speaker, and a poet, he spent his time, after the death of his patron, in travelling through the different cities of Italy, conversing with the learned, and adding to his stock of knowledge.* At Naples he formed an intimacy with Valdes, from whom he imbibed the reformed doctrine;† and, as he possessed great candour and love of truth, his attachment to these doctrines daily acquired strength from reading, meditation, and conference with learned men. During the better days of cardinal Pole, he made one of the select party which met in that prelate's house in Viterbo, and spent the time in religious exercises.‡ When his friend Flaminio, startled at the thought of leaving the church of Rome, stopped short in his inquiries, Carnesecchi displayed that mental courage which welcomes truth when she tramples on received prejudices, and follows her in spite of the hazards which environ her path.§ After the flight of Ochino and Martyr, he incurred the violent suspicions of those who prosecuted the search after heresy, and, in 1546, was cited to Rome, where cardinal de Burgos one of the inquisitors, was ordered to investigate the charges brought against him. He was accused of corresponding with the heretics who had fled from justice, supplying suspected persons with money to enable them to retire to foreign

* Galluzzi. tom. ii. p 76.
† Laderchii Annales, ad an. 1567.
‡ "Il resto del giorno passo con questa santa e utile compagnia del Sig. Carnesecchi, e Mr Marco Antonio Flaminio nostro. Utile io chiamo, perche la sera poi Mr. Marco Antonio da pasto a me, e alla miglior parte della famiglia, de illo cibo qui non perit, in tal maniera che io non so quando io abbia sentito maggior consolatione, ne maggior edificatione." (Lettere, il Card. Reg Polo al Card. Gasp Contarini, di Viterbo, alli ix di Decembre 1541, Poli Epistolæ, vol. iii. p 42.)
§ See before, p. 166.

parts, giving testimonials to schoolmasters, who under the pretext of teaching the rudiments of knowledge, poisoned the minds of the youth with their heretical catechisms, and particularly with having recommended to the duchess of Trajetto* two apostates, whom he extolled as apostles sent to preach the gospel to the heathen.† Through the favour of the mild pontiff, Paul III., the matter was accommodated, but Carnesecchi, to avoid the odium which had been excited against him, found it necessary to quit Italy for a season. After spending some time with Margaret, duchess of Savoy, who was not unfriendly to the reformed doctrines, he went to France, where he enjoyed the favour of the new monarch, Henry II., and his queen, Catharine de Medicis. In the year 1552, he returned to his native country, confirmed in his opinions by the intercourse which he had with foreign Protestants,‡ and took up his residence chiefly at Padua, within the Venetian territories, where he was in less danger from the intrigues of the court of Rome, and could enjoy the society of those who were of the same religious sentiments with himself. Paul IV. had not been long seated on the papal throne when a criminal process was commenced against him. As he did not choose to place himself at the mercy of that furious pontiff by making a personal appearance, he was summoned at Rome and Venice, and failing to appear within the prescribed term, the sentence of excommunication was launched against him, by which he was delivered over to the secular power to be punished as a contumacious heretic.§

---

* See before p. 159. † Laderchii Annal. ad an. 1567.

‡ Laderchius says he formed an intimacy with Philip Melanchthon; but as the latter was never in France, Schelhorn thinks the person referred to might be Andrew Melanchthon, a relation of that reformer, who was imprisoned for preaching in the Agenois. (Amœn. Hist. Eccles. tom. ii. p. 192.)

§ The process against him was commenced October 25, 1557; the monitory summons was issued March 24, 1558, and the excommunication was passed April 6, 1559 (Laderchius, ut supra.) Galluzzi, in his history of the grand duchy of Tuscany, says, that Cosmo, by means of letters of commendation, prorogations, and attestations of infirmity, contrived to avert the sentence during the life of that pope.

When Giovanni Angelo de' Medici ascended the chair of St. Peter, under the name of Pius IV., Carnesecchi, who had always been a zealous friend to the family of this pontiff, obtained from him the removal of the sentence of excommunication, without his being required to make any abjuration of his opinions. The popish writers complain, that, notwithstanding these repeated favours, he still kept up his correspondence with heretics in Naples, Rome, Florence, Venice, Padua, and other places both within and without Italy; that he gave supplies of money to Pietro Gelido, Leone Marionio, and others who had fled to Geneva; and that he recommended the writings of the Lutherans while he spoke degradingly of those of the Catholics. On the accession of Pius V. he retired to Florence, and put himself under the protection of Cosmo, the grand duke of Tuscany, justly dreading the vengeance of the new pope. From papers afterwards found in his possession, it appears that he had intended to retire to Geneva, but was induced, by the confidence which he placed in his protector, to delay the execution of his purpose until it was too late. At a conclave held at Rome for the special purpose, measures were concerted for obtaining possession of his person. Cardinal Pacecco, a distinguished member of the sacred college, addressed a flattering letter to the duke, in which, after praising his zeal for the holy see, and telling him that he could never have a better opportunity of testifying it and gratifying his holiness, he added, that it should not be matter of surprise that such eagerness was shown for the apprehension of one man, as the example would draw after it the most important consequences, in which his excellency himself might share. The master of the sacred palace was sent to Florence with a letter to Cosmo, written with the pope's own hand, and instructions to request him to deliver up a heretic who had long laboured to destroy the Catholic faith, and corrupted the minds of multitudes.* When the messenger arrived and delivered his credentials, Car-

* Galluzzi, tom. ii. p. 78, 79.

nesecchi was sitting at table with the duke, who, to ingratiate himself with the pope, ordered his guest to be immediately laid under arrest, and conducted as a prisoner to Rome; a violation of the laws of hospitality and friendship, for which he received the warm thanks of his holiness.* The prisoner was proceeded against without delay before the inquisition, on a charge consisting of no fewer than thirty-four articles, which comprehended all the peculiar doctrines held by Protestants in opposition to the church of Rome.† Achilles Statius, a native of Portugal, who had formerly held the situation of secretary to him, acted on the present occasion as his legal accuser. The articles were proved by witnesses, and by the letters of the prisoner, who, after defending himself for some time, admitted the truth of the main charges, and owned that the articles contained generally a statement of the opinions which he entertained. We have the testimony of a popish historian, who consulted the records of the holy office, to the constancy and firmness with which the prisoner avowed his sentiments to the last. "With hardened heart," says he, "and uncircumcised ears, he refused to yield to the necessity of his circumstances, and thus rendered the admonitions and the often repeated delays granted to him for deliberation useless; nor could he, by any means, be induced to abjure his errors and to return to the true religion, according to the wish of Pius, who had resolved, on the appearance of penitence, to visit his past crimes with a more lenient punishment than they merited."‡ The same account is given by the historian of the grand duchy of Tuscany, who says

* Thuani Hist. ad an. 1566. Laderchius, who has inserted, in his Annals, the pope's letters to Cosmo, admits the truth of De Thou's narrative as to the manner of Carnesecchi's apprehension, which he applauds—"ex bene acta re et optima Cosmi mente." The letter demanding Carnesecchi is dated June 20, and the letter of thanks, July 1, 1566

† The articles are given at large by Laderchius, in his Annals, from which they have been reprinted by Schelhorn, (Amœn. Hist. Eccles. tom ii p. 197—205,) and by Gerdesius, with some abridgment. (Ital. Ref. p. 144—148.)

‡ Laderchius, ut supra.

that Cosmo, by letters and messages, sought to move the clemency of the pope and cardinals; but that all his efforts were rendered useless by "the fanaticism" of Carnesecchi.* On the 16th of August, 1567, sentence was pronounced against him, and on the 21st of September it was publicly read in the church of St. Mary, near Minerva, along with those of other heretics.† He was condemned as an incorrigible heretic, deprived of all honours, dignities, and benefices, and delivered over to the secular arm; after which he was degraded, and clothed with a *sanbenito*, painted with flames and devils. The final execution of the sentence was, however, delayed for ten days. Whether this delay proceeded from deference to the duke, or a hope of being able to present such a distinguished person as Carnesecchi in the character of a penitent on the scaffold, it may be difficult to determine. During the interval, a Capuchin of Pistoia was incarcerated along with him, with the view of inducing him to recant; but as the labours of the friar proved fruitless, Carnesecchi was brought out on the 3d of October, and being beheaded, his body was consumed in the flames. " His fanaticism," says a historian, who has furnished us with some minute particulars respecting him, " sustained him to the very last moment. He went to execution as to a triumph, and appeared with new linen and gloves, as his inflamed *sanbenito* did not admit of his wearing any other piece of apparel."‡

* Heresy was the word used in the sixteenth and seventeenth centuries; but the writers of the Church of Rome in the eighteenth century substitute the word fanaticism, as calculated to lessen the odium of the severities employed against the Protestants, on the minds of men living in an age more distinguished for its liberality than its faith.

† In the diary of Cardinal Farnese is the following entry, under the 19th September, 1567·—" Sanctissimus Dominus noster hortatus est, et invitavit omnes Reverendissimos Dominos, ut accederent ad videndum, et audiendum abjurationem hæreticorum, qui fieri debet die Dominico proxime futuro in Ecclesia B. Mariæ prope Minervam." To this is added, in the original MS., " Lata est hæc sententia die Sabbathi 16 Augusti 1567 ; die vero Dominico 21 Septembris ejusdem anni, in Ecclesia S. Mariæ supra Minervam publice recitata."

‡ Galluzzi, tom. ii. p. 80 Laderchius expresses great displeasure at De Thou for saying that Carnesecchi was condemned to the fire,

It has been the barbarous policy of the church of Rome to destroy the fame, however well earned, and, if possible, to abolish the memory and blot out the very names of those whose lives she has taken away for heresy. Flaminio himself did not escape this "occult censure," as it has been called; and his name was expunged from letters which were published after his death, though he was never formally convicted of heresy, and had several friends in the sacred college.* The subject is curious, and it may not be improper to adduce an example or two. The celebrated Muretus was engaged in publishing a work which was intended to contain a poem in praise of Carnesecchi. In the meantime, a prosecution for heresy was commenced against the object of his panegyric, which threw the delicate author into great perplexity. Averse to lose the ode, but afraid to associate himself with a person suspected of heresy, he held a consultation on the subject, and the result was, that his caution conquered his vanity, and the poem was suppressed.† Carnesecchi was the intimate friend of the learned printer, Paulus Manutius, and was godfather to one of his sons. In an edition of his letters published in 1558, this scholar, writing to Muretus, had spoken in the most kindly manner of *his* Carnesecchi; but in subsequent editions, including those which proceeded from his own press, we find the harsh name of his friend gratefully softened down to *Molini*.

without saying whether he was to be committed to it dead or alive; and he asserts that the Roman Church never decreed that heretics should be burnt alive. But in his next volume, he found it necessary to correct his error, and to admit the truth of what he had denied. (Annal. tom. xxiii f. 200.)

* " Neque tamen occultam censuram effugit, (Flaminius,) ejus nomine passim in epistolis, quæ postea publicatæ sunt, expuncto." (Thuani Hist. ad an. 1551.) Schelhorn has produced a number of instances in illustration of the truth of De Thou's assertion. Ergoetzlichkeiten, tom. i. p 201—205.

† The passage relating to this subject is in a letter to Paulus Manutius, and begins in the following characteristic strain—" Erat ad Petrum τον ξηρόχρεον (finge aliquod ejusmodi nomen aut latinum aut vernaculum, ita quem dicam intelliges) ode una jam pridem scripta; de qua, quid faciam, nescio," &c. (Mureti Orat. et Epist. lib. 1. p. 442. Lips. 1672.)

Again, in a dedication of the works of Sallust to cardinal Trivulzi, printed in 1557, Manutius mentions "Petrus Carnesecus, the protonotary, an honoured person, distinguished for every virtue, and excelling, in a cultivated mind, all that I have met with in the course of my life;" but in the subsequent editions of the dedication we look in vain for the name of the "honoured" protonotary! The same person printed, in 1556, select letters of illustrious men, containing one written in a laudatory strain by Cosmo Ghieri, bishop of Fano, to "Carnesecchi, apostolical protonotary;" but in an enlarged edition of the work published at Venice in 1568, the office only, and not the name of the person to whom that letter was addressed, appears. "It is not so much to be wondered at," says Schelhorn, when speaking of the verses written in praise of this martyr, "that they should have been afraid to mention, at least in Italian, his name, at a time when the funeral pile, on which his body was consumed to ashes, was yet smoking; but that, at the expiry of nearly two centuries, such innocent and beautiful poems, which do not treat of religion, and had been published, should be still suppressed, merely because they were addressed to Carnesecchi, is a clear proof that the prohibitory laws of Rome continue to have no small authority in the Venetian states."* About the middle of the eighteenth century, an edition of the poems of Flaminio was published by one of his countrymen, who found it necessary, or judged it prudent, to omit the odes addressed to Carnesecchi, "lest he should incur the censure of those who have said and written that Marcus Antonius Flaminius was a heretic, because he cultivated the friendship of Carnesecus."† Nor is this all; for the learned editor, in quoting from a dedication to a former edition of the

---

* Schelhorn, Ergoetzlichkeiten, tom. 1. p. 205—209.

† Flaminii Carmina, ex prelo Cominiano, 1743, p. 375. The editor, Franciscus Maria Mancurtius, had included the odes referred to, in a former edition of the work printed in 1727. (Schelhorn, Ergoetzlichkeiten, tom. 1 p. 189, 191, 197. Conf. Amœn. Hist. Eccl. tom. 11. p 209.) I subjoin one of the poems, from which the learned reader will judge of the violence which the editor must have done to

poems, in which Carnesecchi was highly praised,* suppresses his name; forgetting, perhaps, that the excellent author whose works he was editing had himself been formerly subjected to the same unworthy treatment. It is impossible to say how far this system of suppression was carried. Another instance of it may be given. A letter of Cardinal Maffei to Lodovico Castelvetro, in which his eminence expresses the highest esteem for that scholar, was published in 1556, among a collection of the epistles of illustrious men; but in a new edition of the work which appeared in 1568, after Castelvetro had incurred the stigma of heresy, his name is not to be seen.† These facts are not foreign to our subject. They will suggest to the intelligent reader a train of reflections as to the fatal influence which bigotry and intolerance must have exerted at this time in Italy over all that is liberal in his taste, when he prevailed on himself afterwards to exclude it.—

Ad Petrum Carnesecum.

O dulce hospitium, O lares beati,
O mores faciles, et Atticorum
Conditæ sale collectiones,
Quam vos, ægro animo et laborioso,
Quantis cum lacrymis, miser relinquo!
Cur me sæva necessitas abire,
Cur vultum, atque oculos, jocosque suaves
Cogit linquere tam venusti amici?
Ah reges valeant, opesque regum,
Et quisquis potuit domos potentum
Anteponere candidi sodalis
Blandis alloquiis, facetiisque;
Sed quanquam procul a tuis ocellis,
Jucundissime Carnesece, abibo
Regis imperium mei secutus,
Non loci tamen ulla, temporisve
Intervalla, tuos mihi lepores,
Non mores ipsa adiment. Manebo tecum,
Tecum semper ero, tibique semper
Magnam partem animæ meæ relinquam,
Mellite, optime, mi venuste amice.

* Schelhorn, Ergoetz. tom. i. p. 196, 197. The dedication was addressed to Margaret, sister of Henry II. of France, and contained these words:—"Cum Petrus Carnesecus, lectissimus & ornatissimus vir, de tua singulari erga Deum pietate, et assiduo litterarum studio, ad me multa scripsisset," &c. Mancurti gives the passage thus:—"Cum lectissimus et ornatissimus *quidam* vir," &c

† Biblioteca Modenese, tom. i. p. 437.

letters or generous in spirit. If it is only after the most laborious search, and often in the way of catching at obscure hints, detecting fallacious names, and cross-examining and confronting editions of the works of the learned, that we have been able to discover much of what we know of the Reformation and its friends in that country, how many facts respecting them must remain hid, or have been irrecoverably lost, in consequence of the long continuance of a practice so indefensible in itself and so disgraceful to the republic of letters.

We have already spoken of Aonio Paleario, or, according to his proper name, Antonio dalla Paglia.* On quitting the Siennese about the year 1543, he embraced an invitation from the senate of Lucca, where he taught the Latin classics, and acted as orator to the republic on solemn occasions. To this place he was followed by Maco Blaterone, one of his former adversaries, a sciolist who possessed that volubility of tongue which captivates the vulgar ear, and whose ignorance and loquacity had been severely chastised, but not corrected, by the satirical pen of Aretino. Lucca at that time abounded with men of enlightened and honourable minds; and the eloquence of Paleario, sustained by the lofty bearing of his spirit, enabled him easily to triumph over his unworthy rival, who, disgraced and driven from the city, sought his revenge from the Dominicans at Rome. By means of his friends in the conclave, Paleario counteracted at that time the informations of his accuser, which, however, were produced against him at a future period.† Mean

---

* Tiraboschi, Storia, vii. 1452. The wretched iambics in which Latinus Latinius charges Paleario with having renounced his baptism by changing his Christian name, and alleges that his dropping the letter T from it was ominous of the manner in which "the wretched old man expiated his crimes on a gibbet," have been thought worthy of a place in the Menagiana. De la Monnoye, who wrote an epigram in Greek and Latin in opposition to them, says— "They are so frigid, that they would have quenched the flames in which Paleario was consumed." (Menag. tom. i. p 217.)

† Epistolæ, lib. iii.. Opera Palearii, p. 525—531, 550—554, edit. Halbaueri.

while, his spirit submitted with reluctance to the drudgery of teaching languages, and his income was insufficient for supporting the domestic establishment which his wife, who had been genteelly bred, aspired to.* In these circumstances, after remaining about ten years at Lucca, he accepted an invitation from the senate of Milan, which conferred on him a liberal salary, together with special immunities, as professor of eloquence.† He kept his place in that city during seven years, though in great perils amidst the severities practised towards those suspected of favouring the new opinions. But in the year 1566, while deliberating about his removal to Bologna,‡ he was caught in the storm which burst on so many learned and excellent men at the elevation of Pius V. to the pontifical chair. Being seized by Frate Angelo de Cremona, the inquisitor, and conveyed to Rome, he was committed to close confinement in the Torre Nona. His book on the benefit of Christ's death, his commendations of Ochino,§ his defence of himself before the Senators at Sienna, and the suspicions which he had incurred during his residence at that place and at Lucca, were all revived against him. After the whole had been collected and sifted, the charge at last resolved itself into the four following articles:—that he denied purgatory; disapproved of burying the dead in churches, preferring the ancient Roman method of sepulture without the walls of cities; ridiculed the monastic life; and appeared to ascribe justification solely to confidence in the mercy of God forgiving our sins through Jesus Christ.‖ For holding these opinions, he was condemned, after an imprisonment of three years, to be suspended on a gibbet and his body to be given to the flames; and the sentence was executed on the 3d

---

* Epist. lib. iv.; Ibid. p. 563.
† Halbauer has given the diploma of the civic authorities in his life of Paleario, p. 27—29.
‡ Tiraboschi, Storia, vii. 1454.
§ Palearii Opera, p. 102, 103.
‖ Laderchii Annales, tom. xxii. p. 202.

of July 1570, in the seventieth year of his age.* A
minute, which professes to be an official document of
the Dominicans who attended him in his last moments,
but which has neither names nor signatures, states
that Paleario died confessed and contrite.† The testimony of such interested reporters, though it had been
better authenticated, is not to be implicitly received;
as it is well known that they were accustomed to
boast, without the slightest foundation, of the conver-
sions which they made on such occasions.‡ In the
present instance it is contradicted by the popish con-
tinuator of the annals of the church, who drew his
materials from the records of the inquisition, and represents Paleario as dying impenitent. His words are
—"When it appeared that this son of Belial was obstinate and refractory, and could by no means be recovered from the darkness of error to the light of truth,
he was deservedly delivered to the fire, that, after
suffering its momentary pains here, he might be
bound in everlasting flames hereafter."§ The unnatural and disordered conceptions which certain persons have of right and wrong prompt them to impart
facts which their more judicious but not less guilty
associates would have concealed or coloured. To this
we owe the following account of Paleario's behaviour
on his trial before the cardinals of the inquisition:—
"When he saw that he could produce nothing in defence of his pravity," says the annalist last quoted,
"falling into a rage he broke out in these words—
'Seeing your eminences have so many credible witnesses against me, it is unnecessary for you to give

* Writers have varied as to the year of his martyrdom, which,
however, may be considered as determined by an extract from a
register kept in San Giovanni de' Fiorentini di Roma, which was
printed in Novelle Letterarie dell' Anno 1745, p. 328, and reprinted
by Schelhorn (Dissert. de Mino Celso Senensi, p. 25.)

† Diss. de Mino Celso, p. 26. Tiraboschi, following Padra Lago-
marsini and Abbate Lazzeri, has adopted this opinion, but solely on
the ground referred to in the text.

‡ Conringius has shown this from a variety of examples. (Præfat. ad Cassandri et Wicelii Libr. de Sacris nostri temporis Contro-
versiis, p. 148.)

§ Laderchii Annal. tom. xx. f. 204.

yourselves or me longer trouble. I am resolved to act according to the advice of the blessed apostle Peter, when he says, Christ suffered for us, leaving us an example that we should follow his steps, who did no evil neither was guile found in his mouth, who, when he was reviled, reviled not again, when he suffered threatened not, but committed himself to him that judgeth righteously. Proceed then to give judgment—pronounce sentence on Aonio, and thus gratify his adversaries and fulfil your office.'"* Instead of supposing that the person who uttered these words was under the influence of passion, every reader of right feeling will be disposed to exclaim, "Here is the patience and the faith of the saints!" Before leaving his cell for the place of execution, he was permitted, by the monks who waited on him, to write two letters, one to his wife, and another to his sons, Lampridio and Fedro.† They are short, but the more affecting from this very circumstance; because it is evident, that he was restrained by the fear of saying any thing which, by giving offence to his judges, might lead to the suppression of the letters, or to the harsh treatment of his family after his death. They testify the pious fortitude with which he met his death, as an issue which he had long anticipated and wished for, and that warmth of conjugal and paternal affection which breathes in all his letters.‡ They also afford a negative proof that the report of his recantation was unfounded; for if he had really changed his sentiments, would he not have felt anxious to acquaint his family with the fact? or, if the change was feigned, would not the monks have insisted, on his using the language of a penitent, when they granted him permission to write?

Paleario had, before his apprehension, taken care to secure his writings against the risk of suppression, by committing them to the care of friends whom he could trust; and their repeated publication in Protes-

---

* Laderchii Annal. tom. xx. f. 205.
† He left two sons and two daughters.
‡ The two letters will be found in the appendix.

tant countries has saved them from those mutilations to which the works of so many of his countrymen have been subjected. From his letters it appears that he enjoyed the friendship and correspondence of the most celebrated persons of that time both in the church and in the republic of letters. Among the former were cardinals Sadolet, Bembo, Pole, Maffei, Badia, Filonardo, Sfondrati; and, among the latter, Flaminio, Riccio, Alciati, Vittorio, Lampridio, and Buonamici. His poem on the immortality of the soul was received with applause by the learned.* It is, perhaps, no high praise to say of his orations, that they placed him above all the moderns who obtained the name of Ciceronians, from their studious imitation of the style of the Roman orator; but they are certainly written with elegance and spirit.† His letter on the council of Trent, addressed to the Reformers, and his testimony and pleading against the Roman pontiffs, evince a knowledge of the Scriptures, soundness in the faith, candour, and fervent zeal, worthy of a Reformer and confessor of the truth.‡ His tract on

* Tiraboschi, Storia, vii. 1454—1456. Sadolet says of it, in a letter to Sebastian Gryphæus, "Tam graviter, tam erudite, tam etiam et verbis et numeris apte et eleganter tractatum esse, nihil ut ferme nostrorum temporum legerim, quod me in eo genere delectavit magis."—(Palearii Opera, p 627; conf. p. 624)

† Morhoff says—" Longe aliter sonat quod Palearius scribit, quàm Longolius et alii inepti Ciceronis imitatores." (Colleg. Epistolic. p. 17.) Crenius has collected several testimonies to the merit of Palearius. (Animad. Philolog. et Historic. part. ii. p. 18—23. Conf. Miscell. Groning tom. iii p. 92, 93 Des Maizeaux, Scaligerana, &c. tom. ii p. 483. A Life of Paleario is in Bayle and in Niceron.

‡ The letter appears to have been written with the view of being sent along with Ochino when he retired from Italy; and one copy of it was addressed to Bucer and another to Calvin. Salig gave an account of it without knowing the author; (Historie der Augsburgischen Confession, tom. ii. lib. v. p. 66;) but it was published, for the first time, in 1737, by Schelhorn, along with a short account of the martyrdom of the author. (Amœnit. Hist Eccles tom. i p. 425—462.) The other work, entitled *Testimonia et Actio in Pontifices Romanos et eorum Asseclas*, though intended also by the author to be sent across the Alps, was first found in his handwriting at Sienna in the year 1596, and printed in 1606 at Leipsic. (Halbauer, Vita Palearii, p. 49.) The only peculiar opinion which the author adopted was the unlawfulness of an oath in any case, which he endeavours to support at some length. (Opera, p. 317, &c.) When he calls

the benefit of the death of Christ was uncommonly useful, and made a great noise at its first publication. Forty thousand copies of it were sold in the course of six years.* It is said that cardinal Pole had a share in composing this work, and that Flaminio wrote a defence of it;† and activity in circulating it formed one of the charges on which cardinal Morone was imprisoned, and Carnesecchi committed to the flames.‡ When we take into consideration his talents, his zeal, the utility of his writings, and the sufferings which he endured, Paleario must be viewed as one of the greatest ornaments of the Reformed cause in Italy.§

A number of other excellent men suffered about the same time with Carnesecchi and Paleario, of whom the most noted were Julio Zannetti and Bartolommeo Bartoccio.‖ The latter was the son of a wealthy citizen of Castel, in the duchy of Spoletto, and imbibed the Reformed doctrine from Fabrizio Tommassi of Gubbio, a learned young gentleman, who was his companion in arms at the siege of Sien-

marriage a sacrament, he appears to me merely to mean that it was a divine or sacred ordinance. (Ibid p. 305, 315.)

* Schelhorn, Ei goetzlichkeiten, tom. 1 p. 27.

† Schelhorn, Amœnit. Hist. Eccles. tom. 1. p. 156. Laderchii Annal tom. xxii. p 326.

‡ Wolfii Lect. Memorab. tom. ii. p. 656. Schelhorn, ut supra, tom. ii. p 205. The only writer for two centuries, so far as I know, who has seen the original of this rare work, is Reiderer. The proper title is—Trattato utilissimo del beneficio de Giesu Christo crucifisso, verso i Christiani. Venetiis apud Bernardinum de Bindonis, Anno Do. 1543. (Nachrichten zur Kirchen-gelerten und Bucher-geschichte, tom. iv. p. 121.) An answer was made to it by Ambrogio Catarino, who was afterwards rewarded with an archbishopric.

§ The Italian works of Paleario, printed and in MS., including some poems, are mentioned by Tiraboschi. (Tom. vii. p. 1456.) Joannes Matthæus Toscanus, the author of *Peplus Italiæ*, who was a pupil of Paleario, composed the following verses, among others, on his master:—

> Aonio Aonides Graios prompsere lepores,
> Et quascunque vetus protulit Hellas opes.
> Aonio Latiæ tinxerunt melle Camœnæ.
> Verba ligata modis, verba soluta modis.
> Quæ nec longa dies, nec (quæ scelerata cremasti,
> Aonii corpus) perdere flamma potest.

‖ Thuani Hist. ad an. 1556. Mat. Flacii Catal. Test. Verit. append.

na.* On returning home he zealously propagated the truth, and made converts of several of his relations. During a dangerous sickness by which he was attacked, he refused to avail himself of the services of the family confessor, and resisted all the arguments by which the bishop of the diocese attempted to bring him back to the catholic faith; upon which he was summoned, along with his companions, before the governor Paolo Vitelli. Though still weak with the effects of his distemper, he rose in the night time, surmounted the wall of the city by the help of a pike, and escaped first to Sienna and afterwards to Venice. Having ascertained by letters that there was no hope of his being allowed to return to his native place, or of his receiving any support from his father, except in the way of recanting his opinions, he retired to Geneva, where he married, and became a manufacturer of silk. In the end of the year 1567, while visiting Genoa in the course of trade, he imprudently gave his real name to a merchant, and was apprehended by the inquisition. The magistrates of Geneva and Berne sent to demand his liberation from the Genoese republic; but before their envoy arrived, the prisoner had been sent to Rome at the request of the pope. After suffering an imprisonment of nearly two years, he was sentenced to be burnt alive. The courage which Bartoccio had all along displayed did not forsake him in the trying hour; he walked to the place of execution with a firm step and unaltered countenance; and the cry, *vittoria, vittoria!* was distinctly heard from his lips, after his body was enveloped in the flames.†

But it is time to bring this distressing part of the narrative to a close. Suffice it to say, that, during the whole of this century, the prisons of the inquisition in Italy, and particularly at Rome, were filled with victims, including persons of noble birth, male and female, men of letters and mechanics. Multitudes were condemned to penance, to the galleys, or other arbi-

---

* In 1555. † Histoire des Martyrs, f. 757, 758.

trary punishments; and, from time to time, individuals were put to death. Several of the prisoners were foreigners, who had visited the country in the course of business or of their travels. Englishmen were peculiarly obnoxious to this treatment.* At an earlier period, Dr. Thomas Wilson, afterwards secretary to Queen Elizabeth, was accused of heresy, and thrown into the prisons of the inquisition at Rome, on account of some things which were contained in his books on logic and rhetoric. He made his escape in consequence of his prison doors being broke open during the tumult which took place at the death of pope Paul IV.† Among those who escaped by this occurrence was also John Craig, one of our reformers, who lived to draw up the national covenant, in which Scotland solemnly abjured the popish religion.‡ Dr. Thomas Reynolds was less fortunate. After residing for some time at Naples, he was informed against to the bishop, who sent him to Rome, along with three Neapolitan gentlemen, accused of heresy. With the view of forcing him to depose against his fellow prisoners, he was subjected to the torture called by the Italians *la tratta di corda,* and by the Spaniards *l'astrapado;* and, in consequence of this and similar treatment, he died in prison in November 1566.§ In the year 1595 two persons were burnt alive in Rome, the one an Englishman and the other a native of Silesia; the former having, in a fit of zeal, indiscreetly torn the host from the hands of the priest who was carrying it in procession, had his hand cut off at the

* Histoire des Martyrs, f. 758, a.

† Dr. Wilson, after giving an account of his imprisonment and escape, in a new edition of one of his works printed in 1560, adds facetiously—"And now that I am come home, this booke is shewed me, and I am desired to looke upon it and to amende it where I thought meete. Amende it? quoth I. Nay; let the book first amende itself, and make me amendes. For surely I have no cause to acknowledge it for my booke; because I have so smarted for it. If the sonne were the occasion of the father's imprisonment, would not the father be offended with him, think you?" (Art of Rhetorike, Prologue, sig. A 5. Lond. 1583.)

‡ Life of John Knox, vol ii. p. 55.

§ Strype's Annals, vol. i. p. 526.

stake before he was committed to the flames. The nobleman who relates this fact, and was then studying at the university of Padua, adds, in a postscript to his letter, that he had just heard of some other Englishmen having been thrown into prison at Rome.* Notwithstanding all these severities, persons secretly attached to the reformed doctrines were to be found in that country during the seventeenth century; and some of our own countrymen, who had been induced to expatriate themselves out of zeal for popery, were converted to the Protestant faith during their residence in Italy.†

After these details of cruelty, it may appear a matter of trivial interest to trace the measures adopted for the suppression and destruction of books. From the period of the invention of printing, the regulation of the press had belonged to the civil authorities, who issued, from time to time, orders for suppressing particular books, which were deemed dangerous or unfit for the public eye. In the year 1546, Charles V., anxious to arrest the progress of the new opinions in Flanders, charged the theological faculty of Louvain to draw up a catalogue of such books as ought not to be read by the people; and, ten years after, this catalogue was enlarged, and authorized by an imperial edict.‡ In Rome the laws on this subject were still

---

* Letter from John, Earl of Gowrie, Padua, 28th November 1595; printed in appendix to Life of Andrew Melville. It is probable that the following extract relates to the execution mentioned above —" Il y a eu plusieurs Anglois, (condamnés,) mais sur tout un, qui à Rome au grand temple de Saint Pierre, lors que le prestre consacroit l'hostie, l'arracha d'entre ses mains, le quel fut puny meritoirement. Le Secretaire de Monsieur Dabain m'a dit l'avoir veu executer." (Scaligerana Secunda, art. *Hæretici*.) In bishop Hall's epistles, published in 1614, is a letter "To Mr. John Mole, of a long time now a prisoner under the inquisition at Rome; exciting him to his wonted constancie, and encouraging him to martyrdome." (Epistles, Decade vi. ep 9.)

† Mr. Evelyn, in his travels through Italy in 1646, met with a Scotsman, an officer of the army, at Milan, who treated him courteously, and who, together with an Irish friar, his confidant, concealed their Protestantism from dread of the inquisition. (Evelyn's Memoirs, vol. i. p. 215—217.)

‡ An account of the first register of prohibited books, written in

local, and no attempt had been made to extend their authority over the catholic world. But in 1559, pope Paul IV., emulating the zeal of the emperor, resolved to frame a catalogue still more rigid in its prohibitions, and to make its observance universal. Accordingly, he published an index of books, accompanied with a denunciation of the highest pains at his pleasure, and particularly of deprivation of ecclesiastical benefices, censures, and infamy, against all who should not, before a certain time, deliver such books to the persons appointed to receive them. This index was divided into three classes. The first contained the names of those authors whose whole works, whatever the subject might be of which they treated, were interdicted. The second contained the names of those persons of whose works some only were specified as forbidden. The third pointed out certain books printed without any author's name, and contained a prohibition of all anonymous books published since the year 1519, and of all of the same description which might be published for the future without the approbation of the ordinary of the place and of an inquisitor. To the whole was added a list of upwards of sixty printers, with a prohibition of all works which proceeded from their press, on what subject and in what language soever they were written. Such was the infamous *Index Expurgatorius* of Rome, an engine devised to extinguish letters in Europe, and to reduce it to the barbarism from which it had lately emerged.*

Deputies were despatched without delay to the different states of Italy, for the purpose of promulgating the papal decree in confirmation of the index, and seeing it carried into effect. The doom of the condemned books was the same with that pronounced against heretics—consumption by the flames. The

the language of the Netherlands, and printed at Antwerp in 1540, is given by Riederer, in Nachrichten, tom. i. p. 354—361.

* Index Auctorum et Librorum qui ab Officio Sanctæ Rom. & Universalis Inquisitionis caveri ab omnibus & singulis in universa Christiana Republica mandantur. Hic Index excusus est—de mandato speciali sacri officii, Romæ An. D. 1559. Mense Januarii.

arrival of the deputies at Florence threw Cosmo, duke of Tuscany, into great perplexity. On the one hand, he was afraid of irritating his holiness and his myrmidons; on the other, to execute such a decree would have been to forfeit the glory of the house of Medici, and to desecrate a city which boasted of being the favourite seat of letters and the arts. From this dilemma he expected to be extricated by the determination of his neighbours. But the senate of Venice temporized, while the viceroy of Naples and the governor of Milan referred the matter to Philip II., who was then in Flanders, though the disposition of that monarch to suppress every species of liberty was sufficiently known. Torelli, an eminent lawyer and first auditor of the duke, having been required to make a report on the subject to his master, presented a remonstrance stating, that the execution of this indiscreet law would inflict on the citizens of Florence a loss of more than a hundred thousand ducats, would ruin the printers and booksellers, and reduce to ashes all books printed in Germany, Paris, and Lyons, (which were the most highly esteemed,) including Bibles, Greek and Roman classics, and other works of great value and public utility. The Medicean college, through Andrea Pasquali, the duke's physician, represented the injury which it would inflict on the study of the arts; and the deputies of the inquisition themselves, having been probably dealt with in private by Cosmo, seemed to be ashamed to insist on a rigorous execution of their orders. But the cardinal of Alexandria (afterwards Pius V.) insisted on the promulgation of the papal decree, in which he was zealously supported by the monks. To this the duke partially consented, appointing it to be carried into effect as to all books contrary to religion, or which treated of magic and judicial astrology, but suspending its execution as to others; and the monks of San Maria, who intended to yield implicit obedience to the papal decree, were given to understand that, as patron of their convent and library, he could not agree to the destruction of so many books, the gift of his ancestors. On the 8th of March 1559, the condemned books were accordingly brought out and committed to the flames, with great solemnity, in the piazzas of San Giovanni and Sante Cruce. Notwithstanding the restrictions, the trade suffered so severely, that the magistrates of Basle, Zurich, and Frankfort, applied to Cosmo to use his influence with the pope to obtain some reparation for the loss which their respective cities had sustained.*

In the meantime, the work of conflagration was carried on, without discrimination or remorse at Rome, throughout the states of the church, and in every part of Italy that was under the influence of the papal court, to the dismay of literary men, foreign and native. "At Rome," says Bullinger, in a letter to Blaurer, "Paul IV. has burned all the works of Erasmus, and also the works of Cyprian, Jerome, and Augustine, because they are polluted, as he foully speaks, with the scholia of Erasmus."† "So great," says Simler, "was the number of books condemned by the pope, that the professors in the Italian academies complained loudly that they would be obliged to desist from lecturing if the edict remained in force. The magistrates of Frankfort, as well as ours and those of other cities in Germany, wrote to the senate of Venice, urging them not to admit an edict which would put an end to the mutual traffic in books."‡ An Italian writer of that age says—"The number of books committed to the flames was immense, so that if they had all been collected into one place, it would have equalled the burning of Troy. There was not a library, private or public, which escaped the disaster, or which was not nearly annihilated."§ Another contemporary writer writes thus from Rome to a friend in Germany:—"Why do you think of setting forth new works, at a time when almost all those which have been published are laid under an interdict? No

* Galluzzi, Istor. del Granduc. di Toscano, tom. i. p. 366—369.
† Hottinger, Hist Eccl. tom. ix. p. 408.
‡ Vita H. Bullingeri, p. 33.
§ Natalis Comes, Hist. Sui Temporis, b. xi. p. 263.

one here will, in my opinion, venture for many years to write any thing, except it may be a letter to an absent friend. It is vain for you to labour on the translation of Demosthenes, or the various readings of the Bible. Faernus has been occupied for several days in clearing and purging his library; and I intend to commence the same operation to-morrow, lest some of the prohibited goods should be found in my possession. This shipwreck, or rather conflagration of books will, I doubt not, have the effect of deterring your learned men from writing, and making your printers cautious of what they undertake. As you regard me and yourself, keep your desk close, lest any thing which comes to you should transpire."*

On the death of Paul IV. the inquisition after books was relaxed, and a new index was published by the authority of the council of Trent, which, while it included a greater number of Protestant works under the prohibitory sentence, was more select and discriminate in its censure of other productions of the press. The names of some popish authors formerly stigmatized were dropped, and a distinction was made among the works of others. But this led to a practice as barbarous as the former. The tolerated works were mangled by the censors of the press, to whose correction they were subjected. Several copies of the works of the fathers are still to be found, in which the annotations of Erasmus are so much disfigured, by being cut with knives, torn with pincers, or besmeared with glutinous matter, as to be utterly illegible. One of these is plastered over with woodcuts and figures of different kinds, in such a way as to have the appearance of a historical or cosmographical work, instead of one of the fathers; but, on a more minute inspection, we ascertain that these figures consist of views of fields of battle, tournaments, and executions, maps of cities and countries, drawings of animals, escutcheons, medals, and other prints, which the inquisitors had ordered to be taken out of Munster's Cosmography, and similar

* Latinus Latinius, Lucubrat. part. ii. p. 61.

works, when they were condemned to the flames.* So strict was the search at this period, that domiciliary visits were appointed with the view of discovering such books as were prohibited; and those who were unwilling to have them committed to the flames, or who had neglected to deliver them up within the prescribed time, adopted the precaution of burying them in the earth, or immuring them in their houses. On taking down an old house in Urbino, in the year 1728, the workmen disinterred a copy of Brucioli's paraphrase of Paul's epistles, with some books of Ochino, Valdes, and others of the same kind, which had remained in concealment for more than a century and a half.†

CHAPTER VI.

FOREIGN ITALIAN CHURCHES, WITH ILLUSTRATIONS OF THE REFORMATION IN THE GRISONS.

An account of those exiles who left Italy from attachment to the Protestant cause, forms an important branch of our undertaking. It is important, whether we take into view the testimony which was given to the authority of religious principle and the Reformed faith, by the fact of so many persons quitting their homes and all that was dear to them, in obedience to the dictates of conscience, or consider the loss which their ungrateful country sustained by their emigration, and the benefits which accrued to those countries which, with Christian hospitality, opened an asylum to the unfortunate strangers.

It was calculated that, in the year 1550, the exiles amounted to two hundred, of whom a fourth or fifth part were men of letters, and these not of the meanest

* Schelhorn, Ergoetzlichkeiten, tom. i p. 20—22.
† Apostolo Zeno, Note al Fontanini Bibl. della Eloq. Italiana, tom. i. p. 119.

name.* Before the year 1559, the number had increased to eight hundred.† From that time to the year 1568, we have ground to believe that the increase was fully as great in proportion; and down to the close of the century, individuals were to be seen, after short intervals, flying to the north, and throwing themselves on the glaciers of the Alps to escape the fires of the inquisition.

The settlements which the Italian refugees made in the Grisons claim our first notice. With a few exceptions they all visited that country in the first instance, and a great part of them made it the place of their permanent abode. This was chiefly owing to its proximity to Italy, and its affording them the best opportunities of corresponding with the friends they had left behind them, or of gratifying the hope, to which exiles long fondly cling, of revisiting their natal soil, as soon as such a change should occur as would render this step practicable and safe. But in choosing this as a place of residence, they must also have been influenced by the consideration that the native tongue of the inhabitants in the southern dependencies of the Grison republic was Italian, while a language bearing a near affinity to it was spoken over the greater part of the republic itself. The affairs of the Italian settlers in the Grisons are so interwoven with the progress of the Reformation in that country, that the former cannot be understood without some account of the latter. I shall be the less scrupulous in entering into details on this subject, because it relates to a portion of the history of the Reformed Church which is comparatively little known among us; for while the interesting fates of the Vaudois, who took refuge in the Valais and Piedmont, have attracted the attention of ecclesiastical historians to the Cottian or western range of the Alps, the Rhetian or eastern has been in a great measure overlooked.

To the south-east of Switzerland, in the higher re-

* Vergerio, Lettere al Vescovo di Lesina: De Porta, tom. ii. p. 36.
† Busdragi Epist. ut supra, p. 322.

gion of the Alps, where these gigantic mountains, covered with ice and clouds, are cleft into narrow valleys, and around the sources of the Rhine and Inn, lies the country of the ancient Rhetians and modern Grisons. Secluded from the rest of the world, and occupied in feeding their cattle on the mountains, and in cultivating corn and the vine within their more fertile valleys, the inhabitants, who came originally from Italy, had preserved their ancient language and manners, with little variation, from a period considerably anterior to the Christian era. During the middle ages they fell under the dominion of the bishops of Coire, the abbots of Disentis, and a crowd of other chiefs, ecclesiastical and secular, who kept them in awe by means of innumerable castles, the ruins of which are still to be seen in all parts of the country. Worn out by the injuries which they suffered from these petty tyrants, and animated by the example which had been set them by their neighbours the Swiss, the miserable inhabitants, in the course of the fifteenth century, threw off the yoke of their oppressors one by one; and, having established a popular government in their several districts, entered into a common league for the defence of their independence and rights. The Grison league or republic consisted of a union of three distinct leagues,—the Grey league, that of God's House, and that of the Ten Jurisdictions; each of which was composed of a number of smaller communities, which retained the right of managing all their internal affairs, as well as of sending deputies to the general diet, whose powers were extremely circumscribed. In no nation, ancient or modern, have the principles of democracy been carried to such extent as in the Grison republic; and as the checks necessary to prevent its abuse were not provided by a rude people smarting under the recent effects of tyranny, its form of government, according to the confession of its own as well as foreign writers, not only created great dissensions, but led to gross corruption and bribery in election to offices and

indifferent, and produced unforeseen consequences of the greatest importance. The first public reformation in the Grisons took place in the years 1524 and 1525, when the inhabitants of the valley of St. Anthony, of Flesch, and of Malantz, in the high jurisdiction of Mayenfeld, though surrounded by powerful neighbours addicted to popery, embraced with one consent the Protestant doctrine and abolished the mass.* This produced so great an effect, that within a short time the new doctrine began to be preached by some of the priests, and was eagerly listened to by the people, in various places throughout the three leagues. Among these preachers, the most distinguished were Andrew Sigfrid and Andrew Fabritz at Davos, the chief town in the league of the Ten Jurisdictions: and in the league of God's House, James Tutschet or Biveron, in Upper Engadina; Philip Salutz or Gallitz, in Lower Engadina; and John Dorfman or Comander, who, in consequence of the late regulations of the diet, had been chosen parson of St. Martin's church, in the town of Coire.† The two last afterwards became colleagues at Coire, and they may with propriety be designated the joint reformers of the Grisons, having contributed beyond all others to the advancement of knowledge and religion in their native country. Comander was a man of learning, sound judgment, and warm piety. To these qualities Gallitz added great dexterity in the management of public business, an invincible command of temper, and uncommon eloquence both in his native tongue and in Latin ‡ The conversion of John Frick, parish priest of Mayenfeld, was brought about in a singular manner. Being a zealous catholic and of great note among his brethren, he had warmly resisted the new opinions when they first made their appearance. Filled with chagrin and alarm at the progress of innovation in his immediate neighbourhood, he repaired to Rome to implore the

* De Porta, tom. i. p 57—68.
† De Porta, p. 58, 59, 76—78. Ruchat, Hist. de la Reform. de la Suisse, tom. i. p. 273, 274.
‡ Ibid. tom. i. p. 67, 79; tom. ii. p. 278.

assistance of his holiness, and to consult on the best method of preventing his native country from being overrun with heresy. But he was so struck with the irreligion which he observed in the court of Rome, and the ignorance and vice prevailing in Italy, that, returning home, he joined the party which he had opposed, and became the reformer of Mayenfeld. In his old age he used to say to his friends pleasantly, that he learned his gospel at Rome.*

In the meantime, the clergy, aroused from the slumbers into which they had sunk through indolence and the absence of all opposition, had recourse to every means within their power to check the progress of the new opinions. Bonds of adherence to the catholic faith were exacted from the parish priests. The most odious and horrid representations of the reformers and their tenets were circulated among the people. Individuals belonging to the anabaptists who had been banished from Switzerland came to the Grisons, and laboured to make proselytes among the reformed by pretending to preach a purer and more spiritual religion than was taught by Luther and Zuingle, whom they put on a level with the pope. The popish clergy secretly encouraged these enthusiasts,† at the same time that they had made use of

* Schelhorn, Amœn. Hist Eccl. tom. ii. p. 237. Ruchat, tom. i. p. 275.

† Their leader, who went by the name of Blaurok, in allusion to the colour of his cloak, was an ex-monk of the Grisons, who had made a great noise in Switzerland. At Zurich, he said "he would undertake to prove that Zuinglius had offered greater violence to the Scriptures than the Roman pontiff himself." (Acta Senat. Tigur. apud De Porta, tom. ii. p. 86.) The following is an extract from one of his letters :—" I am the door, he that entereth in by me shall find pasture; he that entereth by any other way is a thief and a robber. As it is written—'I am the good shepherd, the good shepherd giveth his life for the sheep,' so I give my life and my spirit for my sheep, my body to the tower, my life to the sword, or the fire, or the winepress, to squeeze out the blood and flesh, as Christ gave his on the cross. I am the restorer of the baptism of Christ, and the bread of the Lord, I and my beloved brethren, Conrad Grebel and Felix Manx Therefore the pope, along with his followers, is a thief and a robber; and so also are Luther with his followers, and Zuinglius and Leo Juda with theirs." (De Porta, tom. ii. p. 89.) Blaurok and his associates were banished from the Grisons in the year 1525.

their excesses to excite prejudice against the cause of the Reformation.* When the general diet of the republic met at Coire in the year 1525, the bishop and clergy presented a formal accusation against Comander and the other reforming preachers, praying that they might be punished by the secular arm, for propagating impious, scandalous, and seditious heresies, contrary to the faith of the catholic church during fifteen centuries, and tending to produce that rebellion and outrage which had lately been witnessed at Munster and other places. Comander having, in the name of his brethren, declared their readiness to vindicate the doctrine which they held against these criminations, a day was appointed for a conference or dispute between the two parties at Ilantz, in the presence of certain members of the diet. The dispute which ensued added seven to the number of the reformed preachers, who were previously above forty; while the articles which formed the subject of dispute having been printed and circulated throughout the valleys, multiplied converts among the laity.†

In the meantime, an event occurred which had well nigh proved fatal to the reformed party. Irritated by the assistance which the Grisons had given to Francis I., the emperor and duke of Milan encouraged the turbulent John de Medicis, marquis of Muss, to attack their southern territories. Having possessed himself of the castle and town of Chiavenna, he threatened to attack the Valteline. This obliged the republic to recall their troops from Italy before the famous battle of Pavia; but having failed, after all, in recovering the castle, they had recourse to the mediation of the Swiss cantons. The deputies sent by the Swiss were keen Roman catholics, and asserted that they had it in charge from their constituents to obtain a pledge that heresy should not be permitted to spread in the Grisons, without which they could not co-operate in bringing the negotiations to a favourable issue. The

* De Porta p. 87—92.
† Ruchat, tom. 1. p. 408—416. De Porta, tom 1. p. 96—100, 102—130.

marquis covered his ambitious project with the pretext of zeal for the church, and was, besides, under the influence of his brother, then an ecclesiastic in the Valteline, and afterwards raised to the pontifical chair under the designation of Pius IV. Availing himself of these circumstances, the bishop of Coire prevailed on the deputies to insert in the treaty an article which provided for the maintenance of the ancient religion, and the punishment of all who refused conformity to it. An extraordinary diet was called to deliberate on this affair; and so great was the influence of the bishop and mediators, together with the anxiety of the nation to put an end to the war, that a majority voted for the article respecting religion. It was, however, warmly opposed by the representatives of several districts, including the city of Coire, which refused to affix its seal to the decree. The manner in which the decree was expressed seems to intimate that it partook of the nature of an understood compromise and temporary measure; for, while it provided that the mass, auricular confession, and other rites, should be observed, it added that, "along with these the gospel and word of God should be preached;" and in declaring that non-conformists should be subjected to an arbitrary punishment, the diet "reserved to itself the liberty of altering its measures, upon being better informed by disputations, councils, or any other way."* The first effect of this law was the banishment of Gallitz, whose talents and success rendered him peculiarly obnoxious to the abettors of popery. Several of his brethren were also obliged to retire from the country to avoid the processes intended against them. But the city of Coire, in spite of their bishop, maintained Comander in his situation; their example was followed in other places; and though the clergy endeavoured to push the advantage which they had gained, they found that a spirit was abroad in the nation too powerful for all their efforts, even when supported by legislative enactments. The subject was brought before the next national diet by the

* De Porta, tom. i. p. 131—134.

report of the commissioners appointed to attend the dispute at Ilantz; and, after consultation, it was moved and agreed to, "That it shall be free to all persons of both sexes, and of whatever condition or rank, within the territories of the Grison confederation, to choose, embrace, and profess either the Roman catholic or the Evangelical religion; and that no one shall, publicly or privately, harass another with reproaches or odious speeches on account of his religion, under an arbitrary penalty." To this was added the renovation of a former law, "that the ministers of religion shall teach nothing to the people but what is contained in the Scriptures of the Old and New Testament, and what they can prove by them; and that parish priests shall be enjoined to give themselves assiduously to the study of the Scriptures as the only rule of faith and manners."*

This remarkable statute, which, whatever infractions it may have suffered, and whatever attempts may have been made to overthrow it, remains to this day the charter of religious liberty in the Grisons, was formally sealed and solemnly confirmed, by the oaths of all the deputies at Ilantz, on the 26th of June 1526, along with a number of other regulations of great importance. The power of appointing magistrates and judges was taken from the bishop of Coire and his ecclesiastics, and given to the people in their several communities. Where persons had bequeathed sums of money to churches and convents for offering anniversary masses and prayers for their souls, both they and their heirs were declared free from any obligation to make such payments for the future, "because no good ground could be shown for believing that this was of any benefit to the deceased." It was decreed that no new members, male or female, should henceforth be admitted into monasteries; that the existing monks should be restrained from begging; and that after appropriating a certain sum for

---

* Ruchat, tom. 1. p. 416 De Porta, tom 1. p. 146 Anabaptists and those of other sects, if they retained and propagated their errors after due information and admonition, were subjected to banishment.

their support during life, the remainder of the funds should be returned to the heirs of those who originally bestowed them, and, failing them, be disposed of as each league thought best. The power of choosing and dismissing their respective ministers was given to parishes.* All appeals from secular courts to the jurisdiction of the bishop were strictly prohibited; annats and small tithes were abolished, and the great tithes reduced to a fifth part.†

It thus appears that a great deal more was done on this occasion by the authorities of the Grisons than merely recognizing and sanctioning religious liberty. A national reformation was introduced, which, so far as it went, must have been attended with the most beneficial consequences to the state, and to individuals, whether popish or Protestant. The grand principle of the Protestant reformation was, in fact recognized by the legislature, when it declared the sacred Scriptures to be the only rule of religion. Some of the grossest abuses of popery, and those which draw many others after them, were abolished. And the liberties of the Roman catholics were secured, not only against attacks from the Protestants, but also against the more dangerous encroachments and demands of their own clergy, and of a foreign priest who claimed dominion over both. It is impossible to read the document on which we are commenting without being convinced that the Grisons possessed at this period statesmen of enlightened minds and liberal principles. The historians of that country have gratefully preserved the names of the men by whom the deed was drawn up, and through whose influence chiefly it was adopted by the supreme council of the republic. Two of them were distinguished above their brethren—John Guler, whose name often occurs in the history of his country, and

* The words of this article are—" Ad hinc etiam penes singulas parochias esto suos pastores omni tempore eligendi conducendi atque rursus quando lubitum fuerit, dimittendi " (De Porta, tom. 1. p 150.) Formerly the bishop of Coire had the power of appointing and removing the parish priests throughout the whole of his diocese.

† De Porta, tom. 1. p. 148—151. Ruchat, tom. 1. p. 416, 417.

John Travers, neither of whom had at that time joined the reformers. The latter, who belonged to a noble and ancient family of Zuts in Upper Engadina, had received his education at Munich, and improved his mind by travelling in different parts of Europe. His abilities and learning, adorned by the most unimpeachable integrity, secured the confidence of his countrymen, who intrusted him with the highest offices of the state and the management of their most delicate affairs. He was equally distinguished as a soldier and a scholar, a politician and a divine. The first book ever written in the Grison language came from his pen,* being a poem on the war against the marquis of Muss, in which he had himself commanded the forces of his country. The late period at which he renounced the communion of the church of Rome was beneficial to the evangelical cause, as his colleagues in the senate and his countrymen at large entertained on that account the less jealousy of the measures which he proposed in favour of religious liberty. After joining himself to the reformed church, he promoted its interests with the utmost zeal. The Protestant minister settled in his native city being a young man and meeting with great opposition from the principal families of the place, Travers asked and readily obtained from the ministers permission to act as his assistant. The whole country was struck with astonishment to see a man of rank, and renowned for his services in the senate, the field, and foreign courts, mount the pulpit. The Roman catholics tried to conceal the chagrin and alarm which they felt, by circulating the report that he was mad or in dotage; but his performances soon put to silence their invidious and artful allegations.†

---

* It does not appear that this work was printed.
† De Porta, i 229, 233—241. Coxe's Travels in Switzerland, iii. 295—298. A fine letter which Gallitz addressed to Travers, on his application for liberty to preach, has been preserved. "O felicem terram quæ tales*nanciscitur doctores et magistros!—Sed quæ modestia est ista explodenda, imo quod facinus hoc, quod permittis tibi petere a nobis auctoritatem, quum fecerit opus concionandi? Tu, inquam, qui Rhætiæ nostræ primoribus auctor fuisti, veniam nobis concedendi ut prædicemus evangelium," &c.

The publication of the edict in favour of religious liberty was followed by the rapid spread of the new opinions; but the formation of churches was much slower. This proceeded partly from the plan pursued by the first reformers, who, to use their own expression, " sought to remove idols from the hearts of the people before they removed them from the churches;" and partly from the democratical nature of the government, which required the unanimous or at least general concurrence of each community previously to any change on the public worship. In the year 1527, the mass was abolished, images removed, and the sacrament of the supper celebrated after the reformed mode, in St. Martin's church at Coire, under the direction of Comander. The same thing was done at Lavin in Lower Engadina, under the direction of Gallitz; at Davos in the Ten Jurisdictions, under the direction of Fabritz; and at Ilantz, in the Grey league, under the direction of Christian Hartman. The example set by these places was soon imitated by others. The reformed religion was embraced earliest in the league of the Ten Jurisdictions, where it soon became almost universal. Within the league of God's House it prevailed generally in the neighbourhood of Coire, but made little progress in Engadina and other places to the south until 1542, when the Italian exiles arrived. In the High or Grey league the number of its adherents was still smaller.*

Had the Reformation continued to move forward with the same rapidity which marked its progress during the six years which succeeded the declaration of religious liberty, the ancient religion must soon have disappeared before it. Various causes, however, contributed to arrest its progress. One of these is to be found in the languages of the country. The Rhetian, Italian, and German tongues were all spoken in the Grisons, so that the inhabitants of two adjacent valleys were often incapable of understanding one another. This of itself must have proved a great hin-

* De Porta, tom. 1. cap. 8. Ruchat. 1. 274. 417. 418. Coxe, iii 250—253.

derance to the communication of knowledge, especially as the number of teachers was small. But this was not all. The Rhetian or Grison tongue is divided into two dialects, the Romansh and the Ladin, and there was not a single book in either of them at the time of the Reformation. Nobody had ever seen a word written in that tongue, and it was the common opinion that it could not be committed to writing.* There can be little doubt that the rapid and extensive spread of the reformed doctrine among the inhabitants of the Ten Jurisdictions was owing, in a great degree, to their speaking the German tongue, and consequently having access to the Scriptures and other books in their native language. The same remark applies to the citizens of Coire and of some other places. But the inhabitants of those districts where nothing was spoken but the original language of the country, were long confined to oral instruction. The reformed ministers laboured assiduously in supplying this defect, and they at last practically demonstrated the fallacy of the ignorant prejudice which the priests had fostered in the minds of the people. In this respect, their country is under unspeakable obligations to them. Other nations owe their literature to the Reformation: the Grisons are indebted to it for their alphabet. But a number of years elapsed before the preachers, occupied with other labours and straitened in their finances, could bring their writings from the press; and, by that time, the desire for knowledge which the first promulgation of the reformed doctrines had excited must have been in some degree worn off from the minds of the people. A translation of Comander's German catechism into the Ladin, by James Tutchet or Bive-

* De Porta, i. 19; ii. 403. Coxe, iii. 294. In addition to a collection of words and phrases in Romansh, Ebel has inserted a dissertation on the history of that language, (which he calls "la langue Hetrusco-Rhétienne,") by Placidus a Specha, capitular of Disentis. From this it would appear that a number of old MSS., written in that language during the middle ages, were preserved, the greater part of which, however, were destroyed when the French burnt the monastery of Disentis in 1799. (Manuel du Voyageur en Suisse, tom. i. p. 318—337.)

roni, printed at Puschiavo in the year 1552, was the first work which had appeared in the Rhetian language. "At the sight of this work," says a historian then alive, "the Grisons stood amazed, like the Israelites of old at the sight of the manna." Biveroni printed, in 1560, his translation of the New Testament into the same language, which was followed in 1562 by a metrical version of the Psalms, and a collection of hymns, composed by Ulrich Campel.*

Another cause was the poverty of the pastors, which inflicted a lasting injury on the Reformed church.† While the popish priests possessed the tithes, in addition to what they gained by private masses and confessions, the Protestant ministers received a small stipend from their congregations, and, in many cases, were reduced to the necessity of supporting themselves by manual labour. Gallitz, a man of liberal education, states, in one of his familiar letters, that he and his family had been for two years in great straits, were obliged to sleep during the night in the clothes which they wore through the day, seldom tasted flesh, were often without bread, and, for weeks together, lived solely on vegetables seasoned with salt. Yet he trained his son for the church; and when the young man had an advantageous offer made him during his attendance at the academy of Basle, his father declared it would be impiety in him to accept it, when there were so few persons capable of preaching to his countrymen in their native language.‡ But it was not to be expected that the first Reformers would be succeeded by men of the same nobleness of mind. The consequence was, that the people, in

* De Porta, ii. 404—407. The Bible was published in the Ladin of Lower Engadina, for the first time, in 1679, and in the Romansh of the Grey league so late as 1718. (Coxe, iii. 301—304.)

† In Travellers Guides through the Grisons it is to this day a common direction, "If the town to which you come be catholic, call for the curé of the parish, who will entertain you hospitably. if it be Protestant, you may ask for the pastor, who will direct you to the best inn; for the salaries of the pastors are so sorry, and their houses so bad, that, however willing, they cannot show hospitality."

‡ De Porta, i. 181, 186, 187.

many parts of the country, remained destitute of pastors, or were induced to receive illiterate persons of low character, who disgraced the office by their meanness or their vices. "Assuredly," says the excellent man last mentioned, "covetous persons are most cruel to themselves, while they choose rather to be without good pastors than to be at the expense of maintaining them. Oh! the ingratitude of men, who, a little ago, cheerfully gave a hundred crowns for teaching lies, and now grudge to give twenty for preaching the truth!"* Another radical defect of the Grison reformation consisted in neglecting entirely to provide the means of education for youth. This the Reformed ministers exerted themselves to remedy, and they succeeded at last in providing parochial teachers for the chief towns, and in persuading the legislature to appropriate the residuary funds of such monasteries as were suppressed to the establishment of a national seminary at Coire.† These evils were aggravated by the political state of the country. Proud of their liberty, the natives of the Grisons were weakly jealous of those common measures which were in fact necessary to preserve it; while they roamed about their valleys without control, they forgot that savages are free; and, pleased to hear their mountains re-echo the votes which they gave at the election of a municipal *landamman* or of a deputy to the diet, they did not perceive that their voices were in reality at the command of a few men of superior intelligence, many of whom had sold themselves, and were prepared to sell them, to the highest bidder. Foreign princes had their pensioners resident in the Grisons; the chief statesmen were secretly in the interest either of the emperor or of the king of France; and, between the two factions, the country was at once distracted, cor-

---

* Gallicius ad Henr. Bullingerum, 6 Mart. 1553: De Porta, i. 180.

† This academy was opened in the year 1542; and the individual first placed at the head of it was John Pontisella, a native of Pregalia, for whom Bullinger, at the request of the Grison Reformers, had obtained a gratuitous education at Zurich. (Ibid. i. 187, 192—197.)

rupted, and betrayed. Next to his labours in reforming religion, Zuingle is entitled to immortal praise for denouncing, at the expense of incurring the odium of his countrymen, the practice of hiring themselves out as mercenaries to fight the battles of foreign princes. The Grison Reformers imitated his example, and they met his reward; their countrymen, imagining that they were hirelings like themselves, punished them by reducing their stipends!*

The churches in the Grisons were organized in the same manner as those in the Protestant cantons of Switzerland, as to government as well as doctrine and worship. From the beginning, congregations had their consistories. To these were added, probably at a later period, colloquies or presbyteries, of which there were two in each league. The pastors were accustomed to meet together occasionally for consultation about the common interests of the reformed body, for examining and ordaining candidates for the ministry, and for rectifying the disorders which occurred. But these meetings were voluntary, and their determinations were given out in the form of advices. The report having gone abroad that a great scarcity of preaching was felt in the Grisons, numbers flocked into the country from Switzerland and Germany, pretending to be preachers, although they were both illiterate and disreputable in character. Repairing to the valleys, they insinuated themselves into the affections of the country people; and having clandestinely concluded a bargain with them to serve their churches for a small sum of money, they behaved in such a manner as to open the mouths of the Roman Catholics, and bring great discredit on the

---

* In answer to a letter from Bullinger, (Feb 18, 1544,) dissuading him from leaving his station at Coire, Comander writes—"Another reason is, that, six years ago, when I opposed myself to the worthless pensioners in a sermon, as I was in duty bound to do, I excited their rage against me, and they took away thirty-three florins from my stipend, which was before sufficiently small. Hitherto I have digested this injury, and have supplied the deficiency from my own and my wife's fortune; but if I continue to do this much longer, my children must be reduced to beggary after my death." (De Porta, i. 183; conf. p. 256.)

evangelical cause. To remedy this evil, the ministers applied to the diet of the republic for their sanction to the holding of a national synod, which should have power to call to account those who had come from foreign parts, inquire into their qualifications, and exact from them certificates of character; to examine all who should afterwards be admitted to the ministry, watch over their conduct, censure the disorderly, and, in general, preserve the order and promote the edification of the whole reformed body. This petition was granted by the diet on the 14th of January, 1537, and from that time the synod was held regularly every year in the month of June, when the passage across the mountains was easiest.*

Such was the state of the reformed churches in the Grisons, when the exiles from Italy first made their appearance in that country. The encouragement presented to them, in a worldly point of view, was certainly far from flattering; but they had come seeking a refuge, not a fortune. They had left a land flowing with milk and honey: what they wanted was a land of religious liberty, and in which there was not a famine of hearing the word of God. Accordingly, they were received in a very different manner from the vagrants formerly mentioned: the tale of their distress had arrived before them, and their sufferings were held to be sufficient testimonials.

Their first arrival in the country produced an impression highly favourable to the interests of the Reformation. The very sight of so many persons, some of them illustrious for birth, learning, and rank, civil and ecclesiastical, who had voluntarily renounced their honours and estates, left their dearest friends,†

* De Porta, i. 188—192.

† Julio de Milano, writing to Bullinger, from Tirano, in the Valteline, 23d June, 1552, says—" The circumstances of the person who will deliver you this letter are as follows:—God has permitted his two sons to be thrown into prison for confessing Christ, and they will soon either suffer martyrdom or be condemned to the galleys for life. They have wives and thirteen children, the eldest of whom, who may be about thirteen years of age, accompanies the unfortunate old man. Do something to prevent this family from perishing by want." (De Porta, ii. 145.)

and encountered poverty, with all the other hardships attendant on exile, rather than do violence to their consciences, while it established the Protestants in the doctrine which they had embraced, struck the minds of their adversaries with astonishment, and forced on the most reluctant the suspicion that such sacrifices could not have been made on slight grounds. No sooner did the exiles find themselves safe than they detailed the cruelties of the inquisition, and laid open the arts of the court of Rome, with the ignorance, superstition, and vice which reigned in it. They dwelt with enthusiasm on the liberty of conscience and the pure preaching of the gospel enjoyed in the Grisons. They grudged no labour in communicating instruction, privately and publicly, wherever an opportunity offered, by which means they gained many souls to Christ, especially among those who spoke Italian. Some of them made themselves masters of the language of the country, so as to be able, within a short time, to preach to the inhabitants. They made attempts, and often successfully, to preach in parts of the country from which the native ministers deemed it prudent to abstain; and in every place in which they remained for any time, new churches were sure to spring up.*

Bartolommeo Maturo arrived in the Grisons at a much earlier period than any of his countrymen. He had been prior of a Dominican convent at Cremona, and being disgusted at the lives of the monks and the fictitious miracles by which they deluded the people, he threw off the cowl and left Italy. Having preached the reformed doctrines in the Valteline, he was accused to the diet which met at Ilantz in 1529, and had sentence of banishment passed against him. But he was taken under the protection of one of the deputies, and conducted to Pregalia, where he commenced preaching with success. From that place he went into the neighbouring district of Engadina, where Gallitz had hitherto gained very little ground, on account of the determined hostility of the most powerful inhabi-

* De Porta, ii. 36, 37.

tants. The first appearance of Maturo threatened a tumult, but he persevered, and the matter being referred to the suffrages of the community, he obtained a majority in his favour, and preached openly before the eyes of those who in the late diet had voted for his banishment.* Returning to Pregalia, he undertook the pastoral charge of Vico Soprano and Stampa, where he continued until 1547, and died a pastor in the valley of Tomliasco.†

Soon after Maturo's removal, Vico Soprano obtained for its pastor the celebrated Vergerio. It is true the bishop did not distinguish himself by observing the law of residence, having frequently visited the Valteline, beside the journeys which he undertook into Switzerland and Germany, during the period in which he held this cure.‡ Some allowance must, however, be made for the habits of a man who had been accustomed all his life to a change of scene and employment. Besides, he was never idle; and, considering the state of the country at that time, he perhaps did more good by his itinerant labours than he could have done by confining himself to a parish. The stateliness of his figure, his eloquence, and the rank which he had lately held in the papal church, conspired in fixing the eyes of the public upon him; and persons of all classes were anxious to see and hear a man who had repeatedly sustained the office of ambassador from the court of Rome, was supposed to be acquainted with all its secrets, and was not scrupulous about divulging what he knew. In returning from one of his visits to the Valteline, he passed a night at Pontresina, a town situate on the northern base of mount Bernino. It happened that the parish priest had died that day, and the inhabitants were assembled in the evening at the inn to converse with the landlord, who was judge of the village, about choosing a suc-

* Ruchat, ii. 458, 459.
† De Porta, i. 158; ii. 14, 27—30.
‡ De Porta says that, at this time, Vergerio drew the yearly stipend of one hundred and fifty crowns, as ordinary pastor of Vico Soprano; (ii. 46.)

cessor. After engaging their attention by conversing on the subject which had called them together, Vergerio asked them if they would not hear a sermon from him. The greater part objecting to this, "Come," said the judge, "let us hear what this new-come Italian will say." So highly were the people gratified with his sermon, that they insisted on his preaching to them again before his departure. Accordingly he preached next day to a crowded audience on the merits of Christ's death and on justification, with such effect that the inhabitants soon after agreed harmoniously in abolishing the mass and giving a call to a Protestant minister. Having preached, during one of his short excursions, in the town of Casauccia, at the foot of mount Maloggia, all the images in the church of St. Gaudentius were thrown down during the following night; and the same thing happened after a visit which he paid to Samada. An accusation was brought against him for instigating these disorderly practices, but he was acquitted.* His countrymen were no less diligent in planting and watering churches in that part of the country. In general, it appears that the greater part of the important districts of Upper and Lower Engadina, and the whole of Pregalia, a district lying on the southern declivity of the Alps, were reformed by means of Italian refugees. This took place between 1542 and 1552; and, from that time, the Protestants became decidedly the majority, comprehending the greater part of the population as well as the wealth of the republic.†

But the principal scene of the labours of the refu-

* De Porta, i. 231, 232; ii. 46, 47.
† Castanet was reformed by Jeronimo Ferlino, a Sicilian, who was succeeded as pastor by Agostino, a Venetian, Giovanni Batista, a native of Vicenza, &c. Jeronimo Turriano of Cremona was the first minister of Bondo, which enjoyed a succession of Italian ministers. Bevers was reformed by Pietro Parisotti of Bergamo, and Siglio by Giovanni Francesco, who had for his successor Antonio Cortesio of Brescia. Bartolommeo Sylvio of Cremona was pastor at Pontresina; and Leonardo Eremita and several of his countrymen were successively pastors in Casauccia. Vettan was reformed by an Italian named Evandro, who was succeeded by Francesco Calabro. (De Porta, i. 226, 232, 233; ii. 46—48.)

gees was in the provinces subject to the republic, and situate between the Alps and Italy. These consisted of the Valteline, a rich, beautiful, and populous valley, fifty miles long, and from twelve to fifteen broad; the county of Chiavenna which forms the point of communication for the trade between Italy and Germany; and the county of Bormio. To these may be added the valley of Puschiavo, a jurisdiction or community within the republic, and lying to the north of the Valteline. In all these districts the language spoken by the inhabitants was Italian. From the time that the new opinions began to prevail in the Grisons, the attention of the court of Rome was directed to this quarter, and precautionary measures were adopted to prevent them from spreading into Italy. As early as 1523, the bishop of Como sent a friar named Modesta into the Valteline to make inquisition after heretics; but the inhabitants were so incensed at the extortion of which he was guilty, that they forced him to depart, and a decree was passed that no inquisitor should afterwards be allowed to enter that territory. The reformed opinions were brought across the Alps by inhabitants of the Grisons who came to reside in the Valteline for the purpose of trade, or on account of the mildness of the climate; and subsequently to the declaration of religious liberty by the diet, it was natural for them to think that they had a right to profess in the subject-states that religion which had been authorized within the bounds of the governing country.* The increase of their numbers, particularly at Chiavenna, where they were joined by some of the principal families, alarmed the priests. They durst not attack the persons or property of the objects of their hatred, for fear of being called to account by the public authorities, but every thing short of force was employed to intimidate and distress them. The minds of the people were inflamed by the most violent invectives from the pulpit against the Lutheran heresies; and recourse was had to arts of a still worse description. A simple maid was decoyed into the

* De Porta, tom. ii. p. 4.

belief that the Virgin Mary had appeared to her, and given her a charge to acquaint the inhabitants of Chiavenna, that heaven, provoked by the encouragement given to heresy, was about to visit the place with an awful calamity, unless the heretics were speedily exterminated. Processions, accompanied with fasting and prayers, were immediately proclaimed and observed with great solemnity in the town and surrounding villages, and every thing portended some violent explosion of popular hatred against the Protestants; but, in consequence of a judicial investigation, it was found that the whole affair had originated in the wicked device of a parish priest to gratify his lust, under the hypocritical covert of zeal for the Catholic faith.* The detection of this imposture, under a governor who was unsuspected of any leaning to the new opinions, together with the subsequent conviction of some other priests of notorious crimes, silenced the clergy, and contributed to open the eyes of the people to the fanatical delusion under which they had fallen.†

A great part of the learned Italians who fled to the Valteline between 1540 and 1543, after refreshing themselves from the fatigues of their journey, crossed the Alps. But a considerable number of them were induced to remain, by the pleasantness of the country, the importunity of some of the principal inhabitants, who were anxious to have the benefit of their private instructions, and the prospect which they had of being useful among a people who were entirely destitute of the means of religious knowledge. Among these was Agostino Mainardi, a Piedmontese, and an Augustinian monk. Having been thrown into prison in the town of Asti for maintaining certain propositions contrary to the received faith, he was liberated upon the explications which he gave, and went to Italy. At Pavia and other places he acquired great reputation by preaching and disputing in behalf of the truth; and after escaping repeatedly the snares

* De Porta, tom. ii. p. 15—20.   † Ibid. tom. ii. p. 20, 21.

laid for his life, was obliged at last to betake himself to flight. His learning, mildness, and prudence, qualified him for the difficult situation in which he was now placed.* Julio da Milano, a secular priest and doctor of theology, who had escaped from the imprisonment into which he had been thrown at Venice,† proved a zealous and able coadjutor to Mainardi. They were joined by Camillo, a native of Sicily, who, on embracing the Protestant doctrine, took the name of Renato; and by Francesco Negri of Bassano, who is known as the author of several books against the church of Rome, which had an extensive circulation at the time of their publication.‡ The two last were not preachers, as has been erroneously

---

* Raynaldi Annales, ad an 1535. Celio Secundo Curio, De amplitudine regni Dei, p 15 Museum Helveticum Gerdesii Ital. Reform. p. 300. Schelhorn, Ergoetz tom. ii p. 16.

† Gerdes (Italia Ref. p 279, 280) has confounded this person with Julio Terenziano. They were different individuals. Fueslin has published a letter from *Julius Terentianus*, and another from *Julius Mediolanensis*. (Epistolæ Ref. p 304 353.) The former, according to Simler, continued with Martyr from the time he left Italy till his death (Vita Martyris, sig b. iiij.) He was with him in England in 1548 and 1553, retired with him to Strasburg in the end of that year, and was still with him in 1558 at Zurich. (Scrin. Antiq. iv 664 667. 674 Fueslin, p. 313. 318) In 1565, bishop Jewel sent to Zurich twenty crowns, "being an annual pension to *Julius*, who was his dear friend, Peter Martyr's constant servant and assistant." (Strype's Annals, i. 505) But *Julius Mediolanensis* was in the neighbourhood of Chiavenna during all that period (Fueslin, p 359. De Porta, ii. 30. 40) Argelati, in his Bibl. Script Mediol. as quoted by Tiraboschi, (Storia, vii. 383) says, that some sermons by "Giulio Terenziano da Milano" were printed at Venice; but I suspect that these learned writers have mistaken the real author, and that the sermons, as well as the work which appeared under the concealed name of *Girolamo Savonese*, were the production, not of Giulio Terenziano, but of Giulio da Milano.

‡ Bock, Hist. Antitrin ii. 482 Beside the work formerly mentioned, (p 318,) Negri was the author of *Tragedia de Libero Arbitrio*, which Fontanini characterises as "empia e diabolica," and from which Schelhorn has given extracts (Ergoetzlichkeiten, tom. ii. p. 29—31) Verci has given an account of his writings; and the documents which he has produced refute the opinion of Quadrio and others, that Negri was a native of Lovero, in the Valteline. (Scrittori Bassan 1. 60 Tiraboschi, vii. 383) "Antonius Nigrus, medicus," is mentioned by Melanchthon as having come from Italy; (Epist col 749,) and "Theobaldus Nigrus" is spoken of by Martyr as at Strasburg in 1551. (Loc. Commun. p. 763.)

stated by some writers,* but confined themselves to the teaching of youth. Camillo had under his charge the sons of several of the principal gentry, and took up his residence at Caspan, in the Valteline, while Negri fixed his abode at Chiavenna.† To them may be added Francesco Stancari, a native of Mantua, who remained some time in the Valteline, and commenced teaching the Hebrew language, of which, before he left his native country, he had been professor at Terra di Spilimbergo, in the province of Friuli.‡

Among the distinguished citizens of the Grisons who resided in Chiavenna, was Hercules de Salice or Salis, the descendant of a noble family, who had already gained great reputation as a soldier, and afterwards rose to the first employments in the republic. He entertained Mainardi, who pleased him and the friends who frequented his house so highly, that they determined to have the obstacles which stood in the way of his remaining with them removed. The zealous Roman Catholics insisted that it was a fundamental law of the democracy, that no religious service could be set up in any community, town, or village, without the formal permission of the majority of the inhabitants. The Protestants, on the other hand, pleaded the liberty which had been granted to use the reformed worship within the republic. De Salis brought the affair before the national diet held at Davos in the year 1544, which determined that it should be lawful to such as embraced the evangelical religion in the Valteline, Chiavenna, and other places within the dominions of the Grisons, to entertain and keep privately teachers and schoolmasters for the spiritual instruction of their families; and that those who had fled from their native country on account of that religion should be permitted to settle in any part of the Grison territory, upon subscribing the received Protestant confession, and giving such other securities

---

* Fueslin, Epist. Ref. p. 254   Gerdesii Italia Ref. p. 307.
† De Porta, i. 197, ii. 45.
‡ Ibid. p. 127.   Tiraboschi, vii. 1087.

as the laws required.* In consequence of this law, Mainardi was established as pastor of the flock which had already been gathered by his private instructions at Chiavenna; and to this congregation De Salis gave his chapel, called Santa Maria del Paterino, together with a house, garden, and salary, to the minister. It increased rapidly, and great care was afterwards taken to provide Chiavenna with able pastors.†

About the same time, Julio da Milano, after preaching with great success in Lower Engadina, founded a congregation at Puschiavo, which enjoyed his ministry for nearly thirty years, and continued long to be one of the most flourishing churches in the republic. He also laid the foundation of a number of churches in his neighbourhood.‡ About the time of his death, which happened soon after 1571, an able successor was provided for him by the opportune arrival of Cesare Gaffori, a native of Piacenza, who had been guardian of the Franciscans § The first printing-press in the Grisons was erected in the town of Puschiavo by Rodolfino Landolfo, the descendant of a noble family in that place, who expended a large sum on the undertaking. It contributed greatly to the illumination of the country, but was very annoying to the Roman Catholics; and, in 1561, the pope and king of Spain made a formal demand for its suppression as a nuisance, with which however the diet did not comply.‖

* De Porta, ii. 37, 38.

† Mainardi was succeeded by the celebrated Jeronimo Zanchi, who had Simone Florillo, a Neapolitan, for his colleague; after whom Scipione Lentulo of Naples, and Ottaviano Meio of Lucca, successively occupied this important post. (Zanchii Epist. lib. ii p. 376. De Porta, ii. 49—54.)

‡ Brusio, Ponteilla, Prada, Meschin, and Piuri or Plurs, were all in a short time provided with pastors from among the Italian refugees (Schelhorn, Dissert. de Mino Celso Senensi, p. 34 46. De Porta, tom. ii part ii. p. 179) The village of Plurs was overwhelmed, in the year 1618, by the falling of Mount Conto, on which occasion, all the inhabitants, to the number of more than two thousand, were buried in the ruins, with the exception of three individuals who happened at the time to be in the fields. (Ebel, Manuel du Voyageur en Suisse, tom. ii. p. 390, 391.)

§ De Porta, ii. 40, 41.   ‖ Ebel, tom. iv. p. 53.

The Church of Caspan was the first fruits of the Valteline, having as early as the year 1546, met for worship in a house provided by the Paravicini, one of the most ancient families in that country. It was, however, nearly ruined by the imprudence of an individual belonging to the family to which it owed its erection. A crucifix having been found broken in one of the churches, the clergy directed the suspicions of the inflamed populace against the Protestant minister, who, on being arraigned and put to the rack, was made to confess that he had committed the sacrilegious deed. On being liberated from confinement he repaired to Coire, and protesting that the extremity of the torture had wrung from him the confession of a crime in which he had no participation, demanded a fair trial. On examination it was found that the outrage on the crucifix had been committed by Bartolommeo Paravicino, a boy of thirteen, on the night before he set out for the university of Zurich. But though the innocence of the minister was cleared, so strong were the prejudices of the Roman catholics, that it was not judged prudent to permit him to return to Caspan, and the congregation was directed to choose another pastor in his room.* Teglio, the chief town of the most populous district in the Valteline, obtained for its pastor the pious and learned Paolo Gaddio, a native of the Ciemonese, who, after visiting Geneva, had acted as a temporary assistant to the venerable pastor of Puschiavo.† Sondrio, which was the seat of the government, enjoyed for some time the labours of Scipione Lentulo, a learned Neapolitan, who had devoted himself to the service of the Waldensian churches in the valleys of Lucerna and Angrogna, and been exposed to the severe persecution which they suffered, in 1560 and 1561, from Emanuel Philibert, duke of Savoy.‡ His talents and learning were

* De Porta, ii. 41—44.
† Fueslin, p 359. Zanchii Opera, tom. vii. p. 4.
‡ Leger has inserted an account of the deliverance of the Waldenses, in a letter from Lentulus to an illustrious person at Geneva. (Hist. des Eglises Vaudoises, tom ii. p. 34—36.)

of the greatest utility to the reformed cause during his residence at Sondrio, and afterwards at Chiavenna.* Churches were also erected in a number of other places in the Valteline;† and they spread subsequently into the county of Bormio.‡ Upon the whole, the number of Protestant churches to the south of the Alps appears to have exceeded twenty, which were all served, and continued till the end of the sixteenth century to be for the most part served, by exiles from Italy.

I have brought into one view what concerns the formation of Italian churches in this part of the country; but it was after considerable intervals, and amidst the most violent opposition, that permission was obtained to erect the greater part of them. No sooner did the priests perceive the success of the reformed doctrine at Chiavenna and Caspan, than they began to exclaim against the edict of 1544. Not being able, with any decency, to object to the first part of it, they directed their invectives against the liberty which it granted to the Italian exiles to settle among them, exclaiming that it was disgraceful to the republic of the Grisons to give entertainment to *banditti* (as they called them) whom other Christian princes and states had expelled from their dominions. The popular mind was still further inflamed by a crowd of monks who came from the Milanese, and especially by Capuchins sent by the bishop of Como, who, in the fanatical harangues which they delivered during the time of Lent, did all but exhort the people to rebel against their rulers. Failing in their applications to the diet for a repeal of the obnoxious edict, the opponents of the Reformation had recourse to the local government, to which, in the year 1551, they presented a petition, demanding that it should be declared, agreeably to the spirit of an ancient law, that no exile should be permitted to remain above three days in

---
* Gerdesii Ital. Ref. p 281—284. De Porta, ii. 335 495—500.
† Those of Tirano, Rovoledo, Mellio, Morbegno, and Dubino, are particularly mentioned.
‡ Coxe, iii. 102. De Porta, ii. 286, 287.

the Valteline. Anthony de Planta, the governor, was a Protestant; but dreading, from the irritated feelings of the populace, a massacre of the refugees, he gave his consent to the measure. In consequence of this, the preachers were obliged to conceal themselves for a time; and several distinguished individuals, both male and female, among whom were count Celso Martinengho and Isabella Manricha, prepared to remove into Switzerland.* The diet was highly offended at these illegal and disorderly proceedings, but contented itself with renewing, in 1552, its former edict, and charging the governor and vicar of the Valteline to see it strictly observed.

The firmness of the government repressed, without allaying, the hostility of those who had gained the command over the passions of the Roman catholics, which burst forth, on the slightest occasions, in acts of violence against the Protestant preachers. They felt a strong hatred and dread of Vergerio, and during a visit which he paid to the Valteline in 1553, a deputation waited on the governor and insisted on the instant banishment of the bishop; adding, that if their demand was not complied with, "they would not be answerable for the scandals which might ensue." Understanding the meaning of this threat, Vergerio agreed voluntarily to retire; "for," says he, "they meant to oppose me with the dagger, and pistol, and poison." One of the basest methods adopted by the monkish trumpeters of sedition, was to impress on the minds of their hearers that it was unlawful for true catholics to hold civil intercourse with heretics, or to live with them as masters and servants, husbands and wives; by which means they disturbed the peace and broke

* De Porta, ii. 50. Frederic de Salis writes, June 20, 1559, that Isabella Manricha (see before, p. 157) was still at Chiavenna, waiting for her household, and uncertain whether to remain in that place or to remove elsewhere. (Ibid p. 343, conf. p. 170.) Annibale Caro addressed a letter from Rome, April 27, 1548, to this lady, who was then at Naples. There are four letters by the same learned man to her son, George Manricha, from the last of which it appears that this young man was at Milan on the 18th of June 1562. (Lettere Famil del Commendatore Annibal Caro, tomo i. p. 269, 270. 293, ii. 16. 279, edit. 1572.)

up the harmony of some of the principal families in the country. A Dominican monk of Cremona, named Fra Angelo, declaiming from the pulpit at Teglio during the festival of Easter 1556, accused the rulers of the Grisons of listening to heretical teachers, and gave a formal challenge to any of the evangelical party, offering to prove from the Scriptures that those who refused the mass were diabolical heretics, and that their spouses were not legitimate wives, but worse than strumpets. On leaving the church the infuriated audience rushed to the Protestant place of worship, attacked Gaddio the pastor, and wounded several of his hearers who attempted to defend him. Instead of calling Angelo to account for instigating this tumult, the Grison government invited him to Coire to maintain the dispute which he had provoked; but although offered a safe conduct, he refused to make his appearance, and orders being afterwards issued to apprehend him, he made his escape into Italy. The procurator who appeared for those who had been active in the riot, did not deny that it was caused by the monks, and had the effrontery to declare, before the judges appointed to examine the affair, "that there would never be quietness in the republic until that religion of the devil (the Protestant) was exterminated." Yet so forbearing was the government, that it not only passed over the tumult with impunity, but sacrificing private interests, and in some degree the character of the innocent sufferers, to public peace, agreed that Gaddio should remove to another place, although his congregation earnestly petitioned for his being allowed to continue with them.*

This lenity was entirely thrown away on the enemies of the Protestants, both within and without the republic. At the very time that the government was labouring to allay animosities, two brothers, Francesco and Allessandro Bellinchetti, were seized in Italy. They were natives of Bergamo, who, on embracing the reformed religion, had retired into the Grisons and

* De Porta, ii. 147—149, 264—272.

settled in the village of Bergun, at the foot of mount Albula, where they wrought an iron mine. Having paid a visit to their native place, they were thrown into the inquisition, and proceeded against on a charge of heresy. On hearing of this, the authorities of the Grisons immediately sent an ambassador to demand their liberation as citizens of the republic; and being referred, by the magistrates of Bergamo and the senate of Venice, to the inquisitors, they wrote to the prior of the Dominican monastery at Morbegno, in the Valteline, to use his influence with his brethren to obtain the release of the prisoners; but he paid no regard to the application. Upon this the diet met and came to a peremptory resolution, that if the two brothers were not released within the space of a month, all the Dominicans within the territories of the Three leagues should be banished, and the property of the monastery of Morbegno, movable and immovable, forfeited and applied to the relief of the poor and other pious uses. An extract of this deed having been sent to the prior, the prisoners were immediately set at liberty.*

In the meantime, the foreign monks who had invaded the Valteline, confiding in the support of their governments, became every day bolder in their invectives and in plotting against the public peace. Through their influence, persons of the first respectability for birth, probity, and talents, were not only excluded from civil offices, but denied the rites of sepulture, prevented from building places of worship, and exposed to every species of insult. Seeing no end to this illegal and degrading oppression, they at last resolved on laying their grievances formally before the government. Aware of the justice of their complaints, impressed with the equity of extending to the subject-states that religious liberty which had been found so advantageous to the governing country. perceiving that the threats of strangers were heard above the voice of the law in their southern dominions, and convinced that it was high time to adopt

* De Porta, ii. 272, 273.

decisive measures unless they chose to allow their authority to sink into absolute contempt, the diet, which met at Ilantz in the beginning of the year 1557, unanimously adopted the following decree, which, being ratified by the several communities, was enrolled among the fundamental and standing laws of the republic. It was declared, that it should be lawful to preach the sacred word of God and the gospel of our Lord Jesus Christ in all places belonging to the Valteline, and to the counties of Chiavenna, Bormio, and Teglio: that in those villages in which there were a plurality of churches, the Roman catholics should have their choice of one, and the other should be given to the Protestants: that in any village in which there was only one church, the Roman catholics should have the privilege of using it in the former part of the day, and the Protestants in the latter: that each party should be allowed to perform all the parts of their worship, and to bury their dead, without oppositon from the other: that the professors of the Protestant faith should enjoy all honours and be admissible to all offices equally with their fellow-subjects: that no foreign monk or presbyter, of whatever religious persuasion, should be admitted to reside within these territories, unless he had been previously examined and approved by the ordinary authorities in the church to which he belonged—the ministers by the Protestant synod in the Three leagues, and the priests by the bishop and chapter of Coire; and that none should be admitted unless he declared his intention to reside at least for a year, and gave security for his good behaviour. In the course of the same year an act was passed, freeing the Protestants from penalties for not observing the popish holidays; and, in the following year two statutes were enacted, one for extending to the subject-provinces the law which prevented the admission of new members into monasteries, and the other making stated provision for the pastors of the Protestant churches. The former was not executed. In pursuance of the latter, a third part of the ecclesiastic rents of Chiavenna was allotted to the minister of the reformed church in that village, which, by this time, included the half of the population. To the pastors in other places forty crowns a year were assigned, to be taken, in the first instance, from the benefices of absentees and pluralists; and, failing these, from the revenues which the bishop of Coire drew from the Valteline, from the funds of the abbacy of Abundio; or, as the last resource, from the common funds of each parish.*

This was the only legislative enactment by which positive encouragement was given to the Reformed religion in the Valteline; but the Protestant ministers derived little from it except envy, the clergy contriving, by concealment, litigation, and violence, to retain nearly the whole of the funds. It was granted, in consequence of a representation from the Protestants, who pleaded that, though the minority in point of numbers, they contributed the largest proportion to the funds of the clergy, many of whom performed no duty, and the rest confined themselves chiefly to the saying of mass. As is usual on such occasions, those of the laity who contributed next to nothing were loudest in exclaiming, "that they were taxed for upholding an heretical religion;" while the clergy called upon "the Italian deserters of monasteries" to imitate the example of the apostle Paul, who laboured with his hands that he might not be burdensome to the churches, and of the Egyptian anchorites, with Peter the hermit at their head; and insisted that they could not be the followers of Christ and his apostles, inasmuch as they did not work miracles nor live on alms.† It may be proper to mention here another act, though passed at a later period, which gave great offence to the Roman catholics. The diet of the Grison republic agreed to erect a college at Sondrio, in the Valteline.‡ It did not partake of the nature of a theological seminary, but was confined to the teaching

---

* De Porta, ii. 273—276, 283—287.
† De Porta, ii. 287, 289, 560, 561.
‡ Though not erected till 1584, this college was planned so early as 1563. (Zanchii Epist. lib. ii. p. 376.)

of languages and philosophy. The children of papists and Protestants were equally admissible to it, and provision was made for teachers of both persuasions. But notwithstanding the liberal principles on which it was founded, the clergy cried out against it as a Lutheran seminary; formal representations were made against it by the popish cantons of Switzerland and by the court of Milan; and the republic was obliged to send back the principal, a learned and moderate man, whom they had brought from Zurich, and to remove the institution, after it had subsisted for only one year, to the city of Coire.*

The Italian exiles were elated by the laws passed in their favour, and looked forward with sanguine hopes to the speedy triumph of the Reformed cause in the Valteline; but their ultramontane brethren, who were better acquainted with the genius of the inhabitants, and more indifferent judges of the opposition which might be expected from foreign powers, repressed their fervour, and wisely urged upon them the propriety of trusting for success to the gradual illumination of the people, rather than to legislative decrees, which required external force to carry them into execution.† The court of Rome had been, from the beginning, highly displeased at the reception given to the Italian exiles in the Grisons; but its displeasure was converted into a mingled feeling of indignation and alarm, when it saw the standard of evangelical truth planted in one of the suburbs of Italy, from which, if not speedily dislodged, it might be carried into the interior, and, in process of time, might insult the head of the church in his capital. The extirpation of the colony was resolved on; and, to accomplish it, the popes exerted themselves in securing the co-operation of the neighbouring catholic powers, especially the Spanish monarch, who had lately ob-

---

* De Porta, tom. ii. part ii. 32, 37, 48, 53, 57, 58, 332. The erection of a similar seminary in 1614, but on a smaller scale, and without deriving any support from the funds of the Valteline, excited equal hostility, and was made one pretext for the rebellion which followed soon after (Ibid p. 252—254, 322.)

† De Porta, ii. 280, 281.

tained the sovereignty of Milan. It is difficult to say whether ambition or bigotry had the ascendant in the character of Philip II., but both principles led him to embark in this scheme with the utmost cordiality. The Valteline bordered on the Milanese, and had formerly belonged to that duchy. Philip, as well as the dukes who preceded him, had ratified the cession of it to the republic of the Grisons, but that did not prevent him from cherishing the idea of recovering a territory which was the key to the communication between Milan and Germany, and the command of which would enable him at all times with safety to convey troops from Austria to his dominions in the north of Italy. For interfering with the affairs of the Valteline, he found a pretext in the plea, that it was necessary to prevent heresy from spreading in the Milanese, which had already been to no inconsiderable extent tainted by that pestilential malady.

In the year 1559 the government of Milan erected forts on the confines of the Valteline. Under the cover of these the inquisitors entered the country, and as they durst not seize the persons of the inhabitants, collected a large quantity of heretical books, which they burnt with great solemnity. They were followed by a swarm of foreign monks, who, trusting to the garrisons as places of retreat, despised the edict which prohibited them from entering the country, and went about inflaming the minds of the people against the Protestant preachers, and even the local rulers by whom they were protected.* A college of Jesuits was established at Ponte, and maintained itself in spite of repeated orders issued by the diet for its removal.† These strangers kept up a regular correspondence with the heads of their respective orders at Como, Milan, Rome, and other places in Italy, the effects of which soon became apparent. It has been already mentioned that Pius IV., who filled the papal throne between 1559 and 1566, had been a priest in the Valteline; a circumstance which at once disposed

* De Porta, ii. p. 297—299.
† Ibid, p 302—304.

him to take a deep interest in the affairs of that country, and made his interposition the more effective. In 1561 his legate Bianchi, provost of Santa Maria della Scala at Milan, appeared at Coire. Supported by the presence and influence of Ritzio, the Milanese ambassador, the legate made a formal demand on the diet, in the name of his holiness, that they should banish the Italian exiles from the Valteline and Chiavenna, allow free ingress and egress to foreign monks, make no opposition to the Jesuit college at Ponte, prevent the issuing of books derogatory to the church of Rome from the press at Puschiavo, and, in general, overturn all that they had done in relation to religion in that part of their dominions.* But the influence of Pius, who had not left behind him the odour of sanctity in the Grisons, was small compared with that of his nephew, the celebrated cardinal Borromeo, archbishop of Milan. Though this prelate owed his canonization more to his zeal for Catholicism than to his piety, yet his talents and the decorum of his private character rendered him by far the most formidable adversary who had yet appeared against the Protestant interest. It was the great object of his ambition, from an early period of life, to oppose an effectual barrier to the progress of heresy, and to repair and prop the fabric of Popery which he saw tottering on its base. With this view he applied himself to the removal of abuses in Italy; introduced reforms into the morals of the clergy, particularly of the monastic orders; and erected seminaries in which young persons might obtain such an education as should qualify them for entering the lists with the Protestants, and fighting them with their own weapons. Hitherto those who had appeared as the champions of the Church of Rome, though often not destitute in talents, were almost always deficient in learning, and could do little more than ring changes, and that for the most part rudely, on the popular prejudices against innovation and in favour of the Catholic Church. But men of learning now came forward who could "make

* De Porta, ii. 364—371.

the worse appear the better reason"—who, if they did not convince by the solidity of their arguments, entangled the minds of their readers by their subtlety or dazzled them by the splendour of their eloquence, and contrived artfully to withdraw attention from the real image of the Church as she existed, to one which was the pure creation of their own fancy. All the celebrated champions of the Catholic faith, from Bellarmine to Bossuet, proceeded from the school of Borromeo. It would have been well if the cardinal had confined himself to methods of this kind; but, besides abetting the most violent measures for suppressing the reformed opinions within his own diocese, he industriously fomented dissensions in foreign countries, leagued with men who were capable of the most desperate attempts, and busied himself in providing arms for subjects who were ready to rebel against their lawful rulers, and to shed the blood of their peaceable fellow-citizens.*

It is only a general account which I can here give of the course pursued for disturbing the peace of the Grisons, and expelling the refugees from the settlement which they had obtained in the Valteline. The goods belonging to citizens of the republic who traded with the Milanese were seized by the inquisitors, and applications for restitution and redress were almost in every instance refused or evaded. Merchants who visited that country were apprehended on a charge of heresy, detained in prison, forced to purchase their liberty with large sums of money, or condemned to different kinds of punishment. Borromeo was not afraid to incarcerate the chief magistrate of the jurisdiction of Mayenfeld.† At last a new species of outrage, unheard of among civilized nations, was resorted to. Bands of armed men haunted the roads of the Valteline, seized the Protestants unawares, and car-

* The most serious of these charges is supported by the cardinal's letter of the 24th May, 1584, to the nuncio Spezzani, published by Quadrio, the Catholic h.storian of the Valteline, and reprinted by De Porta (Tom. ii part. ii. p. 33—35; conf. part. i. p. 454, 482.)

† De Porta, ii. 455. 461. 482.

ried them into Italy. Francesco Cellario, the Protestant minister at Morbegno, was returning in 1568 from a meeting of the synod held at Zutz in Upper Engadina. He had scarcely left the town of Chiavenna, when some villains rushed from a thicket on the margin of the lake Lario, forced him into a boat which they had ready, and carrying him first to Como and afterwards to Milan, delivered him to the Inquisition. Ambassadors were sent to demand the prisoner, but they found that he had been conveyed to Rome, and were told by the duke de Terranova, the governor, that his abduction was the work of the inquisitors, over whom he had no control.* After being detained nearly a year in prison, Cellario was tried by the Inquisition at Rome, and committed to the flames on the 20th of May, 1569.† The practice of man-stealing now became a constant traffic in the Valteline; and at every meeting of the diet, for a course of years, complaints were made that some persons had been carried off, including not only exiles from Italy, but native citizens of the Grison republic.‡ The investigations into these acts of violence implicated, in most instances, the monks of Morbegno, who were in the habit of regularly giving such information to the inquisitors as enabled them to seize their prey.§ Nor did they confine themselves to this service. After the abduction of Cellario, Ulixio Martinengho, count

* Gabutius, in his Life of Pius IV., gives the duke's answer in these words —"That the pope has an absolute and lawful power over all parts of the world to seize, as often as he pleases, and inflict merited punishment on heretics." (Laderchii Annal tom xxxiii. 6, 198.)

† Laderchius, ut supra. De Porta, ii. 464—476 The first of these writers gives, from the records of the Inquisition, the sentence condemning Cellario to be burnt alive. Gabutius says he recanted when he came in sight of the fire. De Porta, on the contrary, states that a native of the Grisons, who was in Rome and witnessed the execution, deposed that the martyr, on being taken from the fiery stake, refused to confess, and was again thrown into the flames. Cellario had been a Minorite monk of the order *De Observantia*, and was twice imprisoned at Pavia. The first time, he was released on making some acknowledgments, the second time, he broke his chains and made his escape to the Grisons in the year 1558

‡ De Porta, ii 477, 478. 480. 482; part. ii. 7—9. 50. 88. 95.

§ Ibid. ii. 455. 457. 465. 483.

de Barcho, a learned and pious nobleman who had resided for a number of years in the Valteline, officiated in his room until the admission of Scipione Calandrino, a native of Lucca, whom the congregation had chosen for their pastor. The monks, who had looked forward to the dispersion of that flock, were greatly irritated at their disappointment; and two of them entering one day the church at Mellio, fired a pistol at Calandrino, while he was in the act of preaching. An old man observed them levelling the piece, and gave warning to Calandrino, who evaded the shot; upon which the ruffians stabbed the old man mortally, rushed forward to the pulpit, and having wounded the preacher, made their escape, amidst the confusion into which the congregation was thrown by this unexpected and disgraceful assault.*

The most humiliating circumstance in the whole of this affair is the timidity and irresolution with which the Grison government acted. They sent ambassadors, they craved redress, they ordered investigations, and, on making discoveries, they passed threatening votes; but they took no step becoming the character of a free people in defence of their violated independence and insulted honour. Their neighbours showed them an example worthy of their imitation. Cardinal Borromeo, in one of his archiepiscopal visitations, entered the territories of Switzerland. The Swiss government, not relishing the visit, despatched an envoy to request the governor of the Milanese to recall him. No sooner had the envoy arrived at Milan, than he was seized by the inquisitor and thrown into prison; but the governor, as soon as he learnt the fact, ordered his release, and treated him with marks of great respect. On being informed of what had happened, the Swiss authorities sent a message to the governor, signifying that if the same post which brought the news of the imprisonment of their envoy had not acquainted them with his enlargement, they would instantly have seized the cardinal and detained him as a hostage; upon hearing which, his eminence

* De Porta, ii. 483, 484.

retired from the Swiss territories with less ceremony
than he had entered them.* If the authorities of the
Grisons had acted in this manner—if they had, as
they were advised, confiscated the property belonging
to the inhabitants of Milan and Como, and retained
it until their own merchants were indemnified for the
losses which they had sustained—and, above all, if
they had issued peremptory orders to level the monastery of Morbegno with the ground, as a watch-tower
of spies and a den of thieves—the boldness of the
measure, supported by its justice, while it gave courage to the loyal and checked the disaffected among
their own subjects, would have secured the respect
and forbearance of foreign powers. But the counsels
of the republic were distracted by dissensions, and
its arm palsied by corruption. The Grey league,
which was composed chiefly of Roman Catholics,
refused its consent to any vigorous measure. Spanish
gold had found its way into the other leagues; and a
Protestant ambassador returned from Milan, bearing
the insignia of an order of knighthood conferred on
him by a papal brief, instead of bringing the prisoner
whose liberty he was sent to demand. France, on
whose aid the party opposed to Spain placed its
chief dependence, had fallen under the rule of the
house of Guise, which was secretly engaged in the
league for the extirpation of Protestantism; and the
report of the massacre of St. Bartholomew, while it
blew up the hopes entertained from the north, gave
dreadful note of a similar explosion from the south,
which was soon to shake the Grisons to its centre.
The proper season of applying the remedy being
neglected, the evil became inveterate, and all attempts
to cure it served only to inflame and exasperate.
Provoked by persevering injuries, alarmed by repeated conspiracies, and betrayed without being able
to discover or convict the traitors, the authorities had
recourse to violent measures; and courts of justice,
composed chiefly of Protestants, were erected, by
which arbitrary and heavy punishments were inflicted,

* Fra Paolo, Discorso dell' Inquisitione di Venetia, p. 47.

and individuals were condemned on slight or suspicious evidence. These severities were artfully heightened by the representations of foreign agents, and ministered fresh fuel to the existing disaffection. The joint influence of these causes led to the catastrophe of 1620, of which no person acquainted with the general history of Europe is ignorant—the indiscriminate and barbarous massacre of the Protestants in the Valteline, the revolt of all the southern dependencies of the republic, and the temporary subjugation of the Grisons by the combined arms of Austria and Spain. Writers professing to have formed an impartial judgment,* impute these disastrous events, in a great measure, to the impolitic zeal with which the government attempted to introduce the Reformation into the Valteline. There can be no question, that if the Reformation had not been admitted into the Grisons, the republic would not have been exposed to that hostility which they actually encountered from neighbouring powers. But ought they on that ground to have prevented its reception? And having allowed it in the governing country, would they have been warranted in prohibiting it within the subject states? Or, are they greatly to be blamed for having given encouragement to those who were their best subjects, and on whom they could rely for an entire and undivided allegiance? If the subject be impartially considered, it will be found, I apprehend, that the radical and main cause of the disturbances was the retaining of the southern provinces in a state of vassalage, together with the oppression and peculation to which this led on the part of those to whom the administration of their affairs was committed—evils which are almost inseparable from the government of colonies and dependent provinces, whether they belong to monarchies or republics. Had the Valteline and the adjoining districts been received at first into the confederation as a fourth league, and admitted to all its privileges, the inhabitants would

* Coxe's Travels in Switzerland, vol. iii. p. 96.

have turned a deaf ear to the insidious proposals made to them from Milan and Inspruck, and the obstacles to the Reformation would not have been greater in the Cisalpine than they were in the Transalpine departments of the republic.

Before leaving the Grisons, it will be proper to give some account of the internal dissensions which prevailed among the Italian exiles. Though the greater part of them were distinguished for their learning, zeal, and piety, and, by their services, amply repaid the kindness of the country which afforded them an asylum, it was soon found that others cherished in their breasts a variety of subtle and dangerous opinions, which they at first insinuated in private, and afterwards taught and maintained with such factious pertinacity as to bring scandal on the whole body of the exiles, and to give great offence and uneasiness to those who had been most active in procuring them a hospitable reception. It is impossible to give such an account of the opinions of this party as will apply to all the individuals who composed it. While they agreed in refusing their assent to the received creed, some of them cavilled at one of its articles and others at another. The leaders cautiously abstained from disclosing their system, and contented themselves with imparting privately to the initiated such of their views as they knew to be most offensive and startling to the minds of serious Christians. The more forward, who were usually the most unlearned, advanced crude and contradictory notions; and, their minds being unhinged and tossed to and fro with every wind of doctrine, they veered suddenly to opposite extremes, so that it was not uncommon to find individuals maintaining one day that God was the author of sinful actions, and that holiness had no connection with salvation, and the next day inveighing against the doctrine of predestination as leading to these odious consequences. In general, however, they were disciples of Servetus, whose creed was a compound of anabaptism and antitrinitarianism, and had, as we have seen, been embraced by a number of the Protestants in Italy.*

Francesco, a Calabrian, and Jeronimo, a Mantuan, were the first who excited a noise by venting these opinions. They had not been long settled as pastors in the district of Engadina, when the report arose that they were inculcating that infants ought not to be baptized; that God is the author of sinful actions; that the body, flesh, or death of Christ, can be of no avail for the salvation of men; and that the souls of the just sleep till the resurrection. The church of Lavin dismissed Jeronimo as soon as they ascertained his sentiments; but the Calabrian, by his address and eloquence, had so fascinated his flock at Vettan, that they clung to him and regarded all his sayings as oracular. This encouraged him to persevere in the course which he had begun, and to despise the admonitions of his brethren. Loud complaints being made that his doctrine was corrupting the morals of the people, a public disputation, according to the mode of those times, was held, in the year 1544, at Zutz, which was attended by Roman catholic priests as well as Protestant ministers. Francesco, having appeared before this assembly, was convicted of the chief errors imputed to him, and was afterwards expelled the country.†

But it was in the Italian churches erected on the south of the Alps that these opinions were most industriously propagated and excited the greatest disturbances. The author and chief fomenter of these was Camillo Renato, a man of considerable acuteness and learning, but addicted to novelties, captious yet cool, opinionative yet artful and insinuating. As long as he remained at Caspan he had little opportunity of making disciples, though he tainted the mind of Paravicino, in whose house he lived as tutor. But on his coming to Chiavenna, where the Protestants were numerous, he found a more extensive field for propagating his peculiar notions. Mainardi, the minister

* See before, p. 149—156.
† Bock, Hist. Antitrin. tom. ii. p. 410. De Porta, ii. 67—75.

of the Protestant church in that town, perceiving that the minds of some of his flock were corrupted and others scandalized by the opinions which were secretly sown among them, remonstrated with Camillo on his conduct, and endeavoured, by friendly conferences, to effect a change on his views, or, at least to prevail on him to retain them within his own breast. Failing to accomplish this, he first gave warning to his people from the pulpit of the danger to which they were exposed, and afterwards drew up, in the name of his congregation, a confession of faith, in which, without mentioning the name of Camillo, he explicitly condemned his errors. Upon this Camillo and his followers withdrew from the ministry of Mainardi, and began to meet by themselves.

The following are the opinions which are said to have been held by Camillo:—That the soul dies with the body, or sleeps until the resurrection; that the same body substantially shall not be raised at the last day; that there shall be no resurrection of the wicked; that man was created mortal, and would have died though he had not sinned; that there is no natural law by which men can know what to do or avoid; that unregenerate men are irrational creatures like the brutes; that the decalogue is useless to believers, who have no law but the Spirit; that the Scripture says nothing of the merit of Christ; that the Saviour had concupiscence residing in him, was capable of sinning though he did not actually sin, and is said to have been made a curse because he was conceived in original sin, and not because he offered a sacrifice for sin or suffered the death of the cross for sinners; that justifying faith has no need of being confirmed by sacraments; that there is no resemblance between baptism and circumcision; and that baptism and the Lord's supper are merely signs of what is past, do not seal any blessing, and have no promise annexed to them.* It is not difficult to perceive in these propo-

* Mainardi's Confession, which contained these articles, is lost; but Pietro Leonis, a disciple of Camillo, inserted them in a book which he published at Milan, from which they were extracted by De

sitions the elements which were afterwards formed into a system by Faustus Socinus. It is true, Camillo did not profess his disbelief of the doctrine of the trinity, but some of his disciples who enjoyed a large share of his confidence made no scruple of openly disavowing it. He was also wary as to what he advanced on the immortality of the soul, and, when pushed on that point by his opponents, was wont to reply—" Camillo is ignorant whether the soul be immortal or not; he does not affirm that the soul dies with the body, he only says so for the sake of dispute."

Irritated at the detection of his scheme before he had time to mature and propagate it, Camillo complained loudly of the conduct of Mainardi. He drew up several writings, in which, confining himself to the subject of the sacraments, he endeavoured to hold up his opponent as at once ignorant and intolerant, and the true cause of all the discord which had arisen. In this he was encouraged by Stancari and Negri. The former, who, at a subsequent period, excited great contentions in Poland and in Germany, fomented the schism in the congregation of Chiavenna, although in his sentiments respecting the sacraments he went to the opposite extreme from Camillo. Negri, a good but weak man, vacillated between the views of Camillo and Stancari, and lent his aid to the faction.*
The consequence of all this was, that Mainardi incurred the censures of some of his countrymen who occasionally visited the place, such as Vergerio and Altieri; and received letters from the Grisons and Switzerland admonishing him to conduct himself with greater moderation. Knowing that he had good grounds for all which he had done, and that the prejudices raised against him would give way as soon as

Porta. (II. 83—86.) That Camillo carried his scepticism into philosophy as well as divinity, appears from the following article.— " Quod memoria rei alicujus non fiat, ut is qui illam facit, rei vel facti certior fiat"

* Museum Helveticum, tom. xix. p 481—487; where extracts are given from the letters of Altieri and other distinguished persons at Venice, describing the turbulent temper of Stancari.

the cause came to be investigated, Mainardi did not relax in his vigilance. "The favourers of Camillo," says he in a letter to Bullinger, "tear my sermons in pieces. If I hold my peace, the truth is exposed to imminent danger; if I speak, I am a morose old man, and intolerant. Write to Blasio and Comander not to listen to the statements of one party, but to come and examine the matter before the whole congregation. I purposed to retire into England, but providence has kept me from deserting this little flock. Yet I wish they could obtain a better pastor and one of greater fortitude than I." From the time that he came to the Valteline, Camillo had kept up a correspondence with Bullinger by letters, in which he endeavoured to ingratiate himself with him by professing his agreement with the church of Zurich; but when his opponent offered to submit the controversy between them to the judgment of that venerable divine, he declined the proposal. The Grison synod, which met in 1547, called the parties before them, but Camillo neither attended nor sent a letter of excuse, upon which they enjoined him to desist from opposing his minister and disturbing the peace of the church. As he disregarded this injunction, and continued his former practices, a deputation, consisting of four of the principal ministers in the Grisons, was sent to Chiavenna in the close of the year 1549, to inquire into the affair, and put an end to a dissension which now began to make a great noise, and caused no small scandal both among Roman Catholics and Protestants.* The deputation found all the charges brought against Camillo proved, and declared that Mainardi had acted the part of a faithful and vigilant

* On this occasion, a correspondence of a rather singular kind took place. The Protestant deputies, on their arrival, addressed a letter to the Roman Catholic chapter of Chiavenna, intimating the design on which they had come, and inviting them to meet with them, and "confer on those common articles of Christianity about which they were both agreed." The chapter returned a polite answer, but declined the meeting, "because there was a great gulf between them;" adding a number of exhortations to unity and against divisions, the drift of which it was not difficult to perceive.

minister; but, without censuring the former, they, with the view of restoring harmony, drew up certain articles upon the subjects which had been controverted, to which they required both parties to agree. But although Camillo subscribed this agreement, the deputies had scarcely left the place when he resumed his former practices; in consequence of which, the consistory of Chiavenna, agreeably to the advice which had been given them, suspended him from church privileges, and, on his proving contumacious, publicly pronounced the sentence of excommunication against him.* After this we hear little of Camillo.† I have been the more particular in my account of him, because there is every reason to think he had great influence in forming the opinions of Lelius Socinus. By their contemporaries, the former is usually spoken of as the master and the latter as the disciple. It is certain that Socinus had interviews with Camillo at Chiavenna; and the resemblance between their opinions and the cautious and artful manner in which they uttered them, is very striking.‡

Finding themselves baffled in their attempts to propagate their peculiar tenets, the innovators had recourse to a device which had nearly proved successful. They got Celso Martinengho, Vergerio, and some other respectable persons, to subscribe a petition for liberty to the Italian ministers to hold a synod of their own, distinct from that which met in the Grisons. In support of this proposal, they pleaded the difficulty of the journey across the Alps, the difference of languages, and certain rites practised in the Grisons which the Italians disliked, and which other reformed churches had laid aside.§ But the measure

* Hottinger, Helvetische Kirchengeschichte, tom. iii. 762, 791: De Porta, tom. ii cap. 4.
† That he was alive and in Chiavenna or the neighbourhood of it in 1555, appears from a letter of Julio da Milano to Bullinger, in which he speaks of him as requiring still to be narrowly watched. (Fueslin, p. 357.)
‡ Illgen, Vita Lælii Socini, p. 17, 44. Bock, ii. 581, 582. Hottinger, iii. 791. Fueslin, p 356.
§ These rites were the use of unleavened bread in the eucharist, the pronouncing of the angelical salutation (commonly called *Salve*

was quashed by the wiser part, who saw that the preservation of the Italian churches, both from the arts of internal agitators and from the attacks of their popish adversaries, depended on their maintaining their union with the churches of the Grisons inviolate.* "Our churches in the Valteline," says Julio da Milano, "which are planted at Puschiavo, Tirano, Teglio, and Sondrio, continue harmonious in their adherence to the ancient and simple doctrine transmitted from the times of the apostles, and at this day taught without controversy in your churches of Switzerland and ours of the Grisons."†

The noted antitrinitarians, Alciati and Blandrata, stirred the ashes of the late controversy, during a visit which they paid to the Grisons in 1553, on their way from Italy to Switzerland. After this, Michael Angelo Florio, minister of Soglio, and Jeronimo Turriano of Plurs, began to undermine the faith of their hearers in the doctrine of the atonement, by ascribing salvation solely to the grace of God; while the divinity of Christ was directly attacked by others, particularly by Ludovico Fieri, a Bolognese and a member of the church of Chiavenna. In 1561, the synod summoned these persons before them, and drew up certain articles condemnatory of their opinions, which Florio and Turriano subscribed; but Fieri, avowing his sentiments, was excommunicated, and retired to Moravia.‡ There were, however, still individuals secretly attached to antitrinitarianism, who continued to correspond with

Regina) after the Lord's Prayer, and the admitting of godfathers in baptism. In this last character Roman Catholics were sometimes admitted; and Paul Iter, the popish bishop of Coire, occasionally presented the child for baptism to Comander. The ministers of the Grisons were not rigidly attached to any of these rites, and they disapproved of the last mentioned practice, though they scrupled to prohibit it, (especially after the violence manifested by the priests of the Valteline,) lest it should interrupt the friendly intercourse which subsisted between popish and Protestant families. The Italians exclaimed against every thing of this kind as symbolizing with antichrist. (De Porta, ii 66, 226.)

* Bock, ii. 466.
† Epistola ad Bullingerum, a. 1555: Fueslin, Epist. Helvet. n. 81.
‡ De Porta, ii. 397. 497.

their friends in other countries; and, in 1570, the controversy was revived in consequence of the arrival of some distinguished persons belonging to the sect, who found it dangerous to remain any longer in Switzerland. Among these were Camillo Soccini, the brother of Lelius Socinus, Marcello Squarcialupo, a physician of Piombino, and Niccolo Camulio, an opulent merchant, who liberally patronized persons of this persuasion.* Their presence encouraged Turriano to resume his former course, in which he was joined by Sylvio,† the minister of Trahona, and some other individuals. But the proceedings of the synod which met at Coire in the year 1571 induced the visitors to withdraw from the Grisons. Turriano and the other ministers were deposed, but subsequently restored to their churches on making acknowledgments for their offensive behaviour.‡ Alciati and Blandrata visited the Grisons a second time in the beginning of 1579, but were ordered by the magistrates instantly to depart, after which the country does not appear to have been disturbed with these controversies.§ When we consider that the Italians were strangers, that they had obtained an asylum on condition of their joining themselves to the Protestant church already settled in the country and submitting to its discipline, and that the republic was subjected to great odium on account of the harbour and protection which it afforded them, we will be cautious in condemning the magistrates for expelling individuals who fomented discord and endangered the existence of the whole colony, by propagating sentiments equally shocking to the ears of papists and Protestants. Expulsion was the highest punishment which they inflicted; and in one instance in which they threatened to proceed further against an individual, named Titiano, who had provoked them, the ministers interposed and prevailed on them to desist

* Schelhorn, Diss. de Mino Celso, p. 35. Bock, ii. 483, 554, 576; conf. i. 907—910. De Porta, ii. 508, 543, 544.
† Bartolommeo Sylvio was the author of a tract on the Eucharist, printed in 1551.
‡ De Mino Celso, p. 35—37, De Porta, ii. 497—502, 543, 555.
§ Ibid. ii. 632.

from their intention.* I cannot, however, speak so favourably of the sentiments entertained by many of the ministers respecting the punishment of heretics. This question was keenly agitated after the execution of Servetus at Geneva. Gantner, one of the ministers of Coire, maintained that heresy ought not to be punished by the civil magistrate, and was warmly opposed by Eglin, his colleague. The question was brought under the consideration of the Synod in 1571, which decided in favour of Eglin. It is true, the proposition adopted by the synod refers to seditious heretics; but several of the arguments on which it appears to have been grounded, and by which it was afterwards defended, would (if they have any force) justify the punishment, and even the capital punishment, of persons who are chargeable with simple heresy, and consequently must have tended to betray those who held them into measures of persecution.†

Though it appears, from what has been stated, that a number of the Italian exiles were tainted with Arianism, yet several individuals among them have been suspected of this without the slightest reason. Even Zanchi, who succeeded Mainardi,‡ has not escaped the suspicion with some writers,§ although he was the person selected by his brethren as most fit for opposing this heresy, a task which he performed

* De Porta, ii. p. 76.

† Ibid. ii. 533—540. Diss. de Mino Celso, p. 37—44. J Jac. Simler, Samlung alter und neuer Urkunden zur Beleuchtung der Kirchengeschichte, tom ii. p. 805.

‡ Mainardi died in the end of July 1563, in the eighty-first year of his age. (Zanchii Opera, tom. vii. p. 35.) He was the author of the following works:—(1.) Trattato dell' unica et perfetta sattisfattione di Christo, a. 1551. (2.) Uno pio et utile Sermone della Gratia di Dio contra li meriti humani, a. 1552. (3.) L'Anatomia della Messa. The question concerning the real author of this last work, which Bayle has discussed at great length, but unsatisfactorily, (Dict. art. Vergerio,) had been previously settled by Zanchi. (Ut supra.)— I may add here, that Alessandro Trissino, a native of Vicenza, wrote a long letter to count Leonardo Tiene, exhorting him and his fellow-citizens to embrace the reformed opinions. It was dated from Chiavenna, July 20, 1570, and printed two years after. (Tiraboschi, vii. 383.)

§ Bock, ii. 426, 563.

with distinguished ability. His assertion that he was
"neither Lutheran, Zuinglian, nor Calvinian, but a
Christian," is what every person may adopt whose
faith is founded on the word of God, and not on the
wisdom and authority of men. The suspicions against
Celso Martinengho and Vergerio* appear to have
originated entirely in their having at first taken part
with Camillo against Mainardi, before they discovered
the real sentiments of the former. Martinengho afterwards enjoyed the confidence of Calvin during all
the time that he was pastor of the Italian church at
Geneva. Vergerio declared himself openly against
the anabaptists, and gave early warning of the defection of his countrymen, Socinus and Gribaldi, to the
opinions of Servetus.† The fate of this distinguished
man was in some respects hard. He forfeited the
high character which he had held in the church of
Rome,‡ without gaining the confidence of the Protestants. By wavering between the sentiments of the
Lutherans and Zuinglians, he incurred the displeasure
of both. He excited the jealousy of the ministers in
the Grisons by affecting a species of episcopal authority as superintendent or visitor of the Italian churches;
and they complained that he had not laid aside the
mitre, nor forgotten the arts which he had learned in
courts.§ It is not improbable that, in addition to the
finesse which has been supposed to enter into the
Italian character, Vergerio had acquired, from his employments, the habit of using policy to accomplish his
ends, and that he felt some difficulty in reconciling
himself to the simple life of a Protestant pastor after
the splendour and opulence to which he had been accustomed. But if he had not been sincerely attached
to the Reformation, he would have listened to the
proposals made to him by the court of Rome, which,
though it would have preferred seizing his person,
was not unwilling to purchase his faith. Though his

* Bock. ii. 410, 551—553. De Porta, ii. 63, 154—156.
† De Porta, ii. 158, 159.
‡ Bembo, Lettere, tomo iii. p 389.
§ De Porta, ii. 154, 160—166.

writings were not profound and his conduct was marked with versatility, Protestants might have treated with a little more tenderness the memory of a man whose name lent at least a temporary credit to their cause, and who gave the rare example of sacrificing worldly honours and affluence to religious principle. He died on the 4th of October 1565, at Tubingen, in the duchy of Wirtemburg, where he had resided since the year 1553, although he repeatedly visited the Grisons during that interval.*

Ludovico Castelvetro, of whom we have already spoken, was among the learned men who found a refuge from persecution in the Grisons. After his flight from Rome,† he concealed himself in Ferrara; but, hearing that the officers of the inquisition were in eager search for him, left his native country, and retired to Chiavenna, where he found his old friend Franciscus Portus. The removal of Portus, who was called to Geneva, gave him an opportunity of being useful in teaching the Greek language, which served to relieve the languor of his exile. Application was made in his behalf to the council of Trent, but the fathers would not interfere in a cause which was already before the tribunal of the inquisition. Through the interest of his friend Foscarari, bishop of Modena, hopes were given him of a favourable issue to his process, provided he would return to Italy; but he declined this, as well as the proposal made by the nuncio Delfino, who was sent into Switzerland to treat with him, Vergerio, and Zanchi. It was most probably the fears which he entertained for his safety, at a time when many of his countrymen were surprised and carried off into Italy, that induced him to leave Chiavenna and repair to Lyons. But finding himself exposed to new dangers, from the civil war which

* Salig, Hist Auspurg. Confes. tom. ii. p 1180. Bayle, Dict art. Vergerio De Porta, lib. ii cap v. Gerdesii Ital. Ref. p. 346—350. The first volume of a collection of his works was printed in 1563. The *Apologia pro Vergerio adversus Casam*, by Schelhorn, I have not seen.

† See before, p. 203.

then raged in France between the catholics and Hugonots, he retired to Geneva, and soon after returned to Chiavenna, where he opened a private school, at the desire of some young men, to whom he read daily two lectures, one on Homer and another on the Rhetorica ad Herennium. Encouraged by the reception which his brother had met with at the court of Vienna, he went there in 1567, and put to press his celebrated commentary on Aristotle's Art of Poetry, which he dedicated to the emperor Maximilian II. But the plague breaking out in that place, he returned again to Chiavenna, where he continued till his death, on the 21st of February 1571, in the sixty-sixth year of his age. Previous to his last illness, some of his countrymen, who had settled at Basle, requested him to take up his residence with them; an invitation with which he seemed willing to comply. Castelvetro was one of the great literary ornaments of his country; an acute and ingenious critic, and extensively acquainted with Italian and Provençal poetry as well as with the classics of Greece and Rome, to which he added the knowledge of Hebrew.*

It is now time that we should quit the Alps, and take a rapid survey of the Italian churches formed in Switzerland and other countries to the north.

At Zurich the exiles form Locarno obtained from the senate the use of a church, with liberty to celebrate public worship in their own language. They enjoyed at first the instructions of their townsman Beccaria; but as he had come merely to supply their

* Muratori, Vita del Castelvetro. Opere Critiche, p. 33—49. Tiraboschi, Della Letter Ital. vii. 1170—1173. Bibl Modenese, tom. i. p. 456—467. Freytag, Analect. Libr. Rar. p. 219. Jacopo, the son of Gianmaria Castelvetro, who accompanied his father and uncle in their exile, took up his abode finally in London, where, in 1591, he published an edition of the Pastorfido of Guarino, and the Aminte of Tasso. Having been induced to go to Venice, probably by the dissension which arose between that republic and the court of Rome, an accusation was brought against him as a heretic, and he was thrown into prison, from which he escaped by the assistance of Sir Henry Wotton, the English ambassador. (Bibl. Modenese, tom. i p. 432—434) He was in Edinburgh in the year 1592. (MS. in Bibl. Jurid. Edin. A. 4. 18)

present necessities, after labouring among them for a few months, he resigned his place to a person of superior talents.* Returning to the Grisons, he took up his residence in the valley of Misocco, a part of the country which remained in a state of gross ignorance, and in which he was extremely useful, in the double capacity of schoolmaster and preacher, until 1561, when he was expelled through the agency of cardinal Borromeo; after which he retired to Chiavenna.†

Ochino was the person chosen to succeed Beccaria at Zurich. After leaving his native country,‡ he had remained for some time at Geneva, where he acquired the esteem of Calvin:§ but finding himself shut out from employment there, as the only language of which he was master was the Italian, and none of his countrymen had as yet come to that place, he repaired to Basle, for the purpose of printing some of his works, and from that went to Augsburg. The magistrates of this city appointed him Italian preacher, with an annual salary of two hundred florins, partly to provide for his support and partly to gratify the merchants and other inhabitants who knew his native language.‖ He accordingly commenced preaching on the epistles of Paul, in the church of St Anne, to numbers, attracted by curiosity and by the report of his eloquence. For the sake of those who could not understand him, his discourses were translated into German and printed. But the emperor, Charles V., having come to Augsburg with his army in July 1547,

* Schelhorn, Ergoetzlichkeiten, tom. iii. p. 1162

† Beccaria, who also went by the name of Canesa, continued to visit his flock in Misocco down to the year 1571. (Tempe Helvetica, tom. iv. p. 200—202. De Porta, ii. p. 344—350; conf. p. 169.)

‡ See before, p. 183

§ Burmanni Sylloge Epist. tom. ii. p. 230. Lettres de Calvin à Jaque de Bourgogne, p. 36, 108.

‖ Schelhorn, in his interesting collections relating to the life and writings of Ochino, has published two decrees of the senate of Augsburg, in one of which, dated October 20, 1545, they give permission to "Frater Bernhardin Ochinus," along with his brother-in-law and sister, to reside in the city, and in the other, dated December 3, 1545, they assign him the salary mentioned in the text as "Welscher Predicant." (Ergoetzlichkeiten, tom. iii. p. 1141, 1142.)

demanded that Ochino should be delivered up to him, upon which he fled, along with his countryman Stancari, to Constance, whence he went by Basle to Strasburg.* Here he found several Italian refugees, and particularly his intimate friend Martyr, with whom he repaired, in the end of that year, to England, upon the invitation of archbishop Cranmer. Martyr obtained a professor's chair in the university of Oxford,† while Ochino exercised his talent of preaching in the metropolis. But, in consequence of the change of religion produced by the death of Edward VI., both of them retired in 1554, the former to Strasburg and the latter to Basle.‡ From this place Ochino was called to be minister of the Locarnese congregation at Zurich, to the charge of which he was solemnly admitted on the 13th of June 1555, after making an orthodox confession of his faith, and swearing to observe the rites of the Helvetic church and the ordinances of its synods.§

Soon after the settlement of Ochino, his countryman Martyr came to Zurich, to fill the chair of theology and Hebrew, which had become vacant in the university by the death of the learned Conrad Pellican.‖ This was of great advantage to the Locarnese congregation. His interest with the magistrates and pastors of the city was exerted in its behalf; it had

* Schelhorn, p. 994—998, 1142, 1143. Salig, tom. ii. p. 419. Seckendorf, lib. iii. p. 613; et Supplem. num. lvi.

† "Peter Martyr, doctor of divinity of the university of Padua," was incorporated into the university of Oxford in February 1547. (Wood's Fasti Oxon. p. 126.)

‡ Strype's Memorials, vol. ii. p. 189. Burnet's Hist. of the Ref. vol. ii. p. 53, 250. Sanders, De Schism. Anglic. p. 349. During his residence in England, Martyr lost his wife. On the restoration of popery, her body was, by the orders of cardinal Pole, (once the intimate friend of Martyr,) disinterred and thrown into a dunghill; but, after the accession of Elizabeth, it was removed, under the direction of archbishop Parker, and again honourably buried (Historia Vera, De Vita, &c. Martini Buceri et Pauli Fagii; item Historia Catharinæ Vermiliæ, D. Petri Martyris conjugis, f. 196—202. Argent. 1562.)

§ Schelhorn, Ergoetz. tom. iii. p. 1162.

‖ He came to Zurich in July, 1556. (Melch. Adam, Vitæ Exter. Theolog. p. 49. De Porta, ii. 228.)

the benefit of his sound advice in the management of its internal affairs; and he preached to it as often as Ochino was unwell or absent.* It must, therefore, have sustained a severe loss by his death, which happened on the 12th of November, 1562, after an illness of a few days. Of all the Italian exiles, none left behind him a fairer and better earned fame than Peter Martyr. He possessed eminently the good qualities of his countrymen, without the vices which have been ascribed to them; acuteness without subtlety, dexterity without cunning, and ardour without enthusiasm. In Italy he gave great offence by deserting the religion of his ancestors and violating the monastic vow; in England he was opposed to the champions of the Catholic faith, after the government had declared itself decidedly in their favour; at the conference of Poissi he appeared in support of the Protestant doctrine, at a crisis when its adversaries trembled at the prospect of its success within the kingdom of France; and at Strasburg he was involved in a dispute with those who maintained the peculiar sentiments of Luther on the eucharist with more violence than their master had ever shown. But in none of these places did prejudice, strong as it then was, and loud as it often lifted its voice, whisper anything unfavourable to the personal character of Martyr.† His piety and learning were recommended by modesty, candour, and gentleness of manners. As an author, his talents were allowed by his adversaries; and in the reformed church, his writings were, by general agreement, placed next to those of Calvin, for judiciousness and perspicuity. His last years were spent happily in the most uninterrupted harmony and cordial friendship with his colleagues in Zurich. Bullinger, who loved him as a brother, closed his eyes, and Conrad Gesner spread the cloth over his face,

* Zanchii Epist. lib. ii. p 284.
† Speaking of Bucer and Martyr, Walter Haddon exclaims—"O aureum par senum felicissimæ memoriæ, quorum doctrinæ testes libri sunt ab illis confecti, morum tot habuerunt approbatores quot unquam convictores invenire potuerunt!" (Haddoni Lucubrationes, p. 224.)

while the pastor and elders of the Locarnian church wept around his bed.*

The year in which Martyr died was remarkable for the death of one of his countrymen, whose name obtained still greater notoriety than his, though on different grounds. This was Lelius Socinus, who had, for a number of years, been a member of the Locarnese congregation † He was born at Sienna in 1525, and educated under the eye of his father, Mariano Soccini, the younger, a celebrated professor of law. Having testified a decided partiality to the Reformation, he left Italy in 1548,‡ partly from regard to his safety and partly from a desire to see and confer with the leading divines of the Protestant church, whose writings he had read with delight. He came to Zurich at an early period, and lodged with Pellican, under whom he commenced the study of the Hebrew language. Between 1549 and 1551 he resided at Wittenberg, after which he returned to Zurich, where he spent the remainder of his life, with the exception of what was devoted to short excursions into France, Poland, and Italy. I have already given my reasons for thinking that, before leaving his native country, he had not adopted the creed which has obtained from him and his nephew the name of Socinian, and that his interviews with Camillo Renato at Chiavenna had great influence in leading his mind into that train of thinking.§ Soon after his arrival in Switzerland he

---

* Josias Simler, who had been appointed his colleague in the theological chair, drew up his life in the *Oratio de Vita et Obitu D Petri Martyris Vermilii*, to which we have repeatedly referred. There is a beautiful letter in commendation of him, written soon after his death, by Wolfgang Haller to Zanchi. (Zanchii Epist. ut supra) Besides the collection of epistles appended to his *Loci Communes*. a number of Martyr's letters were published by Gerdes, in his *Scrinium Antiquarium*, tom. iv.

† Illgen, Vita Lælii Socini, p. 48. Fueslin, p. 356. 358.

‡ Cornelio, Camillo, and Celso, three of the brothers of Lelius, embraced the same sentiments, and followed him, at a later period, into Switzerland, as did also his nephew Faustus. (Schelhorn, De Mino Celso, p. 35. Bock, ii. 576, 577. 624.)

§ The reader may compare the opinions of Camillo, as already stated, with the doubts started by Socinus in his correspondence with Calvin. The letters of Socinus, indeed, are not extant, but the sub-

began, in his conversations and epistolary correspondence with learned men, to start doubts as to the commonly received opinions concerning the sacraments and the resurrection, and afterwards concerning redemption and the trinity; but he uniformly proposed these in the character of a learner, not of a teacher or disputant, as difficulties which he was anxious to have solved, and not as sentiments which he held or wished to support. The modesty with which he propounded his doubts, together with the eager desire he showed for knowledge, his courteousness, and the correctness of his morals, gained him the esteem not only of Melanchthon and Bullinger, but also of Calvin and Beza. If, at any time, he gave offence or alarm by the boldness with which he pushed his speculations into high and inscrutable mysteries, or by pertinaciousness in urging his objections, he knew how to allay these feelings by prudent concession and ample apologies; and Calvin, after declining farther correspondence with him, was induced to renew it and to return a friendly answer to his doubts respecting the doctrine of the trinity.* In adopting this method toward the more learned reformers, it was probably the object of Socinus to ascertain what they could say against his opinions; but, in other instances, he exerted himself in secretly making proselytes, and not without success.† He carefully concealed his sentiments respecting the trinity from the divines of Zurich.‡ On receiving warning of them from the Grisons, Bullinger, whose affections he had gained, laid the matter before him, and, in a very friendly manner, advised him to remove the suspicions which had arisen as to his orthodoxy. Socinus protested that he agreed in all points with the church of Zurich, and complained of the reports

stance of them is preserved in Calvin's replies. (Calvini. Epist. p. 52. 57; Opera, tom. ix.)

* Colomesii Opera, p. 502. Conf. Calvini Epist. p 57, Opera, tom. ix.

† Zanchii Præf. in Libr. de Tribus Elohim; Opera, tom. i.

‡ Simla, Assertio Orthod. Doctrinæ de duabus naturis Christi, præf. p. 4.

circulated to his prejudice; but, on being dealt with more closely, he owned that he had indulged too much in abstruse and vain speculations, promised that he would guard against this for the future, and subscribed a declaration of his faith, which was satisfactory to Bullinger.* Julio da Milano, who was one of those from whom the information had come, and knew the correspondence which Socinus held with the antitrinitarians in the Valteline, was suspicious of the sincerity of his professions; and though he promised to use his influence to induce his brethren to accept of the pledge which had been given, implored Bullinger to watch over the purity of the Locarnese congregation.† After this, Socinus was more circumspect: we find no more noise made about his opinions during his lifetime; and there is every reason to think that he continued to communicate, as he had formerly done, with the Italian church in Zurich. But after his death, the antitrinitarians who had enjoyed his confidence, thinking themselves no longer bound to secrecy, proclaimed that he was of their sentiments; and as a proof of this, circulated such of his writings as were in their possession.‡ On

* Illgen, p 46—55. Bock, ii. 597—602.
† Fueslin, p. 353—359.
‡ Bock has given an account of his writings. (Hist. Antitrin. tom. ii. p 635—654.) But Illgen has shown greater discrimination in distinguishing his genuine works from those which are supposititious or were written by others. (Vita Lælii Socini, p. 74—85) His work composed on occasion of the punishment of Servetus, and entitled, " Martini Bellii Farrago de hæreticis, an sint prosequendi, et omnino quomodo sit cum eis agendum," was first printed at Basle in 1553. The edition which I have examined wants the words " Martini Bellii Farrago" in the title, and was printed " Magdeburgi 1554." The following is a specimen of the style of reasoning in that work.—" Suppose one accused of disloyalty at Tubingen, who makes this defence for himself—' I believe that Christopher is my prince, and I desire to obey him in all things; but as to what you say about his coming in a chariot, this I do not believe, but believe that he will come on horseback; and whereas you say that he is clothed in scarlet, I believe that he is clothed in white; and as to his ordering us to wash in this river, I believe that this ought to be done in the afternoon, and you believe it ought to be done in the forenoon.' I ask of you, prince, if you would wish your subject to be condemned for this ? I think not: and if you were present, you would rather praise the candour and obedience of the man than

hearing of his death, his nephew, Faustus Socinus, came from Lyons to Zurich, and took possession of his papers, which he afterwards made use of in composing his own works. To this, however, he applied himself at a period much later; for he went immediately to Florence, where he spent twelve years in the service of the grand duke of Tuscany, not in preparing his mind for the task of illuminating the world, (as the Polish knight who wrote his life has asserted,) but in the idleness and amusements of a court, as he himself has acknowledged.*

The Locarnese exiles were surprised and distressed at learning that so respectable a member of their church as Socinus had made defection from the evangelical faith; but their painful feelings were heightened by the report, which soon after became current, that their pastor had followed his example. Socinus had failed in his attempts to warp the judgment of his countryman Zanchi;† but his subtlety and address were too powerful for one who was now advanced in years, and who, though possessed of good talents, had read but little on theology, in consequence of his imperfect knowledge of ancient and foreign languages. Without supposing him to have been the slave of popularity, Ochino could scarcely have failed to be flattered with the crowds which flocked to his preaching in Italy; and he must have felt the change, when, on coming to a foreign country, his hearers were necessarily few, from the circumstance of their being confined to those who understood his native tongue. He had, besides, taken up the idea that the divines of

blame his ignorance; and if any should put him to death on this ground, you would punish them So is it in the question under consideration. A certain citizen of Christ says, I believe in God the Father and Jesus Christ his Son," &c. (De Hæreticis, &c. p 8) No copy has, for a long time, been seen of his " Paraphrasis in Initium Evangelii S. Johannis, scripta an. 1561," which contained the famed interpretation of the first verse of that gospel, " In *Evangelii* principio erat Dei sermo," &c This paraphrase must not be confounded with the " Explicatio Initii Evangelii Johannis," which was the work of his nephew Faustus.

* Bock, tom ii. p 663, 664.
† Zanchii Opera, tom. i. præf. ad finem.

Zurich despised him for his want of learning; and though this suspicion appears to have been groundless, we have his own authority for saying that it soured his mind.* In this state of his feelings, he was more ready to listen to the objections of his artful townsman, though they struck at the root of sentiments which had been the favourite topics of his sermons, and in which he had gloried most when he left the church of Rome.

It appears that surmises unfavourable to the orthodoxy of Ochino had arisen soon after his arrival in Switzerland. We learn this fact from a letter of Calvin, which reflects honour on the heart of that great reformer, and shows that he was far from being of that suspicious and intolerant disposition which many, through ignorance or prejudice, have ascribed to him. "There is another thing of which I must write you, at the request of our friend Bernardin. I understand that it has been reported, through the foolishness of a certain brother, who was one of his companions, that he was somewhat suspected here as not altogether sound on the doctrine of the trinity and person of Christ. I shall say nothing in his exculpation, except simply to state the truth of what happened. As I have not great confidence in the genius of many of the Italians, when he first imparted to me his design of taking up his residence here, I conferred with him freely on the several articles of faith, in such a manner that if he had differed on any thing from us he could scarcely have concealed it. It appeared to me that I discovered, and, if I have any judgment, I can safely attest, that he agreed with us entirely on the article referred to, as well as on all other points. The only thing I perceived was, that he felt displeased with the over-curious discussion of these questions which is common among the schoolmen; and, really, when it is considered how much the airy speculations of these sophists differ from the sober and modest doctrine of the ancients, I cannot be of a different opinion. I think it proper to bear this testimony to

† Ochino, Dialogo, in Schelhorn, Ergoetz., tom. iii. p. 2030.

a pious and holy man, lest the slightest suspicion should unjustly be attached to his character among us; for he is unquestionably a person distinguished for genius, learning, and sanctity."* Calvin retained the same favourable opinion of him at a subsequent period,† and there is no reason to think that the divines of Zurich were of a different mind. But, in 1558, Martyr received a letter from Chiavenna, stating that Ochino and the brothers of Lelius Socinus were secretly undermining the doctrine of the merit and satisfaction of Christ. Even according to his own explanation, Ochino had forsaken his former views on that point; but the matter was accommodated by the friendship and prudence of Martyr.‡ About the same time he gave offence to some of the divines of Switzerland by one of his books; and on this occasion also, though the work was printed without their knowledge and was far from pleasing them, the ministers of Zurich interposed in his favour.§ But he forfeited their protection and exhausted their forbearance, by a work which he published in the course of the year after his countryman, Martyr, died. It was printed privately, not at Zurich but at Basle, and consisted of thirty dialogues, divided into two parts.‖ In the first part he proves, in opposition to a Jew, that Jesus is the true Messiah, and, on the general argument, his proofs are strong; but when he comes to defend the

* Calvinus ad Pellicanum, Genevæ, 14 Calend. Maias 1543: Calvini Epistolæ MSS vol. 1 no 60, in Bibl. Genev.
† Calvin. ad Viretum, 6 April. 1547· MS. in Bibl. Genev.
‡ A letter which Ochino wrote on this occasion has been preserved by De Porta, tom 11. p 392. 393.
§ Schelhorn, Ergoetzlichkeiten, tom. 111 p. 2164. The book referred to was his *Labyrinthi*, in which he discusses the questions respecting free will and predestination.
‖ Bernardini Ochini Senensis Dialogi XXX. Basileæ 1563. The work was printed from a translation into the Latin made by Castalio. It was afterwards disputed whether the work had undergone the examination which the laws prescribed before its being printed. It appeared, on investigation, that the Italian original, in manuscript, had been put into the hands of Amerbachius, the rector of the university, by whom, as he did not understand the language, it was committed to Celio Secundo Curio, who denied that he had ever given it his approbation. (Schelhorn, Ergoetz tom. 111. p. 1185—1188.)

sacrifice and satisfaction of Christ, he argues feebly and inconclusively. It was, however, the second part of the work, in which he treats of polygamy and the trinity, which chiefly gave offence. The first of these questions is discussed in dialogue between Telipoligamus, an advocate of polygamy, and Ochinus. Every argument which had been urged in favour of the practice, or which the ingenuity of the author could devise, is put into the mouth of the former, who reasons at great length and with much eloquence; while Ochinus replies at once with brevity and feebleness, and in the end materially, though not in so many words, yields the point in dispute to his supposed antagonist. The dialogues on the trinity are conducted in the same manner. Some writers insist that Ochino cannot be charged with maintaining polygamy and antitrinitarianism; but it will be difficult for any person to read the dialogues impartially without conceiving strong suspicions of the author's heterodoxy.*

Certain citizens of Zurich, on a visit to Basle, were told in a public company that their town would soon become a sink of vile heresies, as their ministers had already begun to write in favour of polygamy; and on their resenting this as a calumny, they were silenced by the production of the work of Ochino, which had been lately published. Returning home, they gave information to the ministers of the city, and implored them to wipe off a disgrace which had fallen upon their order and upon the whole city.† The divines of Zurich had, at a former period, been greatly displeased at the conduct of such of the German reformers as had countenanced the bigamy of the landgrave of Hesse,‡ which brought so much scandal on the whole evangelical body; and they now felt both grieved and indignant at the conduct of their colleague. Having communicated the fact to the chief magistrate, they, at his desire, translated the dialogue

---

* The dialogue on polygamy has been republished and translated into our own language (among others) by the friends of that practice.
† Schelhorn, Ergoetzlichkeiten, iii. p 2160, 2161.
‡ Fueslin, Epist. Ref. p. 198—200, 205.

on polygamy into German, and laid it, with remarks on the other dialogues, before the senate, which came to the resolution of banishing him from the territories of the canton. Being unable to prevent this sentence, he petitioned for liberty to remain during the winter; but this was refused, and he was ordered to depart within three weeks.*

The banishment of an old man of seventy-six, with four young children, in the depth of winter, was a severe measure, calculated to excite compassion for the sufferer; and had Ochino left this feeling to its own operation, it is probable that the magistrates and ministers of Zurich would have incurred public odium. But he published an apology for himself, which was answered by the ministers, and injured instead of helping his cause.† Besides the charges brought against the senate and pastors in general, he made a personal attack on Bullinger, whom he represented as one who disliked all foreigners, especially Italians, wished to ruin the Locarnese congregation, had opposed his election to be their pastor, and persecuted him because he would not worship him as a pope and a god.‡ Now all this was so contrary to the character of that divine; and his kindness to exiles, his care about the Italian church,§ the tenderness with which he had treated Socinus, and the respect which he had shown for Ochino himself, were all so well known, that the ministers scarcely needed to use their "sponge" to wipe off aspersions which served only to throw suspicion on the pen which had discharged them. Nor was the author happier in the defence of his book. His chief

* Schelhorn, Ergoetz. iii. 2022, 2161, 2166, 2174—2179. Bock, ii. 501—504.

† His apology, entitled "Dialogo, Favellatori—Prudenza humana e Ochino," and the reply to it, entitled "Spongia adversus aspergines Bernardini Ochini," are both published by Schelhorn in the third volume of his Ergoetzlichkeiten. It would appear, from the reply, that Ochino's apology was printed at that time, though Schelhorn thinks it was only circulated in manuscript.

‡ Dialogo, ut supra, p. 2021, 2029, 2030

§ There is an excellent letter by him to the Protestants suffering persecution in Italy, dated 6th January 1561, and published by Fueslin. (Epist. Ref. p. 445—456.)

apology for the manner in which he had conducted the argument was, that "truth does not stand in need of many words like falsehood, for it can defend itself."* As if we were warranted to strip truth, and then place her on the pillory, to be insulted and pelted by the mob, while we stood by and contented ourselves with crying out, "Great is the truth, and will prevail!" Ochino alleges, that one chief reason of the keenness with which the ministers of Zurich had persecuted him was, that, in the obnoxious dialogues, he had exposed their errors and pointed out the defects of their boasted reformation. But, as anything of this kind was put into the mouth of the interlocutor whom he opposed, he, by this allegation, virtually acknowledged the deception which he had practised, and deprived himself of his principal defence.†

On coming to Basle, Ochino was given to understand by the magistrates, that his continuing there would be offensive. After residing for some time at Mulhausen, he set out to join his countrymen of the antitrinitarian persuasion who had gone to Poland. But cardinal Borromeo, by express orders from the pope, wrote to cardinal Hosius to keep his eye upon him and prevent his settlement in that country, a service which was also given in charge to the nuncio Commendone. In consequence of this, he was obliged to retire into Moravia, and died at Slacovia in the end of the year 1564, after having lost two sons and a daughter by the plague, which then raged in that country.‡ Whatever the faults of Ochino were, it is

* "La verità non ha bisogno di molte parole, sicome il mendacio; imperoche la verità per se stessa si difendi, resiste, supera e trionfa; ma il contrario è del mendacio." (Dialogo, ut supra, p. 2018.)

† Dialogo, ut supra, p. 2030—2034. Schelhorn is of opinion that Ochino's Dialogue on Polygamy is not original, and that the greater part of it was borrowed from a dialogue on the same subject, written in defence of Philip, landgrave of Hesse, and published in 1541, under the fictitious name of Hulderichus Neobulus. (Ergoetzlichkeiten, tom. i. p. 631—636; iii. 2136—2156.) There is certainly a striking coincidence between the extracts he has produced from this dialogue and that of Ochino. The charge of plagiarism is, however, weakened by the fact that Ochino was ignorant of German.

‡ Bock, tom. ii. p. 504—508.

impossible to contemplate this termination of the career of a man who had been held in such high estimation and enjoyed so large a share of popular applause, without feelings of the deepest regret and humiliation. The narrative affords a useful lesson both to preachers and hearers: it admonishes the latter not to allow their admiration to usurp the place of their judgment, if it were from no other motive than pity to the gods whom their breath creates; and it warns the former not to trust themselves to the intoxicating gale of popularity, which, after deceiving them, leaves in their breasts a painful restlessness, prompting them to make undefined and perilous efforts to regain what they have lost. The Roman catholics had felt great mortification when Ochino deserted their communion; their triumph was now proportionately great, and his versatility and melancholy fate furnished them with a popular argument against all change in religion and every attempt at Reform.

The Locarnese congregation, however, continued to flourish and enjoyed a succession of pastors until the emigration ceased, and it was no longer necessary to have the public service performed in the language of Italy.* Some of the most distinguished families at this day in Zurich are descended from Italian exiles, who first introduced into it the art of manufacturing silk, set up mills. and dye-houses, and so enriched the city, by their industry and ingenuity, that, within a short time, it became celebrated beyond the limits of Switzerland.†

Basle had long been distinguished as a resort of learned men, which induced many of the Italian Protestants to select it as the place of their residence. I can only name a few of them. Paolo di Colli, the father of Hippolytus a Collibus, a celebrated lawyer and counsellor of the Elector Palatine Frederic IV., was a native of Alexandria, in the Milanese, from

* Hottinger, Helvetische Kirchengeschichte, tom. iii. p. 762—763; Gerdesii Ital. Ref p. 40.

† Zschokke, Schweizerlands Geschichte, p. 258. Tempe Helvetica, tom. iv. p. 173.

which he fled in consequence of the discovery of a Protestant conventicle which was kept in his house.* Guglielmo Grataroli, a physician of Bergamo, was equally distinguished by his piety, his classical learning, and his skill in his own art, on which he published several works.† Alfonso Corrado, a Mantuan, and said to have been the instructor of the wife of Alfonso duke of Ferrara, preached for some time in the Grisons, and published at Basle a commentary on the Apocalypse, "filled (says Tiraboschi) with invectives and reproaches against the Roman pontiff."‡ Silvestro Teglio, and Francesco Betti, a Roman knight, were both learned men.§ Mino Celso, a native of Sienna, is praised by Claudio Tolomeo, and an edition of the letters of that learned man was dedicated to him by Fabio Benvoglienti.|| Having left his native country from love to the reformed religion, he became corrector of the press to Petrus Perna, a Lucchese, and long a celebrated printer at Basle, "whose memory (says Tiraboschi) would have been still more deserving of honour if he had not tarnished it by apostasy from the catholic religion."¶ Mino Celso was the author of a rare work against the capital punishment of heretics, in which he has treated the question with great solidity and learning.** But the

* Adami Vitæ Jureconsult. p. 207. Tonjolæ Monument Basil. p. 124.

† Thuani Hist. ad an. 1568. Bezæ Epistolæ, p. 218, 231. Speaking of Grataroli, Zanchi says—" In his native country he enjoyed an honourable rank and riches: his piety alone has impoverished him." (Epist. lib. ii. p. 390.)

‡ Gerdesii Ital. Ref. p. 231—234. De Porta, ii. 35. Tiraboschi, vii. 383. " Exseceretur me Papa, quærant me principes ad necem, qui sub mentito Inquisitorum hæreticæ pravitatis nomine hæresin pessimam defendunt, &c." (Alph. Conradus, Comment in Apocalypsin, Dedic. sig. ii. Bas. 1574.)

§ Teglio translated into Latin the Principe of Macchiavelli. Betti was the author of a letter to the marchioness of Pescaro, and afterwards became intimate with Faustus Socinus. (Schelhorn, Dissert. de Mino Celso, p. 62. Bock, ii. p. 665, 817.)

|| De Mino Celso Senensi, p. 14—18.

¶ Storia, vii. 1763. A life of Perna was published at Lucca in 1763, by Domenica Maria Manni.

** It is entitled, " Mini Celsi Senensis de Hereticis capitali supplicio non afficiendis. Anno 1584." This is the edition I have con-

most learned person among the refugees who resided in this city, was Curio, whom we have already met with repeatedly in the course of this history. At his first coming from Italy, the senate of Berne placed him at the head of the college of Lausanne, from which he was translated in 1547 to the chair of Roman Eloquence in the university of Basle. On that occasion the degree of doctor of laws was conferred on him sitting, a mark of respect which had been shown to none but Bucer. But greater honour was done him by the numbers who came from all parts of Europe to attend his lectures. He received an invitation from the emperor Maximilian to the university of Vienna, from Vaivod, king of Transylvania to Weissemburg, and from the duke of Savoy to Turin; while the pope employed the bishop of Terracino to persuade him to return to Italy, by the promise of an ample salary, with provision for his daughters, and on no other condition than that of his abstaining from inculcating his religious opinions. But he rejected these offers, and remained at Basle till his death in 1569.* Beside his writings on religious subjects, he published various works on grammar, and editions of the Latin classics, accompanied with notes, by which he did great service to Roman literature and education. Of all the refugees, the loss of none has been more regretted by Italian writers than that of Curio.†
The testimonies which they have borne to him deserve the more attention for this reason, among others,

---

sulted, but the work was first printed in 1577. The author mentions that he was led to treat the question in consequence of his finding it disputed among the Protestants when he passed through the Grisons in 1569. In the work, he points out the distinction between the kingdom of Christ and secular kingdoms, examines the doctrine of Scripture on the subject, produces testimonies from the fathers and Reformers in favour of the opinion which he maintains, and shows that it is not inconsistent with the exercise of civil authority in reforming and supporting religion. His reasoning is not confined to capital punishment.

* Stupani Oratio de Cælio Secundo Curione, ut supra, p. 347—349.

† Tiraboschi, Storia, tomo vii. p. 1559—1561. Ginguene, Hist. Litter. d'Italie, tome vii. p 233—236.

that some of the most important facts relating to the progress and suppression of the Reformation in Italy have been attested by him; and the greater part of the narratives of Italian martyrs proceeded from his pen, or were submitted to his revision before they were published by his friend Pantaleon. The children of Curio, female as well as male, were distinguished for their talents and learning, and among his descendants we find some of the most eminent names in the Protestant church.*

In taking leave of Curio, I am reminded of his interesting friend, Olympia Morata. On retiring into Germany,† she and her husband were kindly entertained by George Hermann, the enlightened minister of Ferdinand, king of the Romans, through whose influence they were offered an advantageous situation in the Austrian dominions, which they declined, as being incompatible with the free exercise of the Reformed religion. Olympia felt herself happy in the affection of the worthy young man to whom she had given her heart along with her hand; and the recollection of the ease and splendour in which she had spent the most of her life was lost in the liberty of conscience and Christian society which she now enjoyed. The letters which she wrote at this time to her female acquaintance in Italy and to her fellow exiles, testify that she was in possession of the richest of heritages, "godliness with contentment." In Schweinfurt, an imperial town of Franconia, and the native place of her husband, she resumed her favourite studies, and her friends congratulated themselves on the prospect of her adding to the literary fame which she had already acquired in her native country; but the muses were soon put to flight by the trumpet of war. The turbulent Albert, marquis of Brandenburg, who had been engaged in a predatory warfare with his neighbours, threw himself into the

---

* It is sufficient to mention here the names of Buxtorf, Grynæus, Freyus, and Werenfels. (Stupani Oratio, p 363, 381, 398. Ryhinerus, Vita Sam. Werenfelsii, in Tempe Helvetica, tom. vi. p. 47.)

† See before, p 205.

city of Schweinfurt, when he was besieged by the German princes.* During the siege, which was tedious and severe, Olympia was obliged to live in a cellar; and when the town was taken, she, with great difficulty, escaped, in disguise, from the fury of the soldiers, and reached the neighbouring village of Hammelburg in a state of exhaustion. "If you had seen me," she writes to Curio, "with my feet bare and bleeding, my hair dishevelled, and my borrowed clothes all torn, you would have pronounced me the queen of beggars."† Her library, which she valued above all her property, including her own manuscripts, was entirely destroyed in the sack of the town. Under this calamity, she experienced the polite attention of the counts of Erbach; the Elector Palatine provided her husband with a place in the university of Heidelberg; and her literary friends united in sending her books to furnish a new library. Their sympathy and kindness soothed her spirits, but could not restore her to health, or prolong a life which was fast hastening to a close. Her delicate constitution had received an irrecoverable shock from the agitation and fatigue which she had undergone; the symptoms of consumption became decided; and after a lingering illness, during which the sweetness of her temper and the strength of her faith displayed themselves in such a manner as to console even her husband who doated upon her, she expired on the 26th of October 1555, in the 29th year of her age.‡ Who would not drop a tear over the untimely grave of the amiable and accomplished Olympia Morata! She ceased not to the last to remember her ungrateful but beloved Italy, though every desire to return to it had been quenched in her breast from the time she saw the apathy with which her countrymen allowed the standard of truth to fall and the blood of its friends to be shed like water in their streets. Be-

* Sleidan, tom ii. p 410, 449, 468.
† Olympiæ Moratæ Opera, p. 160—162. Nolten, Vita Olympiæ Moratæ, p. 138—147.
‡ Olympiæ Moratæ Opera, p. 167, 177, 185—192. Nolten, p. 148—163.

fore she was confined to bed, she employed her leisure time in transcribing from memory some of her poems, which she bequeathed to her friend Curio, by whom her works were published after her death. They consist of confidential letters, dialogues in Latin and Italian, and Greek poems, chiefly paraphrases of the Psalms, in heroic and sapphic verse; all of them the productions of a pious and highly cultivated mind.*

Strasburg, one of the free cities of Germany, opened its gates to the Italian refugees. Paolo Lacisio of Verona, highly praised by Robortello for his skill in the three learned languages, came to it along with Martyr, and obtained the situation of professor of Greek in the academy.† Jeronimo Massario of Vicenza was about the same time admitted professor of medicine. This learned man, beside what he wrote on the subject of his own science, was the author of a description of the mode of procedure in the tribunal of the inquisition at Rome. In this work he describes the trial of a fictitious prisoner, whom he calls Eusebius Uranius, and puts into his mouth, during an examination which lasted three days, the principal arguments from Scripture and the fathers against the church of Rome. Though it contains several facts, yet it is rather a controversial than an historical work, and much inferior in usefulness to the account of the Spanish inquisition by Gonsalvo.‡ The Italians were not so numerous in Strasburg as to require the use of

* Her works were published in 1553, and went through four editions in the course of twenty-two years. The first edition was dedicated to Isabella Manricha, and the subsequent ones to Queen Elizabeth of England. Two of her letters will be found in the Appendix.

† Simler, Vita Martyris, sig. b iiij Gerdes, Scrinium Antiq. tom. iii. p. 17. Colomesii Italia Orientalis, p. 67, 688.

‡ It is entitled, " Eusebius Captivus, sive modus procedendi in curia Romana contra Lutheranos—per Hieronymum Marium. Basileæ." The dedication is dated, " Basileæ iiii Nonas Novembris, Anno 1553." Colomies says that Hieronymus Marius is the disguised name of Cælius Secundus Curio. (Des Maizeaux, Colomesiana, tom. ii. p. 594.) But Zanchi, in a letter to Musculus, says expressly that Massario had gone to Basle to get the work printed. (Zanchii Epist. lib. ii p. 312, 317) He died of the plague at Strasburg in 1564 (Wolfii Notæ in Colomesii Ital. Orient p. 74, 75. Sturmii Institutiones Literatæ, p. 140. Torun. Boruss. 1586.)

a church, but they met in private and enjoyed for
some time the instructions of Jerome Zanchi.* This
celebrated divine was a native of Alzano in the Bergamasco, and descended from a family distinguished
in the republic of letters.† He was persuaded by his
relation, Basilio, to enter a convent of Canons Regular, where he formed an intimate acquaintance with
Celso Martinengho. They were associated in their
studies in reading the works of Melanchthon, Bullinger, Musculus, and other Reformers, and in attending
the lectures of Martyr. They left Italy about the same
time, and their friendship continued uninterrupted till
the death of Martinengho. Having come to Geneva
in 1553, by the way of the Grisons, Zanchi agreed
to accompany Martyr into England; but when about
to set out for this country, he received an invitation
to be professor of divinity in the college of St. Thomas at Strasburg. This situation he filled, with great
credit and comfort, for several years, until, after the
death of James Sturmius, the great patron of the
academy, who had been his steady friend, he was involved in controversy with some of the keen Lutherans, led on by John Marbach, who took offence at
him for opposing their novel notion of the omnipre-
sence of the human nature of Christ, and for teaching
the doctrines of predestination and the perseverance
of the saints.‡ In the midst of the uneasiness which

* Zanchii Epist. lib. 1. p. 131.

† His father, Francesco, is enumerated among the historians of
Italy. (Tiraboschi, tom. vii. p 369.) His second cousins, Dionigi,
Grisostomo, and Basilio Zanchi, were all learned men. The last was
reckoned one of the finest Latin poets in Italy, and a mystery hangs
over the manner and cause of his death. It is supposed that he died
in prison, into which he had been thrown by pope Paul IV. (Ibid.
p. 1182—1184; comp. p 387—389, and Roscoe's Leo X. vol. 1. p. 76.)

‡ He gives an account of this dispute in his letter to the landgrave
of Hesse. (Opera, tom. vii. p. 1—46; tom. iii epist dedicat. Conf.
Melch. Adami Vitæ Exter. Theolog. p. 149.) John Sturmius, who
was rector of the academy of Strasburg, and celebrated for the elegance of his Latin style, wrote a philippic against the adversaries
of Zanchi, to which Melchior Speccer replied in a letter published by
Schelhorn. In this letter he says—" Alterum caput criminationis
tuæ—Zanchium, suavissimas tuas delicias, vitam tuam, et animulam
tuam continet." (Ergoetzlichkeiten, tom. iii. p. 1136.) In a letter

this quarrel gave him, he rejected the proposals made to him by the papal nuncio,* but accepted in the end of the year 1563, a call from the Italian church at Chiavenna.† In the beginning of 1568 he came to the university of Heidelberg, where he taught during ten years; but finding that the prejudice which he had encountered at Strasburg followed him to this place, he gave way to it a second time, and removed to Neustadt, where count John Casimir, the administrator of the Electorate Palatine, had recently endowed an academy. He died in 1590, during a visit which he paid to his friends at Heidelberg, in the 76th year of his age.‡ The moderation of Zanchi has been praised by writers of the Roman catholic church, though his love of peace did not lead him to sacrifice or compromise the truth. His celebrity as a teacher procured him invitations from the academies of Zurich, Lausanne, and Leyden. John Sturmius, called the German Cicero, was wont to say that he would not be afraid to trust Zanchi alone in a dispute against all the fathers assembled at Trent. Nor was he less esteemed as an author after his death. His writings, consisting of commentaries on Scripture and treatises on almost all questions in theology, abound with proofs of learning; but they are too ponderous for the arms of a modern divine.§

Lyons, in the sixteenth century, was a place of resort for merchants from all parts of Europe. The Italian Protestants in that city were so numerous,

to Bullinger, Sturmius praises the learning, piety, courteousness, and placability of Zanchi. (Zanchii Epist. lib. ii. p. 287.)

* Tiraboschi, vii. 369.

† De Porta, ii. 412—421.

‡ Thuani Hist. ad an. 1590. Teissier, Eloges, tom. iv. p. 99—103. Melch. Adami Vitæ Exteror. Theolog. p. 148—153. A life of Zanchi, by Sig. Conte Cav. Giambatista Gallizioli, a patrician of Bergamasco, was printed at Bergamo in 1785. (Tiraboschi, vii. 369.)

§ His works were collected and printed, in eight volumes folio, at Geneva in 1613. Fridericus Sylburgius, celebrated as the author of several learned works, and the editor of many of the Greek and Roman classics which came from the presses of Wechel and Commelin, was for some time the servant of Zanchi, to whom he was indebted for his education. (Zanchii Epist. lib. ii. p. 440, 442.)

that the popes reckoned it necessary to keep agents among them to labour in their conversion. But so far were they from succeeding in this work, that Lyons came to be regarded at Rome as "the chief seat of heresy," and all who visited it fell under suspicion.* Several editions of the New Testament, and other religious books, in the Italian language, proceeded from the Lyonese press.† In the beginning of 1562, the Italians obtained permission to hold meetings for worship, and called Zanchi to be their minister. The magistrates of Strasburg having refused to part with him, he, in the following year, received another pressing invitation from the celebrated Viret, in the name of the Protestant consistory at Lyons; but he had previously engaged himself to the church of Chiavenna. When afterwards deprived of the preacher whom they had chosen, Zanchi received a third call from his countrymen in Lyons, who were again disappointed.‡

Antwerp was, in that age, the emporium of the world, and frequented by men of all nations. The reformed doctrine had been early introduced into it, and continued to spread among the inhabitants in spite of the severities employed for its suppression.§ For many years the Italian Protestants satisfied themselves with meeting for worship along with the French church, which was erected in that city after the Netherlands threw off the Spanish yoke; but as their numbers had increased,‖ they resolved, in the year 1580,

* Fontanini Biblioteca Italiana, tom i. p. 119.
† Besides the translation of the New Testament by Massimo Teofilo in 1551, an edition of Brucioli's was printed at Lyons in 1553, and an anonymous translation in 1558. This last had been published, with a French version, in 1555, by Ludovico Paschali, the martyr; but the place of printing is unknown. (Schelhorn, Ergoetzlichkeiten, tom. i. p. 417—419.)
‡ Zanchii Epist. lib. ii. p. 287, 375—378, 390.
§ Gerdesii Hist. Reform. tom. iii. p. 217, 243.
‖ The Italian version of the New Testament by Brucioli was printed at Antwerp in the year 1538, accompanied with two prefaces, in which the advantages of reading the Scriptures, and the propriety of translating them into the vulgar language of every people, are urged with great force. (Ergoetzlichkeiten, tom. i. p. 408.)

to form themselves into a separate church, and invited their countryman Zanchi to be their pastor. With this invitation, though warmly seconded by letters from the senate and ministers, he did not think it prudent to comply.* It is, however, probable, that they obtained Ulixio Martinenghot† for their minister; for we find Zanchi, about this time, writing his opinion of that nobleman, at the desire of one of the ministers of Antwerp. "I know him well," says he, "and can, with a good conscience and in the presence of the Lord, attest that he is incorrupt and well grounded as to doctrine, possesses no common share of learning, is unblamable in his life as a Christian, zealous toward God, charitable toward his brethren, and distinguished for prudence and dexterity in the management of business, which, as you well know, is a qualification very necessary in the rulers of churches. The only thing of which I cannot speak is his gift of preaching, for I never heard him from the pulpit; but he speaks Italian well. O that I could spend what remains of my life in the company of this excellent servant of God! Believe me, you will find him, on acquaintance, still better than he appears to be; sincere, frank, kind, obliging, courteous, and one who adds lustre to the nobility of his birth by the correctness of his morals as a Christian. I am sure he will greatly please your illustrious prince."‡

Of all the foreign Italian churches, none was so distinguished as those which were established in Geneva and in London. But as their affairs were intimately connected with those of the Spanish refugees who settled in these cities, I shall speak of them in the account which I propose to give of the struggle for reformation in Spain.§ For that work I shall also reserve the remarks I have to make on the influence

* Zanchii Epist. lib. ii. p. 409—414, 424.
† See before, p. 328.
‡ Zanchius Joanni Taffino: Epist. lib. ii. p. 411; conf. p. 366.
§ See History of the Progress and Suppression of the Reformation in Spain, p. 269—276.

which the suppression of the reformed opinions had on the national literature and character of the Italians, which are applicable, with a very little variation, to those of the Spaniards.

APPENDIX.

No. I.

Specimens of the Sermons of Savonarola.

[See before, p. 31.]

In 1540 were printed at Venice a collection of the sermons of this famous preacher, under the following title:—"Prediche del Reverendo Padre Fra Gieronimo da Ferrara, per tuto l'anno nuovamente con somma diligentia ricorette." They had been taken originally from the mouth of the preacher, and were printed from a collation of different manuscripts. The following short epistle to the reader, which is prefixed to them, is given here for the sake of the writer, as well as the testimony which it bears to the work:—

"Accept, then, this small gift—small I call it, in respect of the small hand which I have had in it, though in itself great and very rich, being filled with the most sacred Christian instructions, in reading which your Christian soul may be comforted, while you see this Christian writer with great energy prophesying a universal renovation of the church, which is now at hand and just about to appear, and which may God perfect, that so all people may give praise to the Creator of the universe, and to his Son, Jesus Christ our Lord and Saviour, to whom be honour and glory for ever, Amen.

Antonio Brucioli."

The following extracts will give an idea of the talents and manner of the preacher, and are sufficient to show that he was not that ignorant fanatic which some writers have represented him to be. The sermon from which the last extract is taken was preached at the time when he was lying under a papal interdict.

"I showed, a little before, how necessary and natural a thing it is that bodies, which are perishable in their constitution, should either wholly corrupt and disappear, or else pass into some other condition, according to the maxim of philosophy, *Omne contrarium est corruptibile.* It follows, of necessity, that there is nothing in a state of union under heaven which does not either corrupt and resolve into its first principles, or make its appearance again under a new form. And so it is with spiritual things. The church is so set together in its different parts as to resemble a body, the form of which is the grace of the Holy Ghost, and the uniformity of which, as upheld by this same grace, is simplicity of heart; and no sooner does this fail, than the church falls, since the harmony which preserved its union is departed. It was in the first age of the Christian church that this Christian simplicity was peculiarly exemplified, and, accordingly, she stood fast, and was full both of spirit and of life; but now as this simplicity is lost, so purity is departed from us. The church has lost her primitive and proper form; and if you would find purity of heart in our days, you must go seek it in the hearts of simple young children. The church is now well nigh extinguished, and so we tell you that she must either fall back into her first elements, and altogether evanish, or otherwise be renewed and reformed. It is impossible that she can again revert to heathenism, out of which she came at first, nor can she altogether disappear from the face of the earth; antichrist is not yet so very near; and, therefore, we declare it to be much more probable that she shall again be renovated and restored to her pristine form."—

"When contrary planets come into contact with each other, bad effects are sure to ensue to the world in natural things. You will say, 'Oh! but God can bring good even out of such untoward accidents as these if he pleases, and it is not inconceivable that disunion should continue to prevail among the stars.' And you say rightly; God could do so; but there are many things which it is in his power to do, and which yet he never does. He goes upon a fixed and regular system, which his wisdom has firmly established from the first, and by which it is a settled law that the stars should preserve a mutual harmony and union, before they can exercise their different influences upon our lower world. He has in the same way established a set plan of procedure in the management of his church, by which it may continue to be regulated to the end of the world, since he has instituted in it, as in the heavens, a certain presiding and governing order of angels, who co-operate in bringing forth the elect of God within it. And as all the stars in the firmament stand in their own places, according as the divine wisdom has disposed them, so these servants of God, whom he has ordained for the good of his church, have an appointed order, which is good and profitable for the bringing forth of the elect of God in his church. Now, there are various kinds of prelates or spiritual planets, and their conflicting together is attended with as bad effects to the church as that of the stars would be to the material world. Here you may say again, 'Oh! but God, if he choose, can prevent any injurious consequences of this kind.' True; he could do it now, if he chose, for every thing is in his power; but it so happens that he is never accustomed to do it. For the present he has, by his wisdom, established a certain order, according to which the things which are lower in degree never fail to be influenced by the causes which act above them. Accordingly, at such a time as this, when the higher planets or prelates of the church are thrown into disorder and confusion, how can we look for a reformation, knowing, as we do, that it can be expected only from the outpouring and blessing of the Holy Spirit. Only observe in what a deplorable state the generality of the prelates now are, and you may safely say, that those who are placed under their charge are in no better state, and that any attempt to reform would just increase the evil; but let those in the higher stations be first brought into a right condition, and then there will be less difficulty in restoring those below them to the same. Bad rulers, especially when found in the church of Christ, are the greatest of all scourges, and an evil which points most clearly to a coming judgment. To assure yourselves of this, you need only look into the Old Testament, where you will see that when God would chastise a people for their sins, he gave them bad kings, bad princes and leaders, whom he allowed to give full rein to their wickedness. There also you will find that when he wished to punish his people, he allowed David to fall into sin. So also did he permit that bad king Zedekiah to reign in Jerusalem, at the time when his anger was kindled against her, and he was about to send her into her long captivity. And can the abuse which spiritual rulers make of their power be otherwise than productive of bad effects? What wilt thou then, if the Holy Ghost come and himself commence the work of reformation? This, at least, I make bold to say, that so long as the present misgovernment and disunion continues, there can be no change whatever expected. The sword then must come forth. Therefore have I threatened Italy, and once again threaten her, with her rulers, that she may repent. I have told her that the sword will come. Repent I say, and delay not your repentance till the sword come."—

"My chief reason for appearing here to-day, is that I may prove myself obedient. But to whom? Their lordships? No, indeed. Excuse me, I am not bound to obey what is evil. Well, hast thou come to be persuaded by the people? By no means; it is not to be believed that I would allow myself to be persuaded in this matter by any man. Art thou minded then to obey the higher prelates? Not a word has been spoken to me by any of the prelates. But know, that I have come here to obey one who is prelate of prelates and pope of popes. Wouldst thou have me to act contrary to my nature? I would very willingly remain silent, but it is impossible—I cannot do otherwise than speak: I must obey. I do not appear here this day, as on former occasions, to gain honour and respect, but to expose myself to persecution. I must tell you that these interdicts are grievous. Whoever disobeys them is punished; and I not the least, since, as you well see, I encounter nothing but hatred, and wrath, and shame, and bodily danger, and reproaches on the right hand and the left. In truth, I know not what to say; but I betake myself to God, and exclaim, Thou hast made me for a reproach to all people. I speak of things which are come to pass: straightway one cries out that I am a fool. I change the subject and speak of other things: every one contradicts me. But the more I perceive their contradiction, the more I believe the truth of what I have said. Tell me, ye enemies of the truth, when have ye ever in our days witnessed such a storm of opposition? When have you ever seen, that one preached in a city, and his voice was heard throughout all Italy, and beyond it? Every body contradicts me. One has thereby pocketed six thousand ducats; another says that I have slandered the pope and the cardinals; but nobody thinks of saying, that others have done the same thing, and that publicly. Yes; some who, in public, and indeed from this very pulpit, in presence of the assembled people, have themselves launched out into invectives against the pope, and distinctly mentioned him by name too, have yet blackened my character to him by circulating that I have spoken contemptuously of him. Thus it is that they succeed in bringing me into odium, and themselves into favour. Now may you see how things go. Some there are who write to Rome; and did you but know who they are, and what insipid stuff it is which they write, truly you would wonder! They are a set of shameless men, who, like bugs, smell vilely within and without: at no time do they sleep—through the whole night are they swarming and running about, paying their visit now here, now there, now to this friend, and now to that. When one of these wicked men is converted, the rest cry out, He has become one of the fools! Here I must tell you, that you too easily get alarmed, and allow your spirits to sink, when these base men are slandering you. Know you not that the devil is their head, and that God is the head of the good? Which of these, think you, will overcome, God or the devil? Surely you must believe that God will gain the victory."

No. II.

Letter written from Rome, in 1521, concerning Luther.[*]

[See before, p 50.]

You ask me, among other things, to tell you what we think of Martin and his doctrine; but you do not consider what a dangerous topic this is, especially to beneficed persons. For who would willingly and without necessity expose himself to the indignation of the Roman pontiff and cardinals? I shall, however, comply with your request, on condition that you conceal my name and thus screen me from danger.

Know, then, that there is not an intelligent person in Rome who is not perfectly convinced that Martin has spoken the truth in most things; but good men dissemble from dread of the tyrant, and bad men are enraged, because they are forced to hear the truth. Indignation is mixed with fear in the minds of the latter class, for they are in great alarm lest the affair spread further. This is the reason why such a furious

---

[*] This interesting document, relating to the early history of the Reformation, and the light in which it was viewed by persons residing in Rome, was found, in Latin, among the papers of Bilibald Pirkheimer, one of the most distinguished restorers of letters in Germany. It was in the hand-writing of that Scholar, who had translated it from the original Italian, probably to screen the author from detection. He had marked it with the inscription, *Literæ cujusdam e Roma.* The year in which it was written is ascertained from internal evidence. It is translated here from a copy published by Riederer, Nachrichten zur Kirchen-Gelehrten und Bucher-Geschichte, band i. p. 178—184, Altdorf, 1764.

bull has been issued, in opposition to the remonstrances of many good and wise men, who advised that the matter should be deliberately weighed, and that Martin should be dealt with mildly and by reasoning, instead of being run down by violence and execrations. But indignation and fear prevailed; for the heads of the faction asserted that it was unbecoming the Roman pontiff to treat with so mean a person, and that force should be employed against the obstinate, lest others should be encouraged to use similar freedoms. In support of this opinion, they referred to John Huss and his disciple Jerome, by whose punishment, they said, many were deterred from the like temerity.

One of the chief authors of this advice was cardinal Cajetan, who is unfavourable to the Germans, because, as he thinks, he was not so honourably received and rewarded by them as he should have been, for he returned to Rome disappointed and poor. He had discovered, he said, that nothing but fire and sword would keep the Germans from throwing off the Roman yoke. To him were joined Silvester Prierias and the whole faction of the Dominicans, especially the enemies of Capnio, who accused the pope of too great gentleness, asserting, that if he had repressed, at the beginning, the attempts of Capnio by forcible measures, Martin would never have dared such things; and, on that occasion, they extorted a sentence against Capnio's book, although, a little before, the pope had encouraged some persons to print the Talmud, and granted them a privilege for that purpose. Many good men felt very indignant at this, as unjust in itself and derogatory to the dignity and character of the pope; but the worst part prevailed. We are of opinion, however, that the Dominicans are carried headlong, by the Divine displeasure and their own vices, to the extreme of wickedness. The divines of Cologne and Louvain, and many others in Germany, clandestinely urged the measure, promising certain victory as soon as the Roman ensigns (that is, the terrible leaden bulls) were displayed; and it is also said, that certain German princes, whose names, though I knew them, should be secret, were active in the same cause, more from hatred to their neighbours than zeal for the faith.

Above all, the merchant Fuecker, who has great influence at Rome through his money, and whom we commonly call the king of coins, irritated the pope and those of his faction, not only from hatred, but also for the sake of gain and the traffic in benefices, promising the support of many princes to his holiness, provided he would use force against Martin. For this purpose, he sent to Rome the man of his choice, Eckius, a not unapt instrument of the court of Rome, if you except his sottishness; for he excels in temerity, audacity, lying, dissimulation, adulation, and other courtly vices. The only objection to him was his drunkenness, which, you know, is odious to the Italians; but the favour and power of Fuecker reconciled them even to this, nay, turned it into a virtue, so that they applauded the choice, saying, that nothing could be fitter than to send the drunken Germans a drunken ambassador, and that temerity was to be met by temerity. As it was necessary to find a colleague to him, Aleander was at last pitched on—an illustrious couple of orators! every way suited to the cause, and resembling one another in impudence, rashness, and profligacy. No good man, no person of sane mind, belonging to the German nation, would have undertaken such a task; or if there had, perhaps, been one willing, fear and the greatness of the danger would have deterred him from undertaking it. At first, the Jewish extraction of Aleander appeared to be an obstacle to his appointment, but it was thought that this would be compensated by the drunkenness of Eckius. Thus the purpose, the bulls, and the ambassadors, were completely of a kind; for what need was there for reason, where rashness and dishonesty only were required?

War being thus declared, Eckius was furnished with instructions, promises, and bulls; and being charged to execute his task vigorously, promised his ready service, and offered his life for glory, or rather for reward. But you are deceived if you believe that money was given him by the pope, for his holiness is not accustomed to give but to receive money. If Eckius received any money, it was not from the pope but from Fuecker, though I do not believe even this. The friends of Fuecker say that Eckius was furnished with money; but it is the custom with courts and proud persons to promise much and pay little, and to make you own that you received what you never touched, to avoid the disgrace of appearing to have been cheated.

Nor are you to believe that Eckius has authority to cite and summons whomsoever he pleases. If he has anything of that kind, it is unquestionably surreptitious; for what madness would it be to cite the innocent? No doubt, if he were to cite those who openly defend Martin, the pope and his friends would not be greatly displeased, but, as you write, that would be an ocean. If, among the persons cited, you find any of the friends of Capnio, you will easily understand whence the information has proceeded.

No wonder, then, that these bulls displease many among us, since there are few here who approve them, though they are forced to mutter their dislike; for they know that this is not the way of truth. For what—(to pass by other things, for it does not belong to me to search narrowly into each, I wish they were not too manifest to all)—what can be more unjust than to involve those things which Martin has written piously and truly in the same sentence of condemnation with things which are bad? Such procedure savours more of Jewish perfidy and Mahometan impiety than of Christian religion; for the Turks, knowing that their faith is false, and cannot be proved by reasons, will not permit it to be brought into dispute, but defend it by the sword; and the Jews were accustomed to stone to death those who accused their impiety and wickedness, saying that they had blasphemed God and the lawgiver. God never commanded the Christian faith, which is true, and reasonable, and pious, to be defended by fire and sword; a practice which came from that old deceiver, who, from the beginning, abode not in the truth, for it is not truth, but a lie, cloaked with the appearance of truth and a sophistical garb, that seeks to be defended with such weapons.

Although the friends of Luther could have wished that he had shown greater moderation in some things, yet they know that his adversaries have provoked him to write and teach many things which otherwise he would not have uttered; not that the truth should be concealed, but that we should avoid giving offence. Further it is universally well known that all who have written against Luther, or impunged his doctrine, are persons of bad life and immoral character. What wonder, then, that these writings should savour more of their vices than of Christ and integrity? I speak of Roman writers; what the character of those of Germany is you know better than I, for I do not pretend to be acquainted with them.

The pope and his supporters will therefore strain every nerve to destroy Luther, and to extinguish his doctrine as pernicious, not to Christians, but to the court of Rome; and, if I do not mistake, the chief thing that will be treated at your ensuing royal diet* will be what relates to Luther, who is looked upon as a greater enemy to us than the Turk. The young emperor will be urged with threats, entreaties, and flatteries. The Germans will be tempted with the praises of their ancestors, gifts, and promises; the Spaniards will be threatened with the dangers of the sedition which rages in their native country, and flattered with the promise of investiture in the kingdom of Naples. We will not neglect to besiege the nobility and others about the emperor's court; for we are familiar with such arts, which seldom fail us. But if we do not succeed in this way, we will depose the emperor, free the people from their allegiance to him, choose one in his place who will favour our cause, raise a tumult in Germany similar to that which pre-

* The Diet of Worms.

vails in Spain, summon France, England, and other kingdoms to arms, and neglect none of those means which our predecessors so successfully adopted against kings and emperors; in fine, that we may accomplish our purpose and perpetuate our tyranny, we will set at nought Christianity, faith, piety, and common honesty; we will stand in awe of no power, be it of emperors, kings, princes, or states; the only fear we have is lest God should visit us with a punishment, the heavier that it has been so long delayed, and set his flock free from mercenary shepherds—an issue which many predictions and omens have announced, and which our vices deserve and loudly demand.

No. III.

*Account of an Italian book, entitled, A Summary of the Sacred Scriptures.**

[See before, p. 85.]

CHAP. 1. Of faith and baptism, and what baptism signifies. 2. Additional information as to the meaning of baptism. 3. What we profess in baptism, and what kind of profession we make. 4. Of the Christian faith, and what a Christian ought to believe in order to salvation. 5. Of the sure joy of obtaining one's salvation. 6. How we are saved by grace alone, and not in any other way. 7. To whom the grace of God is given. 8. How faith produces charity, and charity good works. 9. How we should not serve

* The reader will be able to form a tolerably correct idea of the nature of this work, and of the extent of the information which it conveys, from the table of contents, and the extract here given from the prologue. Gerdes, by mistake, calls it *Seminarium Scripturæ*. (Ital. Reform. p. 82.) It was published at least fifteen years before 1549, when Casa included it in his list of prohibited books. Giberti, bishop of Verona, was so much pleased with its form, as to point it out as a pattern to those who composed works for the instruction of such as could not read Latin. (Ergoetzl. ii. 29.) It is reviewed by Riederer. (Nachrichten, iv. 121, 241—243.)

God for reward. 10. How we have disinherited ourselves by our disobedience. 11. Of the two kinds of people living in the world. 12. Of good works, and in what way they are pleasing to God. 13. Of four kinds of faith according to the sacred Scripture, and what Christian faith is. 14. In what Christianity consists. 15. How a man should not be afflicted at death. 16. Of the monkish life, as it was in times past. 17. If the life of a monk is preferable to that of a common citizen. 18. Whence it is that monks do not make progress in the spiritual life, but often become worse. 19. Of parents who wish to enter their children into the religious orders. 20. Of the life of nuns. 21. Of the cloisters of sisters, and their life. 22. How husband and wife should live according to the doctrine of the gospel. 23. How parents should instruct and rule their children according to the gospel. 24. Of the life of common citizens, artizans, and labourers. 25. How the rich ought to live according to the gospel. 26. Of the two kinds of government, secular and spiritual. 27. Information, according to the gospel, concerning governors, judges, and other powers. 28. The Christian doctrine of paying taxes and tribute to rulers, according to the gospel. 29. Of soldiers, and whether Christians can carry on war without sin, an information according to the gospel. 30. How servants and domestics ought to live, a doctrine according to the gospel. 31. Of the life of widows, a brief information according to the gospel.

Because all cannot read or understand every book, in order that they may understand the grounds of Scripture, and what it teaches us, I have comprehended in this little book the grounds and sum of divine Scripture, of which the head and chief is faith, from which proceed hope and charity. Thus every one may know what he ought to believe, what he ought to hope for, why he ought to love God, and how God is our father, and we are the children and heirs of the kingdom of God, as St. Paul teaches in all his epistles. Thus also he may know how we are justified without our own merits, so that we should not put our confidence in our good works, as the Jews did. In fine, it teaches that we must not neglect good works, but need to know how and why we should perform them, hoping for our salvation, not from them, but solely from the grace and mercy of God through Christ, by which I have written this tract.—Such is the matter treated of in the first part of this little book. In the second part, I show how persons of every state should live according to the gospel. By this I intend to convince all, how far removed from the doctrine of Christ their life is, to the end that, through the grace of God, they may amend the same. I do not teach that subjects should not be obedient to their princes, nor that monks should fly from their monasteries; but I show them how they ought to live, and to know their errors and correct them; otherwise it avails more before God to be an humble publican than a holy hypocrite, because God does not look at your external works, but at your internal, and at the intentions and secrets of the heart.

No. IV.

*Extracts from a Treatise by Gabriele Valliculi, entitled, De liberali Dei Gratia, et Servo hominis Arbitrio.**

[See before, p. 178.]

To the very reverend father in Christ and worthy bishop of Luna, doctor Sylvestro Benedetto of Sarsi-

---

* Nothing is known concerning the author of this book. It was printed at Nurenberg in the year 1536; but it had most probably been previously published in Italy. Melanchthon, in a letter to Veit Dietrich, written in 1530, says—" In Italy there has arisen a new Luther, whose propositions I send you." (Epistolæ, p. 432, edit. Lugd.) But we have no decisive evidence that he refers to the author of this book. Valliculi appears not to have been a man of talents, but of warm piety; and most probably wrote this treatise after reading Luther's celebrated work *De Servo Arbitrio*. Silvestro Benetto, to whom it is dedicated, was the nephew of Thomas Benettus or de

na, with the greatest respect and veneration, Gabriele Valliculi, in Jesus the only son of the Virgin, wishes grace, by which we are freely justified, and peace, according to what the angels announced at the nativity of Christ, peace on earth and good-will towards men.

I am placed in a strait betwixt two, being doubtful whether I should keep silence respecting the free grace of God and the enslaved will of man, in which case death awaits me; or whether I should treat of them, and run the risk of falling into the hands of the wicked. But the Holy Spirit teaches me that I should choose to fall into the hands of the wicked rather than to sin in the sight of God. Help me, O Lord, thou who art my hope, my refuge, my leader, my justification, my protector and defender. All my safety and confidence is placed in thee, not in human aid, much less in the enslaved will of man. In thee alone, O God, have I hoped, and on this account shall never be moved. But why am I not confounded when the Holy Spirit cries in my ear, What fruit hast thou of those things whereof thou art now ashamed? It is because I come to thee, my Christ, (not to the enslaved will of man,) and my countenance is enlightened and not covered with shame. When I am confounded by the enslaved will of sin in Adam, I will, by the free grace of God, fly from him to Jesus Christ my Saviour, and then I shall not be confounded. * * * * * Free and deliver me for thy righteousness sake, not for mine, but for thine: if I should say for mine, then I would belong to the number of those of whom the Holy Spirit has said, Being ignorant of God's righteousness, they go about to establish a righteousness of their own. Being wholly depraved, I am not justified by my own, but by thy righteousness, and if not by mine but by thine, then is righteousness imputed to me by thy sovereign grace.

Benedictis, bishop of Sarsina and Luna, succeeded his uncle in that bishoprick in 1497, and died in 1537. (Ughelli Italia Sacra, tom i. p. 556.) The extracts are taken from Riederer, Nachrichten, tom. iv. p. 112, &c.

* * * * * In the first place, then, we are of opinion that the human understanding, from its very nature, is incapable of comprehending any thing but what is carnal, or of distinguishing between good and evil except by a carnal discernment. Poverty, want, ignominy, temporal losses, disease, death, and all worldly misfortunes, it judges to be evil; but wealth, glory, reputation, health, long life, and all worldly blessings, it reckons to be good. It knows nothing of a God merciful, angry, avenging, prescient, predestinating, and producing all things; and this the apostle testifies when he says, For we have not received the spirit of this world, nor of reason, intellect, and will, but of the free grace of God, that we may know the things which are given us by God, and not by the understanding and the will—given, saith the apostle, on account of no preceding merit. If they be given, then they must be free; if free, what merit is there in them? These things I have said, not in the learned words of human wisdom, or of the dreams of the sophists, but by the teaching of the Spirit, comparing spiritual things with spiritual.

* * * * Observe to what length this blindness of heart and foolishness of understanding have proceeded. Men have adulterated the majesty of the immortal God, by shadowing out the image of perishing man, and not of man only, but of brute creatures also: they have become corrupt in their own enslaved will and stupidity of heart, and abominable in their pursuits, because human reason is wholly ignorant of God, and neither comprehends nor seeks after him; and, accordingly, they have turned aside to unprofitable things, not perceiving the things of God. But as, by the enslaved will of man, sin has abounded, so the free grace of God hath abounded much more; and as, by the enslaved will of man, sin reigned to eternal punishment, so, by the free grace of God, the king of Salem reigns to life everlasting. Who is it then that reigns? Not the understanding or will of man, but our Lord Jesus Christ the Saviour, who has given us grace without any merit on our part. The plain truth is, that, in respect of spiritual judgment, the human understanding is entirely ignorant of God; and though it were, by day and by night, incessantly employed in examining, perusing, and ruminating upon the whole Talmud, the Holy Scriptures, and the books of philosophers and divines, both ancient and modern, it could never, without the assistance of the Spirit, comprehend truly his omnipotence, prescience, providence, mercy or anger. It listens to discourses, professes to believe them, and hypocritically imitates them, though, in reality, it is quite unacquainted with God, and looks upon heavenly things as fabulous. Oh the profound blindness of man! as Jeremiah testifies, saying, The human heart is depraved and unsearchable; who can understand it? The Lord searches the heart and reins; but the reason of man is incapable of discerning the things of heaven.

No. V.

*Letter from Tolomei to Ochino.**

[See before, p. 183.]

On my return, a few days ago, from the villa to Rome, I was unexpectedly told a piece of intelligence, which seemed to me not only new, but foolish, incredible, and shocking. I was informed, that you, under the influence of some strange advice, had gone over from the camp of the catholics to the tents of the Lutherans, and devoted yourself to that heretical and wicked sect. On hearing this, I was struck with sudden astonishment, and, as we say, made the sign of the cross. Finding the report confirmed by numerous witnesses, and indeed by every one I met, I was obliged, in spite of myself, to believe it, though the news appeared to me as extravagant as if I had been

---

* Delle Lettere di M. Claudio Tolomei, p. 237—241, in Vinegia, 1578.

told that doves had been transformed into serpents, and kids into tigers. But when I considered that Lucifer, from being a fair angel, became a devil, I began to perceive how easily the horrible transformation might happen in your case. For some days I was in doubt whether I ought to write you, or whether it might not be more advisable to keep silence, and retain within my own breast the grief I felt and still feel on account of the extraordinary and dreadful change which you have made. For, on the one hand, it appeared to me that nothing was to be gained by writing, as you have fixed your affections on this new sect, and shown to the world, not only by your words but your actions, that your mind is completely resolved; and then I was afraid lest, while I hoped to reclaim you from the path you have chosen, my own mind should be disturbed by your answer; for well I know the extent of your learning, and the splendour of your eloquence, by whose attractions I might be beguiled and drawn into danger. But, on the other hand, I was afraid that, by keeping silence, I should be forced to form an unfavourable opinion of you, and that being ignorant of your reasons and motives for departing, I had it not in my power to make a sufficient apology for you to numbers who condemn your conduct, and would be under the necessity of making the common-place excuse, by saying, that I could not believe that a person of so much prudence, such singular goodness, and exalted piety as Frate Bernardino Ochino, would make so great a change in his sentiments and mode of life without good reasons. This excuse, I am afraid, would not be sustained, and it would be said, that to make innovations in matters of faith, to disobey our superiors, and to pass from the catholics to the heretics, is no proof either of prudence or religion; and, in fine, that to depart from that most holy truth which has been handed down from the first apostles to our times, and preserved in the Roman church, is not lawful or permissible in any case; but that, on the contrary, we should endure every thing in confessing and defending it, counting pain to be pleasure, imprisonment liberty, torments joy, poverty riches, and death true and eternal life, as so many ancient martyrs did, who never would be removed from the articles confessed by the catholic church, which (as St. Paul says) is the pillar and ground of truth. When I perceived the manner in which they spoke of you, I was so distracted and grieved, that, at last, I resolved to write, and to beg you earnestly to answer me, and endeavour to dissipate the darkness which hangs over this unexpected change of yours, for if I obtain no other light, I cannot believe that this is the light of God.

Perhaps it may be said, that you left Italy because you was persecuted, and that you have only imitated the example of Christ and of Paul and other holy men, who fled from the hands and the claws of their persecutors; and I may be told, that those who are accused by the world are excused by God, and that those who are despised by the world are honoured by God. But, in the first place, I know not that it is lawful for a person to flee contrary to the commandment and orders of his superiors, to whom he has submitted himself, and whom he is bound to obey, as is the case with you. Besides, I do not understand what was the persecution, what was the accusation, or what the dishonour, to which you were exposed, and which made it necessary for you to flee. I remember well, that, in Italy, you were esteemed, honoured, revered, and, as it were, adored like something divine; and, when you preached the sacred name and true doctrine of Christ, you were listened to with such devotion by all Italy, that you could not desire more favour nor she a better spirit. Nor by being so much honoured and revered by the world, were you (as I believe) in less favour with God, but rather in greater, in proportion to the greater fruit which you produced by inspiring the minds of Christians with the love of God; like your first father and master, St. Francis, who was highly revered by the people and by princes, and yet was so dear a servant of God as to be marked with the sacred scars which the Lord Jesus Christ received on the cross. But, perhaps, I will be told, that, in your last sermons, some things spoken by you were marked, informed against, and accused, as containing unsound and uncatholic doctrine. To this I would say, either the accusation was just or it was unjust. If unjust, what reason had you to fear? Why did not you the rather, when called, come to Rome? Before a just prince who loved you greatly, the opinion which he had of your goodness and virtue would have been refined like gold in the fire. If San Bernardino had come to Rome and cleared himself of the charges laid against him, the sanctity of his life would have shone forth the brighter, to the great edification of the people. The malice of your accusers could not have prevailed over the force of truth, sustained and defended by the favour which you enjoyed, not only in Rome, but through all Italy. But if the accusation brought against you was just and wellfounded, I know nothing that can be said, but that, either through ignorance or through malice, you had spread these doctrines among the people. Now, to speak the truth, the one appears to me difficult, and the other impossible, to believe. But be it so, that it is either by the one or the other. If it was through ignorance, then you are under great obligation to your accusers, who had reason for their charges; and you ought to renounce the darkness of error and return to the light of truth, which is nothing else but to return to Christ, the fountain and author of all truth. If it was through malice, the very thought is so wicked that no defence can be set up for such conduct: it is to be blamed in a man, abhorred in a Christian, censured in a monk, anathematized in a preacher of the word of God; and the person guilty of this is no longer a man but is transformed into a demon. I do not forget that the compassionate God does not abandon any who have recourse to him, and that the fruits of the holy sacrament of penance are sweet, so that there is not a better remedy than, like Peter, to weep bitterly for sin.

But, perhaps, it will be said, that it was neither

ignorance nor malice that led to this change, but a greater illumination in the things of God; and that Christ has laid open much truth which remained hid to this time, as he was formerly pleased to illuminate the mind of Paul, and to convert him from Judaism to the true faith. Did Christ then teach and reveal the contrary to what he had taught the apostles? Did he teach them false doctrine; and is the truth turned into a lie? Were Clement, Anaclet, Evarist, Anicet, and other great spirits of God, deceived; and did they deceive others along with themselves? Did Ignatius, on whose heart was found written the name of Christ, not know the true doctrine of Christ? What shall I say of the successors of these men? Shall I believe that Irenæus, Origen, Cyprian—shall I believe that Athanasius, Didymus, Damascene—shall I believe that the two great lights of Cappadocia, Gregory and Basil—shall I believe that Ambrose, Jerome, Augustine, Bernard, and a multitude of other most holy men and renowned doctors of the Christian faith—were all in error? that, instead of holding forth the light, they were involved in darkness; and, in place of teaching us the truth, they have delivered us over to a lie? No person of sane mind will believe this falsehood, especially as Christ our Saviour hath said—"Wheresoever the body is, thither the eagles shall be gathered together." What shall I say more? Has Christ then, for a long time, forsaken his church? For, seeing the catholic verity was believed by all until the time of the impious Luther, he who believes that it is not true says that Christ has entirely forsaken the church; a thing horrible to think of, Christ having said—"Lo! I am with you always to the end of the world." It is necessary, believe me, that, in this turbid and tempestuous sea of conflicting opinions, there should be one fixed star by which to steer our course in the true way of God; and this, as all holy and learned men have taught, is and can be no other than the Roman church, begun by Peter, upon whom Christ first founded his church, and which, through uninterrupted succession of the popes, has come down to the present times. In opposition to this, it is of no avail with me that you quote places of Scripture, understood and interpreted in your way, for it is enough for me to recollect the good and faithful counsel of Origen Adamantius, that though one should show canonical Scripture in opposition to what the church observes and uses, we must not believe him nor depart from the traditions of the fathers. In fine, I say that no good man will leave the catholic church, and that none who leaves it is to be esteemed good; of which I could give such substantial reasons as would show that perhaps no truth in any doctrine is more true than this truth. Therefore, the more I reflect on this affair, the more do I find myself at a loss in defending your cause; and I would willingly not love you so much, that so I might not feel that grief which I now endure on account of this your recent calamity. I may be allowed to make use of this ambiguous and perhaps unsuitable word, to moderate the error which has sprung from your will. But since the love, with which your singular virtue formerly inflamed me, still lives in me, be pleased to give me some consolation, by acquainting me with the reasons of your conduct, which if they do not relieve me entirely of my pain, may perhaps mitigate and alleviate it in some degree. I would counsel you, if, as I believe, you have left Italy for the sake of personal safety, under the influence, perhaps, of too great timidity, that you keep where you are: do not go further; do not preach, do not write, do not speak anything contrary to the catholic doctrine. On the contrary, for anything said or done by you, refer yourself humbly to the judgment of the Roman church; in which case, as I have said, the only thing which will be found blamable in you will be fear, arising from an excess of counsel. But if you conduct yourself otherwise, by exasperating the matter every day, you will be condemned for obstinate heresy. In the first case, by remaining quiet and humble, all Italy will rise up in your favour; they will desire you, they will call for you, they will petition in your behalf, and, to their great joy, will obtain for you every kind of favour. In the second case, the remains of love to you which are yet warm in the hearts of many, will be quenched; and hatred, scorn, and indignation, will take their place. I am reduced to this, that, whereas formerly, as you know, I often entreated you to pray to God for me, at present knowing that the necessity is on the other side, I cannot do otherwise than pray to God for you; and now again I do humbly beseech him that he would be pleased to illuminate and assist you. From Rome, 20th October 1542.

No. VI.

Extract of a Letter written in prison by Pomponio Algieri, to his friends in the University of Padua.[*]

[See before, p. 264]

To allay the grief you feel on my account, I am anxious to impart to you a share of my consolation, that we may rejoice together, and return thanks to the Lord with songs. I speak what to man will appear incredible; I have found honey in the bowels of the lion, (who will believe it?) pleasantness in a dismal pit, soothing prospects of life in the gloomy mansions of death, joy in an infernal gulf! Where others weep, I rejoice; where others tremble, I am erect; in the most distressing situation I have found the highest delight, in solitude the best fellowship, and in galling chains rest. But instead of the deluded world believing these things, it will be rather disposed to ask, in an incredulous tone—" How, think you, will you be able to endure the reproaches and threats of men, the fires, the colds, the crosses, the thousand inconveniences of your situation? Do you not look back with regret on your beloved native land, your possessions, your relations, your pleasures, your hon-

---

[*] Translated from the original Latin, in Pantaleon, Rerum in Eccles. Gest. p. 329—332.

ours? Have you forgotten the delights of science, and the solace, which it yielded you under all your labours? Will you at once throw away all the toils, watchings, and laudable exertions devoted to study from your childhood? Have you no dread of that death which hangs over you, because, forsooth, you have committed no crime? Oh! foolish and infatuated man, who can, by a single word, secure all these blessings and escape death, and yet will not! How rude to be inexorable to the requests of senators the most august, pious, just, wise, and good; to turn an obstinate ear when men so illustrious entreat you!"

But hear me, blind worldlings, while I answer you. What is hotter than the fire which is laid up for you; and what colder than your hearts which dwell in darkness and have no light? What can be more unpleasant, perplexed, and agitated, than the life you lead; or more odious and mean than the present world? Say, what native country is sweeter than heaven; what treasure preferable to eternal life? Who are my relations but those who hear the word of God; and where shall riches more abundant or honours more worthy be found than in heaven? Say, foolish man, were not the sciences, given to conduct us to the knowledge of God? and if they lead us not to this, are not our labours, our watchings, and all our painful exertions utterly lost? The prison is severe indeed to the guilty, but sweet to the innocent; distilling dew and nectar, sending forth milk and all delectable things. This desert place and wild, is to me a spacious valley, the noblest spot on earth. Listen to me, unhappy men, while I rehearse my experience; and then judge whether there be in the world a more pleasant plain. Here kings and princes, cities and people, pass before me in review. Here I behold the fate of battles; I see some vanquished, others victorious, some trodden to dust, others lifted into the triumphal car. I am caught up to Mount Sion, to heaven. Jesus Christ stands in the front, and around are the patriarchs, prophets, evangelists, apostles, and all the servants of God. He embraces and cherishes me;

they encourage me, and spread the sacrament before me; they offer me consolations, they attend me with songs. Can I be said to be alone while surrounded by so many and so illustrious attendants? My intercourse with them affords me example as well as comfort; for in that circle I behold some crucified and slain, others stoned and sawn asunder, some roasted, others fried in brazen vessels, one with his eyes dug out, another with his tongue cut off, one beheaded, another maimed of hand and foot, some thrown into the fiery furnace, others left a prey to the ravenous birds. Here I have no fixed habitation, and seek for myself in the heavens the first new Jerusalem which presents itself. I have entered upon a path which conducts to a pleasant dwelling, and where I doubt not to find wealth, and relations, and pleasures, and honours. In those earthly enjoyments (all of them shadowy, and fading, and vanity of vanities without the substantial hope of a coming eternity) which the supreme Lord was pleased to bestow upon me, I found indeed transient company and solace; but now I taste what endureth. I have burned with heat, I have shuddered with cold, I have watched day and night; but now these struggles have come to a close. Not an hour nor a day has passed without some benefit: the true love of God is now engraven on my heart; the Lord has filled me with joy; I rest in peace. Who then will venture to condemn this life of mine, and to pronounce my days unhappy? Who so rash as to declare his labours lost who has found the Lord of the world, who has exchanged death for life? "The Lord is my portion, saith my soul, therefore will I seek him." If to die in the Lord be not to die but to begin a blessed life, why does rebellious man cast death in my teeth? O how pleasant is that death which gives me to drink of the cup of God! What surer earnest of salvation than to suffer as Christ suffered! * *
* * * Be comforted, my most beloved fellow-servants of God, be comforted, when temptations assail you; let your patience be perfect in all things for suffering is our promised portion in this life; as it is writ-

ten—" The time cometh, when he who slays you will think he doeth God service." Tribulation and death are our signs of election and future life: let us rejoice and praise the Lord that we are innocent; for it is better, if such be the will of God, that we suffer for welldoing than for evil-doing. We have a noble pattern in Christ, and the prophets who have spoken in the name of the Lord, whom the children of iniquity have slain. Behold! we call those blessed who bore up under their trials. Let us rejoice in our innocence and righteousness; God will reward our persecutors, for vengeance is his. As to what they say concerning the Venetian nobility and senators, extolling them as the most august, wise, just, pious, pacific, and of the highest character and fame, I am willing to give all this its due weight. But the apostle teaches us, "that we ought to obey God rather than man;" and, accordingly, after first giving God the service due to him, then and not till then are we bound to obey the official powers of this world. I grant they are august, but as yet they require to be perfected in the Lord; they are just, but the foundation and seat of justice, Jesus Christ, is wanting; they are wise, but where is the beginning of wisdom, the fear of God? they are called pious, but I could wish they were made perfect in Christian charity; they are called good, but I look in vain for the basis of all goodness, even God the great and the good; they are called illustrious, but they have not yet received our Saviour, the Lord of glory. I am blamed for not yielding to the lords of Venice. If what I declared before them was not true and just, let it be proved, and I will confess that they proceeded from me and not from the Lord. If otherwise, who will lay any thing to my charge? not surely the wise. Who will condemn me? not surely the righteous. But if they should, still the gospel shall not be frustrated, and the kingdom of God shall the sooner come to the elect of Christ Jesus. Lift up your eyes, my dearly beloved, and consider the ways of God: the Lord has lately threatened with pestilence, and this he has done for our correction: if we do not receive him he will strike those who rise up against Christ, with sword, and pestilence, and famine. These things, brethren, have I written for your consolation. Pray for me. I salute with a holy kiss my masters, Sylvio, Pergula, and Giusto, along with Fedele di Petra, and the person who goes by the name of Lælia, whom, though absent, I knew, and the Lord Syndic of the university, with all others whose names are written in the book of life.

Farewell, all my fellow-servants of God; farewell in the Lord, and pray earnestly for me. From the delectable garden of the Leonine prison, 21st July, 1555, the most devoted servant of the faithful, the bound

POMPONIUS ALGIER.

No VII.

*Extract of a Letter from Carnesecchi to Flaminio.**

[See before, p. 270, comp. p. 166.]

I received your letter, in which you enlarge, in the way of instruction and admonition, on those topics which we discussed in conversation. Accept of my best thanks for this proof of your piety and great affection for me. When I reflect on the bitter animosity and furious discord which the recent controversies about religion have produced, and on the license which the contending parties have taken in inveighing against one another, forgetful of their own credit and the salvation of others, which charity and and the divine caution against giving offence bound them to regard, I am charmed with the moderation

---

* This letter is printed at length in Schelhorn, Amœnitates Historiæ Ecclesiasticæ et Literariæ, tom. ii p. 155—170. It is the only production of Carnesecchi's pen which I have met with. As my object is merely to give the reader an idea of his character, I have not inserted that part of the letter which enters into the merits of the controversy respecting the eucharist.

and mildness of your letter, in which you avoid throwing abuse on your adversaries or wounding them with biting sarcasm; and, satisfied with pronouncing their sect execrable, discover your usual impartiality by commending such of them as are distinguished for their talents, and superior to the rest in modesty and good manners. Conduct like this was applauded by the ancients, and our own age as well as the last has furnished illustrious examples of it. We are told that Jovianus Pontanus commended the studies of all, and never spoke detractingly of any man, either privately or in public. M. Sabellicus would not revenge himself by retorting the violent and malevolent taunts of his adversaries, though he was by no means deficient in the graces of a copious and elegant style; a display of generosity which has led some over rigid critics to detract from his genius. Pomponius Lætus, an inhabitant of Rome, would not permit himself to be dragged into personal controversy, and suffered the calumnies which were uttered against him to pass without reply. In our own age, not to mention others, what examples of modesty and mildness have we in Nicolaus Leonicus and Jacobus Sadoletus. But the Philelphi, the Poggii, the Vallæ, and others, their contemporaries, (for I will not name any of the present age,) with what contumely and opprobrium did they not load their antagonists? But you content yourself with simply naming the men who, in your opinion, have injured religion, and treat the subject in controversy with accuracy and gentleness.

With respect to the question itself, I shall, for the purpose of enabling us to judge of it with greater accuracy, state, with your leave, what has occurred to me in opposition to your arguments, with all the freedom which our friendship warrants; and you, according to your piety and learning, will judge whether it has any weight in favour of the sentiment of your opponents. I need not remind you that, as in all discussions, the discovery of truth should be our aim, so you should set aside every thing which has a tendency to obstruct this—all respect to custom, long prescription of time, and the authority of human institutions—and steadily fix your eye on that light which alone can prevent us from wandering in error. You recommend certain books to me, but afterwards, with the view of lessening my labour, are pleased to say that you will rest the defence of your cause on Irenæus, an ancient and approved writer. For this I thank you, for really the reading of so many and so voluminous authors would be an arduous and Herculean task. Besides, as it is the duty of an impartial judge to hear the evidence on both sides, I would need to read all the books which are recommended by your adversaries; and where would be the end of that labour? For you know well what is the consequence of controversies and altercation; both parties wishing to be victorious, each heaps up whatever can be said against his opponent and in favour of his own cause; and this practice having become common to those who pervert truth and those who confute error, truth itself, by being mixed up with artifice, has fallen under suspicion with many, who are afraid that their understandings will be bewildered by the casuistry of disputants. Wherefore passing by these and derogating from none of them, I shall, if you please, proceed to examine and weigh with attention what you have produced from the purer fountains of antiquity. It was unnecessary for you, in writing to me, to establish the authority of Irenæus's works, or to commend the author so warmly; for I have long known the universal esteem in which he and his writings are held, and am myself an admirer of both. I often regret that his works have not reached us in the original Greek, which as appears from the extracts inserted in the books of Eusebius, Epiphanius, and others, he seems to have written with fluency, and not without elegance. I am astonished that a certain learned writer has expressed a doubt whether he wrote in Greek. As to those of his writings which have been translated into Latin, (such as it is,) I cannot vouch for their fidelity to the original—certainly the style is by no means good; for the translator makes use of unmeaning words, and his foreign idiom often prevents the reader from discovering the sense. But in this, as in many other cases, we must take what we can get, not what we would wish. In those books which have been published, there is a good deal of discussion on subjects of great importance. Let us then examine the excerpt from the fourth book of Irenæus against heretics. It is necessary, however, for understanding what is said, that we attend to the design, the occasion, and the subject; for otherwise the mind of the reader will be unable to form a fixed and determinate judgment of the author's meaning. For example, Christ says—"Without me ye can do nothing:" to commit sin is to do something; does it therefore follow that without Christ no sin is committed? Again he says—"Give to every one that asketh;" are we therefore to give to a person what he may ask for a base and villainous purpose? I could bring forward many examples of this kind, but these will explain what I mean. * * * *

Nor does the universal agreement of the catholic church concerning ceremonies—of the Greeks, the Armenians, the Indians, and, if you please, the Ethiopians—help the matter; for the frequency or extent of a corrupt practice will never justify it. It is evident that the purity of religion has been deeply injured in every nation, through the carelessness of those to whom it was intrusted, through ignorance of the polite arts and the turbulency of the times. Consider, I pray you, what is now the universal opinion concerning a barbarous style. Shall we condemn those men who have exploded the rude diction long in use, and introduced a purer and more elegant one in its room? But I need not enlarge on this subject to one of your learning. The rest of your letter consists of several accusations, some of them bitter, which, however, I do not impute to you, but to those who prefer defending falsehood to embracing truth. These persons, if they had common sense, would consider that no reproaches are more futile and ridiculous than those which recoil, or at least can easily be thrown back, on the head of the author. In your letter you censure, with great severity and justice, the obstinacy of those who remain blindly attached to their own opinion, cloak their pride under a false zeal, arrogantly accuse general and established customs, and as you add, are actuated by fears of losing their worldly dignities and emoluments. All of these are bad things. I grant that general and ancient custom ought to be retained, lest the foundations be sapped; but this is the very question in dispute, and it remains still undetermined. Who have transgressed or are opposing the catholic agreement? You say that some have their minds puffed up with contumacy, are blinded by zeal, too confident in their boldness, ambitious, avaricious. Let it then, I would say, be determined who are the persons chargeable with these vices. We know too well how bitterly each party reproaches the other, and how far this evil has proceeded in these dissolute and undisciplined times. In my opinion, we should consider what is true, proper, and laudable in itself—what ought to be done, not what has been done by this or that person. Thus, after deliberation, let us pronounce our sentiments concerning the subject, and then, if it must be so, let us speak concerning the persons. Of these, as I have already signified, I shall say nothing, either in the way of accusation or defence; for what Horace said of the Trojan war, may, if I am not mistaken, be justly applied to this controversy—

> Iliacos intra muros peccatur et extra.

A good man will be cautious what he says to the prejudice of another, lest he spread abroad ill-founded reports. I am led to mention this from your naming Bucer, of whom you seem to speak from the report of some malevolent person, and not from your own knowledge. I have heard many accounts from different quarters, both respecting the man and that affair as to which you wish to depreciate him in my esteem. Many letters which I have seen speak highly of his piety and learning; and it is well known how zealous he has been in healing the wounds of the church. I have been informed that he is of a mild temper, and by no means pertinacious, litigious, or severe, although so firm in the cause of the truth as not to be drawn from its defence by any respect either to dignity, fortune, or life. But, as I have already said, we are not to judge of persons but of things. Thus, you have my reply to your letter, less accurate and perhaps less to your mind than you expected. I hope you will take it in good part, and that it will not prevent you from prolonging the discussion, if you think proper, or from continuing to repeat your instructions and advices; for, in dispassionate controversy between friends who happen to differ in sentiment, the truth is often discovered, and is elicited by the very contention, as fire by the collision of flints. Adieu.

No. VIII.

*Extracts from a treatise on the Benefit of Christ Crucified, by Aonio Paleario.**

[See before, p. 279.]

To the Christian readers. There having come to our hands a work more pious and learned than any which has been composed in our day, entitled, (*Del Beneficio di Giesu Christo Crocifisso verso i Christiani,*) *Of the Benefit of Jesus Christ Crucified to Christians*, it appeared to us to be for your consolation and profit to give it you in print, and without adding the name of the writer, that so you may be influenced by the matter rather than by the authority of the author.

CONTENTS.—Chap. 1. Of original sin, and the misery of man. 2. That the law was given by God,

* These extracts are taken from a review of the original Italian work, by Riederer, Nachrichten, tom. iv. p. 239—241.

to the intent that, coming to the knowledge of sin, and despairing to be able to justify ourselves by works, we might have recourse to the mercy of God and the righteousness of faith. 3. That the remission of sins, and justification, and all our salvation, depend on Christ. 4. Of the effects of a living faith, and of the union of the soul with Christ. 5. How a Christian is clothed with Christ. 6. The remedies against distrust—prayer, the remembrance of baptism, the use of the sacrament of the eucharist, and the knowledge of our being predestinated.

* * * * God has fulfilled his promise in sending us that great prophet who is his only begotten Son, that we might be freed from the curse of the law and reconciled to our God, and has inclined our hearts to every good work, in the way of curing free-will, restoring in us the divine image which we had lost by the sin of our first parents, and causing us to know, that, under heaven, there is no other name given to men, by which they can be saved except the name of Jesus Christ. Let us fly then, with the wings of a lively faith, into his embraces, when we hear him inviting us in these words—Come unto me all ye who are troubled and heavy laden, and I will give you joy. What consolation, what delight can be compared to that which is experienced by the person, who, feeling himself overwhelmed with the intolerable weight of his iniquities, hears such grateful and tender words from the Son of God, promising thus mercifully to comfort him and free him from so heavy a burden! But one great object we should have in view is to be acquainted in good earnest with our weakness and miserable condition by nature; for we cannot relish the good unless we have tasted the evil. Christ, accordingly, says—Let him that thirsteth come to me and drink; implying, that the man who is ignorant of his being a sinner, and has never thirsted after righteousness, is incapable of tasting how sweet the Lord is, and how delightful it is to think and to speak of him and to imitate his most holy life. When, therefore, through the instrumentality of the law, we are made to see our infirmity, let us look to the benign Physician whom John Baptist points out to us with the finger, saying—Behold the Lamb of God who takes away the sins of the world; who, I repeat, frees us from the galling bondage of the law, by abrogating and annihilating its bitter curses and threatenings, healing all our diseases, reforming our free-will, bringing us back to our pristine innocence, and restoring in us the image of God. If, according to St. Paul, as by Adam all died, so by Christ we are all revived, then we cannot believe that the sin of Adam, which we have by inheritance, is of greater efficacy than the righteousness of Christ, which, in like manner, we inherit through faith. Once, indeed, man might, with some show of reason, have complained that, without his own instrumentality, he was conceived and brought forth in iniquity, and in the sin of his first parents, through whom death has reigned over all men; but now all occasion of complaint is removed, since eternal life, together with victory over death, is obtained, in the very same method, without any instrumentality of ours, by the righteousness of Christ, which is imputed to us. Upon this subject St. Paul has written a most beautiful discourse in Romans, v. 12—31. * * * From these words of St. Paul, it is clear that the law was given in order that sin might be known, and that we might understand that it is not of greater efficacy than the righteousness of Christ, by which we are justified in the sight of God; for if Christ be more powerful than Adam, and if the sin of Adam was capable of rendering us sinners and children of wrath, without any actual transgression of our own, much more will the righteousness of Christ be able to justify us and make us children of grace, without any good works on our part, works which cannot be acceptable, unless, before we perform them, we be made good and righteous through faith.

* * * * Let us, my beloved brethren, embrace the righteousness of our Lord Jesus Christ, and make it our own by means of faith. Let us seek establish-

ment in holiness, not by our own works, but by the merits of Christ; and let us live in joy and security; for his righteousness destroys all our unrighteousness, and makes us good, and just, and holy in the sight of God, who, when he sees us incorporated with his Son by faith, does not regard us any more as children of Adam, but as his own children, and constitutes us heirs of all his riches along with his legitimate Son.

No. IX.

Letters written by Aonio Paleario, to his Wife and Children, on the morning of his execution.*

[See before p. 281.]

ARTICLE and Memorial, copied from a record belonging to San Giovanni de' Fiorentini di Roma.

Monday, the 3d day of July, 1570. Our confraternity having been called on Sunday night, immediately preceding Monday the 3d day of July 1570, in Tordinona,† Mr. Aonio Paleario of Veruli, resident at the Hill of Valdenza, was delivered into his hands, condemned to death, in the course of justice, by the ministers of the holy inquisition, who, having confessed and contritely asked pardon of God and of his glorious mother, the Virgin Mary, and of all the court of heaven, said that he wished to die a good Christian, and to believe all that the holy Roman church believes. He did not make any testament, except what is contained in the two under-written letters, in his own hand-writing, requesting us to send them to his wife and children at the Hill of Valdenza.

Copies of the letters *verbatim*.

MY DEAREST WIFE,

I would not wish that you should receive sorrow

---

* These letters, with the introductory memorial of the friars, were reprinted in the original Italian by Schelhorn, in his Dissertatio de Mino Celso Senensi, p. 25—27. They are taken from Novelle Letterarie dell' Anno 1745, p. 328, &c. Firenze.

† Torre Nona.

from my pleasure, nor ill from my good. The hour is now come when I must pass from this life to my Lord and Father and God. I depart as joyfully as if I were going to the nuptials of the Son of the great King, which I have always prayed my Lord to grant me, through his goodness and infinite mercy. Wherefore, my dearest wife, comfort yourself with the will of God and with my resignation, and attend to the desponding family which still survives, training them up and preserving them in the fear of God, and being to them both father and mother. I am now an old man of seventy years, and useless. Our children must provide for themselves by their virtue and industry, and lead an honourable life. God the Father, and our Lord Jesus Christ, and the communion of the Holy Spirit, be with your spirit!

Thy Husband,
AONIO PALEARI.

Rome, 3d July, 1570.

The other letter follows, *verbatim.*

LAMPRIDIO AND FEDRO, BELOVED CHILDREN,

These my very courteous Lords do not abate in their kindness to me even at this extremity, and give me permission to write to you. It pleases God to call me to himself by this means, which may appear to you harsh and painful; but if you regard it properly, as happening with my full resignation and pleasure, you will acquiesce in the will of God, as you have hitherto done. Virtue and industry I leave you for a patrimony, along with the little property you already possess. I do not leave you in debt; many are always asking when they ought to give.

You were freed more than eighteen years ago; you are not bound for my debts. If you are called upon to discharge them, have recourse to his excellency the duke, who will not see you wronged. I have requested from Luca Pridio an account of what is due to me, and what I am owing. With the dowry of your mother bring up your little sister as God shall give you grace. Salute Aspasia and sister Aonilla, my beloved daughters in the Lord. My hour approaches. The Spirit of God console and preserve you in his grace!

Your Father,
AONIO PALEARI.

Rome, 3d July, 1570.

Superscription—

To his dearest wife Marietta Paleari, and to his beloved sons Lampridio and Fedro Paleari, at the Hill of Valdenza, in the suburbs of St. Catarina.

No. X.

Letter from Olympia Morata to Madonna Cherubina Orsini.*

[See before p. 360.]

MY DEAREST LADY CHERUBINA,

To the letter I have already written you, I wish to add a few lines, for the purpose of exhorting you to pray to God that he would give you strength, lest, through fear of those who can kill the body only, you offend that gracious Redeemer who has suffered for our sakes; and that he would enable you gratefully to confess him, according to his will, before this perverse generation, and ever to keep in remembrance the words of David—" I hate the congregation of sinners, and will not sit in the company of the wicked." I am weak, you may be apt to say, and cannot do this. O do not say so. Do you imagine that so many saints and prophets, that so many martyrs even in our day, have remained firm in their own unaided virtue, and that it was not God who gave them strength? Then consider that those whose weakness is mentioned in the Scriptures, did not continue always infirm. St.

---

* Translated from the original Italian, in Olympiæ Moratæ Opera, p. 218—222. Basileæ, 1580.

Peter's denial of his Master is not recorded as an example for our imitation, but in order to display the great mercy of Christ; to show us our frailty, not to excuse it. He soon recovered from his weakness, and obtained such a degree of strength, that he afterwards rejoiced to suffer for the cause of Christ. From these considerations we should be induced, when we feel our infirmity, to apply by prayer to the Physician, and request that he would make us strong. Provided we pray to him, he will not fail to perform his promise; only he does not wish us to be idle and unemployed, but to be continually exercising ourselves in that armour of which St. Paul speaks, in the sixth chapter of his epistle to the Ephesians. We have a powerful enemy who is never at rest; and Christ, by his example, has showed us that he is to be overcome by prayer and the word of God. For the love of Christ, then, who has redeemed you with his precious blood, I entreat you to study diligently the Holy Scriptures, praying that the Lord would enable you to understand them. Mark how frequently and with what ardour the great prophet David prays—" Lord enlighten me—teach me thy ways—renew in me a clean heart;" while we, as if we were already perfect, neither study nor read. Paul, that illustrious apostle, tells the Philippians, that he did not yet understand, but was still engaged in learning. We ought to be advancing from day to day in the knowledge of the Lord, and praying all the time with the apostles that our faith may be increased, and with David—" Hold up my steps in thy ways." We have ourselves to blame for our weakness, because we are continually excusing it, and neglecting the remedies which Christ has prescribed, viz. prayer and his word. Do you think that, after having done and suffered so much from love to you, he will not fulfil the gracious promises he has made by granting your petitions for strength? Had he not intended to bestow it, he would not have invited you, by so many promises to ask it; and, lest you should entertain any doubts on this point, he has sworn that all that you request of the

Father in his name shall be given you. Nor does he say that he will give this or that thing, but everything you solicit; and St. John declares that he will bestow whatever we ask according to the will of God. Now, is it not agreeable to his will that we desire of him faith and fortitude sufficient to enable us to confess him? Ah! how backward are we, and how ready to excuse ourselves!

We ought to acquaint the Physician with our disease, in order that he may cure us. Oh! is it not the proper office of Christ to save us from our iniquities, and to overcome sin? Knock, knock, and it shall be opened to you. Never forget that he is omnipotent, and that, before your hour is arrived, no one shall be able to touch a hair of your head; for greater is he that is in us than he that is in the world. Do not be influenced by what the majority do, but by what the godly have done and still do to this day. May the word of the Lord be a lamp to your feet, for if you do not read and listen to it, you will fall before many stumbling-blocks in the world. I beg you to read this letter to Vittoria, exhorting her, by precept and by example, to honour and confess God; read also along with her the Holy Scriptures. Entreat my dear lady Lavinia to peruse frequently a portion of them, and, in doing so, she will experience the efficacy of the word of God. The Lord knows that I have written these exhortations with sincere concern for your salvation, and I beg of you to read them with the same feeling. I pray God that you may be enlightened and fortified in Christ, so as to overcome Satan, the world, and the flesh, and to obtain that crown which is given only to those who overcome. I have no doubt but that, in following my admonitions, you will find the Lord strengthening you. Do not consider that it is a woman only who is giving you advice; but rest assured that God, speaking by my mouth, kindly invites you to come to him. All false opinions, all errors, all disputes arise solely from not studying the Scriptures with sufficient care. David says—Thou hast made me wiser than all mine enemies by thy law. Do not listen to those who, despising the commandments of God and the means which he has appointed for their salvation, say, if we be predestinated, we shall be saved, although we neither pray nor study the Bible. He who is called of God will not utter such blasphemy, but will strive to obey God and avoid tempting him. The Lord has done us the honour and the benefit to speak to us, to instruct and console us by his word; and shall we despise such a valuable treasure? He invites us to draw near to him in prayer; and shall we, neglecting the opportunity and remaining inactive, busy ourselves with disputes concerning the high councils of God and the things which are to come to pass? Let us use the remedies he has prescribed, and thus prove ourselves to be obedient and predestinated children. Read and observe how highly God would have his word prized. Faith, says Paul, comes by hearing, and hearing by the word of God. Charity and faith I assure you, would soon become cold, were you to remain idle. And it is not enough, as Christ remarks, to have begun; we must persevere to the end. Let him that stands, says Paul, take heed lest he fall. I entreat you, for the love of Christ, not to conform yourself to the maxims of men, but to regulate your conduct according to the word of God; let it be a lamp to your feet, otherwise Satan will be able to deceive you in a variety of ways. Deliver these admonitions to my sister also. Never think who the person is that speaks to you, but examine whether she speaks the words of God or her own words; and, provided the Scriptures and not the authority of man be your rule, you will not fail to discover the path of duty. Ask, seek, knock, and it shall be opened to you. Draw near to your heavenly spouse, contemplating him in the Bible—that true and bright mirror, in which shines all the knowledge which is necessary for us. May God, for the sake of Christ, grant that I have not written in vain. The pain in my breast has been considerably increased by the exertion, but I sincerely wish I were able by my death to assist you and others in the things which pertain to salvation. Do me the favour to send me a single line, to acquaint me with the state of your health.

Your OLYMPIA.

No. IX.

Letter of Olympia Morata to Celio Secundo Curio.

[See before, p. 360.]

MY DEAREST FATHER CELIO,

You may conceive how tenderly those who are united by true, that is, Christian friendship, feel for one another, when I tell you that the perusal of your letter drew tears from my eyes; for, on learning that you had been rescued from the jaws of the grave, I wept for very joy. May God long preserve you to be a blessing to his church! It grieves me much to hear of the indisposition of your daughter, but I comfort myself with the hopes you entertain of her recovery. As to myself, my dear Celio, I must inform you that there is now no hope of my surviving long. No medicine gives me any relief. Every day, and indeed every hour, my friends look for my dissolution. It is probable this may be the last letter you shall receive from me. My body and strength are wasted; my appetite is gone; night and day the cough threatens to suffocate me. The fever is strong and unremitting, and the pains which I feel over the whole of my frame deprive me of sleep. Nothing therefore remains but that I breathe out my spirit. But, so long as life continues, I shall remember my friends and the benefits I have received from them. I return my warmest thanks to you for sending me the books, and to those worthy persons who have bestowed upon me such valuable presents. Had I been spared, I would have shown my gratitude. It is my opinion that my departure is at hand. I commend the church to your care; O let all you do be directed to its advantage. Farewell, excellent Celio, and do not distress yourself when you hear of my death; for I know that I shall be victorious at last, and am desirous to depart and be with Christ. My brother, about whom you inquire is making proficiency in his studies, though he needs the spur rather than the curb. Heidelberg looks like a desert, in consequence of the numbers who have died of the plague or fled for fear of it. My husband sends his compliments to you. Salute your family in my name. I send you such of the poems as I have been able to write out from memory since the destruction of Schweinfurt. All my other writings have perished. I request that you will be my Aristarchus, and polish them. Again farewell. From Heidelberg.*

No. XII.

Letter by Marc-Antonio Flaminio to Carlo Gualteruccio.†

[See before, p. 166]

I am extremely glad to hear that the bull has been expedited, not only for my own sake, though it is no

---

* Curio received this letter by the same post which brought him the intelligence of the death of the amiable writer. It was the last exertion she made. On looking over what she had written, she perceived some mistakes, and insisted on transcribing it; but, after making the attempt, was obliged to desist, and said to her husband, with a smile which completely unnerved him, "I see it will not do."

† Epistol. Reg. Poli, a Quirino, tom. iii. p. 68; tom. v. p. 387. Cardinal Quirini has inserted this letter in his Dissertation " De Viterbiensi Card. Poli Sodalitio," as a proof of Flaminio's orthodoxy, because the work of Thomas a Kempis, which he recommends, contains some opinions condemned by the Protestants, particularly the invocation of saints. But his eminence did not seem to have been aware how strongly the letter, and particularly the exception which it makes to the doctrine of the Imitation, establishes the agreement between Flaminio and the reformers on the leading article of dispute between them and the church of Rome.—Beccatello, after stating that Cardinal Pole drew Flaminio from the society of Valdes in Naples to his own house in Viterbo, adds, that the cardinal used to say, " Che non poco servitio, oltra il benefitio dell' amico, gli pareva haver fatto a' catholici havendo ritenuto il Flaminio, e non lasciatolo precipitare con gli heretici, come facilmente havria fatto "

small matter to me, but also because your excellence is thereby relieved of a great burden, which you have cheerfully borne on my account. As to the advice which you ask respecting the books which you ought to read, what I am about to say will perhaps appear to you absurd and foolish; but, if I would speak what I think, I must say it. I know not any book (I speak not of the Holy Scriptures) which I can recommend to you as more useful than that little work which is entitled, "Of the Imitation of Christ;" provided you wish to read, not for the purpose of gratifying curiosity or furnishing yourself with matter for argument and dispute about Christianity, but that your mind may be edified and you may learn the exercises of the Christian life, of which this is the sum, how the grace of the gospel is received by men, or, in other words, justification by faith. There is one exception, however, which I must make, viz. that I do not approve of the way of fear, which is so often spoken of in that book. But you must observe that I do not condemn every kind of fear; the only thing that I object to is penal fear, which is a sign either of unbelief or of a weak faith. For if I believe, as I ought, that Christ hath satisfied for all my sins past, present, and to come, it is impossible that I should fear condemnation by the judgment of God; especially if I believe that the righteousness and holiness of Christ have become mine by faith, as I must believe, if I wish to be a true Christian. Penal fear, therefore, does not become a Christian, since he ought to cherish filial love. But there is a species of fear which becomes him; he should live continually in fear of himself, being ever afraid lest his affections and appetites should induce him to do any thing unworthy of his profession and dignity, by which the Holy Spirit, who dwells in him, may be grieved. As a good son, the more kindly he is treated by his father, is on that account the more careful to do nothing which may displease his father, so a Christian must be ever watchful over himself, and ever afraid of doing any thing unworthy of a son of God; but he must, even at the same time, trust in

God as an indulgent father, who does not look upon
what he is in himself, but what he is in Christ; for
in Christ the Christian is righteous and holy, inasmuch
as, being inserted into his body, he is already a par-
taker of all his merits. If you peruse the book which
I have named, frequently and carefully, and with the
desire of putting in practice what it teaches, I am
sure you will reap the greatest advantage from it, as
all who have read it in that manner can testify from
experience; especially if you are on your guard
against that blemish which I have pointed out to
you. The less there is of the pomp of eloquence and
secular learning in that work, the more worthy is it
of being read; because the more that any thing possesses of spiritual Christianity, and the greater its resemblance to sacred Scripture, the more perfect it
ought to be reckoned. I could name many books
which are highly esteemed in the world, but, in doing
so, I would speak against my conscience, being persuaded that the reading of them would do more harm
than good; and in this I believe I do not err. Nothing
further occurs to me to say, but that I desire with all
my heart to commend myself to your excellence.

February 28, 1542.

No. XIII.

*Extracts from a Letter of Marc-Antonio Flaminio to Ga-
leazzo Caraccioli, Marquis of Vico.**

[See before, p. 166.]

THE happy news of the conversion of your excellence,
which I received from Signor Ferrante,† and Sig. Giovan-Francesco,‡ gave great joy not only to me, but

* Epist. Reg. Poli, a Quirino, tom. III. p. 59. Brixiæ, 1748.
† A friend with whom Flaminio was accustomed to lodge at Naples.
‡ The cousin of Caraccioli. See before, p. 126. If he is the same

also to the most reverend legate,* and other persons of note; and this joy has been confirmed and increased by the letter you have done me the honour of addressing to me. My honourable and much respected sir, when I reflect on the words of St. Paul, "You see your calling brethren," &c, I cannot but perceive the singular grace of the Lord God to your excellence in putting you into the number of those few great men whom he raises to an illustrious nobility, making them his sons by a true and living faith. In proportion to the singular favour shown you by God, are you bound to lead a life becoming his sons, by taking care lest thorns, that is, pleasures and the deceitfulness of riches and ambition, choke the seed of the gospel sown in your heart. I trust the Lord God, who hath begun, to his glory, that good work in you, will bring it to perfection to the praise of the glory of his grace. I trust he will create in you such generous sentiments, that, whereas formerly it was your ambition to support the dignity of your birth before the world, so now you will study to maintain the honour of a son of God, whom it becomes in all things to imitate the perfection of his heavenly Father, by exhibiting that holy and divine life which he expects to lead in heaven. Honourable and respected sir, remember, in all your thoughts, all your words, and all your actions, that we attain to the dignity of sons of God through Jesus Christ.—If we wish to please him, we must be prepared for displeasing men, and despise the glory of the world for the sake of the glory that is to be enjoyed with God. Did Christ, the only begotten and proper Son of God, willingly bear for us, not only the infamy of the world, but the bitterest torments of the cross? and shall not we, for the honour of Christ, willingly bear the scorn of the enemies of God? Let us then, honourable sir, arm our minds against the calumnies and derision of worldly men with a holy pride, deriding their scorn, while, at the same time,

person who is mentioned in p. 244, then he obtained the crown of martyrdom.
* Cardinal Pole. See before, p 169, 270.

like true members of Christ, we bewail their blindness, and beseech our God to bestow upon them a portion of that light which he has vouchsafed to us, that so becoming the sons of God, they may be liberated from the miserable bondage of the prince of darkness, who, together with his servants, persecutes Christ and his members; a persecution which, in spite of the devil and his ministers, shall redound at length to the glory of Christ, and the salvation of his members, who, being predestinated to reign with Christ, rejoice in suffering for him. Wherever the faith of this exists, it easily resists the persecutions of the devil, the world, and the flesh. Wherefore, my much respected sir, let us assiduously pray our eternal Father to increase our faith, and then our soul will long for those sweet and blessed fruits which spring up in the good ground of all the predestinated to everlasting life. If our faith be fruitful in good works, then we are certain that it is a true and not feigned, a living and not dead, a divine and not human faith; and, consequently, that it is a precious pledge of our eternal felicity. If we are the genuine members of Christ, we will feel that we are already dead with him, and risen and ascended to heaven with him, that so our whole conversation might be heavenly, and his glorious image shine forth in us in some degree. In you this image will be the more lively and admirable in proportion as you are raised above others in birth, riches, and authority. Oh! what a delightful and never enough to be looked upon spectacle will this afford to the eyes of all true Christians, nay, to the eyes of God and all the angels, while, reflecting on the frailty of human nature and the vanity of all perishing things, you say, in the words of Christ, "I am a worm and no man," and cry with David, "Look upon me, and have mercy upon me, for I am solitary and poor!" Oh! truly rich and blessed is that man who, by the grace of God, has attained to that spiritual poverty which leads him to renounce all that he possesses—to become a fool for Christ's sake—in the midst of riches to say from the heart, "Give us this day our daily bread," to prefer the reproach of Christ to all the pleasures and favours of this world, and not to wish to enter into the kingdom of God through any other holiness or righteousness but that which he acquires through Christ. Having entered the kingdom of God, glory in this that he hath shown such mercy towards you. This Christian glorying will make you humble in grandeur, modest in prosperity, patient in adversity, brave in dangers, beneficent to all, firm in hope, fervent in prayer, full of love to God, free from the immoderate love of yourself and the world, and, in one word, a true imitator of Christ. Honourable sir, I have acted contrary to my intention, from a desire to yield to your request; for, by the grace of God, I perceive every day more and more my own great imperfections and insufficiency, and that it would become me better to act the part of a disciple than that of an instructor. But, at present, I have chosen rather to follow the dictates of my affection for you than of my judgment. The most reverend legate loves you as a brother in Christ, and will be glad of any opportunity of testifying his affection for you. The illustrious marchioness of Pescara and other noble persons here join with me in affectionate salutations. May the Lord God grant that you may excel more in poverty of spirit than you abound in the riches and gifts of this life, and that your spiritual poverty may make you rich in all divine and eternal blessings. From Viterbo, the 14th February, ann. 43.

THE END.

www.ingramcontent.com/pod-product-compliance
Lightning Source LLC
Chambersburg PA
CBHW052138300426
44115CB00011B/1432